FORAKER
17.395

WICKERSHAM WALL

CARLSON
CREEK

CACHE CREEK

CLEARWATER
CREEK

6-19
2.500'

TURTLE HILL
3.104

2.200

WONDER LAKE

RANGER STATION

TO CAMP DENA

White Winds

WHITE WINDS

by

Joe Wilcox

HWONG PUBLISHING COMPANY
Los Alamitos, California

Hwong Publishing Company
10353 Los Alamitos Blvd.
Los Alamitos, CA 90720
· U.S.A.

ISBN 0-89260-162-0 (HB)
ISBN 0-89260-163-9 (PB)
LC 79-89099

1st printing May 1981; 2nd printing October 1981.

To those who probe the limits of their imagination, seeking truth wherever they find it—whatever its terms.

Contents

Appendix

Anshel Schiff

A great white mountain rises in the midst of the Alaskan wilderness. Early Indians called it: "Denali" ("The Great One"—"Home of the Sun"). But the ancient Indians never climbed their sacred peak to feel the chill of its eternal winter and the sting of its ice-filled gales. In 1967 a mountain climbing expedition would come to know the mountain intimately, as the birthplace of incredible weather and unendurable winds.

Preface

During the summer of 1967, I led a twelve-man expedition up Alaska's Mount McKinley, the highest mountain on the North American continent. Near the summit of this massive peak the expedition was caught in an awesomely intense storm, a storm that left death and ruin in its wake. What had begun as a rather routine climb ended as America's most tragic high altitude mountaineering accident.[1] Many people, some informed, and some not, speculated about the catastrophe. I realized that I, alone, had the voluminous information necessary to accurately and thoroughly document the climb and its personnel. However, in the completion of this task, I have been a reluctant author; for the disaster was deep and personal—the loss of friends as close as brothers. Many times during the intervening years I have attempted to compile this story, yet each time recalling and reliving the events of the climb became too emotionally painful and the unfinished work was set aside. In a tragedy that leaves deep scars of uncertainty and a fathomless sense of loss, there is a temptation to let things be, allowing them to drift into the forgetfulness of time. Only a strong feeling of obligation to mountaineers, to the public, to history, and to my dead friends has prevailed, driving this work to completion and relieving me of an immense burden.

---

1. It is the nature of a superlative disaster that it can be suddenly surpassed.

In the back of every mountaineer's mind is the subconscious realization that no matter how meticulous the planning and preparation, it is possible to inadvertently encounter conditions that cannot be coped with, conditions that are so decisively devastating as to deem all noble struggles for survival futile. No one would venture on a climb knowing that they would not return, yet all who go, know well the remote risk. A person cannot plan to face the overwhelming; they can only accurately evaluate their capabilities and operate within them, maintaining a supreme hope and faith that nothing more will be needed. This is the story of rivers and mountains, warmth and cold, calm and storm, joy and sorrow, life and death: the story of white winds.

J.W.
Gig Harbor, Washington
January 1981

PART I: STORY

1

Flatlands
to Mountains

I entered the mortal world in the war year of 1943 at Arkansas City, Kansas, and grew up in Neodesha, a small town in the southeast corner of the state. My earliest memories of this gently rolling country are of hot, barefoot summers, of watermelon and fireworks; and cold, wet winters of measles and Christmas lights. My parents had grown up in the depression, were married in their teens, and had four children, losing an infant boy. Two sisters provided all of the sibling rivalry a boy could handle.

In the winter Dad often hunted the raccoons that were a pest to the local farmers. I remember well the long nocturnal hunts through dormant corn fields and along muddy creeks with the fragrant odors of sweaty hounds and kerosene lanterns. I enjoyed the brisk air, open fires, and close companionship.

Occasionally nature disrupted the tranquil atmosphere of the sleepy town. Spring floods sometimes brought the Verdigris River to our doorstep; the excitement of paper boats and skipping rocks was followed by the inevitable typhoid shots.

Although the river was threatening, my keenest perception of natural forces came from the wind. This was the Midwest and no wind blows stronger than a whirling tornado. Often before going to a storm cellar, I would stand on the porch and gaze in awe at the forces around me: fulminating streaks of lightning; two-inch hailstones; and the wind—dipping a menacing funnel from a boiling, black cloud, then another, then up again. The playful frolicking of gods.

Safe in the storm cellar we could hardly talk above the howling wind and deafening thunder. I could sense the giant elms swirling in confusion. When all was calm again, we sometimes piled into the car to view the damage. If a twister had touched down, the destruction was total: trees uprooted, houses exploded into matchwood, and dead livestock scattered far from their pasture. My respect for the wind was complete.

Nineteen fifty-three arrived and with it news that two men had conquered Mount Everest, the highest mountain in the world. I listened intently to the newscast, but lacked the necessary background to fully understand their feat. To me mountains were printed photographs in books and magazines; I had never actually seen one. I could only imagine cascading waterfalls and rivers of ice. My wildest dreams did not suggest that I would someday lead an expedition on a major mountain.

At the age of fourteen, I made my first trip to the Rocky Mountains with a group of Boy Scouts. As the caravan of cars crept across the flat, treeless plains of western Kansas and eastern Colorado, I was tense with anticipation. The second afternoon I watched a long, low, purple shadow on the western horizon. Finally I was sure! These were not storm clouds to be swept away with the next change in weather; these were snowcapped protrusions of rock, reaching skyward, defying gravity. These were the Rocky Mountains! I could not contain my excitement.

During the next few days that we spent in the mountains, my senses were acutely alive. I memorized the sounds of rushing mountain streams, the smell of damp pine needles, the vastness of the wilderness. One day we hiked to the top of a mountain, and on the barren upper slopes I was keenly aware of the wind blowing free and of new feelings within myself. I felt a sense of belonging, of being in the right place. These were deep stirrings, the birth of a restless spirit that would someday drive me to the ends of the earth for fulfillment. I had been to the mountaintop, and I would have to return again. . . and again. . . and again.

Back in Kansas, life went on much as before—only I had changed. I wanted more control of my life, to live wherever I wanted, to climb mountains, to sail oceans, to be as free as the wind.

At sixteen I got my second taste of the mountains, this time on a two week Boy Scout trek at Philmont Scout Ranch in the Sangre de Cristo Mountains of northern New Mexico. By now mountains were getting into my blood. The following summer I attempted a 9-to-5 job with the Kansas Highway Department, but found the work so boring and monotonous that I resigned to return to Philmont and an almost payless position as a ranger guide. My job was to guide groups of Explorer Scouts in a two hundred square mile wilderness area and teach them as much scoutcraft and ecology as time permitted.

I eventually reasoned that the key to the independent life that I sought would be a college education, which I could scarcely afford. As a captain of one of the top-ranked high school football teams in the state, I was sure to receive major college scholarship offers. However, a shredded cartilage in my left knee cut short my last season of competition—and my hopes for a substantial athletic scholarship.

My college aspirations were more than salvaged by a keen interest in astronomy and frequent success with science projects. By graduation I had published three articles in national science magazines, received several national awards, amassed more than six thousand dollars in college scholarships, and was selected as the state's third most valuable student.

In the fall of 1961 I entered the University of Kansas with a bit of apprehension. After initially making the dean's list my academic motivation began to vacillate greatly. By spring I was experiencing an intense restlessness and thought that perhaps the excitement of transferring to another college would refresh my sagging scholastic interest. At the end of the school year I left the University of Kansas—and most of my scholarships.

The following September found me at Kansas State College at Pittsburg, Kansas. In an attempt to earn a scholarship (and perhaps to prove something to myself) and with more enthusiasm than common sense I turned out for football, not telling the coach of my past knee injury. As a wide receiver I tried to improve my less-than-lightning speed and pass-catching ability, subconsciously wondering if the next play would bring a crippling blow to my knee. By some minor miracle I lasted the season on my feet and gained a scholarship.

Then the familiar, dull, toothache pain in my left knee began to occur in my right knee also. To continue to play football would be foolhardy. Just as well—I was once again feeling the restless need for a change in environment. Over the next few school years (without scholarships) I worked as a file clerk, gardener, house painter, trash collector, keypunch operator, janitor, and tutor for a blind student before landing a much appreciated teaching assistantship in mathematics. In the end I would attend Kansas State University, the University of Washington, and Brigham Young University before earning a bachelor's degree.

In contrast to the hard work and anxieties of the school months, my summers in the Sangre de Cristo Mountains were relaxing and therapeutic. Above a high desert plain, these beautifully forested peaks and mesas rise to an elevation of 13,000 feet, which at their mild latitude is less than 2,000 feet above timberline. My job as a Philmont ranger was truly a labor of love. Fording flooding streams, sleeping under the stars, and cooking in the morning chill became second nature to me. The sun baked my skin as brown as the sandstone of the desert floor. I felt a true brotherhood and communion with nature. I never tired of the sweeping freshness of a desert storm or the unmatched grace of a pronghorn in full flight. When given a few days off, I usually stayed in the mountains or went on climbing trips with friends.

Sometimes I went to the mountains alone to experience their serene solitude. I enjoyed hiking the mesa rims and aspen covered slopes, occasionally breaking into a run to catch the natural rhythm of the ground. In the hush of night there was always the hypnotic glow of hot coals, and with the dawn I could break the silence with song or gaze upon a flower that no one else had seen.

Always the time to leave this enchanting country to grind out another year of college came too soon. At times I felt as if I were a strange cross between an electronic computor and a ponderosa pine.

In June of 1963 my growing economic needs required that I seek more lucrative employment, and I accepted a position with the National Park Service as an assistant engineer. I was stationed at Mount Rainier in the Cascade Mountains of Washington. This geologically young, uneroded range is dotted with ice-clad volcanoes, Mount Rainier being the largest at 14,410 feet elevation.

My initiation into the misty marine climate of the Pacific Northwest was uneasy. The seemingly perpetual layer of foggy clouds enshrouding the mountain frustrated me. I began to wonder—perhaps I should have returned to sunny New Mexico.

After a week of rain, the clouds dissipated, unveiling the most striking mountain that I had ever seen. This view was well deserving of the mountain's divine Indian name, Tahoma. Barren above 6,000 feet and draining the moist sea air, Mount Rainier is the most glaciated peak in the contiguous United States. The accumulated snow is compressed by its own weight, forming rivers of ice. Responding to gravity these rivers move slowly down the mountainside at the rate of a few feet per day, developing deep surface fractures where they move over uneven terrain. The resulting crevasses and icefalls present serious hazards to the untrained climber.

I soon realized that my visions of prancing up the mountain every weekend were unrealistic. I was a complete novice in snow and ice climbing; and even if I weren't, there were often severe weather conditions in which no one could reach the summit. The local people were acutely interested in mountaineering. The American Mount Everest Expedition, which had trained on Mount Rainier, had only the previous month placed five Americans on top of the world. Most of these were native Northwest climbers. I was caught up in the excitement that seemed to electrify the air.

Beginning with the basics, I extracted climbing skills and information from anyone who had it to offer, making myself a nuisance to the resident mountain climbers. I joined the mountain rescue team and during glacier practices was always the first to volunteer to be lowered into a gaping crevasse. I consumed mountaineering literature with a famished hunger and nearly memorized the contents of several equipment catalogs. Sometimes I learned from the hard school of experience. Once at high altitude I forgot to apply sun cream and barbecued my face badly in the reflector oven of sun on snow. On another occasion I was returning alone from a hike to Camp Muir, a rock hut at 10,000 feet, when I was engulfed by a soupy whiteout. So dense was the fog that I could see nothing. All directions had the same hazy-white appearance, like being in an opaque bubble. Without a compass, I crept slowly down the mountain, once stepping off a ten-foot snow embankment without even seeing it. Finally I arrived at the

Paradise Ranger Station, much relieved. I gained an instant appreciation for wands, flagged garden stakes placed in the snow at intervals to mark a route on a snow-covered mountain.

My confidence increased proportionately to my knowledge and experience. I soon felt secure in any weather on the lower slopes, and by August I led a summit climb.

Throughout the following summers I made many ascents and partial ascents of Mount Rainier and other major and minor Northwest peaks. Living at Longmire, within the national park and often working at Paradise, I sometimes hiked to Camp Muir after work to keep in shape and to meet the great variety of interesting people climbing the mountain. I met most of the American Mount Everest conquerors on these evening hikes. Once I met Tenzing Norkay who was the first person to climb Mount Everest along with Sir Edmund Hillary back in 1953. Although fifty years old, his well conditioned body looked capable of many more spectacular climbs.

By the nature of its environment, mountaineering involves an element of risk. Mountains move. Among such colossal forces, an ill-timed avalanche or falling rock can casually snuff out a life. While climbing Mount Shuksan in the North Cascades, Loren Stienhower, a climbing companion, was hit by a falling rock and tumbled several hundred feet down the mountainside. He was seriously injured with a fractured skull and broken back. An all-day rescue followed, ending with a hover airlift by helicopter. He was lucky; Loren would live to climb again.

My second summer at Mount Rainier National Park was enriched by a courtship with Cheryl Kehr, a college student working at the Longmire Inn. Cheryl was a member of the Church of Jesus Christ of Latter-Day Saints; so I joined this church in preparation for our December wedding. I had never been strongly indoctrinated into any religion in my youth; however, I had grown up with normal Protestant Christian standards. Although I appreciate the sense of fulfillment of those who participate, I have personally seldom felt the need for the social regimen of organized religion. My life seems more controlled by an internal spirit seeking its proper harmony with the universe. Religiously I feel more kinship with my few Cherokee ancestors than with my predominately European progenitors.

After our marriage Cheryl and I loaded our life's possessions into an old Ford sedan that we affectionately called "Nellie" and set out for Provo, Utah, to attend Brigham Young University. The granite canyons of the Wasatch Mountains were well populated with rock climbers; however, snow and ice climbers were nearly non-existent. Within a few weeks I collected a following from the Alpine Club: Bill Daily, Bruce Knudson, Kim Turley, Sally Gordon, Steve Taylor, and Steve Peterson; and we set about to correct BYU's winter mountaineering deficiencies. Every spare minute was spent in planning a climb, preparing equipment, or making climbs. Sometimes before making a climb we flew photo reconnaissance with pilot John Barainca, an Apline Club member. A couple of our climbs were first ascents and I experienced the satisfaction of accomplishing a feat without prior knowledge that it could be done. Beyond this, the "firsts" quickly merged with the pleasant memories of less exclusive trips.

We grew accustomed to low temperatures, biting winter blizzards, and avalanche hazards. Like seasoned high-wire walkers we could hike a corniced ridge with a guarded relaxation, only inches from a precipice. Our many outings spanned the spectrum of snow conditions that must have inspired early Eskimos to incorporate over twenty snow-descriptive words into their language. We enjoyed the fine fellowship born of earthy living; sharing the same adversities, eating utensils, and water bottles—sharing a common lifeline.

During the summer of 1966 I accepted a position as a surveyor for the United States Forest Service in southeast Alaska. This was my first trip to this lush, moss-carpeted, virgin forest where the yearly rainfall is measured in feet. It seemed almost sacrilegious to slash straight transit lines through this wild land and bring it under man's dominion. The summer was pleasant, marred only by the tragic drowning of a fellow worker in a lake.

I never saw Alaska's great white mountain; yet as I flew back to Seattle, Denali's unseen, but waiting presence invaded my subconscious thought with an elusive premonition. The following summer I would return to climb the most imposing mountain in North America: Mount McKinley.

2
Before Boots
Meet Snow

Men may make weekend climbs for recreation, close companionship, personal challenge, physical exercise, or the exhilarating environment; however, these reasons seem inadequate when compared with the reality of a teacherous mountaineering expedition of a month or more. Most reasons given for such a trip appear to result from the consequences of the venture rather than to be the initial motivations for it. Why do men subject themselves to prolonged severe stress and repeatedly take the supreme risk in a remote part of the world where minor injuries, illnesses, and misjudgments can be magnified to fatality?

Probably no amount of fame or fortune could convince a man to push himself to the brink of complete annihilation. This is an endeavor that he pursues of his own free will—indeed at a great expense of time, energy, and money. Few mountaineers have found fame or fortune. Still fewer have quenched their thirsty quest, have satisfied their lust for seeking the limits of existence. Of course there are reasons, reasons that transcend simplicity and defy precise definition. On the few occasions that I have felt obliged to answer the question "Why?" I have replied that it is the realization of a drive within me, a total self-awareness utilizing my physical, mental, and spiritual strengths to full capacity. Never have I pretended that these exhausted my reasons for climbing or even defined their parameters. I did not try to justify a potential Mount McKinley expedition to myself or anyone else. It was just simply the next logical experience in the natural flow of my life.

The decision to climb a major mountain was not impulsive, but evolved from many contributing factors: mountaineering knowledge and experience, the wisdom and judgment to make crucial decisons, physical stamina and the ability to acclimate to the thin air of high elevations, the financial resources to support the trip, and the ever-present motivation and desire. These factors could not all be simultaneously maximized — any assessment of my readiness was a corporate compromise. If I waited for the wisdom of age or for financial lucrativeness, I might be an old man with arthritic knees. Several apprentice years on Mount Rainier, the historical stepping stone to big league mountaineering, had convinced me that I was physically sound, at least for the present. At some unknown point in my progression a subconscious register indicated my ability to make a major climb. It was now possible to reach for a significant summit, not through clawing and gasping with my last ounce of strength, but through an intelligent, controlled expedition minimizing natural risks. Slowly the internal wheels began moving, gaining increased momentum in the following months.

There are many major mountains in the world. How does a mountaineer choose the mountain that best fits his style and serves his purposes? What matches the mountain to the man or the expedition? Some aspects of these questions are subjectively intangible. They cannot be divorced from the perennial question: Why do men climb mountains? The primary objective criteria are: elevation—height above sea level; accessibility—how difficult is it to reach the base of the mountain; relief—vertical distance from the base (where climbing actually begins) to the summit; knowledge and information—availability of maps, photographs, and reports from previous expeditions; weather—the range of conditions that can occur and must be planned for; technicality of terrain—steepness and the need for artificial aids such as fixed ropes, snow pickets, and pitons; geographic location—latitude and the proximity and disposition of nearby oceans, mountains, and governments; logistics—the collection, organization, and transportation of necessary supplies; and cost—the expense of supporting the expedition which may be partially or completely deferred by a sponsor or scientific research grant. The interrelationship of these factors determine the overall scope of an expedition.

The highest mountains in the world, the high Himalayas of Nepal and Tibet, have to be considered significant by elevation alone. Mountaineers literally climb out of the earth's atmosphere and have to subsist on cylinders of oxygen. Combined with other factors, this makes the Himalayas the most difficult mountains in the world to climb. They are also the most expensive, so much so that the mountaineer of average means does not plan to climb them without the invitation of a wealthy sponsor.

The other mountains and ranges of the world have various degrees of formidability, often subject to the interjections of the personal feelings and biases of the person making the comparisons. Exclusive rock climbers are an entirely different breed. They confine themselves to a contracted vertical world, and some think expeditions to be for old men who can no longer handle prolonged acrobatics.

Rising nearly three and a half vertical miles above the subarctic tundra, Mount McKinley has reportedly the greatest relief of any mountain in the world. Hugging the Arctic Circle, it boasts a hostile environment far outstripping the high mountains of more temperate latitudes. McKinley's relative isolation and proximity to the cold northern seas magnify its harshness. Like other singleton peaks, it makes its own weather: it lifts, bends, and rips the marine arctic air masses. Resulting local turbulences are often multiplied greatly. The awesome garrisons of glaciers on the mountain's flanks stagger the imagination. At an elevation of 20,320 feet, Mount McKinley is also well above the mystical 20,000 foot barrier and has the added charisma of being the highest mountain on the North American continent. It has all of the ingredients of a classic climb.

The layman seldom fully realizes the geometric progression of expedition logistics. If a 14,000 foot mountain can be climbed in two days, then he may reason that a 20,000 foot mountain should take three or at most four days. Not so! The pyramid of supporting logistics is so broad that an expedition of from three to six weeks must be considered. At 29,028 feet Mount Everest requires an expedition, even with the aid of Sherpas and porters, on the magnitude of months. If there were a mountain a few thousand feet higher than Everest, it might still be unclimbed, at least by conventional means. Because of this scope, it is usually an exaggeration to compare Mount McKinley with the much more involved Himalayan expeditions. Under normal conditions, McKinley is an easier, more feasible undertaking; yet its most dangerous hazard is elusive: in the vicious jaws of an arctic gale, McKinley's formidability is second to none.

The first serious effort to climb McKinley was in 1910 by a group of sourdoughs. They mistakenly climbed the North Peak, the lower of McKinley's two widely separated summits, perhaps because it appeared higher to them from the northeast side of the mountain where they lived. Such errors were not uncommon among early ascents of multisummited mountains. Three years later Archdeacon Hudson Stuck's expedition stood on the higher South Peak. In the succeeding half century of climbing, dozens of expeditions comprising perhaps 200 people had conquered the fortress by several different routes. Men did not climb McKinley without great effort, but they did climb it and seemingly at will. It had been climbed in the winter; it had been climbed by several women; one group put fifteen people on the summit in a single day; and another climbed it in a deceivingly easy five-day trek. In the Northwest a number of people had made the ascent; several were numbered among the mountaineers that I knew personally.

Over the years only four lives had been lost on McKinley—none by storm. On a few occasions, injured climbers had patiently and successfully waited out days of storm and wind for a daring rescue to pluck them safely from the giant's teeth. Somehow the mountain had always come up empty. Denali's timing had been off, unable to hit an expedition at its most vulnerable position. Yet the ferocious forces were there, lurking invisibly, occasionally and randomly driving the wind chill factor off the scale and playing out their destiny under the concealment of high velocity, lenticular clouds. Statistics were disproportionately out of balance and the slumbering home of the winds was poised to even the score.

Aside from its obvious attractions, McKinley's popularity is enhanced by its accessibility, economics, and a great amount of published information. Thanks largely to the pioneering climbs and research of Bradford Washburn,[1] there is much knowledgeable, detailed information about the mountain, including numerous photographs and an accurate topographical map. The mountain resides within the boundaries of a national park, which results in a lot of public exposure and adds to its accessibility. This is also a factor in the excellent expedition safety record since the Park Service carefully reviews the qualifications of all groups applying for permission to scale the peak.

Except for research expeditions, the Park Service does not permit glacier landings or air-drops within the park boundaries. Climbers so inclined, however, have circumvented this regulation by hiring a bush pilot to land them just south of the park boundary on the Kahiltna Glacier, a location which is situated a fourth of the way up the mountain.[2] This West Buttress route has become the most used as it reduces the length of the climb and avoids the lower slopes that some climbers view as mostly monotonous.

For me the decisive attraction to McKinley was economics. It was possible to launch an expedition for a few hundred dollars per person, barely within the shoestring budget of a self-supporting graduate student. I wanted to scale the entire massif so I chose the moderate Muldrow Glacier, the trail of the sourdoughs, rather than the standard West Buttress or more exotic routes. Some climbers had described the Muldrow as mundane, yet three of the four climbing fatalities had occurred on this route.

With a mountain, a route, and a projected date of summer 1967, it was time to confront the serious business of organizing the expedition. A climber does not simply decide one day to climb the monarch of the continent, throw a little jerky in his packsack, and set out. The months of planning, decision-making, and hard work preceding an expedition relate to the actual climb like the submerged portion of an iceberg. The mountain is mentally climbed many times and every possible contingency considered long before boots meet snow. There was equipment to be inspected, tested, modified, and manufactured; food to be selected, packaged,

---

1. Director, Museum of Science and Hayden Planetarium, Boston, Massachusetts.
2. Based on vertical climbing, not linear mileage.

and marked as to when it would be used; endless hours of pumping McKinley veterans for every bit of information they could recall; pouring over photographs and reports through long, tireless nights; and the constant analysis and contemplation of potential situations and circumstances.

The first and most vital task would be the selection of expedition members. Expeditions have been doomed from the start by inexperience and social incompatability. In addition to the expected scrutiny of mountaineering backgrounds, careful consideration would have to be given to the nebulous interplay of personalities. Nothing is more paramount than the psychological and emotional checks and balances among expedition members.

Often we are presented with the stereotype of the mountaineer as a bold naturalist, pure ecologist, and heroic humanitarian. Such is sometimes the case; however, on occasion I have observed climbers stampede to the summit looking neither to the right nor left, their route well marked with beer cans and other debris. I also witnessed one group, when confronted with the momentous misfortune of another party, view the gravely injured with a curious eye and then continue their ascent as if nothing had happened.

If mountaineers share a common characteristic, it is perhaps that of reserved introversion shielding a strong and often opinionated personality. Further stereotyping is difficult. Consensus yields to the diversities of humanity. A climber's idiosyncrasies over trivia and patriotic passion for such things as a certain manufacturer of climbing equipment may seem petty at first, but makes a great deal of sense in light of the reliance placed upon such things. In an emergency, a man's life may depend on his understanding of the strengths and weaknesses of his equipment. The analytical mind preparing for an expedition seems to extrapolate automatically; the same exhaustive reasoning used to select an ice axe or sleeping bag is often employed to select a toothbrush or spoon.

The commitments to various climbing philosophies are less obvious yet more strikingly intense. Climbers that may function with equally brilliant success on separate expeditions, if placed in the same group, may not be able to get out of the parking lot without irreconcilable differences.

The best possible combination is a group that has climbed together for years, with an understanding and sensitivity to each other's moods, feelings, and thoughts. Familiar fellowship affords a genuine opportunity to treat uncontrollable drudgeries and defeats with a degree of humor, a desirable disposition in maintaining a healthy mentality. Few and fortunate are the expeditions that exhibit a composition of long-time friends, and even this does not guarantee social serenity. High stakes in a naturally stressful environment have brought the best of friends to blows.

I was the leader of the expedition primarily because I conceived of it and organized it. After some thought I reasoned that a climbing party of about six would be ideal. I knew of only three climbing companions that had the readiness and means for the trip; at least two others would have to be recruited from a sea of strangers. This first compromise of the expedition was perhaps the greatest.

At twenty-four years of age, I was rather non-gregarious, and had a strong straight-forward manner, sometimes lacking in tactful social amenities. Therefore, it would be important to select a couple of unfamiliar climbers who would not be offended by my personality, nor I by theirs. Beyond this they would need to be self-disciplined and completely committed to the climb and to the group: this would not be a trip for the fickle or faint-hearted.

In September, 1966, I returned to college at Brigham Young University and began canvassing my most experienced mountain climbing friends. The results were disappointing. Bruce Knudson had been asked by the church to go on a two-year mission to South America; Loren Stienhower was getting married; and Kim Turley, who lived with his parents, was experiencing a great deal of family disapproval of his mountain climbing aspirations. Two slightly less qualified climbers, Bill Daily and Steve Taylor, were available and quite interested. Both were completing bachelor's degrees in physics at Brigham Young University. They were excellent rock climbers, were involved in the BYU Rescue Team, and were active in winter mountaineering and ice climbing. However, their glacier and high altitude experience was sparse.

I was pondering whether or not to postpone my McKinley plans, when I received a letter from Mark McLaughlin of Eugene, Oregon. He had been highly recommended by one of my Oregon mountaineering acquaintances. Mark had excellent mountain climbing credentials including several climbs of Mount Rainier and a couple of first ascent rock climbs. He was also the chairman of the Climbing and Search and Rescue Committees of the Obsidians, an outing organization based in Eugene. I began to regain my expedition enthusiasm.

Mark had a climbing friend, Jerry Clark, who was even more experienced. Jerry had an extensive mountaineering background and had been on two scientific expeditions to Antarctica. A few years earlier he had been an approved coleader of a Mount McKinley expedition which had been aborted in the organizational phase. Jerry had a master's degree in geophysics and had been doing some PhD work in psychology. He began corresponding from Indiana, but soon moved to Eugene, Oregon. Mark and Jerry were welcome additions to the expedition.

Over the years Jerry Clark had met a lot of excellent mountain climbers and suggested several for the trip. Two of these were soon invited to join the expedition: Hank Janes, a ghetto school teacher in Portland, Oregon; and Dennis Luchterhand, a part-time college instructor who was finishing up a master's degree in geology at the University of Wisconsin. Hank had done most of his climbing in Colorado and Wyoming including a first ascent in the Tetons. Recently he had climbed in the Northwest. Dennis, whose airmail special delivery letter of inquiry indicated his eagerness, ". . .I'd give both buck teeth and a right arm to go. . .," was a past president of the University of Wisconsin Hoofers outing club and had significant mountaineering experience in Wyoming and some in Europe.

I was a bit uncomfortable about leading an expedition composed largely of Jerry Clark's friends. Jerry's complete cooperation and support was reassuring.

With the high educational background and scientific inclination of most of the expedition members it seemed feasible that we might be able to fund the trip with a research grant. Marion Millett, chairman of the geography department at Brigham Young University, gave much encouragement to this idea and suggested several research foundations that we should contact. Proposed research included a theodolite[3] survey of flow and ablation rates on the Muldrow and Traleika Glaciers and the combined glaciers near McGonagall Pass, flow measurements on the Harper Glacier at

---

3. A lightweight surveyor's instrument for measuring angles.

about 15,000 feet elevation, the establishment of survey and photographic stations which could be reoccupied in future years, and high altitude measurements of sodium glow in the atmosphere.

It was decided to expand the expedition to ten members: six highly experienced summit climbers, with some research responsibility; and four less experienced support climbers who would be primarily responsible for scientific work. The support team would operate as high as 11,100 feet. Jerry Clark was designated as the high climbing party deputy leader. Anshel Schiff, an assistant professor in engineering seismology at Purdue University, joined the expedition to head up the scientific/support team. Except for a climb of the Grand Teton Anshel's mountaineering background was rather casual, but seemed adequate for the support team.

Walt Taylor, a seasoned rock climber, was enrolled in an elite combined Medical-PhD degree program at the University of Indiana and became the expedition's pseudo-doctor. He stated his qualifications: "I should be able to name the punctured organ or broken bone and apply Band-Aid." Also added to the expedition roster was John Russell of Eugene, Oregon. John was a part-time student and part-time logger. He had climbed all of the major peaks in the Northwest, was a superb rock climber, and had helped build the Camp Sherman shelter hut on Mount Rainier. John was the only person in the expedition who had not climbed with any of the other members.

Although several research foundations were very impressed with our proposed scientific work, in the end, there was not enough time to secure significant funding. We were fully sanctioned by the American Geographical Society and the Foundation for Glacier Research, but financial support was very meager. Eventually the planned research was reduced to flow measurements (rate of movement) of the Muldrow Glacier near McGonagall Pass, and the establishment of photo stations (taking pictures of the glaciers from specific positions on the mountain). After an interval of years, pictures would once again be taken from these same locations by another expedition. Comparing the two sets of photographs would tell scientists how much the glaciers were advancing (becoming larger) or receding (shrinking). Since glaciers are very sensitive to minor changes in climate, the pictures would provide a bit of evidence in projecting long range global climatic trends. Despite the potential value of this work several expedition members were not pleased with the poor funding. Some people wanted to abandon the scientific research altogether, but it remained part of the expedition as an atrophied (and rather unpopular) appendage.

As a result of the smaller research prospectus, the scientific/ support team was merged with the more experienced climbing team. Considered as a combined summit climbing party, our general mountaineering experience was now noticeably diluted. I had made plans for a two-day expedition workout on Mount Rainier before leaving for Alaska. Hopefully this would result in the assimilation of valuable knowledge by our less experienced members and make our diverse group more homogeneous in climbing technique.

Over the several months of selecting expedition members there were a few fluctuations in personnel. While getting his expedition medical examination, Bill Daily was advised by his physician that his congenital lung weakness might cause him severe problems at extreme elevations. Reluctantly Bill dropped from the expedition. Two other climbers, Steve Wunsch, a Princeton student, and Malcolm Bourne, a well-traveled Wisconsin Job Corp volunteer, were brief members of the expedition, but had to drop out due to financial and personal problems. Several climbers were considered to fill the last vacancy, but for various reasons none were invited to join the expedition. And so we proceeded as a nine-man team with equipment and food for ten.

Since most of the expedition members were widely scattered and several were complete strangers to each other, short autobiographies were written and exchanged:

JERRY CLARK

Hi. I'm Jerry Clark. For those of you who don't already know me, I'm 31—old enough that I should have "learned better than to go off stomping around the hills and such." But that sort of depends on your viewpoint. I happen to think that mountains, wilderness areas, and people who frequent them have quite a bit of offer. In fact, my tastes in creature-comforts in the "civilized" world are rather simple. I don't get much of a kick out of dressing up, polite socializing for its own sake, driving a flashy car (you'd believe it if you saw mine), or trying to prove I'm better than a neighbor. But I surely do enjoy looking at a sunrise across a lake, taking a long, cold drink from a mountain stream, or trying to pin down meanings of life with a friend. . .[4] A huge Kelty [pack] loaded with gear does a good job of hiding me (makes good camouflage for snoozing along the trail). I'm one of the "little guys"—about 5'7" and 145 lbs.

Right now I'm working as an electrical engineer for a basic psychology research outfit—figuring out new goodies to hang on computers, dreaming up new ways to arrange colored lights, writing computer programs, putting up light fixtures, replacing wall sockets, kicking the furnace when it stops running—that sort of thing. Getting here was complicated though.

It all must have started somewhere back when I became a Boy Scout. Gee, that was fun! Don't know for sure what I did before that—possibly just sat around thinking scientific things (like how to wire my brother's bed to give him a real charge). I spent about 12 summers working at a scout camp doing everything from teaching compass to running the waterfront department and health lodge. I was also an assistant scoutmaster and Explorer advisor for about 6 years. . .

Anyway, scouting first provided an appreciable escape route from northern Indiana. . . Not that Indiana was so bad—we and 2500 others lived on a pleasant lake (which became a less pleasant resort area in the summer). . .

My dad was a small town doctor and mother a homemaker with an education in music. . . I have an older brother who is a doctor in what has grown to be a larger small town and also a sister who lives in Milwaukee. Dad was killed in a car accident about 8 years ago.

---

4. Three dots indicate that a portion of a document was omitted.

Engineering seemed like a logical choice, so I sort of drifted to Purdue. . . Then there was the old Purdue Outing Club (POC). Picture an oasis in a desert. Much of Purdue is that desert, and POC is the oasis. . . Must have held most of the jobs there including faculty advisor eventually.

Engineering wasn't the thing though. . . Finally about 1961 I found myself with a master's degree in geophysics. . .

I also got a chance to mosey south for the winter. Way south. The University of Wisconsin and National Science Foundation had this little trip to map the surface and subsurface of Roosevelt Island (about 100 miles from Little America and 400 from the nearest occupied base).

I helped teach mountaineering and ice work at the orientation session and then spent 3 months driving around in a snow cat (sometimes a motor toboggan), setting off explosives and measuring ice thickness with a seismograph, doing electronic distance surveying for a network of stakes to determine ice flow (we wanted to see if this really was a model icecap to be studied in detail); peering down peepholes and twisting knobs on black boxes. Improvising everything almost. One also does many other things—I was radio man and usually weather observer. . .

Antarctica is at once exhilarating and frustrating, unbelievably exciting and fantastically boring. One finds himself alternately dying to leave, yet curiously nostalgic as the leaving date approaches. And soon after returning to civilization you kind of wish you were back. . .

But who knows what he really wants to do? I taught geology a year at Purdue, sitting in on an occasional psychology course. . . I spent most of the summer lazying around nursing a back injury. Hence you don't see me climbing even those "short" Class 5's unroped anymore.

Fortunately that didn't curtail the usual Teton trip or a

return to Antarctica. That time there was 1300 miles of new territory from Byrd Station to the Filchner Ice Shelf and back to be looked at. Air recons showed places where the crevasses were awe-inspiring—so big you don't believe your eyes. But you mark the map and plan to avoid the area religiously. There was the usual hectic pace. . . dashing ahead working 18-hour days only to have to wait interminable days for resupply flights until the right astrological combination of weather and red tape occurs. But there was time for an ascent of an unclimbed peak and a 24-hour attempt at another finished off in a delightful blizzard. . .

One appraises the mystical god science a little differently when in the midst of an expensive, seemingly low-return program. One becomes occasionally cynical and the idol accumulates a little tarnish. Six hours of driving a snow cat across the white desert to the next place to drill a new hole in the snow—day after day—crisis after crisis—gives you a chance to accumulate a little perspective. Your sense of humor takes strange turns. You really enjoy someone timing the hops of a toy duck (left over from a previous trip) with a stopwatch—and writing the results in a fieldbook. Or sometimes the pin-up on the wall looks like she just naturally needs a little parka fur glued on to keep her warm!—But it's a beautiful desert; and like a real desert or a mountain range, there are subtle beauties and sometimes stunning majesty to be appreciated. . .

A gradually increasing interest in what really makes people tick pushed me back to Purdue to a year studying psychology, computers, and statistics. University of Oregon's psychology department was interested and I ended up there last year in a clinical psychology program. The program was exasperating. . . University of Colorado's program looked better. . . it was off to Colorado. . . University of Colorado is delightful. But the psych department suffers from the same delusion that clinicians are interested in (or "need to know" at least) academic and theoretical pseudo-scientific blurb rather than practical matters of helping people. The disenchantment includes finally understanding that clinical psychology is about in the alchemy stage of development and at current rates of progress I'd be a gray old man on Social Insecurity before I could really be confident there was much basis for what I was doing. . .

Anyway, I resigned from another fellowship and decided to drift back to reality. Which eventually brought me back to Oregon to a job with more freedom than most university positions.

Needless to say, I've been too busy to accumulate a wife. In fact I've not even gotten seriously in the running—a point that bothers me—occasionally.

Mountaineering-wise, I've been climbing and informally instructing for about 14 years. . . been on at least 8 serious trips to the Tetons, 2 to the Wind Rivers, a couple to Colorado and have spent a serious summer in the Northwest. . . I have a few first ascents and first routes, sometimes I was more tagging along, sometimes not. . .

I like summit-standing, but it's not a victory symbol. It's the getting there that's fun. . . I'm looking forward to a McKinley trip. . .

HANK JANES

Growing up in Indiana is something that most people don't survive—I was lucky. Probably the greatest threat that someone could make would be to put me back there. Actually, I shouldn't complain; I know a fellow who grew up in western Kansas.

My first major experiences in the out-of-doors were as a Boy Scout. I liked being a scout—it offered many opportunities to raise hell—and almost as good opportunities to hike, camp, canoe, etc. Like all good scouts I learned to cut down trees and inhale.

I was a particularly apathetic high school student—I spent very little time studying, but a great deal of time exploring the woods and creek near our house, riding my horse, etc. As in the Peanuts cartoon, I was going through the identity crisis about this time.

It remained for the Purdue Outing Club (an organization of many virtues) to solve the problem for me—to lead me away from my life of sin—to show me the light (even though it was only carbide). I tossed away my ciggybads, and took up the piton hammer—I even started studying. . .

So anyhow, here I am in Oregon—25 years old and happily unmarried. I'm 5'5" short and weigh 140 lbs. (had to fit that in somewhere). I'm a teacher type—currently enjoying a 2-A deferrment. . . I teach the 7th and 8th grades five days a week and head for the mountains or the coast on weekends.

I'm presently involved in a very interesting and challenging teaching situation—our school is located in the Negro ghetto area of Portland and is designated a "model school." We are in the experimental stages of a program in "compensatory education" for disadvantaged youth. Many of the kids that I deal with have severe learning problems which relate to their environment. It is very demanding work and I go home each day completely exhausted—however, having previously taught for 2½ years in two very blah middle class schools, I welcome the challenge.

I have worked with disadvantaged kids before—3 summers with settlement house kids from Indianapolis in a camp situation. It was those experiences that led me into teaching. Being closely associated with the "other America" has changed my whole outlook on life—I have developed rather strong feelings about civil rights—the poverty program, etc.

For the past four summers I have worked at a private

camp in Colorado—for boys age 8 to 16. I run the mountaineering program which offers instruction in backpacking, first aid, survival, technical rock climbing (for older boys), and basic mountaineering. This instruction is put to practical use on 1, 2, 3, and 5-day backpack trips into the high mountains. Some of the greatest moments of my life have been shared with these kids—standing on one of Colorado's 14,000 foot summits—singing around the campfire—silently watching the sunset—making close friendships—sliding down snowfields—watching a herd of elk race down a talus slope—After McKinley I hope to return to camp for the remainder of the summer.

Looking ahead to the future, I feel that I can be of more help to kids by working with them in an outdoor situation rather than in an academic atmosphere—helping them to develop an awareness of others and of themselves—helping them develop a sensitivity to nature and to life—eventually I hope to start a camp of my own.

I have been doing some graduate work at Reed College under a Danforth Scholarship (MAT Program); however, I haven't reached a decision as to what direction I will head in getting my degree.

Most of my climbing experience has been in Colorado. I've climbed many of Colorado's 14'ers—some of the more significant ones include Mount Sneffles, Carson Peak, the East Face of Longs, Crestone Needle. However, a peak doesn't have to be difficult for me to enjoy it. I remember a moonlight climb of Mount Sherman as one of my favorites. I've climbed in the Tetons—even did a first ascent route on Shadow Peak. Having only been in the Northwest for a little over a year, I haven't made as many peaks as I would like, but I have climbed Hood, Adams, Three Fingered Jack, St. Helens, South Sister, Pinnacle Peak, and did a partial ascent of Rainier. I've done a good deal of rock climbing—mostly in Colorado and at Devil's Lake, Wisconsin. I am a member of Oregon Mountain Rescue.

My other interests include spelunking, skiing, scuba diving—I occasionally dabble in HAM radio (W7DEE)— and I enjoy photography very much. Recently I put together two slide programs—slides combined with music. One to "Finlandia" by Sibelius—the other to "Holy, Holy, Holy" by Gounod. . . Till later. . .

DENNIS LUCHTERHAND

. . .

Age—23, 175 lbs., 6′4″ tall, single, and big footed.

My coming to the University of Wisconsin in 1961 started me off doing all kinds of things for scholarly distraction. Mountaineering, canoeing, skiing, backpacking, snow-shoeing, sailing, biking—all became part of the prodigious scheme of avoidance, actively taken part in with Hoofers—our outing club. Along with this has come a BA in geology, and I'm now pushing through my second year of work towards an MA. If all goes well, by June I should have the THING (my thesis on the origin of a gang of rather rowdy, confused metamorphic rocks located near Torrington, Connecticut) completed. Next, hopefully, comes some study in biology, with concentration on ecology and wildlife conservation. This all should culminate in some breed of conservation work—be it from the biological research end of things or some rather more directly applied branch of conservation effort. Sometime in the next few years I intend to do a spell of Peace Corpsing.

Traveling is one of the staples of life for me. Home has been in Chicago; Madison, Wisconsin; Storrs, Connecticut; Montreal, Canada; Kitimat, British Columbia; New York; and Hannover, Germany; with summers spent on a farm in northern Wisconsin, and almost six years at the University of Wisconsin. Climbing has fitted in nicely with all this—a couple trips into the Wind Rivers, several to the Tetons, one to the Austrian Alps, and a whirlwind two-week trip up the Alcan Highway to Anchorage last

June, from where I spent some time climbing the southern side of McKinley through binoculars! At the time it was so terribly distant, but things are looking much clearer now.

General interests and activities are scattered all over. First come those above. I've had an amateur radio license since high school days when I spent much time jabbering round the world. Foreign languages have been more than school subjects, and my old days of being a "star" eighth grade ice hockey player are just being revived now with the formation of the intramural Geology Aces!! And when all is lost, I revive myself by playing some music on my recorder or a piano, reading Dylan Thomas, or heading off to the woods to see if I can find an owl.

MARK McLAUGHLIN

I, Robert Mark McLaughlin, was born in Palo Alto, California, September 24, 1943. My mother had lived in Eugene most of her life, and so, within a year, we had moved back to Eugene. Except for one year in Santa Rosa, and 10 weeks in Katmai, Alaska, Eugene has been home. My earliest exposure to the great out-of-doors was from the Boy Scouts, then Explorer Scouts. When I was 16, the summer between my junior and senior year in high school, my younger brother read about a climbing school being put on by the Obsidians, and since he was only 11, I was talked into going with him. I liked it, had enough money to start, and got up 5 mountains my first summer. This summer will be summer number 8 in the mountains and I still enjoy it all, well almost all. The Obsidians are a local club, some 300 members, of which about 50 are climbers; the rest hike or socialize. The club runs a climbing schedule of about 30 climbs. In October of '65 I was elected to the 9-man board of directors, and the summers of '66 and '67 was, and/or still am, chairman of the Climbing Committee, and the Search and Rescue Committee.

Climbing experience includes some 17 different mountains in Oregon and Washington. I've been in the Olympics two times, and to the top of Mount Rainier four times. Last Memorial Day F. Jerry Clark and I and two other friends did Nisqually Icefall. Also have done the north side of Adams, and St. Helens twice. Back in Oregon, I have done Hood, Jefferson from the East Face, and Jeff Park Glacier. Have also done all Three Sisters and others. Two first ascents to my credit, one a 150' rock pillar in the Umpqua area, Old Man Rock. The other a first on the west face of Three Fingered Jack, direct. . . Also have done Jack in the winter and lots of tries on others—tried several in the winter. Snowshoes could be interesting, as I ski, but find myself like the ugly duckling on snowshoes.

I graduated from South Eugene High School in 1961, somewhere near the middle of my class of 505. The next fall I enrolled at the University of Oregon in the Architecture and Allied Arts School. After a year of painting and sculpture, I decided that it wasn't for me, and got into the Geology School. One term later I flunked out of school. I went nights for 2 or 3 terms, just messing round, so gave it all up. This last fall I finally realized that I didn't want to spend my life working at some half-assed job, and started back to night school, to get my grades up and my study habits into some sort of shape. Fall term U.S. History 201—grade "A." Hope to apply to the University of Oregon for readmission fall term '67, and have a job on campus fall term. Still planning to major in geology. . .

I am tall, 6'½"; well-built, 150 lbs.; and full of humor. . .

Personality-wise I am sort of a loner. Not that I don't get along with people, I do, very well, with most everyone. But I am kinda for people doing for themselves. With my limited education, I have a little trouble with conversation that is "intellectual," but do OK on semitechnical matters and enjoy solving problems of a practical nature.

Marital status: single—looking, sort of.

I have a few outside interests other than mountaineering: University of Oregon Alpine Club; Mountain Search and Rescue; Federation of Western Outdoor Clubs. Also am a rather inactive Jaycee. Also work. I spend about 50 hours a week working for Oregon Screw Products Company, a wholesale fastener store. I fill orders for nuts and bolts, washers, wood screws, tapping screws, brass, stainless steel, silicon bronze, aluminumumum. Also answer the phone, wait on the counter, put up stock, sweep, make coffee, get the mail, deliver, anything else that needs to be done I get to do also. It is a small store—2 salesmen, 1 bookkeeper, 1 boss, me, and 1 boy afternoons.

Politically I am a Republican—not too interested in politics, more interested in putting the cross back up on the butte, or in keeping the loggers out of Jeff Park and the Mount Jefferson Wilderness.

This will be my first really major mountain expedition and I am looking forward to lots of work but lots of fun and good times. This is the attitude that I take with me as this undertaking gets underway.

Thanx. . .

JOHN RUSSELL

I was born (1944) and I have had the usual stresses applied to my life with a few additional ones.

I went to high school in Canada and England. On a cultural kick of my parents, I learned riding and the "art of etiquette." After graduating from high school I turned to a life of wandering. In the last five years I have been a part-time laborer and a part-time student. Jobs I have had include: sheet metal journeyman, alidaner, electronics assembler, calculator and adding machine repairman, cab driver, games keeper, sandal maker (boot repair might be a useful skill on the climb). My schooling includes math, biology, chemistry, history, philosophy. I have traveled in Europe, Central America, with a short stay in Fairbanks that I no longer remember.

For the last ten years, my first love has been climbing. The most peaceful times that I can remember have been in the mountains. Devil's club, unstable ice, falling rock, and people under stress are the things I have had the best success in coping with. Two weeks alone in the High Sierras consummated the religion of the mountains for me. Since then, I have climbed in Washington and Oregon and have learned only a little of what I would like to know about the mountains. Some of the things I have learned are how to make a boot axe belay in less than a second and how it feels to have frostbite and how to help fellow climbers in trouble (two years of rescue experience). I want to climb McKinley to learn and teach the mountains and to gain friends or to make respectable enemies.

In my climbing I have found myself constantly using unconventional equipment and methods. I use a hammock at low altitudes and a waterproof tent at high altitudes. My manila rope has held a 30-foot leader fall (I wish I could afford braided nylon). My knee belay has held a 20-foot leader fall. As an aside, I believe in short axes and long ropes.

I am now working as a logger in central Oregon. This is probably one of the most strenuous jobs around these days. I have in the past carried loads of over 100 pounds to over 10,000 feet, and I expect to be able to carry loads of up to 150 pounds by June, if necessary.

What more can I say? It is for you to ask and for me to answer as best I can. . .

P.S. I play the harmonica.

ANSHEL SCHIFF

I am 30, single, 5'10", and 175 lbs. I was born and raised on the north side of Chicago. From my twelfth year until I entered college I was very active in scouting. While my scouting experience did not provide the arduous adventures of the "Outward Bound" type, I did develop a keen interest in camping, hiking, and similar outdoor activities. After high school a 7,000-mile car camping trip to the western U.S. and Canada introduced me to the mountains. I have spent a portion of each summer since then in the West. Most of my effort has been spent hiking, packing, and scrambling as opposed to climbing. In 1954 I entered Purdue University to study mechanical engineering. I started skiing at this time and have had the good fortune to be able to ski out West (Colorado, Utah) during successive winter vacations. Unfortunately, since PU is located in Laf a Lot (Oops! for some of you this may be your first exposure to a Clarkism. This is an affliction similar to leprosy in that it grows on you. While it may be your first, I am sure it will not be your last exposure.) Lafayette, Indiana, my skiing has been restricted to one week a year.

After getting my BSME I had an enjoyable 6 months in the army and then returned to PU for a master's in engineering sciences. In 1962 I finished my master's and prelims and got a grant to study at Cal Tech (engineering seismology) for a semester. It is here that I got interested in rock climbing. After returning to PU, weekends were often spent at a local area and occasionally at Devil's Lake. Last spring I had the pleasure of tramping around Europe and returning to PU to finish up my PhD. I now have an appointment in the School of Engineering Sciences at PU as assistant professor. I teach basic mechanics and various courses on instrumentation. My research interests are in stochastics (random processes) with emphasis on random vibrations of mechanical systems. Right now I am studying earthquake resistance of engineering structures. While the expedition could provide an opportunity for field tests, I prefer leaving the investigation of the response of mountain tents to violent ground motions to the laboratory and let others perform the field tests.

Other of my hobbies would include canoeing and the design and construction of camping and climbing equipment. Politically I have liberal leaning but I am not an activist. I would classify myself as an introvert. . .

STEVE TAYLOR

I was born August 12, 1944, in Portland, Oregon, in a Catholic hospital. The Sisters were very nice to my mother and tried to influence the naming. Since I wasn't Becky Ray and my mother hadn't thought of that possibility, they had an open field. They, of course, presented only biblical names and this irked my mother so she finally decided on a name of lesser importance. So this possible Peter, Paul, or Christopher fell from grace to a mere Stephen. . .

I was reared in Aurora, Colorado, which at that time was just a little suburb for those people who didn't like Denver. . .

My father, who works for United Air Lines, was transferred to Pittsburgh, Pennsylvania. I spent my junior and senior high school days there. I was in the band and played clarinet and saxaphone. I was quite reserved and was somewhat embarrassed when I had to kiss a girl on stage during our senior class play.

My mother is an English and grade school teacher and that influenced my only sister, who is older than I, to become a teacher also. She graduated from Slippery Rock State Teacher's College. This is the school that is always reported at the end of the national sports scores. This is because so many national coaches graduated from there. She is now living in Portland with her husband and three little girls.

I met Joe Wilcox in a physics class a few years ago and he told me a little about mountain climbing. I got interested and joined the BYU Alpine Club. It is basically a rock climbing group but we also do winter climbs, caving, river running, and skydiving. . . I've only made *one* jump so far but I do intend to go back—just keep putting it off.

I graduate in May in physics. I intend to return to school to get a master's in business administration after I get away long enough to appreciate it.

My church has been a very strong influence in my life and I am considering going on a mission for about two years for the Church of Jesus Christ of Latter-Day Saints (Mormon). I am presently single and intend to have only one wife—but then there was my great-great-grandaddy [Brigham Young] who had 26 wives back in the good old days—or was it? I think they're more trouble than they're worth.

I'm what you would call skinny: 6'2", 155 lbs. I enjoy life and live it fully. My parents don't think it is such a swinging idea, my jumping out of airplanes, etc., but I won't let life pass me by; and when my tide comes I will be ready to take it at the flood.

. . . looking forward to getting to know all of you. . .

WALTER TAYLOR

I am twenty-four years old.
I weigh one hundred fifty-five pounds.
I am five feet eight inches tall.
I have flat feet.

I grew up in Indiana.
I went to high school in Indiana.
I went to college in Indiana.
I have a burial plot reserved in Indiana.
I plan to die elsewhere.

I am enrolled in the Indiana University Graduate
    School of Arts and Sciences.
I am working toward an MA degree in philosophy.
I am completing the first two years of medical school.
I used to study biological sciences.

I like J. Brahms, the Beatles, J. Sutherland, yodelers,
    M. Heidegger, J. Barth, L. Durrell, G. Herbert.

I first learned to climb with Jerry Clark.
I first learned to water ski with Jerry Clark.
I first learned to snow ski with Jerry Clark.
I first learned spelunking with Jerry Clark.
I first learned scuba diving with Jerry Clark.
I learned to smoke and drink on my own.

I used to climb mountains to tell people I climbed
    mountains.
I used to climb mountains to get to the top.
I used to climb mountains to test my courage.
I fell thirty-five feet two years ago and landed on my
    head.
I climb mountains to look at the climbers and the sky
    and the rock and the snow and the flowers.

Gentlemen and fellow climbers. Please accept my apology
for the tardiness with which I have completed this, my
first assigned task in the ascent of Mount McKinley,
and do not regard either its brevity or its seeming
flippancy as a reflection upon the conscientiousness or
seriousness of mind of its author. I wrote eleven
autobiographies in preparation for this distillation and
synthesis of biographical data and psychological
revelation. But there are those of us possessed of a certain
turn of mind who when obliged to choose between two or
several possible moves are overwhelmed by the laudable
qualities or crippling limitations of any one and yet of all,
and given the obligatory task of choosing between two
seemingly identical toilet bowls would inevitably wind up
befouled in between with one hand in each bowl. So it

was that I hesitated again and again to choose between those aspects of my conscious behavior which would credit myself most highly in your favor and yet not be totally inconsistent with that which will not credit. One of the more insidious dangers of autobiographical statements exchanged between persons as yet unacquainted is that in addition to pointing out areas of mutual agreement and understanding, oftentimes alienating aspects emerge on paper which would never have arisen in the more nearly balanced in-person impression. But then again one of the more insidious dangers of in-person impressions is that oftentimes alienating aspects emerge in person which would never have arisen on paper. . .

Semester break came and with it an opportunity for an extended winter climb. I wanted to test some ideas on equipment and my own physical condition. A downhill skiing mishap had left me with a severely pulled back muscle and reinjured knees. I began to wonder how a wheelchair would fare treading icefalls and steep ridges.

I and two nonexpedition climbing friends, Bill Daily and Kim Turley, chose Wheeler Peak, Nevada, as our objective and set out in a blizzard (Steve Taylor was to meet us, but got badly snowed in at Provo). For five days we battled storm and cold. The winds nearly blew apart our high camp and literally lifted Bill off the ridge on our first summit try; luckily we were roped. I filed many mental notes for future reference and evaluation before McKinley. Upon descending, the rangers informed us that this was probably the first midwinter ascent of the peak. Bill commented that it was no small thing, even if it had been done a thousand times. Having incurred some minor, but irritating, frostbite to my fingers, I readily agreed. Returning to Provo, I plunged back into expedition planning, shedding several layers of finger skin in the following weeks.

As I thought about the expedition I pondered my own objectives. Certainly there was the summit. I knew from the inception of the trip that I would make the top. As I considered the scope of the expedition, it seemed inadequate to spend most of a month to reach the summit and then only stay there a few minutes. The exposed summit would be no place to be in ill weather, but what if fate blessed us with ideal conditions? It intrigued me to think of spending hours on the top or even overnight—to feel catapulted into the center of the swirling sphere of stars, riding the pinnacle of intense impressions. Surely others had entertained such thoughts—perhaps others had done it.

There were many "ifs" in planning a camp on the summit: weather, logistics, acclimation, time. Two things seemed advantageous in such planning. It would sharpen our awareness to the conditions we might encounter high on the mountain and it would gear our thinking (logistically and psychologically) beyond just a summit climb.

One last winter climb was in order, so Bill Daily, Kim Turley, Sally Gordon, Steve Taylor, and I attacked Utah's Mount Nebo. This ascent of a very exposed ridge involved nearly every form of snow conditions and types of weather imaginable and consumed 17 hours.

With the expedition members spanning more than half the continent, it was necessary to delegate major organizational responsibilities. One technical part of the route would be a knife-edge ridge requiring fixed rope for added safety. To secure the rope on the snow-packed ridge we planned to use long aluminum poles (pickets) that would be driven into the snow. In addition to his scientific obligations, Anshel Schiff was placed in charge of the design and construction of the pickets. They were subsequently sent to Oregon for testing. Anshel also dabbled in modifying the expedition stoves in an attempt to decrease weight and improve efficiency. Jerry Clark was responsible for the selection of two-way radios for use in communicating between camps and hopefully communicating with the McKinley Park rangers. Wands and expedition cooking gear were handled by Mark McLaughlin with help from Jerry. Hank Janes tested tents and made recommendations. Dennis Luchterhand introduced the expedition to new untested and controversial plastic snowshoes (Snowtreads). We tested the lightweight Snowtreads plenty and eventually most of us took them on the expedition; however, they remained controversial. Steve Taylor and I were to assemble the necessary medical supplies (including some very potent drugs) and were faced with the massive packaging of expedition food. We were assisted in both of these tasks by the professional recommendations of Paul Sondrup, a BYU Health Center doctor who had a keen interest in sports and mountaineering medicine. I had met Paul during my two years as technical advisor to the BYU Rescue Team. Walt Taylor and John Russell had joined the expedition late, but still offered generous opinions on many matters. Several expedition members negotiated group discounts from various mountaineering outfitters. I also succeeded in getting a sizable discount from Perma-Pak for the bulk of the expedition freeze-dried food supplies.

To keep the expedition members updated on organizational progress I sent a series of dittoed newsletters. These newsletters were also sent to several friends of the expedition which resulted in some beneficial advice. Vastly greater than the expedition newsletters, however, were the reams of correspondence and hours of long distance telephone conversations between expedition members. Detailed objective evaluations and pseudo-objective (thinly disguised politicking) points of view were exchanged on science, summit camping, packs, snowshoes, skis, fixed line, pickets, stoves, tents, peanut butter cups, and Jell-O flavors. Jerry and Mark wanted to take skis for use on the glacier instead of snowshoes which caused a mild polarization between those who supported this view and those who felt that the use of skis on a glacier was too dangerous. In the final expedition ground rules, skis were permitted with the stipulation that they be used as snowshoes. There would be no downhill skiing. Another topic of discussion was our proposed nonstop drive of the Alcan Highway. Like many decisions this one was a compromise of several factors. At one end we could not all get together until June 10 for a Rainier workout — at the other end, good climbing weather on McKinley reportedly disintegrates rapidly by the end of July. We could forego the Rainier workout or climb into August or rush up the Alcan. I had no desire to take a group on the mountain who had not recently practiced methods of crevasse rescue nor did I want to be caught on the mountain late in the season. The least threatening compromise was to drive the Alcan with few stops.

One Park Service requirement for McKinley expeditions was that they secure the agreement of a qualified rescue group to come their aid should an emergency occur. The most prominent such group was the ARG (Alaska Rescue Group) based in Anchorage. Previous expeditions had indicated that Park Service permission was routine once ARG approval was given. Winter mountaineering had alleviated the weak experience of some of our members and we were readily approved by the ARG. Surprisingly, the Park Service was hesitant. They questioned Steve Taylor's qualifications and mentioned a four-man Colorado McKinley Expedition which also planned to climb the Muldrow route—hinting that they should join or combine with our group. (Both the Park Service and the ARG had apparently made this same recommendation to the Colorado climbers.) I asked Steve Taylor to complete an updated climbing resume including rescue experience to be resubmitted to the Park Service. I could recall Steve's cool-headed performance on a difficult rescue the preceding fall—among falling rocks and whirling chopper blades.

The suggested combination of our group with the Colorado McKinley Expedition was perplexing. The thought of joining two expeditions with separate logistics and leadership seemed to be asking for a lot of internal problems. The lengthy process of organizing an expedition develops a rather inflexible pattern of ideas and expectations. We had already excluded a number of excellent climbers for personality quirks and lack of safety consciousness. Perhaps the Park Service would be satisfied if the two groups agreed to coordinate some activities and watch out for each other on the mountain. I sent a letter of inquiry to Howard Snyder, leader of the Colorado McKinley Expedition. He shared my concerns and sent me copies of their climbing experience forms. I examined these forms with interest as I was curious as to their difficulty in gaining approval; there had been several successful four-man McKinley expeditions in the past. Two of the Colorado climbers had good altitude experience, having climbed several high volcanoes in Mexico. These peaks are lightly glaciated and require only one and two-day climbs at their low latitude; still they rise to 17,000-18,000 feet and give an indication of immediate physiological reaction to high altitude. I suspected that the key to the Colorado group's approval difficulties was their glacier experience; two of their members had very little. If we were to coordinate closely with them on the climb, I was convinced that they should attend the Rainier workout and dangle in a few crevasses along with our less experienced expedition members. Several letters and phone calls later, Howard and I agreed to a semi-merger of the expeditions. We would share campsites, radios, wands, fixed rope, and pickets along with appropriate expenses. Half of the cost of the fixed rope and pickets would also be paid by the MCA (Mountaineering Club of Alaska) Expedition which planned to climb the Muldrow route a couple of weeks behind us. We would leave the fixed rope in place on the mountain for their use.

I and several other members of our expedition were more than a little apprehensive about close coordination with the Colorado McKinley Expedition, but it did gain the necessary Park Service approval even if it was only a marginal approval. Among other minor things, the Park Service required that if our party was split, one of the two most experienced members (Jerry Clark and myself) accompany each team. The Park Service letter was both joyful and depressing. Likely none of the park officials had participated in a McKinley expedition yet they still had the combined resources of fifty years of McKinley mountaineering history to draw from.

Like many other expeditions, we investigated the possibility of testing mountaineering equipment in exchange for the privilege of using it on our trip. Most of the gear we intended to use had already been well tested on other expeditions; however, Heath Company did offer to supply us with radio transceivers if we could guarantee news media coverage or some unique advertising benefit. We knew that the significant newsworthiness of our trip would not reach beyond localized areas. Perhaps a feature in a Sunday newspaper supplement or a local television travelogue[5] would satisfy the Heath Company criteria. Should we happen to place climbers on both summits simultaneously perhaps a radio transmission between the peaks would be "unique" even though the distance involved would be only two miles.

On one of our many food runs to Salt Lake City, Steve Taylor and I stopped by KCPX-TV and talked to the news director, Roy Gibson. He was very excited about the trip and thought that we should film a documentary for his TV station, suggesting that the

---

5. Before he dropped out of the expedition, Malcolm Bourne had been investigating the possibility of filming the climb.

station might have someone who could go along on the lower parts and perhaps train someone to film the high scenes. I advised Mr. Gibson that this would require clearance by the Park Service and create an extra burden of supplies and film to be transported up the mountain. We could only justify that if the compensation to the expedition were worthwhile. Mr. Gibson said that he could make no commitments without talking to his general manager, but that things looked good.

At our second stop William Smart, Executive Editor of the *Deseret News,* indicated that the paper would have a reporter in Alaska covering the Alaska '67 Centennial Exposition in Fairbanks. He might come over to McKinley Park to do a feature article on the expedition. Mr. Smart asked if we had any interesting or different plans for the climb. I mentioned the possibility of climbing both peaks simultaneously and my desire to camp on the summit. He asked if these things had ever been done on McKinley. I replied that I didn't know. Realizing that newspeople might sensationalize our minor alterations of a standard climb into "fantastic firsts," I knew it would be well to set the matter straight before any embarrassing news releases. Mr. Smart asked us to bring some climbing gear the following week for a pre-trip interview. It seemed strange and a bit uneasy to have the news media aware of our trip. We had operated in a silent vacuum for so many months. I wrote a hurried letter to Bradford Washburn to ask if any of our proposed activities on the mountain had been done before.

The possibility of partially financing the climb with a film was short lived. A week later Roy Gibson notified me that his general manager would not underwrite the project. I felt a sweeping relief; as I analyzed the vast amount of work to be done in the next few weeks, I simply did not have time to replan the trip around a film. Steve and I cancelled our newspaper interview in favor of making and packaging 150 pounds of high-energy fudge. At this hectic time, publicity without financial support served no useful purpose and subsided as quickly as it had risen.

As my attempt to gain financial support for the trip through publicity became common knowledge among expedition members, I was bombarded with letters of philosophical disapproval of such activities. Also vetoed was my interest in camping on the summit.

This desire would have to wait for another day on another mountain under different circumstances. Publicity and summit camping were never mentioned seriously again.

Then came an astonishing letter from Bradford Washburn. Apparently my query to Washburn had been ambiguously worded as he had gotten the impression that our expedition had been designed for the specific purpose of seeking publicity. Washburn began by classifying our trek as a weird undertaking and ended by suggesting that we all fall simultaneously into the same crevasse. I was completely befuddled. Washburn knew very little about our expedition. How could a man in his high position of public respect moralize on such little evidence. Besides, wasn't this the same Bradford Washburn on whose published accounts of McKinley exploits I had cut my climbing teeth? He had certainly received more publicity than any other McKinley climber. With a kindled temper I wrote Washburn a searing letter and discarded the matter as unsalvageable. I felt an empty sadness at the crumbling of a childhood idol.

Washburn's misjudgment of our expedition had drifted to the back of my mind until one evening when I received a call from Boyd Everett, who would be leading an attempt on McKinley's South Face. He wanted to know if I had any plans to contract glacier pilot, Don Sheldon, that might conflict with his needs. I replied no; we would not be using Sheldon at all. Boyd then mentioned that he had heard of my conflict with Washburn and he wanted me to know that he and most of the mountaineers he knew felt that Washburn, of all people, was in no position to complain about others receiving publicity on McKinley. I was surprised to learn that Washburn had apparently launched a correspondence campaign to discredit our expedition. I thanked Boyd and suggested that he express his opinion to Washburn. He said that he didn't want to right now as there were still a few climbs in Alaska that he wanted to do. Quite shocked, I asked if he really felt that Washburn could or would try to block an expedition. Boyd replied that Washburn had a great deal of influence and he didn't want to take a chance. The telephone conversation was a revelation to my naiveté. The misunderstanding with Washburn continued as an embarrassing shadow over the expedition.

A very busy school year was coming to a close. The increased cerebral activity caused by the expedition planning had some spin-off. I was at the top of my math classes and was awarded a graduate fellowship in physics. Although I had completed my undergraduate work fall semester, I waited until May to graduate with my wife, Cheryl. The long-awaited college diploma was finally mine. Steve Taylor also collected his bachelor's degree. Cheryl's parents, August and Gloria Kehr, drove down from Washington to attend the graduation ceremonies. I broke the news as gently as possible that a full expedition with all of their equipment would soon descend upon their household in final preparations for Alaska.

I gave a little thought to things I might wish to take to the summit (flags are traditional). I settled on school pennants from the five colleges I had attended, a small Kansas flag, and a large pennant from my hometown of Neodesha, Kansas.

Time was short now, and Steve and I suspended our long conditioning runs in the Wasatch foothills. We rented a large trailer which I had initially considered pulling with my Ford sedan. Second thoughts, however, convinced me to buy a sturdier vehicle —a 1951 Chevrolet carryall. Food and equipment were carefully organized and packed in the trailer and a borrowed tarp secured. The hum of the telephone ceased and the last of the well-wishers left with only a few hours remaining before departure to the Northwest. There was time for a tender good-bye to Cheryl and plans for a post-expedition rendezvous.

3
Gathering
and Approach

The morning of May 28 found us leaving the quiet, unsuspecting town of Provo, Utah, and nosing the old carryall up the freeway ramp with the trailer bouncing uncooperatively behind. A few miles and several severe gyrations later, we were persuaded to stop and redistribute the weight in the trailer. We traveled on without further incident through alternate spring squalls and misty rainbows, each of us silently and separately contemplating the immensity of our venture. My untrained ears analyzed the low whine of the engine, and I occasionally interrupted Steve's thoughts to help me repair the one semi-operating windshield wiper. When night came we unrolled our subzero sleeping bags among desert sagebrush and gazed at the stars.

Our anticipation built throughout the following day. Several of the expedition members were gathered in Portland, and we were about to meet Jerry Clark, Mark McLaughlin, John Russell, and Hank Janes for the first time face-to-face.

Everyone was much as I had imagined them, yet somewhat different: Mark was a little taller and more outgoing: Hank was a little shorter and more reserved; Jerry was somewhat quieter; and John was less inhibited and a great deal poorer. It was like meeting people for the first time with the feeling that you have always known them. There was some expedition business to transact; however, most of the evening was spent in getting acquainted. It would take time to regain the openness that we had achieved and enjoyed through correspondence.

Jerry informed me that the Heath Company had sent radios after all, despite the fact that the expedition would receive no publicity. Ironically the radios did not work well when several days later they were cooled to low temperatures for testing. Jerry had to take out a loan to purchase other transceivers. He had drained his cash reserves with loans to John. We could not afford to buy tents so Hank was authorized to modify two four-man Logan tents and one two-man Mountaineer tent from the Alpine Hut. (Hank had previously reserved these rental tents). The Logan tents had been successfully tested in 100 mile per hour winds during a recent Antarctica expedition and were the best expedition tents available. Together with Mark's three-man homemade tent we would have accommodations for thirteen men, enough for good flexibility in logistics and a separate cook tent if desired. Hank would also be driving his Dodge van to Alaska. We settled on using polypropylene water ski tow rope for the fixed line.

The following morning, Steve and I drove to Puyallup, unhitched the trailer in the driveway of my in-laws, and set out for Mount Rainier. There we met Kim Turley for a two-day climb of the mountain via the Nisqually Icefall. To me a climb of Mount Rainier was like coming home, reliving memorized sensations: the evergreen taste of timberline meltwater, the brash coolness of gaping crevasses, the damp smell of sweat-soaked wool, the oily paste of layers of sun cream, and the cerebral throbbing of a rapid gain in elevation.

It was the opening week of climbing season and even on this rather difficult route we were accompanied by several other parties. Once we had to wait on a steep slope while a group above us negotiated a technical pitch. As I turned toward Steve, I saw his mitten slide down the slope and disappear into a crevasse. No words were spoken; there was nothing to say. He located a spare mitten in his pack and we continued. A mental note was made: our mittens would be secured by sleeve cords on McKinley.[1] Suddenly with a deep groan the glacier moved beneath us. Hearts stopped

---

1. Howard Snyder had suggested this procedure earlier.

and minds raced until all was stable again. The ice had moved less than a foot.

We arrived at the eastern rim of the snow-filled summit crater late in the afternoon. The summit register was on the opposite rim, a quarter of a mile into the cold west wind. We concluded that a scribbled signature was not worth the effort and descended the peak uneventfully.

The first to arrive in Puyallup was Anshel Schiff, a casual scientist with a pleasant disposition, yet fully capable of subjecting me to a pestering inquisition on matters of the trip which he felt needed clarification. Anshel had made or altered most of his climbing equipment, and it reflected his meticulous eye for minute detail. Next came exuberant Dennis Luchterhand. I had no trouble locating Dennis' gangly frame in a crowded airport. Anshel and Dennis immediately left for Rainier to meet Mark McLaughlin for hiking and a climb of the Ingraham Icefall. I took the 4 x 5 Speed Graphic press camera (borrowed for photo station use) to Seattle for winterizing.

Then came a phone call from Howard Snyder. One of his expedition members had been injured in an auto accident. They were now only three, and below the minimum set by the National Park Service. There was no longer a Colorado McKinley Expedition. Howard asked if the remaining three could join our group. Such a decision should be carefully considered, but there was little time. Quickly I had to evaluate the options. If we didn't adopt the Colorado climbers, we would lose their financial support for the fixed rope and radio equipment. Complete merging would in the long run be better than the awkward coordination which we had previously planned.

The social adjustment would clearly be greater for the Colorado group. After months of preparation for a small, close expedition of familiar and predictable friends, they would have to completely revamp their thinking and be willing to endorse the good of a larger group composed mostly of strangers and accept leadership of perhaps strikingly different temperament. This adjustment would be particularly difficult for Howard, who had several years of preparation in anticipation of leading a major mountaineering expedition. Howard assured me that he and the other two climbers, Paul Schlichter and Jerry Lewis, understood the implications of joining our expedition, namely, the forfeiture of the autonomy of the Colorado group. I indicated that I was agreeable to the merger, but could not at this late date give final approval without the support of the entire expedition. The Colorado group had thought of climbing in British Columbia should they not be permitted to climb McKinley, so I told them to come to the Rainier workout where everyone could assess the situation thoroughly face-to-face.

Because our expedition's scientific research status was insufficient to gain Park Service clearance for air-dropping supplies, we had contracted a horse packer to transport most of our food and equipment for about the first twenty miles of the trek: from our starting point at Wonder Lake, across the McKinley River and tundra to as close to the Muldrow Glacier at McGonagall Pass as terrain and snow conditions would permit. Since this would put us several days ahead of the Colorado climbers, I was adamant that Howard contact the horse packer immediately to see if he could also get his group's supplies transported. To expedite matters with the Park Service, Howard and I agreed to write letters indicating that they had joined our group. During the next few days as people began to gather in Puyallup, there were varied reactions to the news of the Colorado group and a lot of deep thinking.

Our preparation activities at the Kehr residence increased with a seemingly endless crescendo. Everyone who arrived was equipped with some small invention of cleverness or convenience which after inspection seemed indispensable to all. John Russell had thought of sewing sections of ski climbing skins to his nylon overboots to increase traction; someone else attached a piece of ensolite to a web belt to form a "beaver tail" for protection from the cold while sitting in the snow; and another person sewed patches of leather to his nylon overboots to protect them from being worn by crampons (metal frameworks of spikes which are strapped to a climber's boots for better traction on snow and ice). The sewing machine ran night and day, reproducing each brilliant invention nine-fold. Under this onslaught, the Kehrs, our gracious hosts, took to coming home only for meals and sleep, after a time only to sleep, and finally they seemed to abandon the house altogether.

A daily auto shuttle service developed to transport last-minute shoppers to the various climbing supply stores in the Northwest. As a jolly group of young men jammed into a car and cruising through

Seattle, we were conspicuous by our normality: satirically critiquing the latest movie or hit song or commenting on the impressive natural endowments of a cute car-hop. Yet individually and privately we were each sobered by moments of truth and doubt.

On the eve of our departure for the Rainier workout, Jerry called to say that he and Hank would be held up. Jerry was making some modifications on the new citizens band Lafayette transceivers, and Hank was bogged down in some minor alterations of the rented tents.

Six of us piled into two cars and drove to Longmire where we inquired about the Colorado climbers. They had not arrived yet. We left word of our whereabouts and proceeded to the Longmire bridge for prussiking practice (a method of climbing a rope by using several smaller ropes). I had discovered years before that this wooden structure fifty feet above the racing Nisqually River was a near ideal practice area. Later we had an early dinner in the dining room of the Longmire Inn. I chatted with a few Park Service employees that I knew from my summers of living there. As we were leaving, the desk clerk, who was also the postmaster of the Longmire Post Office which occupied a corner of the lobby, gave me a letter. I was at first puzzled as I was not expecting any mail at Mount Rainier National Park. The letter was from Berle Mercer, the horse packer, and was addressed to the Colorado McKinley Expedition in care of me. This could be something important regarding the packing schedule. I thanked the clerk and indicated that I would deliver the letter that evening. Evening gave way to night and morning followed—and still no Colorado climbers. Also Walt Taylor had not made his appearance in the Northwest. We drove the ten miles up the mountain to Paradise, the official meeting place. The large, saucer-shaped visitor center forced its shadow through the fog that completely obscured the mountain and reduced visibility to a few yards. I recalled my many days working at this site in 1965 when this stone and concrete monster was being erected. Somehow I preferred the rustic log beamed structure that had been razed to make room for this monolith to progress.

We parked in front of the ranger station and waited and waited, far past the rendezvous time. Eventually there was a cheery "Hello!" and Sally Gordon appeared through the dampness. She had come up from her home in Seattle to wish us luck, and she was accompanied by two young brothers and a large chocolate cake. What a pleasant surprise! We all retired to the shelter of the ranger station to share our bounty.

After a brief party it was time to start; we couldn't wait any longer for the others. I contemplated the letter from Berle Mercer: maybe it contained information that would require immediate attention, a change in schedule or plans, a phone call, perhaps decisions that could not wait for two days while we were on the glacier. I opened the letter and examined its contents. It confirmed that Mercer could pack the Colorado gear—on a second trip, after taking our gear in.

Six variously attired, heavily-ladened climbers ascended quietly through the misty fog to a steep hill several hundred feet above Paradise. Here at Alta Vista we would begin the workout.

In a fall on an ice-clad mountain, the two most important items of equipment are the climbing rope which holds the climbers together and their ice axes which hold them to the mountain. Expert knowledgeable use of both was mandatory for expedition members. We had all practiced self-arresting (a method of checking a sliding fall with an ice axe) many times before; still, it would be reassuring to refresh our sensation of this maneuver. The steep side of Alta Vista with a gentle run-out was a safe practice area. We moved to the top, checked the consistency of the snow, and individually began sliding down the slope, stopping ourselves periodically with self-arrests. Soon we were as excited as children on a sledding hill. Our antics gathered greater speed and variation—backwards, headfirst, cartwheels—until we were sure that we could not be disoriented by an unexpected tumble on McKinley. We then roped up and practiced self-arrests in threes: one man running full steam down the slope to simulate a fall, while his ropemates stopped the rope with self-arrests. It is considered polite for the falling climber to warn his companions with a loud "falling!"; however, such a courtesy is seldom managed in reality. To be realistic, we executed a few unannounced falls—tumbling ropemates head-over-heels. We were thankful that we had taped some of the sharp edges of our ice axes to avoid inadvertent injury. Finally we were confident and satisfied in each other's abilities and broke for lunch.

After eating, we packed up and began making our way toward

the Nisqually Glacier, stringing out a little along the way. There were some groups of people from the Seattle Mountaineers climbing club also headed for the glacier. There appeared one man apparently unattached to the other parties. He was wearing ancient, oversized, wool suit pants with large suspenders, an orange stocking hat, several days' growth of dark beard, and white sun cream on his nose and lips. Perhaps he was a clown lost from a nearby circus. The man steamed up to me with obvious purpose. I asked if I could help him. "Yes," he said, "I'm looking for Joe Wilcox." Walter Taylor had arrived. In the following weeks Walt would prove the quick-witted morale booster that Jerry Clark had promised. Underneath this humorous, yet functional, garb was a handsome man with a keen analytical mind and magnetic personality. I also understood from those who knew him well that Walt possessed a certain charisma with the ladies, the type of guy who could attend a party without a date and leave with two. Walt brought no word of the Colorado climbers.

We roped up and stepped onto the glacier, our perception distorted greatly by the dense whiteout. Weaving our way among crevasses, we traveled until we surmised that we were near the middle of the glacier; here, near several large crevasses we would camp for the next day's activities. An area was carefully probed to expose any crevasses in the camp that might be dangerously concealed by a thin layer of snow. The perimeter of the safe area was marked with wands and we unroped. Without most of our expedition tents, we were forced to shelter in plastic tube tents which were to be used for food storage on McKinley. John Russell grabbed a stove and began cooking dinner with authority. Although a short man, John was exceptionally strong and decisive in his mannerisms. When he handled a piece of equipment, no one was quite sure whether he was operating it or effecting a forcible disassembly. Anshel could only look on with concern at his newly modified and pampered stove.

After dinner, Dennis gathered up the food wrappers and inquired the whereabouts of the trash sack. I replied that the only trash sack available was the deep crevasse just outside the camp perimeter. What happens to trash dumped into a crevasse he quizzed skeptically. "Probably," I answered, "it will eventually reach the giant grindmill formed by fragmented rocks frozen into the bottom of the glacier and be ground to glacier silt. Someday it will leave the glacier snout and enter the Nisqually River unnoticed." (I have since learned that at our low elevation on the glacier the garbage is likely to reach the snout before reaching the bottom and be released into the river in much the same condition as when discarded.) Dennis walked toward the crevasse, then hesitated and walked away.

I was awakened in the drippy morning by the sound of voices out on the glacier—many voices! I crawled out of the tent and stared into the whiteness. Slowly, like the ledgendary buffalo herds of the plains, a multitude of Seattle Mountaineers materialized out of the fog and descended upon the crevasse field. Promptly they began rescue practice, occupying all of the nearby crevasses. Faced with this unexpected population problem we ate breakfast, roped up, and went in search of a suitable chasm. After a while we found what we were looking for, a wide crack of indeterminate depth.

One has only to be lowered dangling from the end of a rope into a yawning fissure and sense its beckoning throat curving into blueness far below to realize that crevasse rescue "practice" is a gross misnomer. This was not "practice" — this was the real thing. Having visited the cool depths a half dozen times before did not alleviate the twinge of anxiety which I felt. Adjusting my slings, I industriously began the monotonous misery of prussiking with a full pack. After a time, a rope was lowered to lift up my pack, and I quickly pulled myself over the lip of the crevasse onto the glacier surface. One by one the others repeated the exercise, each being lowered by a boot-axe belay with the rope secured to an ice axe driven into the snow to the hilt perpendicular to the pull of the rope. (Experience had taught me that this was a good anchor; the ice axe shaft would actually break before pulling out of the dense glacier snow.) Occasionally a chunk of snow would be accidentally or purposely kicked into the crevasse to provide adequate realism, usually inciting a profane response.

Anshel exhibited an elaborate nylon webbing harness of his own design and construction. He also had a length of webbing and a carabiner (an elongated metal ring with a side gate for clipping into a rope or other object) designed to lift the weight of his pack from his shoulders should he take a fall. This was a valuable idea: a heavy snapping pack at the end of a long fall can fracture ribs and break backs. After everyone was relatively calm and comfortable as a crevasse victim, I introduced a simple quick pulley method of rescue. Even though it was used in my first introduction to crevasses, I had never seen it explained in any mountaineering technique textbook. To implement the rescue, a pulley is lowered on a loop of rope and attached by the victim to his waistline. One end of the rope is anchored and the other end is a haul line for the topside rescuers. The victim can aid in his own extraction by pulling hard on the anchored end of the rope which reduces his effective weight. Two men tied to the hauling end can walk away and literally catapult a man from a crevasse. All were impressed by the ease and simplicity of the procedure, and we spent some time popping in and out of the crevasse like jack-in-the-boxes. Exhausted and confident we returned to camp for lunch.

"Look!" Dennis proclaimed at the close of lunch, "I have been reformed and converted." Then he guiltlessly and shamelessly cast his food wrappers into a crevasse.

When we returned to the Paradise parking lot in midafternoon, Dennis spoke to me aside. "I'm not going," he said.

"Not going where?" I questioned.

"Not going on McKinley," he replied. We had just had an excellent technical workout and Dennis was the most enthusiastic member of the expedition. I laughed to join in with his obviously facetious joke. "I'm not climbing McKinley!" he repeated firmly in a tone that left no doubt that this was no joke.

I was completely taken back. "Why on earth not?" I asked in amazement. Anshel and Steve were near and came over; the others had gone to the visitor center for refreshments.

"I'm not sure," he said. "I just don't feel good about it; I have a feeling that there will be problems on the climb."

"Can you be specific?" I queried. "A particular thing, a particular person?"

"I'm not sure," he replied. "I didn't feel very well on the summit during my climb with Mark last week, but mostly it's just a 'gut' feeling that something will go wrong."

"Nearly everyone living at a low elevation greatly notices the altitude when climbing Rainier in two days," I advised. "On McKinley we will have three weeks to gradually acclimate, even though the altitude will be much higher. A quick climb of Rainier is not always an accurate measure of acclimation capacity. Anyway, a person who acclimates poorly on one climb may experience little difficulty on another."

I told Dennis that I respected his decision and asked that he rethink it carefully before we repacked food and equipment. I also informed him that we couldn't possibly give him a money refund until after the trip. From his knowledge of expedition finances, Dennis already understood this. As Dennis began gathering his gear into the car, I asked Anshel for his evaluation of Dennis' sudden change in disposition. Anshel could not shed any light on the situation; perhaps Jerry Clark could probe the real cause of Luchterhand's reluctance when we got back to Puyallup.

Suddenly we were interrupted by Mark who informed us that the rangers had John and Walt. They had been apprehended while climbing the rock wall of the visitor center. God! I mused privately as I commenced to walk to the scene of the crime; this group is beginning to resemble a pack of Cub Scouts.

When we arrived, the rangers seemed more perplexed than upset. Perhaps there was no Park Service code covering rock climbing on visitor centers or perhaps the code did not elaborate on the consequences of such an infraction. Apparently there would not be a fine involved; the rangers seemed content to detain them for a lecture.

We left Steve Taylor with the carryall to chauffeur the dubious duo to Puyallup, following their compulsory class in public building appreciation. The rest of us piled into the second vehicle and set out to locate the Colorado climbers who, we learned, were camped at Cougar Rock Campground. (When I first came to Mount Rainier in 1963, my first job was surveying a section of woods for the construction of Cougar Rock Campground.)

Physically, the three Colorado climbers were impressive: all were over six feet tall, trim, and well-conditioned. Excellent mountaineers come in all sizes, yet these three seemed nicely matched to each other.

Howard Snyder, a geology student at the University of Colorado, was the twenty-two-year-old former leader of the Colorado McKinley Expedition. At 6'2" and 175 pounds, Howard was lean and wiry. His creamy complexion was characteristic of that which precedes a heavy beard. I was struck by his young appearance, although he was only a couple of years younger than I. Howard had climbed extensively in the Colorado Rocky Mountains in all seasons. A trip to the European Alps included ascents of the Matterhorn, Monte Rosa, the Eiger, and Mount Blanc; and his climbs in Mexico rounded out an excellent preparation for high altitude. Howard had, by far, the most mountaineering experience of the three, and it was reflected in his conversation.

Paul Schlichter, a twenty-two-year-old cadet at the Air Force Academy, was 6'4" and 200 pounds. He had been introduced to mountain climbing by Howard and was a carbon copy in both technique and strategy. Paul had climbed in the Rockies, including some winter treks, and had taken the trip to Mexico with Howard to climb Orizaba, Popocatepetl, and Ixtacihuatl—three high volcanoes.

Jerry Lewis was a veteran of the army, working on an electrical engineering degree at the University of Colorado. He was thirty years old, and at 6'5" and 220 pounds the largest man on the expedition. Jerry's mountaineering experience was mostly in the Colorado Rockies with a few climbs here and there during his well-traveled military career. As a group, the Colorado climbers were quiet and reserved. Howard was the most talkative, although his lack of genuine warmth caused me to suspect that he sometimes concealed his true feelings. Paul seldom offered any striking opinions of his own. For the most part, he was content to echo Howard. Jerry Lewis was very quiet in matters of expedition organization and leadership, yet his personality and disposition were evident in subtle mannerisms. He was the most likeable and predictable of the Colorado group.

As we pulled into their Cougar Rock campsite, Howard approached us with a beaming smile. We managed a cordial, but short, greeting. I was more than a little disappointed that they had missed the Rainier workout and quickly turned the conversation to serious matters. Howard explained that they had arrived late and did not think that they could locate us on the glacier in the foul weather. I agreed that it might have been difficult for a group unfamiliar with the area and explained that the details of the pulley rescue method would be demonstrated to them (as well as to Jerry Clark and Hank Janes) somewhere along the way, before we got into a position to have to rely on it. I told Howard that a letter from Mercer had been sent in care of me, and when they hadn't shown up, I took the liberty of opening it on the chance that it might contain something requiring an immediate change of plans. I related that the letter only confirmed their expected packing date, and I would give it to him later as it was in the expedition file in the other vehicle. Howard acknowledged this information and indicated that they would be in Puyallup the next day to meet the rest of the group. I requested that he proceed to Puyallup that evening to avoid further delay in the details of the merger. The group began packing up their gear as we hastily departed. Our first meeting with the Colorado climbers had been a little uncomfortable. Both groups were feeling out the trust necessary for functioning properly together in an expedition. We stopped for dinner, and when we arrived in Puyallup, we were pleasantly surprised to find everyone there.

Jerry Clark had already been informed about Dennis' disposition, and they were standing at the side of the driveway talking privately. A short while later all twelve men congregated on the back lawn to discuss the assimilation of the Colorado climbers. If anyone had any anxieties or could foresee serious situations or problems, now was the time to speak up and express them. The meeting was long and varied, sometimes directing questions to the Colorado group, sometimes taking the form of a propositional debate amongst ourselves. Normally shy Steve Taylor came out boldly and strongly against the merger. Some of his thoughts seemed well reasoned, some did not. Mark supported the merger as did I. Jerry Clark was mildly opposed, and Walt Taylor was mildly supportive. Both spoke few words, but pointed out some of the subtler consequences that we might be overlooking. Dennis was moody, yet caught up in the conversation at times. John, Anshel, and Hank seemed neutral. Some of us were concerned with the differentiation in the amount of food and equipment of our respective groups. We had scientific gear and a total of 47 days of food for ten men,[2] including food to be cached for a hopefully leisurely trip down the mountain. This figured to be more than 52 days for our nine-man group, which could in bad weather be stretched possibly to 60 days[3] of food for use on the mountain. The

2. The Wilcox group originally packaged 48 days of ten-man rations; however, one day of rations had been used at the Rainier workout.

3. Our rations averaged 4,998 calories per man-day not including supplementary and emergency food.

Colorado group had 30 days of food which they did not plan to begin using until McGonagall Pass. An expedition cannot possibly carry all of its supplies at once and can only proceed by making several trips or relays between camps situated a day's journey apart. The extra time required for our relays of additional food would be irritating to both groups. Also if by choice or chance the expedition found itself on the peak for a lengthy time, the extra food would serve all twelve members of the expedition equally. We secured the agreement of the Colorado climbers to share in relaying the extra supplies and the flexibility of splitting their group between camps when expeditious to the objectives of the climb.

Howard answered most of the questions directed to the Colorado climbers, with Lewis and Schlichter agreeing or adding a comment now and then. After most apprehensions were arrested, we retired to the kitchen to compose a formal written agreement.

I was unfamiliar with the food and equipment of the Colorado group and asked to inspect it. Their adequate supplies, which were similar to ours, were carefully packed in the back of Jerry Lewis' new Dodge Power Wagon pickup, their transportation to Alaska. I repeated the advice which I had heard from several people who had been there: that the key to climbing McKinley is to pack a lot of supplies high on the mountain and wait for a break in the weather. Relating information from one expedition report, I indicated the possibility of storms as lengthy as 17 days.[4] Howard looked at me in disbelief. I told him that we had 20 days of high altitude rations which we hoped to pack above Karstens Ridge (days 21-30 were scheduled for 15,000 feet and days 31-40 were scheduled for our highest camp near 18,000 feet). Although it was past midnight, the Colorado climbers left, indicating that they had to pick up some items in Canada and would meet us at McKinley Park or perhaps along the way.

We had planned to leave for Alaska on June 12, but the day arrived with an excessive number of loose ends. Jerry eventually had persuaded Dennis to stay with the group and he attended to expedition matters with increased interest. We needed large nonabsorbent bags to hold quantities of our smaller 2-man-day

---

4. The Log of the Swarthmore Denali Trip—1966 had mentioned meeting a Fairbanks party that had been caught in a lengthy storm. The Fairbanks group had sheltered for 13 days in a crevasse at 17,200 feet on the Harper Glacier.

food bags[5] for ease in handling on the climb. A parachute was cut up and the pieces sewn into bags large enough to hold ten 2-man-day bags of rations, the expedition food required for two days. When packed, these bags each weighed about fifty pounds[6] and would constitute an individual hauling load for relays on the mountain. Extra bags were made to hold plastic jars of group food, cooking gear, and 40 pounds of assorted cheeses. Walt Taylor paused on the back step once while bringing a bag from the sewing machine to the yard to be loaded. This hastily sewn bag was especially lopsided and holding it in front of him, Walt proclaimed his modeling of the latest Paris fashions for 1967.

Examining a wand that had been used on the Rainier workout, I discovered that the glue holding the flag to the stake was failing. I searched for a stapler to effect a more secure fastener, while at the same time lightly ribbing Jerry Clark for his eternal faith in Pliobond cement. A last trip was made to Seattle to accommodate Walt who had not wanted to buy his down pants through the mail. On this trip we also picked up several bamboo poles from a carpet store. These would be used by rope leaders on the glacier to probe for crevasses on the route and to probe campsites. Realizing that they might also be used to mark caches occasionally, someone proceeded to spray the top couple of feet of each pole with some fluorescent paint which we were taking to help mark photo stations. A few people saw this as an opportunity to color code their personal gear, and soon there were several brightly colored pairs of snowshoes and ski poles. John was the most prolific. When he was finished, his ice axe was almost entirely yellow (including metal parts), his pack had a large orange section (frame and bag), and his water bottle was green.

Eventually the backyard emptied of expedition gear, exposing the lawn once again. The trailer tarp was secured with Hank Janes adding a stenciled "Mt. McKinley." The cargo compartment of the

---

5. Small sealed quantities of food containing enough food for two men for one day.

6. The average weight per man-day of food (not including packaging) was 2.64 pounds. The large parachute bags each contained 20 man-days (ten 2-man-day bags) of food and ranged from about 40 pounds to about 60 pounds.

"Hankmobile"[7] was converted into a mini-Pullman for the grinding Alcan run, and gas tanks were filled. All was ready.

"We have to get some flowers," someone announced and began a collection.

"For what?" I asked, somewhat puzzled.

"For the Kehrs," several people answered indignantly, properly embarrassing me for taking the hospitality of my in-laws for granted. The next morning we set out a day behind schedule, leaving some roses to ease the inconvenience of our household disruption; perhaps in time when the dust settled, the Kehrs would return.

We headed slowly north, checked through Canadian customs, and blended into the summer traffic touring the scenic countryside of beautiful British Columbia. On the following day, eight hundred miles later, we arrived at Dawson Creek, the end of the pavement and the beginning (mile zero) of the infamous Alcan. Although only two men had to drive while the other seven rested or slept, we were still beginning to feel the fatigue that is characteristic of the biological disruptions of long, continuous travel. Bankrupt John Russell had thought incorrectly that expedition food would be used on the Alcan and resorted to eating odds and ends left over from the food packaging. Only a grubstake from my in-laws spared me a similar fate.

Stretched before us was 1200 miles of unpaved road in various stages of disrepair. The Alcan was everything we had feared and more; its worst sections were amplified by the pressure of our hectic pace. Certainly no one should let life slip by without traveling the Alcan—once. To repeat the experience, however, may cast doubt on one's psychological stability and risk being accused of having a masochist mentality. At times we could cruise along at 40 miles an hour; at other times we were reduced to a crawl, our teeth clattering from the rutty jolts of the nonexistent road bed. And always there was the inferno of dust penetrating everything. It caked the vehicles, settled in our clothes and hair, and finally coated our skin. Although there was some interchange of passengers, usually Walt, Steve, Anshel, and John rode with me in

---

7. Jerry Clark's name for Hank Janes' Dodge van. Jerry also named my Chevrolet carryall the "Green Bomb."

the Green Bomb, while the others occupied the Hankmobile. By the next day, June 15, we had made it to the Yukon Territory. While stopped near Teslin Lake to change a flat tire, a familiar Dodge Power Wagon sped by, came to a stop, and backed up. It was the Colorado group. Their horse packing date was three days after ours, and they could afford a more leisurely Alcan journey. We would pass them again in the evening when they stopped for the luxury of stationary sleep.

The coil springs in the trailer were too light for the load we were carrying and eventually had to be replaced. At one stop for roadside repairs, Steve had some trouble in positioning the jack under the trailer. John became impatient and grabbing a nearby log jacked the trailer up caveman fashion. By now Bradford Washburn's letter to me had been read by most of the expedition members, with rather predictable responses. I noticed that some sly insulter had inscribed in the dust of both vehicles, "Brad is a no-gooder and a do-badder."

We took a swing through historic Whitehorse and continued on. There were few towns on the Alcan, and most locations were described in terms of mileage on the highway (mileposts). Daylight had increasingly invaded night, until now it yielded only to twilight. Our cooperate scientific intellect confirmed the roundness of the earth. There was also evidence of another natural law: the price of gasoline increased proportional to latitude. That night, my relief driver was dozing peacefully so I continued my graveyard shift, the rhythm of the road soothing my mind. Suddenly I was startled by the lurching of the vehicle and quickly stopped to find myself off of the road. I was a bit shaken as I had not sensed any real sleepiness. So slight was the difference in terrain that some people weren't even awakened, and the Hankmobile pulled up and someone asked why we were stopping here. There was no apparent damage, although subsequently the whine of the engine seemed a bit different.

Later we happened upon an abandoned late model Cadillac sitting in the middle of the road fully ablaze. Near the Alaskan border we stopped at a roadside "exhibition" of dozens of tall poles littered with signs and auto license plates, perhaps the totem symbols of victims of the Alcan. There were now some concerned grumblings about our marathon driving and quite justified, since we were ahead of schedule, barring any mechanical breakdowns. Tonight we would spend horizontal on solid Alaskan soil. Finally reaching the border was cause for celebration, although most of us had been to Alaska before.

The quiet smooth pavement brought with it the sound of a distinct rattling vibration in the engine, and we stopped at Northway Junction to inspect. A mechanic confirmed our suspicion that the engine bearings were going out in the Green Bomb. Several reasons were suggested for the disorder: the heavy load we were hauling, the grind of fast, rough driving, the devastating Alcan, and the unplanned stop off of the road. No one observed that at sixteen, the Green Bomb might just be succumbing to old age. We assembled at the inn to discuss our options over lunch. With luck, we could make it the 500 miles to McKinley Park, but then the damage would probably be beyond repair. Or we could, at the expense of valuable time, order parts from Fairbanks and have the engine repaired. The third option, and the one ultimately accepted, was to have the Colorado climbers pull the trailer, while all nine of us crowded into the Hankmobile. Sentinels were posted at the edge of the road to flag down the Colorado group when they came by. John and Walt decided to tear into the Green Bomb engine for a closer look at the disorder.

Upon learning that we were mountaineers, the inn manager related the story of a Japanese climber who had been killed in the nearby mountains and how his family back in Japan felt that it was an honorable way to die. We listened with interest. Our consensus, however, was that we much preferred longevity to honor. As the saying goes: "There are old climbers and bold climbers, but no old, bold climbers."

The Colorado group arrived late in the afternoon. A trailer hitch was fashioned for the Power Wagon, and we were ready to resume our journey. Howard indicated that he would compute the increased gas consumption caused by the trailer-laden Power Wagon. Being very short of funds, I suggested that the cost of the trailer hitch and our shared excess of food might compensate for any increase in their travel expenses. Howard agreed. Off again, we must have appeared an unlikely group of college educated men doing more credit perhaps to the image of early day migrant workers. At the U.S. Customs Office near Tok, the officer viewed the slumbering lot and asked the driver how many animals he had.

I really appreciated a good night's sleep at Moon Lake Campground a few miles later. My morning contemplation of this wild wilderness was interrupted by Walt Taylor who suggested that the group was too loosely organized, that I should exert more leadership authority. A half hour later I was approached separately by Jerry Clark who indicated that I was exerting too much leadership authority. With these divergent views, we would clearly have to have further group discussions to firm up organization and leadership roles.

We started checking along the way for white gas in lightweight Blazo cans. Unexpectedly, they were not readily available. One service station attendant suggested that we call Fairbanks and have cans of Blazo sent to McKinley Park on the Alaska Railroad. After a few phone calls, Blazo was located at Delta Junction, and we picked it up en route. The Colorado group had gone on ahead.

Good weather had graced Alaska for two weeks, and June 17 was no exception. The 300-mile panorama of the white tumbled peaks of the Alaska Range was breathtaking. Some of these impressive peaks were probably yet unclimbed, being bypassed in favor of the range's monarch, which had not yet made an appearance.

Along the Denali Highway, I sensed the presence of something of paramount prominence, with lesser peaks dancing before it in a vain attempt at concealment. Slowly and with authority, Denali claimed the horizon in a massive advance of stately splendor, leaving other peaks to scramble for lesser glories. My visions and dreams of this huge mountain were shattered. Any fabrications of the mind are ridiculously inadequate, when confronted with the absolute reality of the majesty I beheld. McKinley's foreboding presence was tempered by a distance of 80 miles. It loomed calmly above us until it was once again hidden, this time by our proximity beneath its foothills.

We passed through the park headquarters at 9:00 PM, its bright daylight dormancy appearing strange, and headed for Wonder Lake, the last 82 miles of our journey. Encompassing 3,030 square miles, Mount McKinley National Park is second in size only to Yellowstone.

After a time, McKinley appeared again, this time in more

detail, and began filling the sky. Wildlife was everywhere profuse, and at one rest stop, Dennis sent us all scurrying after the cry of a loon. Our appreciation was distracted, however, by McKinley, the object of our quest, presenting our intended route so openly. Eyes searching the tundra for wildlife were soon drawn upward in increased concentration, probing the secrets of Denali's thick mantle of fractured ice.

We stopped at Eielson Visitor Center to discuss and confirm radio communications with the seasonal rangers who managed the center. From this position, 33 miles directly northeast of McKinley's summit, they would be in line-of-sight with most of our route once we got above 8,000 feet. Hopefully radio contact would be established by the first of July. The rangers could also visually survey our progress with the telescopes provided for public use.

There was an aura of gossip and curiosity among the park employees resulting from our misunderstanding with Washburn. No one said anything openly; yet it was clear that some half expected to see us arrive with a press bus in tow. It would be folly to try to debate Washburn's prejudice here on his own turf where he was a living legend, and I didn't try.

Jerry Clark gave the rangers a copy of a map on which he had marked all of the line-of-sight radio communication sections of our intended route, and we were off again for the last leg of our auto trek.

As we traveled the short 20 miles to Wonder Lake, a half moon hung in the midnight mellow sky complementing the alpin-glow[8] on Denali's silent Wickersham Wall, perhaps the greatest continuous upslope of land in the world. John had told me earlier that he was thinking of a Wickersham Wall climb for 1968.

Upon arriving at Wonder Lake Campground, we were informed by the Colorado group that the packer and ranger would see us in the morning. We settled down for a restful sleep, glad to have the driving done with. The next morning Beryl Mercer came by and said that he would prefer packing the next day. Being slightly disorganized we readily agreed. At about 11:00 AM the District Climbing Ranger, Wayne Merry, came down and spent a couple of

8. The red, orange, or pink hue sometimes seen on mountain slopes when the rays of the sun are low such as at sunset or sunrise.

hours chatting with us and looking at some of our gear. Wayne was a quiet, but openly personable man of genuine friendliness, somehow escaping the plastic phoniness and procedural preoccupation affecting many bureaucratic employees. He brought with him a series of organized 8 by 10 photos depicting the Muldrow route. Nodding to the dusty inscription on the Hankmobile he said lightly, "Do you want to see what the no-gooder has to say about the mountain?" Washburn's binder of pictures was passed around with the Colorado group finally monopolizing it.

Merry confirmed that Washburn had written the park in regard to our expedition. "We answered that he had greatly misunderstood the letter from you," he added. I thanked Wayne for supporting the principles of a public domain.

As the climbing check-out ranger, Merry was particularly interested in our footgear, frostbitten toes being the most common injury on McKinley. Clark, McLaughlin, and Steve Taylor all had chosen double boots of leather; Schiff, Janes, and Luchterhand had white Korean boots; Walt Taylor had regular black Korean boots; John, the three Colorado climbers, and I had felt boots with down liners. Most of us had brought a second pair of boots to wear at the lower elevations. Everyone had insulated overboots. Merry's inspection seemed slight to those of us who were accustomed to rigorous check-outs at Mount Rainier.

Still cognizant of the Park Service's assessment of our expedition strength, I asked Merry, who was himself a competent mountaineer, for his opinion. "On paper," he replied, "you are the best organized party to ever assault the peak." I was not completely reassured. This was not a paper mountain.

From a vantage point my eyes traced out the 20, almost treeless miles to McGonagall Pass. McKinley rose more than 18,000 vertical feet above the Wonder Lake Campground[9] with the South Peak just hidden from my view.

Mosquitoes are the tundra's most prolific life, breeding in plague-like waves of bloodthirsty siphons. Repellent was effective only if applied in sufficient quantity to drown the beasts, and we quickly resorted to headnets to avoid terminal anemia. We took

9. Elevation of the Wonder Lake Campground is about 2,200 feet. Elevation of the South Peak is 20,320 feet.

little comfort in the fact that only the females are vampires.

I called an afternoon meeting to discuss the expedition's organization. I expressed concern about the divergent views about my role as leader. There was also a deficiency in group orientation: we seemed to be a loose collection of individuals climbing the mountain separately. I explained that this was not a Sunday hike where important decisions can be cast to the momentary whims of the majority. This was a venture bigger than any of us had tackled before. Our objective could only be accomplished if we were a solid team. Walt observed that "no one opens anything with gusto." Perhaps our lethargy was due to adjusting to a new environment, or perhaps we were still recuperating from the Alcan, but one thing was certain, we had a ways to go before becoming a cohesive group with "group" expectations and "group" direction. Several group tasks were discussed. Walt volunteered to take charge of organizing the supplies to be packed in by the horses.

I asked if anyone had any comments on the expedition ground rules distributed before the trip; there were no questions. I stated that we all had different reasons for climbing the mountain, but we had to climb it together. Then I added with humor, looking around at the empty landscape, "As you can see by all of the news photographers, I am climbing for publicity."

The meeting was adjourned. With the sparsely interacting discussion, I did not feel that a great deal was accomplished. Perhaps a few seeds of thought had been planted. We did at least agree to call other such meetings whenever serious problems arose.

Jerry Clark and I drove to the ranger station several miles away for a meeting we had scheduled with Ranger Merry. The cabin also served as a home for the Merry family. I took with me a few postcards for mailing. Over tea we had a two-hour discussion of various matters, including radio communications, and thoroughly scrutinized Washburn's photos of the route.

Wayne's primary mountaineering expertise was in rock climbing, having been one member of a three-man team to make the first ascent of the South Buttress on El Capitan in Yosemite National Park. Although he had not made a climb of McKinley, Wayne exhibited a keen knowledge of the inner workings of an extensive expedition. We agreed to a 7:00-8:00 PM radio schedule, information that Wayne would pass on to Eielson.

Jerry and I returned to camp to find dinner in progress. No kitchen duty assignments had been made, and none would be necessary as long as jobs got done. John Russell was late for dinner, and I found him in another campsite in the midst of a group of Boy Scouts who were completely engrossed in his tales of the mountains. John was obviously enjoying himself, exhibiting a gentle side to his normally rough character. There was a lot of food left over from dinner. I knew from past trips that it would seem to decrease in quantity and increase in quality the further we got from civilization.

Steve confided to me that he felt weak and ill. "What a hell of a time to catch a bug," I thought, "on the eve of the expedition." I advised him to stay at Wonder Lake for three more days. If it was nothing serious, he could hike to McGonagall Pass with the Colorado group, but if he didn't feel better then, he should forego the climb. Steve agreed to stay.

I explained the situation to Howard and suggested that Jerry Lewis accompany the first group in to operate the theodolite during the science work on the Muldrow. Several of us, including myself, could operate the instrument; however, this would be a good opportunity to melt the icy bubble that seemed to surround the Colorado group. The auger for drilling deep stake holes in the surface of the glacier was stranded at the train station 84 miles away near park headquarters, making the already questionable flow measurements a task done more from momentum than for significant purpose. The change in personnel was acknowledged, and behind the tent flaps I closed my thoughts for the night.

The expedition was imminent now, and we would have to live with the sum total of our organizational efforts (our successes and our failures) and hope that we had not made any disastrous oversights.

4
Ascent

DAY 1 — JUNE 19

LOG:[1]

"Packer arrived at 7:00 AM two hours behind schedule and began loading. Wayne Merry stopped by and told us that the McKinley River was very high. . ."

The McKinley River was the first major obstacle and blocked our path only two miles away. The river is a glacier stream born at the snout of the Muldrow. When warm weather causes great melting it can be an unfordable torrent. I placed Walt in charge of the horse packing and with Mark and John, departed to investigate. We angled toward a location upstream where the river was reportedly easiest to cross. With ice axes, but without packs, our fast walk soon became a broken-paced jog across the lumpy and tufted tundra. I remarked that it seemed a little like broken field running in football. John said that it was like jogging through the woods with a logger's axe. Mark, who apparently had neither

---

1. Excerpts from the *Expedition Log* which I kept on the trip.

experience, observed that it seemed a great deal like jogging across the tundra with an ice axe. We covered the 3½ miles to the crossing area in about 45 minutes.

The river was guarded by a shallow spruce forest stunted by the latitude to a height of barely fifty feet. As we emerged from the damping effect of the forest, our ears were filled with the deafening roar of angry, murky, silt-filled water, frantically seeking the sea. The river was more than a mile across and braided into a dozen swift channels. We chose the widest part in hopes that it would also be the shallowest and commenced to find a suitable passage, marking our route with stick poles and survey flagging. I wore tennis shoes which I had brought specifically for the river crossings.

My shoes were soon filled with penetratingly abrasive glacier silt that felt like crushed glass, until the icy water numbed my feet and legs; then I could feel nothing. An hour later we arrived at the far bank and radioed Jerry Clark that the river was passable and that they should proceed immediately. To save time I suggested that Howard, Paul, and Steve bring our three packs down to the river. It would give them a break from sitting around camp and allow them to reconnoiter the crossing area. They agreed. I took off my shoes and socks to inspect my feet, and as the feeling returned, I reclined and massaged them in the dry earth and dozed in the sun's warmth.

I was awakened by Mark shouting that the others had arrived. John had already left to guide them over. I returned my tender feet to the damp tennis shoes and reenacted the painful trip across the river to fetch my pack. The second group had saved themselves a mile of hiking by crowding into the Hankmobile and driving up the road about three miles.

By 1:00 PM everyone was across without incident, and we took a lunch break at the edge of one of the many pothole lakes that dotted the landscape. Silt-filled socks were rinsed, and tender toes were soaked. The lake's shallow warmth was soon overpowering, and all clothing was discarded for a complete immersion. Back to reality, we bushwhacked to the top of a low rounded mound (slightly out of our way and a thousand feet above the river bed), called Turtle Hill, to assure that we would get at least one summit on this venture, and then set out across the open tundra, like brightly colored bugs on a shaggy green carpet. We followed game trails when possible for easier walking. While the supplies for the horse packer were being weighed that morning at Wonder Lake, I had, out of curiosity, weighed my pack—it was a little over 80 pounds. The straps soon cut deeply into my unconditioned shoulders, forcing me to tighten the pack's waistband to shift some of the weight to my hips. By 8:00 PM, we came to the high bank of Clearwater Creek. Its lightly tinted blue-green appearance indicated that it was not a glacier stream. The singly divided stream was deeper and swifter than those we had crossed on the McKinley River. John probed for a passage as I followed. After a few feet, he was nearly swept away by the current, and as he reached back for my hand, his eyes displayed genuine fear. Perhaps he was a nonswimmer. Walt had made a couple of successful crossings up channel, and we followed suit with the aid of a fixed line which we secured. John, Hank, and I crossed, with Hank taking a drenching splash. The others decided to wait for morning in hopes that the creek would be lower. Although glacier streams normally run shallower after a cool night has checked melting, I doubted that the Clearwater would drop appreciably. I had hiked more than eleven miles on this first day of the expedition so I did not mind that the others wanted to camp.

We had planned to meet the horse packer in this area as he had our tents and food. Scouting both sides of the Clearwater, however, did not turn up a horse camp, so we settled down for a bivouac, unwinding by nibbling on our survival rations and shouting obscenities back and forth across the creek. Finally we were quieted by a dripping shower. As I watched a menacing cloud cross Denali's face, I thought of an old mariner's adage, "The good sailor weathers the storm he can't avoid and avoids the storm he can't weather." Realizing the circularity of this reasoning, I pondered, "What if we can't avoid the storm we can't weather?"

DAY 2 — JUNE 20

LOG:
"Troops up by 8:00 AM—northside gang crossed Clearwater with Dennis taking a spill. . ."

As we prepared to leave the night's encampment, I advised that we had gotten a little strung out on the previous day and should try to hike more as a group today. But as we approached the mountain through scattered showers, excitement was difficult to contain, and we became an ever elongating snake of hikers. Finally I decided to leave my position near the rear and catch the head to slow it down. Jerry Clark was left in charge of the caboose. I steamed forward over the treeless uplands, after a while realizing that I was not gaining on the few lead hikers. These were not Boy Scouts or tourists, but mature men, every bit as physically capable as myself. Late in the afternoon, Mercer's empty pack string passed by en route back to Wonder Lake.

> LOG:
> ". . . Russell, Luchterhand, and Walter Taylor were in the first group. . . arriving at the cache at 5:00 PM. They set up camp and greeted everyone with hot stew and drink. . ."

I arrived next at the Horse Cache, dumped my heavy pack, and climbed a nearby slope to observe the stragglers, feeling a little like a mother hen. I knew that hiking alone in this wilderness was a dangerous proposition. I had heard tales of lone hikers drowning in ankle deep streams, apparently after a concussion fall on slippery rocks in the stream bed. We had crossed a couple of small streams during the day. I had also heard of Alaskan natives becoming hopelessly disoriented on such vast trackless tundras, tundras that could swallow a lone hiker without a trace. I was unhappy that we had not traveled as a group; at least we would be roped together once we got to McGonagall Pass only two miles beyond the Horse Cache. The day's hike had been about eight miles, our pace slowed by the lack of a proper meal. After dinner I examined the supply cache and surveyed the camp. At 4,500 feet the Horse Cache was high enough that I could see most of our route from Wonder Lake. By now Mercer's empty pack string was probably back to the McKinley River. It was a peaceful evening: soft music from John's harmonica drifted across the gurgling creek, while a rock rabbit scampered in search of food. For a moment I lost all desire to climb the mountain. who could ask for more contentment than to be allowed to tarry in this soothing setting?

DAY 3 — JUNE 21

LOG:

"Packed one load up to McGonagall Pass—general recuperation from forced fasting; showers."

The packer had been stopped by the steep snow-filled gully of boulders leading to the pass. We loaded supplies and slowly trudged up this ravine. Other mountains had taught us that stepping too close to large boulders can result in a shin bruising plunge through under-melted snow. We also took care to avoid walking over the stream which audibly undercut the snow.

Twelve hundred vertical feet later, we topped McGonagall Pass. I could only take a deep breath and silently stare in reverence at the panorama before me. High icy mountains and ridges walled this glacier-filled valley, decisively sealing it off from the outside world. This was a world within a world. A world sculptured by the elements from the beginning of time—indeed—a world without time. My eyes moved rapidly up the Muldrow, danced along Pioneer Ridge, and finally came to rest on the lofty North Peak shining in the solstice sun. The higher south summit was hidden by intervening peaks and ridges. I sensed the spiritual mystique historically associated with high mountains. This was not Mount McKinley, the namesake of an aspiring politician; this was Denali—harsh, untouched, primeval, devastatingly beautiful, yet without emotions or feelings. She would give no quarter to those who challenged her, and she would not easily forgive an error or miscalculation. This world was not meant for man; we were visitors packing our sustenance on our backs. So total was the demarcation that I turned to reaffirm the world from which I had come. We returned to the Horse Cache for the night. During the following days, McGonagall Pass had the same terminator effect each time I approached it.

DAY 4 — JUNE 22

LOG:

"Moved camp from cache area 2 miles up to McGonagall Pass. Sunny most of day with view of North Peak. Wilcox and Janes' blisters fine — V-Cillin taken. Line laid out across glacier by Russell, Clark, Wilcox, and

Schiff with Lewis on the theodolite. Glacier very slushy with streams and lakes on the surface."

As a glacier slowly chisels at the sides of its valley, undercut rock falls onto the ice surface and is carried along. These lateral moraines combine at the confluence of two glaciers into medial moraines down the middle of the combined glacier. The Traleika Glacier, joining the Muldrow just below McGonagall Pass, exhibited several stripes of medial moraines indicating that it was formed by the joining of several tributaries. The Muldrow above the pass, however, had only a few clumps of moraine—it seemed largely a singleton glacier. Ten years earlier the Muldrow had surged rapidly for a time, now it seemed quite sedate. There were no trees or other familiar objects of uniform structure and our perspective of size and distance was difficult.

Camp I at McGonagall Pass was at an elevation of 5,720 feet and situated on a uniform area of angular rock rubble generously littered with the discarded relics of a dozen previous expeditions. A small creek provided our water. Discovering a crude plaque, apparently left by the 1952 Mexican Expedition, which was the first foreign group to ascend McKinley, Mark suggested that we should leave such a marker. "Perhaps on the 15th Annual Memorial Joseph F. Wilcox, Mount McKinley Expedition," he said. This was a good-natured stab at our expedition name, or lack of it. Although McKinley expeditions are often referred to by the name of their leader, they usually have official names depicting their composition such as a mountaineering club, college, or state. Throughout our organization no such term had evolved to encompass our great diversity of personnel. We became known simply as the Wilcox-McKinley Expedition.

DAY 5 — JUNE 23

LOG:
". . . high 72°F, low last night 37°F. . . Walt, John, Jerry Clark, Dennis pack loads to base of Lower Icefall—put in Camp II."

It was an exciting milestone when the first rope team stepped onto the mile-wide river of ice to wand a route and establish Camp

II, 4½ miles away at the base of the Lower Icefall, although their trip could hardly be called "climbing" as the location of Camp II at 6,500 feet represented an elevation gain of only 780 feet.

I watched as the advanced team skirted a meltwater lake on the surface of the glacier and invaded the sea of whiteness, soon becoming insignificant specks. Only their high motivation and combined intelligence seemed a match for the vastness.

Mark, Hank, and I turned our attention downward to the Horse Cache to pack up more supplies. This was the hottest day of the expedition, magnified to a sultry uncomfortableness in the narrow access valley of snow. Halfway down we met Howard and Paul on their way up. We exchanged greetings and I inquired the whereabouts of Steve, not knowing if he had decided to come on the expedition. "He's a ways behind and will be along soon," I was told.

When we arrived at the Horse Cache, we found that Mercer had already unloaded the second pack string and was camped nearby. There was no sign of Steve. Hank began loading up while I proceeded to Mercer's camp to conclude business. Mark came with me to give the packer a letter to mail.

Mercer had packed 1,942 pounds for us. The personal gear that we had packed in ourselves was 60-80 pounds each. I wrote an expedition check to complement the deposit which we had made earlier. Steve was still not in sight so I visited with Mercer for a while. He was a friendly man, showing a great deal of contentment in running his own business and being his own boss. He told of giving Howard, Paul, and Steve horseback rides across the McKinley River and Clearwater Creek and of nearly losing a horse in the McKinley. Mercer knew about Washburn's misunderstanding and offered that no one had received more publicity on McKinley than Bradford Washburn. "When Washburn is on the mountain," he added "there are helicopters and planes flying everywhere, like an invasion." I acknowledged Mercer's comments, but was beginning to grow weary of the Washburn controversy. I wondered if it would follow us clear to the summit.

Mark was anxious to return to his packing duties, so I borrowed a piece of paper from him for a letter and continued waiting for Steve. A light rain forced me to huddle beneath my Cagoule (a baggy, water-repellent, pullover-type wind parka) to finish a letter to Cheryl.

Finally a red speck appeared on a faraway slope and a half hour later Steve sauntered up, noticeably upset. I asked how he felt, and how he managed to get so far behind. He replied that he was still weak, but felt that he was going to be all right. He then related that Howard and Paul had forced a fast pace—goading, ridiculing, and insulting him whenever he fell behind. Finally, when he was unwilling to push himself beyond reason in his recuperating condition, they had abandoned him altogether on the previous evening.

"Do you mean that they haven't been in contact with you since yesterday?" I asked in amazement.

"That's right," Steve said with resignation.

"Did they tell you that they were going ahead without you and that you were on your own?" I asked.

"No," he replied. Steve started up the gully and I began loading my pack, with my temper beginning to burn. Steve had the gentle forgiving disposition of a religious saint; it would take a great deal for him to claim that someone had been rude to him. Perhaps Howard and Paul were trying to get even with Steve for opposing their joining the expedition. Or even more serious, perhaps they saw nothing wrong with leaving a lone man simply because they were more comfortable at a faster pace. Pushing for fourteen hours with 75-pound packs was no way to treat an ill hiker, especially when such a grind was completely unnecessary. They had no reason to keep up with the horses once Mercer had helped them across Clearwater Creek, which he had done about lunchtime on the previous day; yet apparently they had pushed on until nearly midnight. Whatever their reasons for such an action, they had better be good ones.

I didn't have to wait long as Howard and Paul soon arrived back at the cache. "Why did you leave Steve?" I demanded with obvious emotion. Surprised by my tone, Howard hesitated, then said that they had pointed out the route to Steve and that there was no danger in him hiking alone. "There is no trail, and there are several streams to cross," I retorted. Howard then became very defensive. Paul joined in, and they began attacking Steve, relating how slow and incompetent he was, and how when he got behind once, he got lost following a caribou trail. They said that Steve should not be on this climb and that I should consider sending him back. Howard added that Mercer could verify how slow Steve was.

Howard said, "Besides Mercer said that the first group was strung out when they hiked in." I could not believe my ears! Howard was telling me that Steve could take care of himself, and at the same time, what a blundering hiker he was, with no sense of direction.

It was true that Steve was slow compared to Howard and Paul, and justifiably so in his illness. Even so, Steve had made the trip from Wonder Lake faster than any of us in the first party. Howard's inability to see any difference in his overnight abandonment of Steve Taylor and the afternoon strung out hike of the first group astonished me. I was further disturbed by the fact that they had not gone back to look for Steve when he failed to show up at their camp the previous night. Their lack of group commitment and concern was unacceptable. "The only thing I'm considering is whether or not to send you two back. It seems that you are still the Colorado group, just worried about yourselves," I said with a flushed anger that ended the conversation.

I started hiking, leaving Howard and Paul muttering to each other. If they could abandon a man so easily on the tundra, I thought, how easy would it be for them to abandon someone on the mountain where things could really get rough. I was laboring under a hundred pound load and the two Colorado climbers soon caught up to me. Howard spoke for them both and apologized for any trouble their actions might have caused. They had apparently sensed correctly that my threat to send them back was real. They also apologized to Steve.

DAY 6 — JUNE 24

LOG:
"Rain all day. Mark, Hank, Jerry Lewis, and Wilcox made trips with loads to Camp II. Everyone else packed up remaining gear from the Horse Cache, about two loads each. Russell carried 115-pound load. Low last night 40°F, high 46½°F."

The argument from the previous day was beginning to cool, and it felt great to hike to Camp II and let the tents of McGonagall recede behind. It was a little like being the only occupants of a large empty pavilion, and our voices were pitifully faint, being almost completely absorbed by the wide, white valley. A section of curious cross-glacier moraine served as a dry halfway resting station. Camp II was well located near the base of the Muldrow's lower and very tumbled icefall. It would be a challenge to find a suitable route through this chaos of massive ice blocks and crevasses guarding the upper Muldrow basin. Camp II also had its own water reservoir—a small surface lake. This would conserve our fuel, since we would not have to melt snow for water. However, the lake might at any time be drained by a fracturing glacier movement. We added our loads to the growth of the Camp II supply cache and headed back. These first long days of packing loads over gentle terrain offered little technical challenge, and we prided ourselves on the size of our loads, weighing them with the spring scales which we had transported as far as the pass. The foot-deep slushy snow, covering rock-hard glacier ice, was inconsistent and unpredictable. Once I stepped into a pothole, filling my boot with enough frigid meltwater to give me a numb wrinkled appendage by the time I returned to camp. We suspected that the greatest danger on this first glacier trail was falling into a water-filled crevasse and drowning.

With the Horse Cache gear packed up to McGonagall Pass, we were well supplied for the siege ahead. We had begun using our food at Wonder Lake and had used one day's ration at the Rainier workout, but we still had 45½ days[2] left (41 ten man-days[3]). The Colorado group had about 29 days[4] of food remaining.

There was no designated latrine, and late in the evening, Walt unexpectedly strolled by an area I was using. "Excuse me," he said, "I didn't know that this was the executive washroom."

DAY 7 — JUNE 25

LOG:
"Rain, drizzle, snow all day with one short hour of sunshine. Everyone packed loads to Camp II. Low 36°F, high 58°F."

---

2. This does not include supplementary food and cheese which would increase this estimate by a few days.

3. Normally 9 men consumed the 10-man ration.

4. This does not include their supplementary food.

Our tents were designed for high altitude, purposely nonwater-proof to prevent damaging condensation from breathing and cooking. Crudely fashioned rain flys for low elevation had been ineffective against the driving drizzle. Moisture found its way unreasonably into every item of gear, no matter what the precautions to foil it. During the morning we were desperately hoping for a break from the misery and a chance to dry our gear. The sun soon began playing peek-a-boo with the clouds, which caused Dennis to coax, "Come on, Lord, bring the sunshine." To which Walt advised, "If the Lord brings the sunshine, then he also brings the rain." And then, as if to forsake his gloomy logic and embrace a blind faith, Walt offered, "Come on, sun! Show us you haven't forgotten your children." He then offered a sacrifice to the sun god. "Lord! If you let the sun shine, we'll all take off our clothes and sunburn our weenies." The sun came out for a while, and when no one obliged Walt's promise, the rains came again.

The five members of the expedition who had not practiced the pulley crevasse rescue were instructed in its technique, without the benefit of actually going in a crevasse, as we could not risk an accident.

Upon arriving at Camp II, I dumped my heavy pack load and watched the drifting weather—dense clouds with an occasional break. A patch of blue appeared and for the first time I saw the upper part of the mountain from Camp II. I was surprised to see a low white knob peeking over a ridge. The mound of snow looked inconsequential nested to the left of the towering North Peak; however, I recognized it as the faraway object of our quest—the South Peak. The vicinity of Camp II would be our only view of the summit from our route on the Muldrow Glacier, our last view until we topped Karstens Ridge.

Anshel, Steve, and Dennis were on my rope team to Camp II this day. On our return moraine rest break we were overcome by a tempting pile of rocks perhaps 25 feet high and proceeded to climb it without removing our snowshoes. We planted a wand on the summit, took a picture, and proclaimed the first ascent of Mount Moraine. Dennis accepted the highest honor as he had made the ascent with long wooden trail snowshoes, being the only member of the expedition to reject completely the use of plastic Snowtreads (Jerry Clark and Mark McLaughlin had brought skis in addition to Snowtreads, and a couple of people had brought both trail snowshoes and Snowtreads).

The last group to return to Camp I was the rope team of Clark, McLaughlin, Russell, and Janes. I was standing alone about 100 feet above the glacier edge where they unroped and John immediately steamed up the slope directly toward me. "I want four days of food, a tube tent, and a stove. I'm leaving the expedition," he pronounced with an anger that contrasted his strained red face with his blond curly hair and beard. "Can I have them?" he demanded, before I had a chance to speak.

"Sure John," I answered, "but I would like to know why you have decided to leave the expedition."

John calmed down a bit and explained his reasons. "This is a group, leading itself in 12 different directions," he said. "The Colorado group is a clique; Clark, Janes, and McLaughlin are a clique; and everyone else is strung about in no-man's-land. Some people obviously don't respect some of the ground rules of the expedition. Clark and McLaughlin were downhill skiing today and nearly pulled me off my feet. Also 120 feet of rope is not enough for roping up four people." John pointed out still other indications of separatism in the group, and although his manner was blunt, his perception was keen. He was also concerned about the great mass of expedition supplies and suggested ways to eliminate unnecessary weight.

I pondered John's comments. There were only a couple of short segments of trail between the pass and Camp II where a person could actually approach a posture resembling downhill skiing. However, I had noticed Mark descend to the Horse Cache on the previous day in what would technically have to be called downhill skiing, although it was hardly anything to excite anyone on a beginner's slope. Jerry Clark and Mark had also requested to travel as a rope team of two on skis, a request that I had denied as being too dangerous. Perhaps not dangerous on the lower Muldrow, but here we were forming patterns and habits that would stay with us the entire expedition. At what nebulous point of the climb would safe become unsafe, and who would make such a decision? True, Mark and Jerry were excellent ski mountaineers, yet as I gazed across the glacier to the ridge separating the Muldrow and Traleika, my eyes rested on Mount Carpé which hid Mount Koven, the memorial namesakes of Allen Carpé and Theodore Koven, two previous climbers who thought that they could ski the Muldrow

Glacier. I agreed with John that the safest way to travel was in long rope teams (150-200 feet) of four climbers each, minimizing the possibility that a falling climber would pull a second man into a crevasse and maximizing a rope team's self-rescue capabilities.

The most disturbing problem, however, and the one which I could no longer ignore, was that the group had not accepted a common code of conduct. The range of leadership expectation was also extreme. The group was too large and heterogeneous to sustain loose group consenses in decision-making, yet I did not want to assume a dictatorial role.

I had not been vigilant in my support of the expedition regulations and on a couple of occasions had even been a party to their circumvention. The regulation to use a rope while crossing the McKinley River, adopted at the recommendation of another expedition, in reality appeared to present more of a hazard than a help. After visualizing entire rope teams tumbling down the river hopelessly entangled in their rope, the regulation was properly disregarded, but improperly it was disregarded without discussion. Also the rule to purify tundra water had been ignored. I had almost forgotten the pre-trip agreement not to use skis on route-finding teams and hadn't made the slightest comment when skis had been used in pioneering our first glacier route.

The symptoms were only minor irritations, but the disease could be fatal. It would be foolhardy to let our loose organization proceed on its casual course to some potentially disastrous end high on the peak.

A mail-order expedition like ours had had its leadership fall apart on the treacherous Karstens Ridge a few years earlier. The situation was serious, and I would have to force the issue now, even at the risk of aborting the expedition if necessary. I asked John to wait until morning on his decision to leave. "We'll hold a group meeting and discuss everything, and if nothing constructive results I may join you on your hike out," I added. I retired to my soggy tent for a night of fitful sleep.

DAY 8 — JUNE 26

LOG:
"Low 32°F, high 68°F. Rain in morning, then 1½ hours of sunshine. Everyone put things out to dry. Storm moved in fast up McGonagall Pass. Cold sleet and snow for two hours. . ."

Mountaineers choose brightly colored equipment and clothing for greater visibility. The various pieces of drying gear at McGonagall Pass made camp look a bit like a carnival, until the weather changed and sent everyone scrambling.

Just before the storm began, we gathered for the inevitable meeting, and the weather tormented us greatly, increasing the agony of our verbal ordeal. I opened the meeting by stating that it was time to get down to the brass tacks of living together and hash out problems that were smoldering under the surface. Russell immediately brought up the ski use controversy which precipitated a lengthy argument. I reminded Mark and Jerry of the pre-trip agreement to use skis only as snowshoes. They countered by pointing out the trivial nature of their infringement of the expedition ground rules and stated that they were the expert ski mountaineers in the group and should be permitted to decide for themselves when, if, and how they should use skis. Russell questioned whether or not a man on skis could effect a self-arrest as well as a man on snowshoes. Jerry and Mark argued that a man on skis can edge in and hold a fall better. Although I agreed that a man standing on skis with sufficient warning to edge in can hold a fall well, I also knew from personal experience that a climber does not usually have the courtesy of a warning, his first knowledge of a fall being when he finds himself being yanked ass-over-teakettle. I had to agree with John: I could think of no more helpless creature than a skier being pulled headfirst down a slope; he may not even be able to orient himself to attempt a self-arrest. At this point, Russell became unnecessarily belligerent toward Mark and Jerry, and stated that he wouldn't climb on a rope team with skiers. The group seemed strongly divided on this issue, and someone suggested that the skiers be spilt up and climb on separate rope teams. Another person observed that our discussion was purely academic as no crevasses had been found between Camps I and II, and we really didn't need to rope up at all. Several people agreed. This was the igniting spark. "Only clumsy people fall into crevasses they see," I said angrily. "People fall into crevasses they don't see. Only a few months ago on this very mountain a man[5] died while hiking unroped in an area where he

---

5. Jacques Batkin — a member of the Winter Expedition.

had found no crevasses. People simply cannot act on their own without concern for the group." My runaway imagination pictured a search for an overdue rope team without knowing their assumed regulations for the day or even whether or not they had bothered to rope up. Battle lines were being clearly drawn for group versus individuals. Does the individual have the right to choose a course of action which may endanger only himself? My position was firmly no! A man who endangers himself endangers the entire expedition and its objectives. If someone sustains an injury or falls victim to an accident, others must effect a rescue, no matter what the risk. Those evacuating an injured man to civilization would most likely forfeit their opportunity to climb the mountain.

I then stated with more emotion than I intended, "Before the expedition, I submitted a list of regulations, at which time I received no objections. Now it seems that some people do not respect these rules. I am purposely forcing the issue now, essentially before the climb, rather than at 18,000 feet. I know that the rules are conservative, but we have to be overly cautious on a climb of this magnitude. For those of you who feel that this mountain or route is not a worthy challenge, I suggest that you hike out and climb Mount Logan or some other peak. For myself, I agreed to assume the responsibility of leading this expedition under a set of ground rules, and I am willing to continue only if I have your full support." After a long moment of silence, I asked if there were any other complaints. Walt replied, trying to ease the burden cast before us, "I didn't have any until we called this meeting. Now I'm all wet." As people left the meeting entranced in deep thought, Walt said to me half joking, "Leading is a lonely position." And then he added with concern, "I don't like to see our two leaders not getting along."

Slowly, everyone prepared to pack loads to Camp II and in so doing each silently signified his willingness to sacrifice personal feelings in order to support the group regulations. Individuals had lost, and there were a few strained friendships, but the group had won. For the first time we were actually a group with group identity, group expectations, and group commitment. We would have to wait until tempers mended to be a well-oiled team, but we had taken the important first step.

I felt badly that Mark and Jerry Clark had been the butt of the meeting. Their actions had certainly been no more serious than those of others. They had triggered the internal organizational struggle, but a dozen other situations in the past several days could have served as well. Mark and Jerry were men of strong character and I knew that they would rise above this consternation. Had another person been the expedition leader, the ground rules may have been somewhat different, but they would have been just as necessary. In reality the conflict had not been personal; it was the sweaty labor of a group desperately fighting to be born.

Jerry Clark had earlier discussed the logistics of the trip with me. His idea was to "climb high and sleep low." By not having to relay most of the food consumed during the days of moving a camp to a higher camp, we could save perhaps a day or two on the overall length of the climb. Also altitude acclimation would be easier if a person had climbed to a given elevation several times before he was required to camp there. This effect would be smaller late in the climb when there would be less food and consequently fewer relays between camps. To avoid bottlenecking in the deep snow during the slow analysis of route-finding, a four-man advanced team would normally be stationed one camp ahead to open a highway for the human beasts of burden to follow. Half-loads would be carried by the advanced team to give them greater mobility for their other responsibilities. (Sometimes only three half-loads were carried by the advanced team to free the leader for difficult route-finding.) Once a safe route was determined, everyone would stay on the wanded trail to lessen the danger of a crevasse fall. A long bamboo pole served as a trail probe for the advanced team.

I asked Howard to lead the first advanced team which also included Jerry Lewis, Steve Taylor, and Mark McLaughlin. They would move up to Camp II and penetrate the Lower Icefall the following day. The four began packing their personal gear.

Jerry Clark assumed the awesome logistics of the expedition. With some help from Walt, it was his responsibility to assure that the mass of supplies was kept organized, food was relayed in labeled order, fuel conserved, planned food caches made and marked, and new camps properly equipped before occupation. Jerry also had the major responsibility for outside radio communications.

Luchterhand, Janes, and Schlichter were on my rope team for the day, and we shared our moraine rest break with the team of Snyder, Lewis, Walt Taylor, and Russell. They were en route to Camp II and we were returning.

I had read a lot about the Eiger and its incomparable North Face, so I asked Howard about his climb of this European mountain. He said that he had only taken the tourist walk-up route on the Eiger.

Hank and I became interested in the Mexican volcano-climbing trip taken by Howard and Paul, and we talked with them for a while about the details. These volcanoes can best be climbed in the winter and I thought that such a trek would be a good Christmas break the following year.

Back at McGonagall, I watched in astonishment as two rope teams of two climbers each arrived back from Camp II. Clark's rope team was to swap two men at Camp II for the return trip, leaving the proper advanced team personnel. Russell had made good on his threat not to rope up with a skier and had refused to rope up with Clark. I immediately took John aside. "Listen, John," I began, "you were the one bitching the most about people not following expedition ground rules and now you pull a stunt like this. If today is indicative of your attitude, I would prefer that you left the expedition." John apologized saying that Clark had riled his anger at Camp II. "I don't give a damn what happened," I retorted. "Jerry is the deputy leader of this expedition, and I fully expect you to follow his direction. When convenient, I have no objection to your climbing with whomever you want to; but, when necessary, you must be willing to rope up with any other member of the expedition and even risk your life for that person." John was calmer now than he had apparently been at Camp II, and he quietly agreed. My last comment was not needed: I knew that John would risk his life for a man, regardless of his personal feelings. He had the type of unreasoned self-abandonment that I would want in someone attempting to rescue me in a tight situation. Henceforth, John discreetly found it convenient not to travel on Jerry Clark's rope, although after a while it seemed more from habit than conviction.

We collected together the last of the supplies to be relayed. It would be a heavy carry the next day, but preferable to prolonging our stay at the pass. Around the McGonagall kitchen, we gazed with anxious envy up the glacier toward Camp II, as if we could see the advanced team. Our silence wished them Godspeed.

DAY 9 — JUNE 27

LOG:
"Low 30°F, high 54°F. Rose at 10:00 AM. Have bonfire at trash heap. Spent two hours packing cache food into several metal containers[6] to make. . . somewhat safe from bears, rodents, and birds. Jerry Clark, Paul, and Anshel hiked to top of Oastler Peak where they took several photo station pictures. We packed up camp at McGonagall and moved everything up to Camp II. . . Several loads were as heavy as 120 pounds. . ."

We could not afford many expensive items of freeze-dried food for the entire climb, but in the four-day McGonagall cache were several cans of freeze-dried steaks—a victory banquet for our outward hike. A couple pairs of trail snowshoes were left at the pass. Soon Dennis would be the only non-Snowtread climber. As I sat waiting for others to pack up, I cut a piece from a discarded plastic jar, lined it with Moleskin, and taped it to my goggles for a nose shield. We would be climbing more than halfway through the mass of the earth's protective atmosphere and already I had found it difficult to keep opaque sun cream on the sun sensitive skin of my nose. Fair-skinned John Russell watched my project with interest and then fashioned a similar nose shield for himself. When finished, John pondered for a moment, apparently dissatisfied that his product looked identical to mine. Then he located a can of spray paint and painted his nose shield fluorescent green. It seemed like such a natural thing for John to do that I hardly took notice.

I pondered our mountainous packs for a minute and gave mine a half-hearted tug without budging it. "When you hoist up a pack of this size," I told Dennis, "you speak kindly and say please." I left McGonagall Pass without looking back.

We hiked the 4½ miles in a driving snowstorm which abated

---

6. These were old bulk milk cans left by another expedition.

briefly as we approached Camp II. We arrived just after the return of a noticeably excited advanced team. Jerry Lewis had taken a ten-foot crevasse fall, and he exhibited the fatigue-forced alertness of someone who had just had his adrenalin banks drained. Mark was completely recovered from his morose anger of the previous day. We listened to the recount of the crevasse rescue: how an ice screw was used as an anchor in the rock ice, and how the pulley method was used for extraction. Steve was a fine ice climber, and Howard's opinion of his ability seemed much different than what he had expressed a few days earlier. Steve privately told me that it was a good thing we had shown the pulley method to the Colorado climbers. "I don't think they've done much training in a real crevasse before," he added. I suspected as much later when I learned that their route skirted the icefall completely, running directly beneath the hanging glaciers of the lower Pioneer Ridge and across the dingy amalgamated rubble of recent avalanche cones. Several people expressed concern about the highly exposed route.

We pitched a Logan tent, securing the guy lines with metal "coolie hats" buried in the snow as anchors. I crawled inside and began dinner. John brought a pail of water from the reservoir. Alone in the tent, I discovered that the stove was empty and using a funnel I proceeded to fill it with Blazo. I miscalculated the tank capacity and fuel ran onto the tent floor, forcing me to stop and mop it up with tissue paper. Priming the stove, I struck a match and with a "whump!" the floor of the tent was ablaze. Instinctively, I grabbed the pail of water and extinguished the superficial fire. John was just entering the tent and our yells of excitement brought the others. "Our Fearless Leader just tried to burn down the tent!" John exclaimed. (John and Walt had begun calling me "Fearless Leader" after the group meeting at McGonagall.) Surprisingly, there was no damage to the tent. I quickly advised a new expedition regulation: stoves would not be refueled in the tents. Relighting the stove I began cooking a big pot of chili.

The last rope team arrived from the pass collecting the trail wands en route. We had cut our umbilical cord with the outside world. The second Logan tent was pitched connecting with the cook tent, giving us the capability of having breakfast in bed if we desired.

Late in the evening I stood studying the Lower Icefall and the hanging glaciers of the right valley wall. Perhaps there was no passage through the icefall, but it would be worth another try. We were trained in pulling people out of crevasses; we were not trained in fending off tons of falling ice, rock, and snow. Anyway, the present route offered no protection from crevasses as Jerry Lewis could testify. Tomorrow we would attempt a safer route. I retired to my tent which was facing Gunsight Pass, a low portion of the right ridge. The snow-streaked rock appeared like newsprint pasted on a tagboard sky.

DAY 10 — JUNE 28

LOG:
". . . Low 28°F, high 56°F. Several people stick legs into crevasses. . . fair weather."

After Lewis' crevasse fall, it was advised that everyone carry an ice screw for emergency anchors. Walt selected a tubular ice screw from the cache and inquired somewhat in jest, "How do you use this—screw it in or hammer it in?"

"Damned if I know," I answered with a grin. "I don't have much faith in those new fangled gadgets. I'll let you use one of my ol' reliable Austrian 'coat hanger' ice screws." Walt agreed.

I was not at all sure that we could find an alternate route, so I asked the other eight men to remain at Camp II with their relay loads until we radioed our findings. We entered the icefall with only a fourth of the half-mile wide glacier to our right. I had always considered myself skilled in crevasse maze route-finding, but this mass of confused, upturned blocks of ice and criss-cross chasms was totally taxing. Time and again I stuck my foot into a concealed hole or collapsed a weak snow bridge, requiring yet another backtrack until our options were exhausted. As the glacier forced us to the right toward Pioneer Ridge, I noticed that the crevasses seemed shallower, being partially filled with avalanche debris. Finally after a tedious 800 foot climb we topped the icefall only a few yards from Howard's cache of the previous day. We radioed Camp II that they could begin, and after a short rest we set out on much more negotiable terrain.

I looked back as the steep icefall fell away from my vision and clouds filled the lower Muldrow. We were actually on the mountain now. The relatively flat, fluffy, white surface beneath our snowshoes was easy going, and we quickly crossed over and skirted the left end of a series of long traverse crevasses conspicuous by their covering of sunken snow. We could see more of the mountain now as features memorized from photographs and maps before the trip came into full view. There were two large rock protrusions squeezing the Muldrow from the right. One was low and flat, called the Flatiron, and further up was a high buttress named Taylor Spur. Mount Carpé, rising 12,550 feet, claimed the left ridge. Part of the Harper Icefall was visible, indicating the hidden presence of the high Harper Glacier separating Denali's two summits.

It was refreshing scenery; however, I was purposefully preoccupied in scanning the seracs of the Muldrow's Great Icefall, our next immediate obstacle. We passed a large raised area of intense crevassing resembling the stripes of a zebra, known as the Hill of Cracks and at a point chosen by the decreased tempo of the rope team, I dropped my pack. At an elevation of 8,100 feet, this would be Camp III. Four days' rations of food started the cache. Our downward steps were lightened by the satisfaction of the day's success, and I expressed my feeling that this was our first day of real mountaineering. There was no sign of the other eight climbers, and upon reaching Camp II we discovered that they had chosen to wait for the coolness of the psuedo-night when avalanches were less frequent. John was exuberant. "Joe put up a beautiful route through the icefall," adding in jest, "I don't know who put up that suicide route under the avalanches." Snyder did not laugh. The only thing beautiful about my route was that it was possible at all. It was tenuous at best and with luck might hold up a week under the warming air of an Alaskan summer. The trail did, however, offer some protection from the hanging glaciers, with a few intervening crevasses that would swallow an avalanche as impartially as a climber. We had made an ally of an adversary. Several people wanted to leave the rope partially uncoiled to save time in roping up the next day. They argued that the wet rope would dry more in the open air than in the cache. I agreed if the rope was not left where it could be stepped on and if it was draped over ice axes to prevent burial in a fresh snowfall.

Dennis was pleased that his long trail snowshoes had prevented him from breaking through some soft areas, and he announced that he was going to wear them clear to the summit. "The Hill of Cracks is colder than a witch's heart," Dennis advised. "Better dress warm if you're going up there at night." Heated by the internal furnace of trail-breaking, I had not noticed the cold. Steve donned his face mask in anticipation of Dennis' prediction causing Walt to muse, "If they find the body, they'll never believe it." Awhile after the load carriers left, we noticed that the weather was changing abruptly. Emerald-gray clouds, low, dark and muscle-striated, swept across our silent valley, casting a cool shadow. I wondered what meteorological phenomenon presented such an impressive vanguard.

DAY 11 — JUNE 29

The early morning return of the packers informed me that it was snowing like crazy outside. I briefly stuck my head out into the thick soft snowfall, its gigantic flakes reducing vision to a few feet, and then returned to my sleeping bag. "It's winter already," I thought. "Maybe next year the Alaskan summer will fall on a weekend."

LOG:
"Snow begins about 4:00 AM. Snows all day, depositing 3 feet of snow on camp. . . Low 26°F, high 34°F. . ."

The snow became deeper during the day, and our tents required several shovelings. Soon everything was engulfed in a uniform blanket of whiteness: packs, ropes, and snowshoes were first buried, followed by vertically standing ice axes and the wands marking the perimeter of our camp. Our food cache was a slightly raised hump in the midst of camp. The trail to Camp III was gone. Not one wand was visible. The concealing snowfall had made the icefall a treacherous death trap. The valley walls echoed with the muffled rumble of distant avalanches. There would be no climbing until the fresh snow had consolidated and equalized with its new environment. The day was spent in uncovering the cache, packs, and other equipment and in idle amusements. Snowballs were soon flying through the air from the hands of men expressing their fond memories of boyhood. Steve and I began a game of chess in which he quickly gained the advantage. Faced with the prospect of a long, eventless day and not wishing to concede defeat, I stalled the game as long as possible. Hank read aloud from a book entitled *Zen Zen*. He read an anecdote about a man who found himself cornered by hungry tigers. Faced with imminent death the man plucked a nearby wild strawberry, ate it, and observed that it was the finest strawberry that he had ever eaten. I thought the story curiously odd and returned to the hopeless chess game. Since most of us were of draftable age, the conversation eventually turned to the Vietnam War, and how it was that we were here and not there. Several people had deferments; several others had fulfilled some form of military obligation. I had been drummed out of a regular NROTC program because of my bad knee. Hank was teaching deprived kids in a ghetto. Mark said that he had asthma which became chronic whenever he got within two blocks of his draft board, and John stated that he had been declared unregimentable. No one doubted John's statement. Dennis pined that this was his first all-male mountain trip. I answered that the best female prospect, Sally Gordon, had been grounded by her parents since an encounter with a pelvis-crushing rock on Rainier the previous year. Since then she had only managed one undercover climb of Mount Nebo. Finally Steve's patience gave out, and he consented to a draw in the marathon chess match.

DAY 12 — JUNE 30

LOG:
"Clear and sunny. Low 24°F, high 36°F. Avalanches coming off of Tatum and Pioneer Ridge. Everyone dries gear and soaks up sun. . ."

"I had a strange dream last night." John related.
"What was strange about it?" I asked.
"I dreamt that a large jet full of people landed here," he said. As I gazed across the glacier, absent-mindedly searching for a suitable jet airstrip, John continued, "They were going to heaven and they wanted me to come along."
"And what did you tell them?" I asked.
"I told them that I couldn't go now because I was climbing Mount McKinley," John answered matter-of-factly.

I had had a taste of the upper Muldrow and was anxious to get back. Impatiently I waited for the snow to consolidate and contemplated the wisdom of trying the icefall during the day. Suddenly a sharp crack emitted from high on the shoulder of Mount Tatum, followed by the rumblings of a newly-born avalanche. My searching eyes soon located the cascading snow, and I watched in awe as it gathered in intensity filling my ears with a deep roar. It hit the bottom of the slope defiantly and shot halfway across the gaping Lower Icefall before being fully arrested. A fine white mist was suspended in the air for several minutes. Traveling would have to wait for night. I stretched out my foam pad and let the sun's warmth massage my pack-sore back. In the heat, the snow receded like the tallow of a heavy wicked candle.

With the coolness of evening we all packed up to climb to Camp III. Our wands were visible again, and Dennis led in order to rebreak the route with his long trail snowshoes. Paul, Hank, Anshel, and I would stay at Camp III to become the advanced team for the Great Icefall. By rotating the advanced team's roster, everyone would get a chance to be on a route-finding team. Also, it afforded the opportunity for each person to become familiar with climbing and tenting with every other individual. Darkness was just beginning to expand the night again, making my final trip up the Lower Icefall a winter wonderland draped in deep hues of blue and purple.

DAY 13 — JULY 1

Above the icefall, as morning approached, fire-like alpin-glow danced across the surface of the snow, glistening on the partially melted mantle. We hiked slowly in a burgundy sea of rubies and diamonds until all motivation for movement ceased. I noticed that others were experiencing the same intense beauty. Sitting and standing we separately absorbed the fortunate circumstances of our environment. Few words were spoken. None were adequate. Like all supreme experiences, this one was fleeting and soon passed, leaving our three rope teams to finish the hike strung out on the naked morning whiteness of the glacier. As we approached camp, I noticed that someone had broken a parallel trail for a few yards, forming an island on which was inscribed "DO NOT CROSS

MEDIAN."

At the cache Luchterhand dropped his load, and the second man, John Russell, moved in, dumped his load, and unroped, apparently thinking the campsite was already probed. Clark was on the second rope team, and seeing the situation, shouted a stern reprimand to John from a distance. John glared back, shrugged his shoulders in contempt and then slowly and reluctantly roped up again. Although I was on Clark's rope, I did not intervene in the confrontation. I didn't understand why John had unroped as he was returning to Camp II on the same rope. I probed the campsite, and we began to set up camp.

The third rope team moved in and dropped their loads. Howard asked me if I was going to leave the camp at this site. I looked around trying to detect any gross deficiencies in the area. Howard gestured across the glacier toward a triangular rock face on Pioneer Ridge. "The Hill of Cracks camp is over there," he said in a knowledgeable tone.

"Where?" I asked somewhat puzzled, searching the homogeneous glacier surface in vain for a spot with obviously superior campsite qualities and half expecting to see a posted sign.

"Washburn says that the Hill of Cracks camp is over there," Howard added.

"Oh," I said without emotion or further comment.

LOG:
"Low 22°F, high 33°F at Camp III. Sleep all day. . .
First contact with Eielson about 8:30 PM. Able to contact them from both Camp II and III."

Our first radio contact was an exciting moment. The seasonal rangers monitoring the Eielson radio were George Perkins and Gordon Haber. (Their Lafayette 525 citizens band transceiver was on loan from park employee, George Robinson.) We had brought two Lafayette radios with us on the mountain: a five-watt transceiver which we called "Unit One," and a three-watt "Unit Two." Both had internal batteries as well as auxilary plug-in battery packs, designed so that they could be kept warm by body heat to prolong their life. Incubating the batteries was a job which was rotated without complaint.

At about 11:00 PM the advanced party set out to tackle the Great Icefall. It was a slow climb as our snowshoes were sinking a foot and a half into the soft snow. The Great Icefall was a giant version of the Lower Icefall with monsterous ice blocks and crevasses. These definite, clear-cut barriers were decisively insurmountable, making route-finding less ambiguous than that which we had experienced in the Lower Icefall. We swung around the right of the major disruption and then back toward the middle of the glacier.

DAY 14 — JULY 2

The deep powder snow was a stubborn antagonist, draining our energy and greedily consuming time, until we were forced to turn back short of our hoped for 11,000 foot destination. We dropped our loads at about 10,200 feet near the Flatiron and returned to Camp III exhausted, having been on the trail more than fourteen hours. Switching rope leaders in a heavily crevassed area is not safe, and I was especially tired from having led all of the way.

As we descended the foothills of the Great Icefall, we were treated to a colorful sight: the other eight climbers had moved up to Camp III, and our broadside view of their one-street settlement was impressive. A short distance to the right, Walter Taylor was putting some finishing touches on a snow fortress heavily decorated with wands. Closer inspection revealed that this two-sided structure was a throne, indeed, complete with buttocks-protecting slats from a Blazo crate. Walt's creation was the subject of considerable discussion and perhaps the world's most photographed outhouse.

LOG:
"Four advanced party arrive back Camp III about 1:30 PM. . . Low 18°F, high 54°F. . ."

The only available source of water at Camp II was contained in our solid white surroundings. On warm days some snow was successfully melted by spreading it thinly on a black sheet of plastic; more often, it had to be melted in a heated pot. With the increased stove use, Dennis removed the flimsy muslin cloth frost liners[7] from the Logan tents as a safety precaution. He said that

---

7. Frost liners are used in cold weather to collect freezing breath moisture and prevent its falling on sleeping bags and other gear where it could cause dampness.

some of the pump gaskets were starting to wear out already. Shortly after 8:00 PM we had our second radio contact with Eielson. The rangers said that they had spotted our Camp III tent the night before by telescope; we were now in the public eye. Hank asked them to send his summer employer a postcard indicating that he would report for work a little later than expected.

Late in the evening eight pack mules descended the darkened icefall to bring up the last of Camp II while the remaining four of us rested in anticipation of a daytime assault to push the upper Muldrow route.

DAY 15 — JULY 3

LOG:
"Low 22°F, high 34°F. . . necessary to rebreak trail most of way as it. . . snowed all day and the night before. . ."

It was a frustrating day treading the Great Icefall with full loads, as our deep trail of the previous day was completely filled with new and wind-blown snow. A dense, dry snow was falling, as I moved in a mechanical trance through an audio-vacuum. There was only the soft squeak of the snow compressing under my Snowtreads and the light rasp of my breathing to keep me company. Whenever I paused, there was such absolute silence that I could sense individual snowflakes striking my nylon wind clothes. Our pace slowed as the situation resembled a rerun of the day before. Paul suggested that he might break trail for a while, and I readily agreed. We found a relatively safe area and switched rope leaders. Another two hours found us creeping up to the Flatiron cache. We dumped our loads without speaking and headed dejectedly back to Camp III—defeated again.

When we got back to camp the others were awake from their daytime sleep and had already completed the evening radio contact with Eielson. They reported that Mark had chatted with one of his classmates who was visiting Eielson for the day. She had asked about the temperature—to which Mark had replied that they were all wearing Bermuda shorts and planned to wear them to the summit.

I was not pleased to learn that extra packages of food had been burned in the Camp II trash fire which had also been helped along by some of our precious fuel. We had a liberal surplus of both food and fuel, but unpredictable circumstances in this remote land could quickly reclassify surplus items as necessary items, making a premature destruction of excess commodities disastrous. There was a rumor that both skiers, Clark and McLaughlin, had had problems negotiating the Lower Icefall in the changing snow conditions. Subsequently I noticed that the skis were cached at Camp III and not used again.

Later in the cook tent, Dennis good-naturedly complained, "What's so damn depressing about this pack mule business is that the glacier is creeping downhill, while we're trying to go up—like going up the down escalator. And everytime we stop to sleep, we lose ground."

"Think what a great help it'll be when we descend the mountain," I offered. Dennis was not reassured. Searching for something more convincing, I finally observed, "It seems to me that the higher we get on this mountain, the further we will be from the center of the earth, and consequently the pull of gravity will be less, lightening our loads." We both laughed at my struggling attempt at consoling humor.

DAY 16 — JULY 4

LOG:
"Low 18°F — Greeted with a day of sunshine. Spent two hours taking group pictures. . . Missed radio check with Eielson. . ."

The day began with a pop! John had brought a 3-inch firecracker for the occasion, having carefully protected it from the penetrating dampness. Unfortunately, the acoustics of the upper Muldrow were bad, and the explosion sounded like the breaking of a small balloon.

What began as our first real act of togetherness, a group picture, soon became a serious proof sitting. Each photographer in turn had to carefully adjust his camera, strap it to an ice axe, and set his automatic shutter release. Of course, to assure a good picture, several exposures had to be made at several different camera settings. After a long hour, people began fidgeting and looking forward to the end. John was the first, cleverly stepping behind someone as the shutter clicked, and probably laughing to himself at the thought of a meticulous photographer later viewing an incomplete group photo. Finally John disappeared into a tent and could not be coaxed out. Before the ordeal was over,

I was getting concerned that our photo project was chewing a significant hunk out of a perfect climbing day. John expressed my feelings exactly as he stated indignantly, "When we run out of film, we can start climbing this damn mountain."

Howard approached me requesting what plans I now had for high camps and summit climbing. Although I had made no statements on the matter, there were apparently rumors of all kinds. Howard said that he wanted to express his feeling that it should be 12 men to the top on the same day. I replied that the logistics were greater for a massive 12-man high camp, and it was common and conceivable in a group of this size for one or more people to be unable to acclimate properly. This, of course, I wouldn't know until we started noticeable altitude gains. I added that until such time as possible problems and desires made themselves known, I would be planning on 12 summit climbers.

The long trail snowshoes of Dennis Luchterhand were once again marshalled to the rescue of an expedition in deep powder. Dennis led the first rope team to break a trail to 11,000 feet and Camp IV. A second team followed and Howard, John, Walt, and I formed the third: we would occupy Camp IV as the next advanced team. I turned for my last look at Camp III and Walt's now-sagging structure. It had served us well. The Great Icefall was brilliantly intriguing as I hiked through it for the first time on a clear day. Our winding, well-packed trail resembled a giant game of fox and geese. We passed the Flatiron cache and continued toward the walls that encircled the head of the Muldrow Glacier. Directly in front of us and becoming more menacing with each step of our approach was the Harper Icefall. It was in reality an ice cliff—a tongue of deeply fractured blue ice, 500 feet thick hanging 3,000 feet down a precariously steep slope and there, poised at the edge of a sheer black wall 500 feet above the Muldrow. This dark granite wall was an exposure of the resistive batholithic core which had intruded into the Mesozoic rock to form this skyward uplift of land, a monument to natural forces. The icefall was fed by the high Harper Glacier, and it in turn fed the Muldrow in frequent thundering avalanches that filled the Muldrow cirque with a lingering cool mist. Our camp was protected by only a few intervening crevasses, not enough for great comfort. The Harper Icefall was catastrophic, and I was content to view it from a distance. I surveyed the steep skyline ridge to the left, known as

Karstens Ridge. It looked none too secure, yet it was the only known route around the Harper Icefall. I felt a pang of vulnerability; tomorrow we would assault the ridge, a day of truth. After a sponge bath, I changed my underwear for the first time on the trip. There was very poor laundry service in this part of the world.

Resting sleeplessly in my sleeping bag on this brisk, near zero night, I pondered the strengths and weaknesses of the group's interpersonal relationships. When twelve human beings are isolated together, there are inevitably some friendship preferences and personality clashes. These make themselves evident in tentmates, cooking groups, and assimilation of rope teams, as well as the more obvious consensus or conflicts of philosophy. Aside from the selected advanced party, a rope team on a particular day may determine itself simply by which four men are first standing around ready to go; however, long range trends usually reflect either a conscious or subconscious assessment of friendships and projected hiking paces.

The close pre-trip friendship of Jerry Clark and Mark McLaughlin continued throughout the climb; they usually hiked and tented together whenever convenient. Jerry came to the climb in less than superior physical shape and took a while to regain proper conditioning. Mark did not seem to mind the necessary slow pace; however, later he climbed more frequently with Hank and Dennis, while Jerry gravitated to the more agreeable pace of Anshel and Steve. Jerry never hiked with John after their Camp II blow up (by John's choice). Mark never roped up with Walter, and seldom with Anshel, although he seemed friendly with them in camp. Mark's subtle humor sometimes surfaced. I was told that he once tried to check through the rigorous Mount Rainier equipment inspection with a balsa wood ice axe.

Hank maintained his quiet, friendly disposition which was neither timid nor overbearing. He and Dennis struck up a friendship which amplified their unmatched frames, truly the Mutt and Jeff of the group. Hank also climbed a lot with Paul Schlichter and I, but never with Steve, Walt, or Howard. Hank kept his personal gear meticulously well organized.

In contrast to his good friend Hank, Dennis was an extrovert and was also an openly noticeable "group" man. He seemed always to be cooking or melting snow and was the first in the chow line with his one-quart Tupperware measuring cup which he called his "fair share cup." His striking facial features were accented by a weird hand-knitted stocking hat which he wore perennially, a gift from a girlfriend. Dennis and Walt developed a habit of exchanging greetings at marginal earshot distances with a loud "mathah," perhaps a satire on the ringing trills of alpine yodeling. Dennis seldom hiked with Jerry Clark or Anshel, and never with Howard Snyder. Underneath, Dennis was a profoundly intricate thinker on expedition matters and sometimes exhibited hints of his pre-trip apprehensions.

The strongest and most unlikely friendship was between Walt Taylor, the witty humorist, tactful conciliator and lubricator of organizational gears, and John Russell, the brash individualist who reveled in insulting Anshel's educated etiquette and goading the silent tempers of Howard Snyder and Jerry Clark. Walt and John were well matched in physical ability and among the strongest climbers in the group. I did not think John the saboteur that others did. Behind his barroom rhetoric was a concealed devotion to the group. He often greeted a descending party with a hot meal, feigning complaint to avoid receiving compliments, and routinely packed the heaviest loads. True, John was the biggest abuser of group equipment, but he was also the most conscientious mender. The only irritation which I got from John was his relentless insistence on reducing the weight of the expedition, even suggesting that we discard the wrappers on items in the first aid kit. He also continually complained about the "company matches," wax-coated matches that did not light very well unless all of the wax was carefully peeled off.

Steve Taylor and Anshel Schiff were two introverted loners, brought together mostly by the similarity of their hiking speeds. Anshel was the one man on the trip whose physical conditioning did not seem to improve. It was my initial impression that Anshel was deliberately dieting as a means of losing weight; however, I later learned that he suffered acute heartburn and could not eat either before or during each day's hike. Anshel had apparently anticipated such problems and was able to conceal his condition from almost everyone on the expedition by relying on his personal supply of antacid tablets, which he consumed at the rate of a dozen per day. His physical weakness was a temptation for Anshel to carry less than a full load whenever the opportunity presented itself. He was more realistic than apologetic about his capabilities and avoided hiking with John Russell, probably due to their intense disagreement on the use of group equipment. Steve was slow on the trail but never tired. He preferred maintaining a large reserve of energy for possible emergencies. In forming rope teams, Steve avoided the Colorado climbers and never hiked with Hank. Straitlaced and proper Steve enjoyed an unsuspected friendship with the Taylor-Russell duo. Walt once told me, "Steve is such a nice guy that he embarrasses me. Here I am reduced to a grabbing gluttony, wiping the stew out of my beard with my shirt sleeve, and Steve says in his best banquet etiquette, 'Pass the salt please.' "

Hank, Dennis, and Anshel frequented my rope team while Walt, Steve, and Jerry Lewis did not. Low on the mountain, Jerry Clark and I were usually separated by our respective leadership responsibilities; however, we later had an opportunity to climb together and revive the friendship and mutual respect of our pre-trip planning. Mark, Steve, and I had brought hard hats which we wore as far as the top of Karstens Ridge.

When the Colorado climbers were on separate rope teams, Paul Schlichter and Jerry Lewis were quiet, yet congenial and genuinely friendly. Howard, however, maintained a cold veneer, an edge to his disposition that was perplexing. I knew that my perception was subjectively influenced by an emerging personality clash, but still imagined that Howard felt himself a displaced leader. He seemed bothered by many of my leadership decisions and the relative inefficiency of our larger group, and I suspected these concerns were simmering and smoldering unpredictably in silent indignation.

Howard had alienated several expedition members with his hiking habits. Leading a long rope team on undulating terrain requires a great deal of consideration for others. While the leader is stepping gingerly down a slope, his ropemates may still be negotiating an upgrade. The situation has a whiplash effect, increasing with the length of the rope. To avoid fatiguing the other climbers, the leader must assume a moderate pace. Both Steve Taylor and Mark McLaughlin on separate occasions submitted to me that they no longer desired to hike on Howard's rope because of his insensitivity to this problem. Howard's pace seemed devoid of knowledgeable use of the energy-saving rest step technique (a momentary pause between each step) and was usually near the exhaustion level of the slowest hiker on his rope team. He apparently did not realize that should he take a fall, the fumbling efforts of that drained climber may be the only thing standing between him and a blue eternity. A rope team is only as strong as its weakest member. Howard maintained that speed is safety in the mountains. I agreed that one must be able to move fast, but practicing it as a matter of course is dangerous. The other two Colorado climbers amplified Howard's torrid pace when the three were on the same rope.

One possible reason, I discovered, was that the low altitude rubber boots of the Colorado group were poorly insulated and they were hiking fast to keep their feet warm. In reality, the pace of the Colorado team had the reverse effect whenever circumstances dictated relative inactivity during the hike. It was almost a comical drama. A rope team meandering up the trail leisurely taking pictures and perhaps pausing for a quarter hour to soak up the beauty would block the path of an overtaking, huffing and perspiring Colorado group, who when suddenly halted, would go through impatient antics of fidgeting and stomping designed to salvage their cooling toes and dissipate their growing irritation. Jerry Lewis nearly always hiked on Howard's rope, and sometimes after a ride on this fast freight he looked really tired. I was concerned with his stamina. The Colorado group did not make more relays or carry heavier loads; they simply spent less time on the trail and more in their tent. In camp the Colorado group was even more distinct, isolating themselves and offering essentially no social interaction. They had every appearance of being a separate three-man expedition, climbing the mountain and camping in our campsite only to satisfy the regulations of the Park Service. They were unquestionably committed to the climb. I hoped that I would not have to depend on their commitment to the group.

The other nine climbers were open and explicit in their feelings and disagreements, giving an aura of reassuring predictability. One always knew what Walt or Dennis would do in a given situation. When the chips were down, a John Russell would not hesitate an instant in pulling a Jerry Clark from a crevasse, although he might bitch and curse during the process. We were like the siblings of a large family: sometimes irritated by close living, yet with an underlying bond of brotherhood stronger than life. The Colorado climbers seemed at times bewildered by this paradox.

DAY 17 — JULY 5

LOG:
"Establish radio contact about 9:30 AM.[8] Able to hear
Eielson too, but they are unable to hear us. . . Avalanches
from Harper Icefall about every twenty minutes. . ."

We left Camp IV in late morning and traveled left, up the
glacier to the base of the ridge. Here we cut sharply to the left
above a steep crevasse, whose lower lip had collapsed forming a
jumbled ice wall, and angled toward a saddle on the ridge 500 feet
above Camp IV. The slope was steep enough to avalanche
and I felt helplessly awkward wading waist deep on Snowtreads.
With Walt and John sharing the lead with me, we managed to
wallow to the ridge crest in four hours. Walt was leading and
immediately began forcing a trail up the steep knife-edge ridge. We
soon called a halt to this activity as being too dangerous. We would
have to break the ridge route without snowshoes no matter how
deep we sank into the boggy snow. The view from the ridge crest
was an exhilarating change from the blinders of the Muldrow's
walls. There was valley after valley and ridge after ridge of
impressive peaks—in staccato, appointed with glimmering alabas-
ter robes and templed against the sky. The fingers of the Traleika
Glacier were blocked by Denali's high East Buttress. Karstens
Ridge above us fell away sharply to either side, almost too steep for
self-arresting. Should someone slip off the ridge down a
hard-packed slope probably the only hope would be for another
man on the rope team to jump off the other side—a "jump ridge"
I called it. A slip was unlikely in the deep snow, and I felt a false
sense of security, not fully appreciating that a seductive avalanche
could easily break beneath our steps and sweep us off the ridge,
perhaps into one of the gaping crevasses of the Muldrow or maybe
down the 3,500 foot rock studded wall leading to the West Fork of
the Traleika Glacier.

We were tired, and the lateness of the hour was chilling so we
called it a day, scooping out a platform on the saddle of the ridge
to cache our loads. Camp IV was visible below us as we watched a

8. With Camp III.

team of packers begin their return to Camp III. A faint "mathah" floated up accompanied by an arm wave from a tall figure. Walt bellowed in return with a volume that threatened to precipitate an avalanche. John and Walt spent a few minutes demonstrating to their own conviction the infeasibility of an ice axe belay on our fluffy footing, and then we descended to Camp IV in 20 minutes. The day's work had been a little over a half mile of trail breaking. As we were preparing dinner, the second pack team arrived.

During the period that I was not breaking trail in the day's floundering onslaught, I had experienced the deep-freeze of cooling sweat so this would be the last day for my low altitude footgear. I unpacked my felt boots and insulated overboots, priming them for their maiden voyage.

DAY 18 — JULY 6

LOG:
"Advanced group packs full loads to crest of Karstens where half-loads from day before were cached. Pick up half-loads and break trail up the ridge. . . Rest of group move camp from III to IV. . ."

A hundred yards out of camp the hinge snapped on my right Snowtread. I unshouldered my pack, located some nylon cord, and commenced the quarter hour repair procedure of lashing the boot binding to the Snowtread base. Once mended, I hefted my heavy pack, stood on the mended Snowtread, and then shifted my weight to my left foot to begin hiking again. Snap! The whole process had to be repeated for the other Snowtread. After repairs we made good time to the ridge crest at 11,500 feet and paused there to switch loads. By now the temperature was cold enough and my whiskers were long enough to collect ice from wind and storm and from the moisture of breathing. I noticed that Howard was applying liberal amounts of sun cream to his blush burned face, perhaps compensating for an oversight of the previous day.

I began the snowshoeless struggle up the ridge's ascending curved spine. The snow depth increased with altitude. Hip deep became waist deep, chest deep, and finally shoulder deep. I began to think that I would soon need a snorkel to continue. The situation was further frustrated by a whiteout that persisted in reducing visibility to a few feet. At times the ridge seemed to end altogether, and I could only proceed by following what I sensed to be the highest part of the ridge, correcting myself periodically whenever the slope lurched sharply down to the right or left. I accidently kicked off a few small cornices and avalanches that cascaded across our access trail to the ridge. Suspecting that other cornices might fall at an inopportune time, John purposely dislodged a few. Walt heavily wanded the deep trail. After a time made exceedingly long by our inability to switch trail-breakers, I topped a narrow level shelf at 12,100 feet, which was the only possible campsite on Karstens Ridge. This would be Camp V. I probed the area, we dumped our loads, and descended to the saddle to relay full loads. The weather was clearing and Walt's startling "mathah" with a delayed echo brought my gaze to Camp IV and the arrival of Luchterhand's rope. Howard was complaining of cold feet so we quickened our pace back up the ridge to Camp V. Before our descent I paused to assess the now visible upper ridge. From this close vantage position, it was not a continuous ridge, but an irregular confusion of oddly pitched segments intersecting at various angles. (Reportedly Karstens Ridge was a much simpler obstacle before it was shattered by an earthquake in 1912.) Small overhanging cornices liberally graced both sides of the lower ridge making it difficult to determine the prevailing wind direction.[9] A shallow glacier covered the Muldrow side of the ridge. One bergschrund[10] was visible just downslope from the campsite; another much larger bergschrund had parted from the very crest of the ridge for several hundred yards just above camp. Beyond this, the major disruptions of the ridge were two gigantic snow

---

9. The prevailing storm systems move out of the Aleutian Islands to strike Mount McKinley from the southwest, on the opposite side of the mountain mass from Karstens Ridge. Obviously, the direction and velocities of winds on Karstens Ridge are drastically affected by the orographic disruptions of the mountain itself. We experienced winds from both sides of the ridge during our climb; however, the largest cornices and cornice remnants were on the northwest (Muldrow) side of the ridge indicating that the major storm winds probably blow across Karstens Ridge from the southeast (Traleika) side.

10. As a glacier moves downslope responding to gravity, it pulls away from its headwalls. The crevasse at the head or beginning of a glacier is called a bergschrund.

bulwarks, likely the remnants of years of tremendous cornicing activity. The 50-foot vertical northwest faces of these snow bulwarks exhibited many layers, the sedimented record of storms, seasons, and years. Evidently these snow bulwarks were permanent features of the ridge, providing perennial footing for cornices.

An uncheckable fall on Karstens Ridge had cost the life of McKinley Park ranger Elton Thayer in 1954, and I was glad that we had brought an adequate supply of fixed line for the more exposed sections. Our return to the Muldrow found the bustle of a reunited 12-man camp. Two days' rations of food had been cached at Camp III for the descent.

John, Hank, and I worked on an outhouse recessed, shoulder deep, into the glacier surface, with access stairs and graffiti. To save weight, we had not carried snow shovel handles, using ice axes for handles. The combination seemed to work well. Jerry Clark rigged a dipole antenna to improve the propagation of radio waves from this colony of humanity, tucked snugly into the high glacier cirque. His efforts were applauded as successful during the scheduled radio contact with Eielson.

Dennis became very interested in Gordon Haber's study of wolves, and they chatted for a while about Gordy's latest observations. Dennis stated that he would just as soon be helping with the wolf study as living in this sterile environment although there were some compensations. "At least," he said, "there are no mosquitoes up here."

Hank, Mark, Dennis, and I would occupy Camp V the next day, accompanied by fixed line and pickets for the next ridge assault. In the cook tent there was an ongoing discussion on the effects of various hallucinogenic drugs, while John was massaging Walt's pack-sore back. Several of us looked on with silent envy, frequently readjusting our stiff bodies, as if we could vicariously feel the soothing massage. "You know," Walt reminisced, "girls are very vulnerable to backrubs. A girl will do just about anything if you give her a backrub." We listened with heightened curiosity, expecting Walt to share his amorous secrets and relate to us the details of the great loves of his life which had been precipitated by backrubs. Walt did not elaborate.

DAY 19 — JULY 7

LOG:

". . . Snow during the night and all day leaving a foot of fresh powder on the trail. Low last night 5°F. . ."

I asked if anyone would be willing to hike a mile back down the trail and relay the six-load Flatiron cache to Camp IV, in addition to a regular carry to Camp V. John, Paul, Steve, and Walt volunteered and made the heavy carry with load-and-a-half packs. Jerry Lewis had a painful case of apparent snowblindness in his left eye, so I agreed to allow him to remain alone in Camp IV for the day. Ideologically, I was opposed to leaving a lone man in camp; however, Jerry couldn't travel safely, and another man left with him would mean one less load up to Camp V. Besides, Jerry would be within sight and earshot of the rest of us for most of the day's packing hike. The advanced team shouldered their personal gear and headed for the ridge which was almost calm, with very lightly drifting fog. On the crest I could see my shadow on a fog bank a hundred feet down the Traleika side of the ridge, and the suspended moisture around my warm body created an optical effect, a rainbow halo was visible around my shadow. Shadows of my ropemates were also visible, but without halos—each person could see only his own rainbow and not that of the others.

We had pitched tents at Camp V and eaten lunch before the other two rope teams arrived in close succession to each other. Howard, Anshel, and Jerry Clark were just leaving camp as John quickly examined the cache and vocally expressed the urgent need for a group meeting. We all paused from our activities to listen to John. Howard was 50 feet down the trail and waited there. "Anshel, there's a rumor that you are only carrying half loads," John accused. Anshel was silent as John's glare demanded an answer. Finally Jerry Clark spoke up. "John, you weigh 180 pounds to my 145 and I resent your implication that I should be able to carry as much as you. It's just not realistic."

John calmed a bit. "I don't mind carrying a heavier load," he said. "It's just that I don't like people carrying lighter loads on the sly; if you're going to do it, do it openly so everyone knows what's going on." Apparently, John was also upset that Howard, Anshel, and Jerry Clark had not yet left Camp IV when he returned from the arduous Flatiron carry; next he addressed me, "The Fearless Leader should be out every morning, assigning duties and rope teams." He then looked at Clark. "And the Deputy Fearless should be helping him."

"No," Dennis countered strongly, "it's not their job—it's yours and mine. We're adults and we know what has to be done each day. It's up to us to get things rolling." The meeting adjourned indistinctly, and the two rope teams descended. John had surfaced some concerns that were irritating a lot of us. Only the night before, Steve and I had privately discussed some of the same problems, the normal frustrations born of deep snow and communal living. John's one-man show was a non-threatening source of reprimand, causing a dissipation of anxiety. I could feel it in myself and sense it in the others. We could almost laugh at the situation.

There were four of us now in the cramped quarters of Camp V, a relatively flat 50 by 30 foot safe area of the ridge. On either side the slope dropped off steeply 1,000 feet to the Muldrow and 4,000 feet to the Traleika. Our home was a precarious perch in an otherwise vertical world and as night closed on this catwalk in the sky, I felt a little uneasy.

DAY 20 — JULY 8

LOG:
"Got a foot of snow. . . winds (night) on ridge. Ridge team unable to move entire day, others do same. . . Nearly everyone switched to high altitude cold weather footgear by this camp. Able to get Anchorage radio station[11] — listen to hit tunes, news. . ."

We spent this day of bad weather mostly confined to our tents; Hank and Dennis in the Mountaineer and Mark and I in his homemade Cascade. This was my first one-to-one pairing with Mark and we spent the day getting better aquainted, exchanging philosophies of life and lesser matters.

In the early afternoon I began hearing a faint but distinct repetitious scraping sound, like something digging. The map showed no evidence of mining activities in the area and the number of biological entities on the ridge was well inventoried. I stuck my head out of the tent, just in time to see a flurry of white being

---

11. On Mark's transistor radio.

thrown from a hole in the snow slope a few feet away. "Hey!" I hollered, and the head of Dennis Luchterhand appeared from the snowbank with a look of deep concentration. "What are you doing?" I asked.

"Digging a snow cave," Dennis answered. "Want to help?"

"Sure," I replied. I joined Dennis in the snow cave that was already large enough for several people. I started pushing dislodged snow toward the entrance while Dennis continued digging with the vigorous tempo of an architect who has not nearly completed his creation. "What are you digging?" I finally asked, "A 12-man snow cave?"

"That's the plan," he replied matter-of-factly. "We may need it," he added. "The fiberglass side supports on the Mountaineer tent snapped in that high wind last night." I crawled out to daylight to investigate. Sure enough, the sides of the Mountaineer tent sagged helplessly inward, resembling the windward side of a baggy sail. The damage was somewhat surprising as we had trenched the tents into the ridge about three feet deep. I had heard reports of respectable tents being actually blown apart on this ridge. The snow cave was perhaps more than bad weather amusement. We continued our work as "My cup runneth over with love. . ." blared from Mark's radio.

We had planned to leave two days' rations at Camp IV; however, in a radio conversation with Walt he convinced me that this made little sense as we had already left a large cache of food at Camp III. It was decided to transport the two days' rations higher on the mountain. They were not high altitude menus and would serve only as emergency backup food.

So far, our food selection seemed quite palatable, aside from the natural boredom that comes from trying to consume massive amounts of calories in dehydrated form (5,000-6,000 calories per person per day). The most often uneaten items were the bulky cracker-type rations. Some drink mixes were left unused low on the mountain, but this situation corrected itself in the high dry air. Cheese was used so little early in the climb that I was almost persuaded to leave it at McGonagall Pass. Consumption picked up with altitude, however, and few chunks were left after our highest camps. Fruit-filled Jell-O, chilled in the snow, was relished by all. The soybean bacon-bits were eaten at an increasingly slower rate; "fakey bacies" Jerry Clark called them. Fudge (fudgies) early ascended to the pinnacle of food preference, the highest denomination of barter exchange. Vitamin and mineral pills were taken religiously and were jokingly referred to as birth control pills. Except for Anshel, no one seemed to be losing weight. I actually felt a little heavier than my normal 185 pounds. The Colorado climbers also seemed to be doing okay on their food, with Jerry Lewis appearing a bit thinner. Like most expeditions we were not bothered with contagious illnesses; unless germs are brought in with a group, there aren't many to be found on high icy mountains.

DAY 21 — JULY 9

LOG:

"Weather clearing. Ridge team leaves camp at 11:45 AM; find going up ridge very hard with snow up to 5 feet deep. . . use about 500 feet fixed line; spent 9 hours on ridge. Rest of group bring camp up from IV. . . Steve, Clark, Schiff, Walt make two trips. Trail from IV to V completely snowed and blown over, requiring rebreaking. Wind 20-30 miles per hour on ridge all day. . ."[12]

We were very anxious to make progress up the ridge, but were once again foiled by deep snow. On this long day we gained only 600 vertical feet of the ridge, that is, to the top of the second snow bulwark. Again, I led all of the way without relief. Hank wanded, while Mark and Dennis installed the pickets and fixed line. We carried no supply loads. At one point the snow suddenly gave way under my step. I fell to my right knee, with my left leg dangling in air. A cornice had broken under me, and I watched as it slid, tumbled, and rolled out of sight beginning its 4,500 foot journey to the Traleika Glacier. A man could not survive such a fall.

Besides the diurnal energy fluctuations of work and rest, there is an underlying reservoir of life energy that must be occasionally tapped to overcome exceptional circumstances. Once drained, this inner core takes a lengthy time to regenerate. A person's success on

---

12. The expedition carried a small anemometer for measuring mild and moderate winds. To the best of my knowledge it was never used. Wind velocities reported by the expedition were human approximations.

the climb would depend on his judicious conservation of this psychologically and motivationally controlled resource. Having done most of the route-finding trail-breaking since Camp II, I was beginning to feel the inner energy drain. If this continued I might forfeit my chance at the summit; it would be vain and unwise to continue constant leading, especially while others were just as capable of the job.

On the descent to Camp V, the deep, trough-like trail seemed bombproof, yet I felt more secure being able to clip a carabiner into our newly installed fixed line. The eight climbers had arrived at Camp V and were industriously setting up tents and stomping the powder into a surface that would support Snowtreadless walking. The small figures looked insignificant from my position several hundred feet above them. Suddenly, and as quietly as thought, simultaneous avalanches swept a feathery foot-thick blanket from both sides of the ridge beginning within a few feet of the camp perimeter and the lower trail. "Look!" I shouted, my heart skipping in anticipation of Camp V disappearing in a puff of powder. The avalanches quickly descended their respective slopes in accelerated animation. Eventually, muffled rumbles drifted up from the deep valleys.

I was solemn at the mountain's show of might; we were insects on the back of a gargantuan giant who could cast us down without meaning to, indeed, without awareness. I felt small; at a hundred times my size I would still be small. Man doesn't belong here; there's no logical reason for it. What insanity had driven me to this tightrope in space, playing courtship to eternity? There was no comfort in questioning, only satisfaction in doing. Climbing a mountain is a strong, yet sensitive affair of the senses—of snow, sun, and storm, hardship and humor, drudgery and delight, risk and reward.

When we reached camp I inquired if anyone had noticed when the avalanches took off. "Hell, yes!" came the reply, "the whole camp settled." I asked Paul to replace me on the trail-breaking team for the next day. Walt's face sported a dark red tan from hiking all day with the sun on his front quarter. "You know," he remarked, "before this trip I had visions of going up Karstens Ridge, flinging my ice axe, the sun over my shoulder, and the blue ice chips a flyin'. Now here I am wading snow up to my ass, with the sun in my eyes."

DAY 22 — JULY 10

LOG:
"Mark, Dennis, Paul, Hank leave 9:30 AM to put in fixed rope on ridge. . . Very windy all day drifting [snow] over trail between rope teams and often between members of the same rope team. . ."

There was not much point in waiting in step behind the necessary creeping pace of the advanced team so we remained a few hours at Camp V. By noon a strong clear wind swept over Pioneer Ridge and across the Harper Icefall, lashing at our Karstens trail. The soft crest was easily eroded as tons of snow plumed off the leeward side of the ridge. It blended into a foaming whiteout high over the cooler Traleika basin, amplifying the demarcation effect and delineating the air mass determinator with precision. The tiny advanced team above us was treading the edge of a witch's boiling caldron. As the day warmed, the whiteout receded and the wind lifted toward a high gracefully curved arch known as the Coxcomb. Its wide steep access pitch was the most dangerously exposed of the ridge. Above the Coxcomb and standing sentry at the head of Karstens Ridge was a rock buttress called Browne Tower. The wind ripped a perpetual veil of feathery snow from the top of the Coxcomb and hung it over its Traleika face which was graced with a giant glistening patch of blue ice. From a distance the situation was more picturesque than threatening. My contemplation was interrupted by the low hum of an aircraft engine. Within a few minutes a Cessna appeared from the northwest, swooped low over our ridge, and dipped its wings in recognition. It was probably glacier pilot, Don Sheldon, perhaps accompanied by Chief Park Ranger, Art Hayes. The momentary intrusion of civilization into this bright day with the advanced team waving and the snow plume blowing from the Coxcomb gave an artificial sensation to the scene, like a Hollywood movie production. I almost expected a brass band to strike up.

I watched as the plane continued around the mountain, possibly checking on Boyd Everett's South Face team. Its rapid shrinking and faint buzz revealed the immensity of the Traleika chasm. The aircraft was but a flighty mosquito riding the massive mixed-up air currents. The airplane left as lightly as it had come, and the resumed silence of the ridge seemed lonelier.

Dennis was doing a great job of leading the advanced team: they cached their half-loads near a granite boulder at 13,000 feet, and pushed 300 feet up the steep Coxcomb pitch before they ran out of fixed line and turned back. Paul led the last 200 feet of this assault. At Camp V the rest of us prepared to pack loads up the ridge. Jerry Clark and Anshel discussed the various locations on the ridge where they might want to pause for a photograph, "pornographs" as Jerry called them. John uninvitedly reaffirmed his opinion. "When you guys run out of film, we can start climbing." The accumulated delays for picture taking had certainly been noticeable. I was very glad that we were not filming a documentary. Having never carried a camera on previous mountaineering trips, I had bought one especially for the McKinley climb. I was taking as many pictures as anyone, not realizing until after the expedition that the harsh elements had fouled my shutter at Camp II. A great deal of film and time was wasted with my non-functioning camera.

The ridge trail was distinctly different from the day before. Several feet of snow had been blown away and the trail was now shallow powder over a strong wind crust. Rebreaking the trail was painful in my high altitude footgear. For better insulation the front of my boots were quite roomy, leaving several inches between the end of my toes and the forward slant points of my strapped-on crampons. The short steep steps of the trail offered only enough room for the very front of my boots, and climbing was a teetering proposition at best. Constantly fighting the tendency for my toes to fold upward soon caused excruciating cramps which felt like my toes were being ripped from my feet. I welcomed the pleasantly distracting breaks to take pictures and enjoy the scenery. To the west across the Harper Icefall, our horizon was the high Pioneer Ridge which fell off sharply at Taylor Spur to its lower profile along the Muldrow. The snow of the glacier was ivory in the evening's pale light. Except for the Camp IV cache and a thin trail toward the ridge, the Muldrow seemed cleansed of our passing. The Camp IV cache contained the low altitude footgear of several people and I was glad to see it well marked. I was later told that it sported a super-wand, fabricated from eight regular wands. Directly down the ridge behind us, Camp V was a small multicolored dot. Beyond the camp was the sharp summit pyramid of 12,210 foot Mount Koven silhouetted against the slightly larger Mount Carpé. The West Fork of the Traleika Glacier wound around the spur of Mount Carpé to join its mother body; in the distance to the east-northeast, was Mount Tripyramid, and to the east was Mount Silverthrone. Denali's East Buttress was our southeast skyline. With so much upthrown white wilderness in our vision, we didn't have to stop long to observe an avalanche or two, wondering if it was by choice or chance that we weren't beneath them.

Anshel, Steve, and Jerry Clark shared my rope for this late evening climb. Anshel and Jerry Clark were still tired from their two Camp IV relays of the previous day, and our pace slowed with each hour. I quietly grimaced with each toe-pulling step, finally muttering under my breath, "Damn you, mountain! You may kill me, but I'll climb you if it's the last thing I ever do." I was startled by the folly of my muffled outburst. The mountain seemed insistent on teaching me at least one virtue—patience. A rope length from the Coxcomb cache, Jerry had to rest again. The third rope team had left Camp V an hour behind us, and following our partially broken trail, they had now caught up to us. After a time, and with some encouragement from the third group, we moved slowly to the cache area. The rope team of John, Howard, Jerry Lewis, and Walt followed. John produced his spray can of fluorescent green paint and brightly marked the cache boulder. "This will be a great spot for a photo station," he told Anshel.

"Yes, but on the way down after the summit," someone replied. "We can't afford any delay in getting up this ridge."

I thought it unwise to continue farther with a tired rope team so we began a weary descent. The other group had pulled up some of the nonessential fixed line from below for use on the Coxcomb and John commenced leading a grinding five-hour ordeal up the climb's steepest pitch.

DAY 23 — JULY 11

I was awakened at 4:30 AM, when the Coxcomb team arrived. John collapsed immediately into his sleeping bag. "The Coxcomb was really hellish," Walt told me. "Heavy, but weak—sastrugi wind slab with several feet of powder underneath," Walt continued. "John gave it all he had for 1200 vertical feet. He really burned himself out." For a couple of days, John was not his usual overbearing self.

The Coxcomb crest had been gained. We now controlled nearly all of Karstens Ridge. An early advanced team would push the route out onto the Harper Glacier to about 15,000 feet, and Camp VI would soon be ready for occupation. Anshel, Steve, and Jerry Clark were scheduled to move up to the proposed Camp VI with me. I expected Anshel and Steve to have the hardest time with acclimation and wanted to check their reaction to altitude early. If they had problems, there would still be opportunity for them to descend Karstens Ridge before the rest of us moved on toward the summit. Anshel approached me with the proposition that he be allowed to go high on the peak, if only as a Sherpa. "Let's see what happens at 15,000 feet, before we plan further," I advised.

Jerry Clark asked me why we were discarding the Park Service stipulation requiring the party leadership to be split whenever the group was. "Do you really want both leaders to move to the higher camp?" Jerry asked without conviction. "I don't give a damn what the Park Service thinks," I replied. "We're the ones climbing this mountain." We looked at each other and exchanged knowing grins. This was Jerry's first crack at being on an advanced team, and he was noticeably pleased.

> LOG:
> "Dennis, Hank, Paul, Mark leave early and finish breaking trail to 15,000 feet. Put in 200 feet more fixed line near top of Coxcomb. Took 11 hours. . . Clark, Wilcox, Steve, Schiff take 8 hours following. . . Rest of group hike during night. . . Several people begin to notice symptoms of altitude: headaches and indigestion. Low 2°F."

Jerry Clark had recovered from his exhaustion of the previous day, and we ascended the ridge with renewed ease. We passed over the trail with little notice, as our thoughts were directed upward to our new home. By now, the Coxcomb was a well-broken staircase with a handrail of fixed line. I sympathized with the efforts of John's nocturnal struggles. At the top of the Coxcomb, the gradient of the slope moderated. The broad shallow milky cwm[13] of the Harper Glacier was walled on the right by the upper Pioneer Ridge and North Peak, and on the left by the rocky Browne Tower ridge. And beyond, low in our view, was the snow dome of the elusive South Peak, the top of the continent. It was little more than a vertical mile above us now; we were right under Denali's nose. We called a rest stop at 14,500 feet, where John's team of the night before had cached their loads, and took one last look down the ridge and the Muldrow. I looked in vain for signs of the MCA (Mountaineering Club of Alaska) Expedition which was a week or two behind us on this route. They would have the advantage of following our established trail, except perhaps, for the Lower Icefall and should be traveling faster. I could see far down the Muldrow and wondered what could be detaining them. Turning upward, I inspected our new environment a little closer. The Harper was a gently rising glacier of about the same width as the upper Muldrow; its size and the mildness of its gradient were distorted by my having just come up the knife-edge of Karstens Ridge. The Harper was crossed by twin icefalls, evenly spaced and offering little technical challenge. The expected corridor skirting the right edges of the icefalls and on to Denali Pass at the top of the glacier appeared quite feasible. Ascending to the summit looked deceivingly simple.

The advance team had pushed the route to 15,000 feet, near the left side of the Harper, made a cache, and were now traversing back under the Browne Tower ridge. This half-mile trail was completely visible from our rest stop, and when still several rope lengths away, Dennis exploded in exuberance, waving his ice axe in the air. "We're going to get this mathah!" he shouted. I was taken a little by surprise; I had not sensed such excitement in Dennis since his pre-trip correspondence. Soon we were all waving victoriously and congratulating the advanced team for a splendid job of trail-breaking. "Just a few more days, and we'll be on top of the mountain," I proclaimed. "Yeah, then comes the damnable 17-day storm," Dennis replied only half-jokingly. Dennis' premonition of a storm troubled me a bit, as it seemed completely out of character.

"It's cold up here," observed Hank. "We'll have to unpack our fluffy down clothes."

---

13. A Welsh word meaning a hollow in a mountainside.

"Then we'll find out who the arctic experts are," Mark added, priming a joke.

After a puzzled pause I bit, "Okay, what's an arctic expert?"

"According to Clark," Mark replied, "an arctic expert is a fellow who can take a leak through six inches of down clothing, without getting anything wet."

The cold began hovering around us so Dennis' team dropped over the Coxcomb, and alone on the Harper, we headed for Camp VI. The snow crunched and crumbled under our steps as we entered a bleached desert which was every bit as dry as the Sahara. We would pay a premium price in fuel to drive water from this sea of white rock powder.

Arriving at Camp VI in the middle of the night, we pitched camp: 600 feet higher than the summit of Mount Rainier, and 300 feet above the Matterhorn. I packed down the campsite with Snowtreads, back-lapping in lawn-mowing fashion. It seemed too good to be true. We were actually camped above the ridge! Walt was bringing up a team a few hours behind us to increase our toehold. Karstens Ridge had taken a week, and for the past several days it had been necessary to assault the ridge relentlessly day and night—now it was subdued—now it was ours. I was pleased with our victory and our cooperative effort. Individuals may have packed loads on the Muldrow, but it had required a team to conquer the ridge. We were close now, banging at the door. A strong team on a long calm day might actually claim the summit from here. I had no thoughts of such a try, but it felt good to know that we were within striking distance. Browne Tower was now revealed as the lower end of a rock ridge; it had appeared as a tower from below. I could almost see forever across the rivers and lakes of the distant tundra. A thousand pothole lakes stared back at me in the reflection of indirect light. A dark sunset-sunrise hung off the shoulder of Taylor Spur for hours. Somehow I felt closer to civilization being able to see so far; I felt sure that I would be able to see the lights of an auto if it chanced along the park highway. I strongly sensed, however, that I was in a new world with new adversaries. The familiar foes of avalanches and crevasses were somewhat less now; Denali augmented their demise here with an awesome arsenal of treachery. I kicked the snow with my foot; this snow lay in a perennial arctic climate; it had never experienced the melting sweat of summer warmth. From now on the bitter cold would snap and bite unceasingly at any flesh that happened to be exposed. Constant vigilance would be required in this frigid freezer; there would be no coming in out of the cold. Altitude also made its presence distinctly felt with throbbing drains on our psychological and physiological resources. It would soon reduce us to slow motion replicas of our low elevation selves. Actions and activities would now have to be carefully considered; there would be little excess energy for error. Our labored breathing in the thin dry air would sap our body moisture like a sponge; drinking a gallon of liquid a day might not be sufficient replacement. I sat in the soft defused light of night and gazed at the strangely sculptured snow carpet. The calm glacier floor was as haunting as an empty freeway. Denali's greatest ally was the insidious invisible force that had driven the glacier surface into submission, periodically blasting these heights with abandon. There was no confusion as to who ruled this lofty realm. The goddess of wind would command respect or blow her invaders to oblivion.

DAY 24 — JULY 12

The morning found eight of us camped at 15,000 feet. There was some discussion about our physical condition after the uncommonly difficult ridge struggle. "Your horses are really tired," Walt observed. We finally decided that it would be unwise to continue without a day of recuperation. Ironically the day proceeded in calm perfection, one of the dozen or so ideal weather days that visit this domain in the course of a year. I had a slight headache which was relieved with a single aspirin and did not recur. Steve also experienced an altitude headache. Anshel was weary but not ill, and Jerry Clark actually seemed stronger. His altitude acclimation was remarkable. John and Jerry Lewis were quietly tired, while Walt and Howard were none the worse for wear. I was anxious about being immobile on such a great day. I located a shovel, then noticed that Howard had already began construction of a latrine. "Well, what the heck," I thought, "there could be no harm in two outhouses." I broke the surface for a second privy a few yards from Howard's. The snow had a very good density for digging and my structure was easily formed. It would have been a minor matter to dig a snow cave in this snow, but the warm sun discouraged me. Faced with a possible afternoon of boredom, I continued elaborate refinements: a curved staircase, an ensolite seat cover, and a small frozen vanity shelf complete with hand lotion, a small metal mirror, and a flower fabricated from a wand and survey flagging. With adhesive tape from the first aid kit and a pair of Snowtreads, I fashioned signs: "MEN" for Howard's functional latrine, and "WOMEN" for the frilly facility.

LOG:
"Sack day for people at Camp VI — crew at V move up camp arriving about 12:00 PM. . . . Eielson radio contact reveals people have spotted us from Eielson and Wonder Lake by telescope."

DAY 25 — JULY 13

LOG:
"Mark, Dennis, Hank, Paul sack day. Walt, Steve, Lewis, Russell pack up last loads from 12,100 foot camp. Rest push route up Harper. . . find going very easy after first half mile — snowshoes not needed. . ."

Howard was scheduled to be on the last relay carry from Camp V; however, just after breakfast he approached me and requested to accompany the advanced team on the Harper. He wanted to switch with Steve Taylor and had apparently already talked to him. Steve joined us, and I explained that I had placed Steve on the advanced team for easier acclimation; clearly the Harper hike would be the easier of the two assignments. Howard then explained that his toes really bothered him on the steep slopes while wearing felt boots. I empathized with his foot problem and Steve was agreeable, so the switch was made. Individual strengths and weaknesses fluctuated a great deal on the climb, surfacing and fading.

The advanced team first relayed the 14,500 foot cache to Camp VI. Then Dennis loaned me his trail snowshoes for easier trail-breaking, and we began our upglacier hike. I angled across the glacier below the first icefall and then up to the firmer footing above it. A small glacier merging down Pioneer Ridge appeared harmless. Jerry switched with me at about the 16,000 foot elevation and broke trail to 16,500 feet, midway between the icefalls where we cached our loads.[14] Nearby on a raised portion of the glacier

---

14. Twenty man-days plus a Colorado 9 man-day bag (total 29 man-days of food.)

were several discarded butane cartridges, indicating that this area had been used as a campsite by a previous expedition. Howard suggested that he and I continue on to Denali Pass. I declined as I didn't want to reinstate two-man rope teams. It appeared that we would be able to travel on the upper Harper without snowshoes, so I left Dennis' trail snowshoes to mark the cache, and we turned downward.

The icefall to our right was intricately intriguing, huge ice blocks and seracs scattered with less organization than we had yet encountered. These randomly situated monoliths had lost their granular appearance under the onslought of wind-driven snow. They resembled, in texture, the finely eroded wind and sand sculptured rocks of desert regions. This indiscriminate scene, smoothly pitted and polished, was alien to my perception, resembling an oddly mined quarry of white marble. "The wind must really get fiendish here," I thought.

At Camp VI another warm, nearly perfect day continued. Brightly colored clothing has excellent radiant heat absorption qualities, and we were literally steeping in the direct sunshine, even though the air temperature was well below freezing. We stood around in light clothing, Dennis in his fire engine red longjohns. Someone suggested that Dennis' attire might be indiscreet as tourists were likely watching us from Eielson. We had constructed an outdoor kitchen at Camp VI, wind-shielding the stoves with discarded nylon food bags. In the early evening we stood around sampling various brews and identifying our past route across the tundra far below. Looking past Browne Tower we could see the banded Muldrow below its junction with the Traleika. For the first time, to my knowledge, people began to talk seriously about their plans after the expedition. Great feasts and celebrations were planned for Fairbanks and Anchorage. I hadn't thought much about after the climb; my thinking was still geared totally upward. The sun dropped below Pioneer Ridge and, as if it were connected to a switch, the temperature seemed to drop 40 degrees instantaneously. Everyone scrambled for warmer clothing.

After the evening radio contact we ate dinner and then gathered in the cook tent to discuss plans for our imminent assault on the summit. The high altitude frost liner had been reinstalled, making our crowding even cozier. The Colorado climbers were in their tent, and few were concerned that they be involved in the meeting. Some people had observed that the Colorado climbers were avoiding the energy draining task of trail-breaking. Of the 3,000 vertical feet of our route up Karstens Ridge,[15] I had led 1,200 feet, Dennis 400 feet, Paul 200 feet and John (in one foray) 1,200 feet. Also Mark had broken 500 vertical feet of trail above the ridge. Since the trail often drifted badly between teams, rope leaders Jerry Clark, Walt Taylor and Steve Taylor had also done some significant struggling on the ridge. Howard, physically one of the strongest climbers on the expedition, had relinquished his usual Muldrow rope leading position and had assumed a much easier interior position. He had not led a single pitch on Karstens Ridge. The suspicion was that the Colorado group was saving themselves to improve their summit chances, while we consumed ourselves in arduous trail-breaking. I had also noticed the pattern change in rope teams, but I didn't think that it was a conscious conspiracy. Nevertheless, the meeting commenced without a Colorado representative.

First, I gathered information on our physical and logistical status. Anshel and Steve were the only ones feeling the altitude beyond the inability for prolonged exertion, which everyone experienced. Both were eating and drinking without difficulty. Physically, we were as sound as could be expected. Foodwise,[16] there were 5½ days of rations at the base of the Coxcomb at 13,000 feet, a day of rations cached at 12,100 feet, and 2½ days of rations at 16,500 feet. The 2½ day food cache at 14,500 feet had been moved to camp, so that we now had 6 days of rations at the 15,000 foot camp. I addressed Jerry, "What is the weather forecast?"

"Eielson says that the next two days will be perfect," he replied.

"And after two days?" I asked.

"They only have a two-day forecast. I guess they're just getting it from a radio station," Jerry advised.

---

15. From the ridge saddle at 11,500 feet to the top of the Coxcomb at 14,500 feet.

16. These food quantities are for the combined groups (Wilcox and Colorado) and do not include supplementary food. Each member of the Wilcox group also had about a day of emergency food remaining (we had used about half of our two-day supply when we missed the rendezvous with the horse packer the first night of the expedition). The Colorado group had less than 10 days of rations, so we anticipated sharing our extra food with them.

"At least two days of perfect weather," I silently pondered. "Okay," I said to the waiting group. "My feeling is that we should make a run for it—all of us pack up five days of food to 18,000 feet tomorrow and climb to the summit the following day. If we are delayed at 18,000 feet, there would be the 2½ days of rations at 16,500 feet that could probably be relayed up. If we get immobilized by stormy weather, our bodies will require less fuel, and we can eat half rations as other climbing parties have done."

A strongly opinionated discussion followed concerning various assault plans. Mark said that we were climbing too fast and needed more time for acclimation. He suggested that we establish an intermediate camp at 16,500 feet, as some previous expeditions had done. Dennis pointed out the vulnerability of not bringing up the Coxcomb cache. "If a windy storm traps us above the ridge, that food will be useless," he said. Several others joined in agreement. The point was well made; however, it would take four men a short day to bring up most of the Coxcomb cache. The other eight might just as well move up to 18,000 feet and establish the high camp (highest camp from which summit assaults would be made). With many comments and finally a unanimous agreement, the plan was formulated. Steve and Anshel would stay low another day—along with two of the expedition's strongest climbers, Walt and John. They would pack 60 man-days of the Coxcomb cache up to Camp VI, while the rest of us moved up to 18,000 feet with four days of food[17] for a July 15 summit try. The low camp would move up to the high camp on the 15th, with 3 additional days of food[18] for a summit climb one day behind us. I suspected that Anshel and possibly Steve would not be going to the summit, which would leave compatibly matched Walt and John as a two-man assault team. The first summit group would serve as a support team for the second party, relaying more supplies to the high camp if necessary.

"I wonder what the Colorado guys will think of this plan?" I asked.

"They're just interested in getting to the top," came the reply. "As long as they're in the first summit group, they won't care what

---

17. 40 man-days of food. For the hopefully short time that the entire expedition would be at the high camp, we would stretch the Wilcox group's ten-man rations twelve ways. Supplementary food would also be taken.

18. 30 man-days of rations.

the rest of us do."

"I'll go get their reaction," I said.

"You're the leader," Mark advised. "Don't ask their opinion. Just tell them what we plan to do." I went to the nearby Colorado tent which seemed quiet in anticipation.

"Howard," I called.

"Yes?" came the immediate reply.

"The good weather is supposed to hold for at least two more days," I related. "Eight of us will be going up tomorrow for a summit climb the next day. The other four will bring up most of the Coxcomb cache and follow a day behind us."

"And the Colorado group?" Howard asked.

"You will all be on the first team," I replied. "John and Walt are staying low with Anshel and Steve." I explained a few of the details to them and then returned to my tent. (The entire conversation had occurred through the wall of the Colorado tent.) The camp soon began buzzing with the excitement of the final push. John was placed in charge of sorting the food and supplies to go with the first group. To save weight and energy, only essential items would be taken: a few pots, the two best functioning stoves with full fuel tanks, two snow shovels, wands, a first aid kit, two gallons of Blazo, the five-watt radio, and various other items. The cook tent would be left at Camp VI during our summit assaults.

"Just three more days," I thought, "and then it will be all downhill."

DAY 26 — JULY 14

At 8:00 AM Hank, Walt, Steve, John, Dennis, and I were in the cook tent, when one of the cook stoves began to malfunction. When Walt inspected the gas tank release valve, it popped off, permitting fumes to escape which were ignited by the second stove. Apparently the muslin frost liner acted as a vaporwick; with a loud "whump!" the entire tent ceiling exploded in terrifying flames above our heads. Six panicked bodies scrambled for the two exits. I could see Steve Taylor ahead of me with a fiery halo. I held my breath to avoid inhaling deadly superheated air, threw my arm across my eyes, and dove for the doorway which vaporized before I reached it. Exiting where a wall had just been I plunged into a snowbank and rolled over and over to extinguish any clothing that might be burning. I expected to hear the cries of people with burned eyes and singed lungs. Even worse, maybe someone didn't get out. I turned and was amazed to see that the tent was completely gone except for the doorway zippers and the floor. The fire had lasted only a few seconds. The others were also sprawled out in the snow, miraculously no one was seriously injured. We all sported singed hair, eyebrows, and beards. Hank incurred a small cut above his eye from fielding a frantic foot in the scramble. Walt had tried to throw the exploding stove out of the tent and had burned his hand and face slightly. Smoldering relics of the catastrophe littered the neoprene-coated tent floor. A sputtering stove sat in the midst of the mess. John stood with his hands on his hips, then gave the stove a good kick, perhaps misjudging the force and direction of his blow. Trailing flaming fuel, the stove sailed across the corner of the other Logan tent pitched a few feet away. Several people quickly smothered the fire, simultaneously reprimanding John in terms exceeding his own temperament.

As the electrifying situation calmed and our adrenalin consumption moderated, we objectively assessed our losses. John had been living in the cook tent and his sleeping bag was a pile of singed down and melted nylon. Walt's down parka had also been in the cook tent and was likewise destroyed.

Mark had brought a double sleeping bag and loaned half of it to John for the remainder of the trip, and Anshel supplied Walt with an extra parka.

Other losses were minor. Sitting in the middle of the tent floor, having somehow escaped the inferno of heat, was a bundle of matches. "There's one thing that didn't burn!" John exclaimed, "the company matches!" The biggest sentimental loss was Dennis' multicolored, custom knitted hat. Careful and repeated sifting of the area did not turn up any evidence of its passing. I suspected that in the shuffle it might have gotten buried in the snow. The cook tent was convenient, but admittedly an unnecessary luxury. Content with a dual function for the sleeping tents, we could still proceed as planned. Walt's burns were treated, and Anshel helped him bandage his hand which had blistered. Infections have plagued small injuries on past expeditions, so Walt was also given penicillin.

"The fire was my fault," Walt stated, realizing the tent had been rented. "I'll pay for the tent when we get back."

"No!" I replied. "It seemed like an honest accident to me, it could have happened to anyone. We will count it as an expedition loss and share the expense."

"I insist," Walt countered. "I can afford it, and if I fall in a crevasse you can get the money from my parents. They took out a big life insurance policy on me just before the trip."

"They must have a lot of faith in your mountaineering abilities," I said, then laughed.

It's strange how surviving a close call can precipitate illogical elation. As the cleanup progressed and the packs were made ready for the day's climb, morale was noticeably heightened; the atmosphere was bubbly.

> LOG:
> ". . . Walt, Steve, Anshel, John pack up. . . loads from
> Coxcomb cache. Rest of group pack camp to 17,900 feet
> on Harper, taking minimum supplies. . ."

At about 10:00 AM Dennis, Hank, and Mark roped up with me and we entered the dry fog which had enveloped the preoccupied camp unnoticed. It burned off before we reached the first icefall, exposing another flawless day. The played tension on the rope increasingly slowed my pace until we finally stopped. Dennis indicated that he was feeling ill. I placed a Gelucil tablet in the snow, and the rope team moved up so that Dennis could reach it. We began a long rest stop to wait for the antacid tablet to take effect. The footing was firm, and the second rope team soon caught us: Howard was back in his rope leading position, setting a fast pace which by now did not seem unusual. Short-legged Jerry Clark was bringing up the rear and propositioned our resting team, "Do any of you want to ride this express train?"

"No," Dennis answered for us all. "We'll stay with the slow freight."

Howard's team stopped beside us as two jet fighters streaked close over the mountain. All heads lifted. They seemed closer than they probably were because of the unaccustomed noise. After a few minutes Howard suggested that his team take the lead and establish the high camp. I agreed and advised that it be located as close to 18,000 feet as possible, taking advantage of any natural wind shields that were available. The second team took the lead, and I couldn't avoid noticing their pace. We were climbing at 16,300 feet with 60-pound packs, and Howard was not rest stepping. Instead he was pausing briefly every few dozen steps. Lewis looked silently exhausted as he passed. A few minutes later we resumed our ascent. I was perhaps affected by watching the rhythm of Howard's pace; after a while a loud "Hey!" came from Mark at the end of my rope. "Slow down—my leg hurts," Mark added.

"What's the trouble?" I asked.

"We're climbing this mountain too fast," Mark replied in a tone that reflected more frustration than conviction. I moderated the pace and we moved up to the 16,500 foot cache for a rest. Dennis claimed his snowshoes and we marked the cache with wands. As we reached the bottom of the steeper slope skirting the highest Harper icefall, the other rope team was topping it and disappearing from our sight. As Jerry Clark struggled to match the pace of his ropemates who were above the steep pitch, we heard an indignant outburst. "God dammit! Slow down," Jerry blasted in a manner that would have done credit to John Russell. We topped the icefall at 17,400 feet and proceeded at about half cadence behind the lengthening gap to the other party. At about 7:00 PM, the lead group dropped their packs and began pitching camp. They were only a few hundred yards above us; however, it would take us another hour to arrive. Behind us, the flattening terrain began hiding the steeper slopes, the lower of the two high icefalls, and Camp VI until our horizon etched itself across the broken clouds. We had come a long way from Camp VI, yet the summit didn't look much closer.

Camp VII was situated at 17,900 feet, near the right side of the upper Harper. There was no wind barrier for camp; however, a cursory survey for a more sheltered campsite in the surrounding area revealed that only predominately psychological wind breaks were offered. We were near the crest of this broad, smooth pyramid and the whiteness was at an unprotectingly low angle. Pioneer Ridge to our right exhibited steep, low relief, wind-scarred, ascending granite spines. Seeking shelter here was like trying to hide in the cracks of a sidewalk. I began leveling a tent platform. Dennis and I would share the Mountaineer tent, while Hank and Jerry Clark joined Mark in his tent. The snow was ideal for digging, and I was tempted to construct a snow cave. Only the good weather forecast and the reservation of my energy for the summit stayed my hand. Camp VII was not in line-of-sight with Eielson, so Jerry Clark stretched out the dipole antenna as cloud layers began playing about us. Eielson tape-recorded part of our 8:00 PM radio contact and said that they would try to record us when we got to the summit. There was a breaker (a third radio transmission audible in our conversation) who joined this radio contact, apparently a fishing boat near Sitka, Alaska 700 miles to the southeast.

Before retiring to the tent, I secured my pack against high winds by running the shaft of my ice axe into the snow between the bars of the pack frame. I also carefully threaded the nylon lashing straps repeatedly around the frame bars, an action that was more tidy than vital. I used this small task of habit as a barometer of the effects of altitude which can creep into the mind and body without detection. If the time came that my will revolted against this unnecessary strap wrapping, then I would know that I was being affected.

Dennis had vomited after arriving at Camp VII. Vomiting is a tremendous sapper of body energy and moisture, and I was relieved later when he was able to retain his dinner. Jerry Clark joined Dennis and I for a leisurely meal and a lengthy chat. The proposed uniqueness of the following day required several changes in my evening chore patterns. A sealed plastic bag was opened, and its contents of summit banners was inspected and prepared. For half an hour a can sat thawing in the heated pail of drinking water. This was a summit treat which I had carefully concealed from the others—a can of cola—not exactly worthy of a king's toast, but enough for our meager ceremonial demands. The can of cola and my water bottle would spend the night in the warmth of my sleeping bag.

Camp VII enjoyed the largest surrounding area of gentle terrain since the Muldrow, yet somehow I felt that I was sleeping at the edge of space. Almost subconsciously, I braced myself against the tent floor as if it were improperly leveled. I also felt alone, even though Dennis was right next to me. On the Muldrow the segment of humanity comprised of the expedition members completely filled each camp with the vitality of living. On Karstens Ridge and at Camp VI this human warmth had been confined to separate tents.

Now it failed to penetrate the thin icy air even a few inches to Dennis' sleeping form. It was as if I had come on this journey in a space capsule which had gradually shrunk, until its shell was the very surface of my skin. I peered out of my eyes as if they were windows. My boots and other gear sat in starkness next to my sleeping bag, my confined strength unable to shield them.

We were camped at the upper surface of the earth's life zone for the human species—a zone three and a half miles deep—yet from this vantage point appearing to be a paper-thin layer of life covering the earth and frighteningly responsive to a delicately fragile balance of forces. Tomorrow as we stepped above 18,000 feet, we would enter a dominion whose scarcity of oxygen would tax our bodies beyond their ability to acclimate, a dominion where dead body cells cannot be replaced. Although fatal to the species, hearty individuals with careful attention to maintaining their physiology have lived in this realm for periods of several weeks without lasting ill effects. Uninterrupted and undetained, our brief foray to the summit would hardly be cause for serious concern: still, knowing that we would be living on biologically borrowed time was not comforting.

DAY 27 — JULY 15

I was awakened by the snapping of the tent, buffeted by 50 mile per hour winds. It was not a good omen. "Damn," I thought. "Had we come this far, had we struggled for weeks to the very threshold of victory, only to be denied?" Through the long morning I dozed off and on; the wind was dying down, or was it just my wishful imagination?

Impatiently, I waited as morning slowly faded. If the wind continued much longer, we would have to forfeit a summit try today. Finally at 9:00 AM, it calmed. A canvassing of the camp turned up only three others ready for a summit assault, the Colorado climbers. Dennis said that he felt much better, but would wait to climb with the second team tomorrow. Jerry Clark spoke for the others, stating that they would wait and watch the weather; perhaps he and Mark would climb North Peak today. Climbing North Peak before bagging the summit seemed somewhat backwards to me. As expedition leader I had planned to stay at Camp VII until it was vacated; it made little difference which summit team I accompanied. Denali doesn't indulge mountaineers with an abundance of summit opportunities. I felt neither overly tired nor ill, and I had come to climb the mountain. I would climb today. We had already been in contact with Eielson a couple of times checking on the weather, and scheduled frequent contacts during the day to let them know our progress and get updated weather information.

> LOG:
> "Wilcox, Snyder, Lewis, Paul leave for summit at 12:00 noon. . . Rest decide to stay in camp. Clark and Mark talk of climbing North Peak. . ."

At an elevation of 17,900 feet anoxia (oxygen starvation) affects the thinking processes. Simple tasks like strapping on my crampons required great concentration and an unreasonable amount of time. The alarming revelation was that this functional slowing did not register mentally. I felt that I was performing at my accustomed speed. My watch seemed to be running fast! Altitude is a famished consumer of time. I excavated my pack from the drifting snow and roped up. Only one bundle of wands (about 50) could be located in camp. "What a blunder!" I thought. "How could John have sent us barely half the number of wands needed to mark the route from high camp to the summit? Perhaps he had not realized that we had to use some wands yesterday to mark the route from the 16,500 foot cache to high camp."

Our wands would have to be broken into short 2-foot half-wands, making trail-marking a tricky business. I told Howard to lead off: Jerry Lewis was second; Paul third; and I brought up the rear, marking the route with alternating bare stakes and flagged sticks at 150-foot intervals. Little more than a foot of wand projected above the snow surface. We were off, although the flat terrain made us more strollers than climbers. So gentle and gradual was the change in gradient as we approached Denali Pass that my perception overtook the pace and sensed a downgrade prematurely. A broken cloud blanket hovered at 12,000 feet. As I pondered the others at Camp VII who had passed up a near perfect summit day, I thought, "Of course! Only Dennis was ill. The other three had not suddenly been overcome with weakness or caution. Together with Dennis and Walt they constituted the friendship alliances stemming from Jerry Clark over a period of many years. I should have realized this before—Jerry, Mark, and Hank were waiting to share the culminating climb with their close friends, Dennis and Walt."

A short hour brought us to Denali Pass, the 18,200 foot saddle between the mountain's two summits, and a view of the other half of the world which had been concealed by the mountain massif. We paused to absorb the new view. Mount Foraker, the Alaskan Range's second highest peak, assumed her secondary role in contented dignity. She was not intimidated by her proximity to Denali. We had climbed beyond her 17,395 foot summit without seeing her. Our last view of Mount Foraker had been from near Wonder Lake. At the pass we saw several covered caches from previous expeditions. We didn't inspect any of them, although we did notice that one cache in wooden crates had been opened, possibly by the Winter Expedition whose descent had been delayed a few days here by a severe storm. We had the five-watt Unit One radio with us and tried to reach Eielson at 1:00 PM with no results. I surveyed the ridges and couloirs[19] of North Peak. Mark and Jerry had not started their proposed climb, nor did I think they would; their statement had most likely been just a polite way of preserving their preference without insult or justification. We turned to the left ridge and continued our ascent. Above the pass we were relieved to find the route already wanded, probably the work of a recent West Buttress expedition. That route merged with ours at Denali Pass. Another radio try at 1:55 PM blasted in loud and clear; we were now in line-of-sight with Eielson. Unit Two (Camp VI climbers) joined our transmission.

Gordy said that he would really like to be up there with us. "Frankly," I replied, recalling the past month of winter living, "I would just as soon be relaxing on a sunny beach." Gordy laughed at my half-serious statement.

My nearly empty pack was the lightest of the trip and climbing seemed much easier than I had anticipated. Physically, several days had been more demanding, yet here altitude was a subtle adversary, draining my strength even when I wasn't moving. And when we were climbing it was so slow that my muscles did not

---

19. French word meaning a steep, snow-filled gully.

tire, giving me a false sense of well-being. Jerry Lewis soon slowed our progress by demanding rests at steadily shorter intervals.

By 4:30 PM we had climbed to 19,550 feet and crested the low ridge behind Archdeacon's Tower, a large rock outcropping. We took a long rest as we looked at the wanded route ahead of us. It dropped fifty feet to cross a quarter-mile wide flat basin then steeply ascended 500 feet to the top of the summit ridge, there traversing left to the summit which was still hidden. I cached the remaining wands (about 35) to further lighten my pack and we continued. The shallow basin was like crossing Mount Rainier's summit crater; however, the following upslope again convinced me of our greater altitude. There were still a few footprints left from the West Buttress expedition. Across the Harper, I could see the tent dots of Camp VII and above them the North Peak whose summit we had now surpassed.

We had reached 19,700 feet by 5:00 PM and talked with Eielson about the possibility of setting off an orange smoke flare on the summit to see if they could see it by telescope. As I teetered on the slope, the battery jack accidentally pulled out of the radio, and Eielson blasted in with grand clarity. The internal reserve radio batteries were in good shape. I replugged the jack. The summit ridge had many cornices over its South Face, a near vertical 8,000 foot wall. We stayed a safe distance from the ridge crest, its white edge serrated against a blue-black sky.

At about 6:15 PM Howard ventured a few feet toward the ridge crest and excitedly proclaimed that he could see the summit. After taking a picture he moved on. When my turn came, I stepped to the ridge. Less than 200 yards away and 150 vertical feet above us was the object of our quest. Littered with brightly colored pickets and wands protruding at various angles, it resembled the tired banderilla-pricked shoulders of a bullfight beast—subdued, but not humbled. For it was I who was humbled, a frail figure creeping to the sacred altar—three gasping breaths between each step. The mountain was a mistress that allowed herself to be taken at her own choosing; we were not conquerers.

Eielson monitored and recorded the last ten minutes of our climb as I kept the transmitter key pressed. Unit Two shared this broadcast for the first few minutes. Mostly Eielson recorded only my heavy breathing and small talk among the rope team. Escaping the auditory record were the surprising ramblings of my thoughts. I had expected to be elated at this momentous moment; yet as the summit approached and the skylines receded on all sides, I felt strangely disappointed—not in the summit itself, for I felt a deep respect for the mountain, but in the relative insignificance of the day's climb. The summit stood nearly four vertical miles above sea level, halfway through the earth's troposphere, yet the fulfillment of my elusive reasons for climbing the mountain were not here; they were hidden in the mental sweat of pre-trip planning, the pounding dust of the Alcan, the mosquitoes and rivers of the tundra, the storms and crevasses of the Muldrow, the wind and deep snow of Karstens Ridge, and the cold thin air of the Harper. The fulfillment was in the shared struggle of twelve men matching their intelligent might against the unknown. I fully appreciated now why those at high camp were waiting for their friends. The summit was necessary, but not sufficient: it was the final lunge of a well-run race.

Howard was first on top, reeling in Jerry Lewis, and in turn Paul. As Paul coiled the rope between us, and my legs took the last few uphill steps, I felt an emotional nostalgia. For twenty-seven days I had been training my body for upward climbing; it had responded well, giving me the best physical toughness of my life. In over a hundred miles of route-finding and supply relays I had climbed more than six-and-a-half vertical miles. I had nearly climbed the mountain twice. So serene was this feeling of physical competence that abruptly ending its need caused me to subconsciously search for another slope stretching upward as if I could climb forever.

I stepped onto the top of the continent in soberness; not in triumph, but with endless gratitude at being permitted this unique experience in life. I hardly felt like proceeding with my planned summit rituals, but with mechanical feeling did so, in order to complete the momentum of the situation. Getting here from Wonder Lake had seemed impossible. Yet eventually the repetition of the possible mundane toil of each day's labor prevailed. For no mountain can withstand the persistence of continuously upward steps.

Standing on the summit I was psychologically insecure with everything sloping downward, and I braced myself against the light breeze. The footing seemed stable, yet I restrained a temptation to have a look down the South Face. With our climbing rope coiled and tangled, dislodging a small cornice or section of packed snow could send us all on a mile-and-a-half plunge to the Kahiltna Glacier. Stepping a few comfortable feet below the top, I resumed talking to Eielson on our continuous radio transmission. The time was 6:30 PM.

RADIO TAPE 6:30 PM:

. . .[20]

Joe: "Ah, this is Joe Wilcox of the Wilcox-McKinley Expedition. Ah, we're on the summit of the mountain now. Ah, with me are Howard Snyder of the Colorado group, Paul Schlichter of the Colorado group, and Jerry Lewis of the Colorado group.
The weather's just fine. Some clouds at about seven thousand; ah, high cirrus. We've been in the clear all day. Light breezes from the ah, south I guess."
[Above my accustomed landmarks, I had to swing a panorama and locate North Peak to be sure about directions.]

Joe: "It's ah, quite an exhilarating experience. We've all been planning for this for years. . . we're all glad to be on top."
[Wayne Merry tried to talk to us through Eielson where a crude radio patch had been attempted.]

Wayne: "Well, congratulations, Joe. It's real good to hear you from up there. It's the first time we've talked to anybody ah, on top of the mountain."[21]
[We were unable to hear Wayne although he could hear our transmission. Howard said a few words and then handed the radio back to me.]

. . .

---

20. Three dots indicate that a portion of the tape transcription was omitted or a portion of the radio transmission was inaudible.

21. Although this may have been the first time that the park had talked with anyone on the summit, a more remarkable communicative feat occured at 1:00 PM on July 9, 1964 when Chuck DeHart of the Seattle Mountaineers Mount McKinley Expedition called friends in Seattle from the summit using a phone patch with a radio telephone (Voice Commander).

Joe: "Ah, I don't ah, know if any of these guys have a few more words to say. We're not going to really do much up here; take a few pictures. I think ah, we have a few banners. I have banners from all five of the universities I've been to and one from my home town at Neodesha, Kansas; and ah, one from the State of Kansas, since I think I'm the first Kansan to climb Mount McKinley;[22] and that's all I have to say. I send my greetings to everyone there. . ."

[Howard and Eielson ranger, Gordon Haber, spent nearly ten minutes synchronizing the igniting of a couple of orange smoke flares. There were a lot of tourists at Eielson looking through spotting scopes. Paul did the honors of holding the flares.]

. . .

Howard: ". . .two, one—the flare ignited its generating smoke. Now it's starting to generate enough smoke to be seen. There it goes—now it's off. Can you see us? Over."

Gordy (Gordon): "Yeah, we see you. . . 10-4 we can see it! We can see it! 10-4."

[The orange smoke dissipated quickly in the thin breeze. Paul tried a night flare, but understandably it could not be seen from Eielson 33 miles away. The South Peak is barely out of view from Wonder Lake and Wayne apparently could not see any of the flares. I produced the cola and passed it around. Howard did likewise with a hunk of chocolate.]

. . .

Gordy: "How's your temperature and wind and so on and so forth up there?"

. . .

Howard: "The wind is about ah, 15 or 20, with gusts up to 25."

Gordy: "Well, that doesn't sound too bad—ah, pretty cool up there?"

. . .

---

22. We were the fiftieth expedition to climb the South Peak successfully. It's likely that another native Kansan could have previously climbed the mountain.

Howard: ". . . The temperature we just checked is 6 degrees. . ."
[One of the tourists at Eielson was Ethyl Worthington, Jerry Lewis' next door neighbor back in Colorado. They chatted for a bit over the radio and she said that she would wire the summit news to Lewis' mother. I asked Gordy to send a postcard to Cheryl telling her that I would be home in two weeks.]
. . .

Gordy: "Okay, we got that and we'll sure send this postcard off—ah, glad to do it, and again I say—congratulations!"
. . .

Joe: "Ah, thanks a lot. This is KHD6990 Unit One clear with Eielson."

Gordy: "KHD6990, ah, Eielson clear with Unit One on the summit of Mount McKinley."

There had been a lot of verbal backslapping during the radio contact and it somehow seemed a bit premature. The trip was far from over. Eight people would make their summit try tomorrow after which we would begin our descent—faster, but every bit as hazardous as the climb—perhaps even more so because of our fatigue and the complacency of victory. Many mountaineering tragedies occur after the summit, and I knew from past climbs that my most vulnerable lassitude and physical weakness succeed the summit. The proper time for congratulations and thanks would be at Wonder Lake after every man had safely crossed the McKinley River. Then we could properly claim a successful expedition.

I put the radio away and took another look around. My roll of banners and flags was unfurled, and Jerry Lewis snapped supposed pictures with my camera as I held each up in turn. There were two sets of banners: one set to stay on the summit, and one set to be taken back with me. Howard attached a Confederate flag to the spare ice axe which he had carried the entire trip. Apparently the ice axe belonged to the fourth member of their group who had been injured just prior to the trip. After a picture, Howard produced a Colorado flag and an American flag for further photographs. "That's strange," I thought, "I carried seven flags to the summit, but somehow overlooked bringing the American ensign."

Howard took several individual and a group picture as my thoughts turned toward the long return hike to camp VII. We untangled the rope and without ceremony I led the descent. We had spent nearly an hour and a half on the summit, much longer than my inclinations. I had purposely prolonged the stay in case I should later regret a short stay. The descent to high camp was uneventful, but tiring with the freshened wind of evening. The cached wands were left undisturbed, more out of rest than reason. Surely the low party would be bringing up more wands in case they were needed. Gusting winds were especially uncomfortable on the ridge above Denali Pass, and at one of the few rest breaks I considered the possibility of hiking on the sheltered lee side of the ridge. After fifty feet of thigh-deep snow and complaints from my companions, I was happy to return to the sound footing of the windy ridge. At Denali Pass we switched the lead to share the trail-breaking chore, made exhaustive by the pace of our descent. Some of our short wands were already buried in the drifting snow. We arrived at camp at 10:00 PM, only two hours from the summit. It was a gothic scene in the pale shadow of North Peak. The party coming up from Camp VI was just outside of camp, their almost motionless pace giving them the appearance of time hardened statues against a backdrop of distant broken clouds. They had been on the trail for ten hours. From the end of the rope, I shouted to the others to drop their packs in camp and continue down to help the approaching team. There was no response, so I repeated the request as packs were unshouldered. We moved down to relieve the heavy packs of the low party. Walt and Steve balked at receiving help so close to camp. Surprisingly, John had become ill during the day and had given half of his load to Walt and Steve.

The low group had packed up 30 more man-days of food and 3 bundles of wands (125-150). John carried a bamboo pole decorated with strips from the floor of the burned tent. He planned to adorn the summit with this warrior's staff. The camp was quickly enlarged to accommodate the 12-man group, and dinner was begun. I was disappointed to discover that the next numbered food bag (#29) had been carried to the high camp in error (#31-#40 were intended for Camp VII). I did not cook the beans of the chili menu, but instead sautéed the hamburger sauce in a half package of cheese, an appetizing meal. Dennis seemed much better today.

However, John was weak and could not hold down much food. Little was said about the day's summit climb as others were still anticipating theirs. I didn't do much celebrating, although my face was beaming openly. All was in readiness for another summit assault on the morrow, but the mountain had other plans.

DAY 28 — JULY 16

The wind increased sharply during the night, and a twenty-four hour immobilizing storm moved in. For a while there would be no movement up or down the peak. The storm was no great surprise as we had earlier noticed its vanguard—high cirrus clouds.

> LOG:
> "Wind begins during night. Blasts up to 70-80 miles per hour. Snowstorm begins about noon. . . Tempers flare over use of stoves in tents and distribution of food. . . Mark's tent and Mountaineer drift badly on uphill windward side. . ."

The saggy Mountaineer tent made a very good snow fence, and Dennis and I took turns with the necessary shoveling. At first the task was exhilarating, but the relentless disruptions of our sleep soon changed my attitude. I considered digging a snow cave, but the secure marginality of the present shelter beckoned me back inside for a period of peace. Besides, when it needed shoveling again, it would be Dennis' turn. It was difficult for people held up in four tents to cook with only two stoves and this lowered morale. Three quarts of fuel, half of our reserves, stored outside the Colorado tent apparently drifted under and were lost. Walt helped morale by distributing food and filled water bottles.

My physiological processes seemed normal. I was not dehydrated or constipated and ate anything I wanted, including a package of mixed nuts, supposedly difficult to digest at high elevations. The second night of shoveling snow and little sleep, however, made inroads into my stamina. Some of the more conservative climbers, such as Jerry Clark, were seriously considering abandoning summit aspirations and dropping down at the first break in the weather. Radio contact was weak but clear by using a dipole antenna. Good humor managed to survive in our naturally stressful environment. Dennis started it by howling like a dejected dog; soon the entire camp was howling in hilarious unison.

DAY 29 — JULY 17

After a restless night of flapping tents and drifting snow, we were greeted by clearing weather, not unlike the first summit day. It looked very promising. Perhaps the storm was ending, although we couldn't be certain. In mid-morning, as the camp began stirring, I crawled out to assess the situation and to consult with Jerry Clark. "What are your druthers?" I asked. Jerry surveyed the unstable sky. "I think we'll just wait and see what the weather does." Jerry had already made two morning radio contacts trying to get a weather report. I meandered around and collected the disposition of the camp, then returned to chat with Jerry. "Looks like everyone wants to stay and try the summit except Anshel, so I'll send him down with the Colorado climbers. That'll conserve our low fuel supply. I'll stay here while you guys try the peak," I added.

"That really won't be necessary," Jerry indicated. "We have the majorty of the strongest climbers with us, and besides it would further conserve our fuel for you to descend to Camp VI." Dennis joined in and was also insistent that I go down to help conserve the high camp supplies. "Okay," I finally agreed. Besides, Jerry Clark knew most of the seven high climbers better than I did.

An hour later I began packing my pack and the Mountaineer tent which would go down to 15,000 feet. Dennis and I dug out three of the coolie hat tent anchors. I worked rapidly, and my efforts swiftly reminded me of the altitude, requiring me to rest for a minute. Walt excavated the last anchor and Dennis strapped the tent onto my pack.

"I have a feeling that I should have climbed with you guys the other day," Dennis offered with concern.

"Nonsense," I said. "Today might turn out to be every bit as good a summit day as we had." I made one last round. "Sure you don't want to go down with us, Steve?" I asked.

"I think I'll just stay with the high group," came his reply.

I walked over for a last talk with Jerry Clark who was standing outside his tent with Hank and Walt. Jerry had been in radio contact with Eielson again since I had talked to him earlier. "What does Eielson say about the weather?" I asked.

"They haven't been able to get an updated forecast," he answered.

"Well, I guess you'll be in charge of the high camp," I said.

"No problem," he replied. I described my recollection of the summit route and suggested that it might now be poorly wanded. I continued, "My recommendations are that as few as two people can try for the summit providing both are strong climbers and at least two people remain at high camp to support them. As few as four people can try for the summit without a support group at high camp, and if someone wants to descend to 15,000 feet as few as two people can make the trip down. This should give you a great deal of flexibility," I added. Jerry agreed to the guidelines. "If you find the lost fuel and end up staying several days waiting for a summit try, you may have to send a couple of people down to the 16,500 foot cache for more food. I'll try to get a couple of the Colorado climbers to help me pack you up some more food and fuel, but they've got the summit now and you know how they are."

"Yeah," Walt said, "The cows are headed for the barn." Jerry nodded his understanding. Taking another look at the weather I added, "Don't take any chances, Jerry; it's not worth it." Knowing Jerry, I felt this statement was a bit redundant. I offered it more out of official duty than real concern.

"Don't worry," Jerry replied, "If we can't climb today, we'll probably go down tomorrow."

"Good luck," I said as we parted with a mittened handshake.

I returned to my pack and shouldered it. "Do you think I should take my sleeping bag in case we have to bivouac?" Dennis asked.

"We didn't," I replied. "If you want to as a safety precaution then fine, but I don't think that you should start a summit climb with a bivouac as a planned option. Your taking a sleeping bag would only make sense if everyone else took one."

"Would we all have to take a sleeping bag? Couldn't we double up?" Dennis suggested.

"Yeah," I replied, "two to a bag. You would also need shovels for digging snow caves."

"I had already planned to take a snow shovel," Dennis answered assuredly.

"You'd better discuss the matter with Jerry," I concluded.

"He'll be in charge." I roped up at the end of the long five-man rope and with a wave to the good-spirited, busily preparing camp, we began our descent, the wind playing waves of loose snow around our feet. It was high noon.

Some wands had been blown out between Camps VI and VII, making our previous route hard to follow. We wandered off the trail toward Pioneer Ridge a few yards once, dropping Paul nearly up to his waist in a crevasse. The weather improved as we descended, and the rest stops called by Jerry Lewis and Anshel became less frequent. Lewis had been very weak during our last day at high camp, not eating much, and unable to strap on his own crampons. Jerry seemed somewhat improved with the drop in elevation, I also felt a resurgence of strength in my limbs.

LOG:
"Wilcox, Schiff, Paul, Jerry Lewis, Howard descend to 15,000 foot camp. . . necessary to break trail all the way back to camp. . . Calm back at 15,000 foot camp. . ."

We arrived back at 15,000 feet about 3:00 PM and began re-establishing Camp VI. Anshel and I pitched the flimsy Mountaineer tent broadside to the slope of the Browne Tower ridge. This, we thought, would give us more protection from the winds coming down the Harper.

I was shocked when Paul emptied a Colorado food bag from his pack. He had apparently picked it up at the 16,500 foot cache, reducing the food available to the high camp by more than a day. The 15,000 foot camp already had an 11-day food reserve for our five-man party. True, unless they had found the lost fuel, Clark's party still had more food than fuel. Yet, we had spent a month carrying as much food as possible, as high on the peak as possible, for the optimum support of the summit assaults, and I had even committed the low group to make another supply carry to high camp if necessary. How could anyone think of packing food *down* the mountain? I started to say something, but couldn't think of anything appropriate. Anshel and I cooked up a feast of macaroni and cheese mixed with peas. There was nothing to do now, but relax and wait.

A shallow fog covered the summit slopes throughout the evening. Otherwise, the sky was clear. At the 8:00 PM radio contact, we were unable to hear Unit One directly and information had to be relayed through the stronger station at Eielson which was in line-of-sight with both groups. The high party was having difficulty following the route in the whiteout; apparently the storm of July 16 had blown a lot of the wands away. They asked if there was a large cornice on the summit. I knew that the summit ridge was well corniced, requiring extreme caution. Under optimum conditions, cornices can come and go in a single storm. I had no way of knowing the status of the summit after the storm of the previous day, but little harm could result in being overly cautious. "Roger," I replied. Howard protested strongly that there was no cornice on the summit. After Unit One signed off, Eielson informed us that there were six men in Clark's summit party and that they expected to reach the top in a half hour to forty-five minutes. I asked Eielson to try and find out what climber remained at high camp.

A half hour later I switched on the radio, but after ten minutes of silence I switched it off again to conserve the batteries. Apparently the upper group was not on the summit yet.

RADIO TAPE 9:30 PM:

(A very weak transmission from Unit One)[23]

Gordy: "This is KHD6990 Eielson, go ahead Unit One."

Jerry: "Gordy, this is a real problem up here. Ah, do you have any arrangements to contact ah, Unit Two [Camp VI at 15,000 feet]?"

Gordy: "Ah, I tried to call him just a little while ago and I couldn't get an answer. Why don't you let me try it again—stand by. KHD6990 Unit Two, Unit Two, this is KHD6990 Eielson Base. KHD6990 Unit Two, Unit Two, this is KHD6990 Eielson Base. Ah, I don't get an answer Unit One, Jerry. Ah, I originally had told them we'd—you'd probably be calling about a quarter to nine and so they said they'd be listening in. I imagine they had

---

23. Radio communications were weak and difficult to understand at times during the climb. It required several months of tedious work to accurately transcribe the radio tapes.

their radio on and shut it off. But they might—they might turn it on periodically, ah, although I don't know when. I don't imagine they'll leave it on the whole time 'cause of the batteries. What's the problem?"

Jerry: "We don't know; it's not well wanded at all. We've lost the wands. We're just floundering around. We don't know whether we're on the summit ridge or not. We don't know whether the summit ridge is supposed to be wanded or not- - and ah, we just thought we'd check it out. We've been getting pretty close to the summit, but, ah, we can't tell. We're just floundering around on the flat here. Visibility is about 400 feet."

Gordy: "Ah, I didn't understand all of that, Jerry. I got—I think I got the gist of it. . ."

Jerry: "We're not even sure we're on the summit ridge now. We don't know whether the summit ridge is supposed to be wanded. Ah, we've lost the wands. The wands are set too far apart—can't find out where they left the ridge."

Gordy: "Okay, we're still a little fuzzy there, but I think I understood you to say that you don't know where the summit ridge is—and you have lost the wands because they are too far apart. Is that correct?"

Jerry: "Roger, we're at the summit ridge. We have followed the wands to what we think may be the summit ridge. I'll say that over again. We have followed the wands to what we think may be the summit ridge. And if we find one more wand. . . one more wand, it'd probably be enough, ah, to tell us which way we have to go on the ridge. That would be enough for—to tell us which way to go on the ridge."

Gordy: "Ah, Jerry, ah, I don't know if your batteries are warm enough or not or what, but I couldn't get too much of that. . ."
. . .
Jerry: "Cannot retransmit. We have cold batteries. We have cold batteries."

Gordy: "You have cold batteries. Is that what you said?"

Jerry: "The rest are at the camp."

Gordy: "Okay, is there any chance that you can let 'em warm up a little bit and then we can try again?"

Jerry: "Roger."

Gordy: "Okay, let me stand by here for a few minutes then. . ."

Gordy: "KWA701 this is 702."[24]

Wayne: "701, go ahead."

Gordy: "Yeah, I just got a call from Unit One and they're having problems up there right now. Ah, I don't know what's going on yet. But their batteries are cold and I told 'em to warm 'em up a little bit so I could understand more what they're saying. But it appears as though they're—they're kind of lost or something. . . I want to get back to the radio right now. . . just wanted to let you know what was happening. 702 clear."

Wayne: "10-4, ah, I'll be outdoors about five minutes but I'll be back after that. . . Thanks a lot."

RADIO TAPE 10:45 PM:

Gordy: "This is KHD6990 Eielson. Go ahead Unit One."

Jerry: "Eielson, I read you too—over."

Gordy: "Ah, say again. Go ahead Unit One — this is Eielson."
[Long pause]

Gordy: "KHD6990 Unit One this is Eielson. Go ahead."
[Continued silence]

---

24. Park Service radio call letters for Wonder Lake were KWA701. Eielson radio call letters were KWA702.

At Camp VI, I switched the radio on periodically to try and catch a summit announcement, but finally relented to the cold, still, arctic night.

DAY 30 — JULY 18

A calm coolness prevailed through the morning with the summit sometimes free of its pesty layer of fog. The summit team should have gotten back to high camp about midnight, and I reasoned that they would start down to Camp VI by noon. They would not arrive early enough to continue down Karstens Ridge as the high camp climbers had hoped, so we didn't pack up the camp.

RADIO TAPE 11:30 AM:

. . .

Gordy: "What happened last night? Ah, you called about ah, quarter to eleven I guess and, ah, I heard you call and I answered, but you didn't, you didn't acknowledge. I thought maybe you had radio trouble."

Jerry: "We probably didn't copy you, ah, we had some weak batteries. In fact they're still weak right now, ah, we ended up bivouacking as a matter-of-fact. It got so fogged-in that we couldn't go up or we couldn't go down."

Gordy: "Well, you're coming in loud and clear right here now. Ah, how long do you plan on staying on the top?"

Jerry: "Oh, five or ten more minutes, Gordy. Ah, kind of cold up here. . ."
[Mark continued the summit broadcast.]

Mark: "Hey, Gordy, you still sending postcards from the summit?"

Gordy: "Ah, yeah, go ahead."

Mark: "I'd like to send one to my parents. Have you got a pencil and paper there?"

Gordy: "Go right ahead."

. . .

Mark: "Dear Mom and Dad. Radio from the summit. A-okay. See you in a week or two. Love, Mark."

Gordy: "Okay, got that. Ah, how about giving us a little description of what you can see up there. Ah, tell us how the view is right now."

Mark: "The view consists of, ah, four other guys at the moment. That's all. It's completely whited out. The—we're sitting just below the summit. You can see the wands on the summit. That's all, over."

Gordy: "Well, you didn't luck out like the last four, I guess. They had a real good view when they were up there. Ah, do you mind just, ah, naming off the people that are up there right now?"

Mark: "Ah, sitting on the summit: Jerry Clark, Hank Janes, Dennis Luchterhand, ah, Mark McLaughlin. Oh! and Walt Taylor. Wouldn't want to forget him—he led all the way up."

Gordy: "Okay. Say when I talked to Joe last night—Wilcox—ah, he was wondering what had happened to the seventh man. He thought seven were going to try for the peak. . ."

Mark: "Ah, seventh man is Steve Taylor and he didn't feel good at all—so he stayed in camp at ah, 17-9.[25] He's probably wondering where we are at the moment."

Gordy: "Yeah, I imagine he is. . ."

. . .

Mark: "Jerry wanted to say—all five of us got to the summit at exactly the same time."[26]

---

25. Abbreviated for 17,900 feet.

26. This probably means that they stepped onto the summit shoulder-to-shoulder, perhaps with their arms around each other.

. . .

[Mark tried to give an address for his postcard, but the transmission was weakening.]

Gordy: "Ah, I didn't read that, but we can find your address somewhere else. I think someone else ought to have it here on record."

. . .

Mark: "Well, I guess that's about all the talkin' we can do—especially when you're not copying us. . ."

Gordy: "Okay, thanks a lot for the call. Yeah, I can't read you very well at all any more. You're. . . very indistinct. I think your batteries are going down. . . Ah, just before you do cut off. . . what time do you want us to stand by for the next call?. . ."

Mark: "Just 8:00, I guess—and that's all I have."

Gordy: "Okay, 8:00 PM. Then we'll—we'll have someone here then. Ah, be looking forward to talking to you and congratulations again. Ah, if nothing further then this is KHD6990 Eielson Base clear."

Mark: "Thanks very much KHD6990. Unit One clear."

At Camp VI the wind increased strongly about noon, whipping down the Browne Tower ridge to catch our baggy tent broadside. A snowstorm commenced, reducing visibility to a couple hundred feet. "Damn," I thought, "with the poorly marked route from high camp down to us, the upper party may have to wait and come down tomorrow." The waiting game was producing a little anxiety; we were all ready to descend and be done with the mountain.

LOG:
"Radio contact with Eielson reveals. . . made summit at 11:30 AM. Strong winds from southwest all day. . ."

The bivouac news of the summit team surprised me a great deal. I was a little reassured that it came before, rather than after, the summit. If they were still motivated to climb upward, then the bivouac may not have been too rough on them. There was no contact with the upper party at the scheduled 8:00 PM contact, but this did not concern me as radio schedules had not been kept religiously throughout the trip. I presumed that they were very tired upon returning to high camp and sacked out early.

Anshel and I visited far into the evening. "Listen!" he said suddenly. "I hear voices." I listened to the faint sound for a few seconds, then unzipped the tent and stuck my head out into the blowing snow. The sound was gone. Mountain winds have a way of distorting acoustics. It's often difficult to tell whether a sound has been carried for a great distance or perhaps just a mumbling from an adjacent tent. We weren't expecting the high camp to come down this soon. "Probably just the Colorado climbers or the wind," I said and returned to my sleeping bag.

DAY 31 — July 19

LOG:
"Strong winds all night until noon. Northern storm moves in and dumps a foot of snow. . ."

During a brief mid-morning clearing period, I saw fragmented cirrus clouds draped around both summits giving the mountain an eerie appearance. "Those are hellish high wind clouds," I thought. "We'd better get the expedition down Karstens Ridge before those wind monsters drop." It was uncomfortable to be outside and too miserably cramped to be inside. Anshel gave me a *National Georgraphic* magazine to kill time reading. Someone had carried it along for just such a contingency. It contained a lengthy article on the recent American Antarctica Mountaineering Expedition. The article was interesting, but reading about the struggles of mountainers was not the diversion I needed at the moment. I found a more refreshing article on turtles in the Tonga Islands.

I watched periodically for evenly spaced dots descending the upper glacier, and when the obscuring noon snowstorm moved in, I was very disappointed. "Damn, they waited too long to break camp," I thought. "They're going to be stuck in high camp for another day. At least we'll find out their status at the 8:00 PM radio contact." One more day, and victory would be ours.

5
All Is Not Well

As the evening radio contact approached, something didn't seem right. There was something strange about the storm we were in. What fate had Denali prepared for us for daring to tread the summit snows? Perhaps the wind had already delivered her measure of retaliation. Eight o'clock came and with a nervous premonition, I launched the antenna into the swirling wind and switched on the radio. I talked to Eielson for a few minutes; then everyone listened intently for a call from high camp. Stillness saturated the haunting silence—nothingness permeated the quiet. A sinking emptiness gripped my emotions. We had never missed radio contact on successive days. If Unit One did not call, they could not call. An error in scheduling was not likely as Eielson had been monitoring the airwaves all day for a possible call. Either the radio was not functional or else no hand was capable of pressing its transmitter key. Jerry Clark knew the radios inside out. He had made pre-trip modifications on them and could probably repair any minor malfunctions. The situation had all the aspects of an emerging emergency. There were no options to consider; our only course of action was to climb back immediately to the high camp to investigate.

Howard was outside the tent listening to the radio conversation, so I announced the obvious.

"Howard, there's some kind of trouble at the high camp. You, Paul, and I will start back up as soon as we can get ready. We'll travel light with only our sleeping bags, a snow shovel, and fuel. We can pick up some of the food at the 16,500 foot cache."

"We can't go up tonight, Joe," came the reply. "Let's wait until morning."

Howard's reply caught me completely by surprise. I exploded, "What's the matter? You guys have already made the summit and now you don't want to go up any more, even when people are in trouble up there."

"Look, Joe," Howard replied, "there's a snowstorm out here, and besides, it's getting dark at night now, in case you hadn't noticed."

I unzipped the tent flap and stuck my head out. The weather was uncomfortable, but it was not impossible. And it certainly wasn't dark. At this time of the year, there are less than four hours between sunset and sunrise—much of this twilight, with only about a half hour of total darkness. And even in darkness, visibility on snow is usually good. Realizing that I would not be able to budge Howard and Paul out of camp until morning, I reluctantly agreed to wait. I tried to contain my boiling temper in fitful sleep. I could not understand Howard's attitude. I could recall answering rescue calls in mid-sleep and mid-meal, struggling up unstable avalanche slopes, and climbing frozen, rotten rock faces by flashlight. I didn't want to battle up to the high camp any more than Howard, but rescue is not a matter of what a person wants. Our commitment to the upper party was as total as if we shared their climbing rope.

Perhaps I was overreacting. The high camp might be in fine shape, troubled only by dead radio batteries. And after all, Howard and Paul *had* agreed to go up with me. The restless storm prevailed; it seemed to be a constantly oscillating struggle between a northeast snowstorm and a strong southwest windstorm. The snowstorm periodically moved up the mountain to dump heavy snow on the camp; then it would be driven back by strong winds over the summit. Drifting snow became an ever increasing problem, as our snow fence shelter required shoveling with increased frequency.

DAY 32 — JULY 20

The wind died at 5:00 AM, and I was awakened by the sudden

cessation of the tent's flapping. It took us only half an hour to prepare to leave. We had four gallons of Blazo, so I emptied a gallon into a pressure cooker, the only available container in camp. The other three gallons would go to the high camp. Anshel moved into the Colorado tent with Jerry Lewis. "How long should we wait for you?" he asked.

"Two days," I answered. "If we're not back by then, descend the mountain. Take only the Mountaineer tent and as much food and fuel as you need to get to the next cache. Leave everything else."

"Well, I think I'll take all the film in the cache and any notebooks or diaries I find," Anshel advised.

"Okay," I agreed, realizing that Anshel was considering the possibility that we might not return at all. There was a pause as the rope was uncoiled; the unspoken understanding was clear: I would not only be packing the extra 20 pounds of fuel, but I would also be breaking trail. Wordlessly, I strapped on my Snowtreads and assumed my position at the head of the rope team. Paul and Howard followed.

A soupy whiteout rode the light breeze. I stepped out of camp and my snowshoes were engulfed in a foot of snow. As I floundered to find the trail, I plunged in even deeper, convincing me that I had already been on the trail. Blindly I felt my way along the crest of our old route and we crept onward, as Camp VI disappeared into the whiteness behind us. The wind increased strongly, whipping the snow into a ground blizzard. Snow burned my face, and wind caught my pack, giving me extremely poor balance. At times I had to stop for minutes to catch a glimpse of the next wand; at other times I had to fall to my knees and brace myself against the wind. Energy was sapped seemingly without effort and time passed without progress. Many of the wands had been blown away and there had been none in Camp VI to bring with us. With our trail obliterated as quickly as we broke it, we were in danger of cutting off our retreat; perhaps we would be unable to find our way back to the 15,000 foot camp. Still, I pressed upward into the wind, able to breathe only between gusts. Somehow I felt that this would be our only chance to get up to the high camp, a hope that was rapidly fading. The situation became more desperate with each step, and my silent curses gave way to soft but audible pleading prayer. I was amazed at myself as I had never prayed with real meaning before. But praying I most certainly was, to whatever power or purpose willing to help us climb through the storm.

Finally I stopped beside a half-buried ice block near the base of the first icefall. Two indistinct ghostly shadows followed the pull of the rope and joined me. We had come less than a mile in four hours in a storm that had tattered and drained us. For the last several hundred yards I had not seen a single wand. There was nothing to discuss; it was the will of the wind that we climb no farther.

I switched on the radio and asked for an updated weather forecast. As usual, Eielson did not have one.

I began chipping a depression in the ice. "We'll leave the fuel here," I said. "We can pick it up on our next try."

"Let's take it back to camp," Howard advised. "If we leave it here, it won't do anyone any good."

"No, we'll leave it here," I insisted. "It took a lot of energy to get it this far, and we can't waste that energy." Our chances of getting to the high camp now were going to be marginally measured in calories. I secured the fuel cache and we started ploddingly downward, our pace goaded by the strong tail wind. Mentally I formulated the next course of action.

Anshel scrambled out of the tent when we stumbled into camp. His hopeful anticipation of seeing the high camp party quickly turned to disappointment. Only three vanquished men, gaunt and gasping, greeted him.

LOG:
"Wilcox, Paul, Howard start out from 15,000 feet with fuel to check on high camp team. . . 4 hours and only 3/4 mile in windy blizzard conditions we. . . are forced to turn back."

Under the present weather and snow conditions it would take us perhaps 24 hours to reach high camp, if indeed we could do it at all. I called Howard to my tent to listen to the next radio communication. I asked Eielson to contact the Alaska Rescue Group with the following instructions: if there was no radio contact with Camp VII at 8:00 PM, I wanted an aircraft overflight of the high camp to drop fuel, a radio, and to determine the number of people there. The transmission was a bit weak, so I asked Anshel to locate the extra radio batteries. "They're cached at the 11,000 foot camp," he replied. (Fresh batteries had been put into the radios at Camp IV and the partially drained batteries cached.) "A lot of good they'll do us there," I thought.

Shortly after noon the weather cleared, and we could see to the top of the mountain which was enshrouded in thin wispy ice clouds. This calm lasted for three hours, and I was almost sure that we would see seven men descending any minute. Even a very conservative leader would take advantage of such a weather break. We were not in line-of-sight with the high camp, but we would be able to see them once they got a couple of hundred yards below Camp VII. My eyes strained at the top of the second icefall, but no dots were visible. I considered starting back up, but didn't as the weather began to deteriorate again. What could be keeping the upper party? Perhaps there would be a clue in their summit broadcast, if Eielson had recorded it. I called Eielson, but they could not readily locate the tape to play back to me. Relaying information to Wayne Merry through Eielson, I agreed that the expedition would charter Sheldon if for some reason ARG could not fly.

Anshel and I rotated the tent shoveling, which was now an hourly task. Anshel was on the uphill side and was able to retard the drifting somewhat by propping Snowtreads inside the tent and periodically readjusting them to form an airfoil from the tent wall to sweep away drifted snow in pulsating waves. We talked quietly about what could have happened to the upper party. Anshel asked me about details of the summit route and the summit itself. He asked if it was possible that someone could have fallen off the summit down the South Face, perhaps dragging the others with him in the tangle of ropes. I answered that it was possible but not likely. I could not envision a summit accident, but then something unusual had obviously occurred. "You know," Anshel said, "I think to not try the summit with the second team was the most important decision I have ever made in my life." A moment of gloom filled the tent and stopped our conversation. I thumbed through the *National Geographic* magazine for the umpteenth time. The Antarctica expedition had used Alpine Hut Logan tents, and they had held up well in a 100 mile per hour storm. This was reassuring; at least the upper camp had the best mountaineering tent available to fend off this gale. At the evening radio contact I talked to seasonal ranger, George Perkins:

RADIO TAPE 8:00 PM:

Joe: "Have you heard from Unit One?"

George: "Negative—we've heard nothing."

Joe: "Ah, neither have we, and, ah, we have seen nothing all day. . . Go ahead with the, ah, air observation."

George: "Okay, ah, little more, ah, information that, ah, Wayne wanted from you. First of all, ah, how's your weather; temperature, wind, and visibility?"

Joe: "Ah, visibility is good. Ah, temperature has been—never been below zero. Ah, the wind. . . is inconsistent from the, ah, southwest.[1] Ah, the wind chill factor[2] is tremendous. I'd say it'd be equivalent to 40 below. . . shoveling out the camp."

[I told Eielson that the wind was gusting to about 50 miles per hour with quite a bit of blowing snow, that we could see as high as the top of the lower icefall, and that we would make another attempt to reach the high camp, probably in the morning.]

Howard was outside the tent during the radio contact. "Are you planning to make another try for the high camp?" he asked in a skeptical tone.

"It's not a matter of choice," I replied. "We have to start back up as soon as the weather breaks."

"I guess you're right," Howard agreed unconvincingly.

Sleep came and to my surprise brought with it erotic dreams of seductive, redheaded women. Periodically, Anshel would rudely awaken me for a shoveling dash into the insulting weather. The chore completed, I happily returned to the pleasurable dreams. Such an indulgence of the libido seemed completely inappropriate considering our perilous circumstances.

---

1. According to the National Weather Service this part of the storm was blowing from the west northwest. The wind was apparently being deflected by the Browne Tower ridge above Camp VI.

2. The effects of wind chill are extreme. For example, at zero degrees in a 50 mph wind, exposed flesh will likely incur frostbite in less than a minute.

DAY 33 — JULY 21

By our scheduled morning radio contact with Eielson the wind had increased to about 65 miles per hour and I estimated it to be at least 80 miles per hour at the high camp. I radioed Eielson that we were considering building snow caves.

A growing coolness had been building between Howard and I concerning the feasibility of another try to climb to the high camp. Apparently in an effort to dissuade my stubborn position, Howard asked, "Look, Joe, what can we accomplish by returning to the high camp? If seven men have gotten themselves into a situation they can't handle, we won't be able to help them. If we go up there, we'll just collapse on top of them. We'll be in as bad shape as they are." He apparently thought the logic sound, as he repeated it a little later. I could not reply without anger, so I did not reply at all. I suspected that the probable grimness of the high camp was what was really bothering Howard. They were out of fuel by now; undoubtedly dehydration had caused extensive frostbite. Perhaps death had already claimed the weak. It was psychologically easier to remain at Camp VI shielded from the desperate drama, than to climb to the confrontation of the high camp and have to make face-to-face life and death decisions.

The storm continued to increase its fury. The vindictive wind was howling through camp at more than a hundred miles per hour now, venting its full wrath on our destruction. Our frail toehold in the sky was vanishing. In only a few hours our role as rescuers was reversed. About midday Anshel struggled through the tunnel entrance of the tent on his elbows, holding his unclad hands lifelessly in the air. He had been outside briefly and had exposed his hands to the icy winds which were lashing the camp. He tried unsuccessfully to put his gloves on and as frustration gave way to alarm, he turned to me pleadingly. I quickly unzipped my sleeping bag and put his hands in my armpits. After a while, warm circulation returned to his numb hands.

We were now reduced to sharing our very body heat. We tied up the tent's tunnel entrance, but it was a lost cause. Snow sifted through the tent zippers and appeared to be driven through the very fabric, filling the tent with a fine white mist. The body warmth which was preserving our lives was also melting this snow, resulting in damp sleeping bags. It was only a matter of time until our gear would be too wet to afford much insulation. The radio was left silent, and the log book lay unopened.

The interval between tent shoveling shrank, until it seemed that Anshel and I were passing each other at the doorway exchanging the snow shovel. On one occasion I noticed that the pressure cooker of precious fuel was not in its expected place. I sighted it forty feet down glacier; it had been blown from its snowy shelf, spilling most of its contents. With the aid of an ice axe, I retrieved the nearly empty vessel. Then I stood momentarily above the tent to assess its shoveling needs. A gust of wind buoyed my body as if on a pillow. My feet left the ground, and I was airborne. Reacting quickly, I grabbed a tent guy line as I sailed by. It held. I located the shovel and crawled back to the drifted side of the tent; I was more cautious this time. During the strong gusts I could only hug the surface, unable to shovel or even breathe. Between gusts, I shoveled and breathed as best I could. My footing felt insecure, and Anshel's muffled but frantic yell told me that I was standing on the tent wall. The snow was drifting faster than I could shovel, and the tent was going under. I crawled back into the tent to consider our immediate danger of being trapped and buried in a collapsed tent. I cursed myself for having repeatedly passed up opportunities to dig a snow cave. Too late to ponder what might have been. In our present circumstances we had only two options: to dig a snow cave, or to move into the Colorado tent which by some aerodynamics of design or terrain was not drifting badly. The intolerability of existing outside in the raging storm reduced our options to one.

"Well, Anshel," I concluded, "we'll have to move in with the Colorado climbers for a while. You go first, and I'll follow after I secure a few things."

Anshel looked at me for a moment and then asked in all seriousness, "But what if they won't let us move in with them?"

"Don't ask them," I retorted. "Just tell them that we're moving in."

Anshel's concern was unfounded, as the Colorado climbers readily accepted us into their tent. I got out of the collapsing tent first to give Anshel room to gather up his gear. He handed me his foam sleeping pad through the tent portal. As I grabbed it firmly with one hand, a savage gust ripped it from my grasp. There was a wisp of blue down glacier—then nothing. "Sorry about that," I said. "I'll give you mine." With critical items tucked in his iron gripped sleeping bag, Anshel made a crouching foray to the Colorado tent and after a moment disappeared within. Suspecting that the abandoned tent would soon be blown apart and its contents lost to the wind, I emptied all valuable items into my pack which I in turn anchored near the Colorado tent. I pulled my ice axe from its guy line anchor and used it to improve the security of my new home. Placing the radio, my water bottle, and some high-energy food in the foot of my sleeping bag, I pulled it into the storm. The tent was now jettisoned. The camp was in shambles, and I briefly surveyed the grim scene, then let go of the nearly buried tent and began the 30-foot journey to safety. Halfway there, a confused turbulence caught my sleeping bag. I grabbed the bag with both arms and fell to the snow, wrapping my legs around it. If the bag was to be blown away, I would go with it. I would not give it up. It was my frail lifeline to survival, my umbilical cord to the warmth of living. To lose it now would mean certain death. I lay prone for a couple of minutes braced against the screaming high-pitched wind. The whole camp appeared to be floating in a crystal cloud and for a time it was deceptively pleasant. It seemed as if I weren't really there, but casually observing these happenings from afar, like watching a movie. Perhaps I could just relax and witness my own death. I forced reality through this strong temptation and crawled the remaining distance to the safety of the blue Colorado tent.

It felt odd for alienated personalities to be thrust into the cold mechanics of close living. The tent offered each man a section of sleeping space less than a foot and a half wide with both head and feet pressed tightly against the drifted side walls. The cramped quarters were improved somewhat by sleeping head to foot. My parcel was next to the entrance which meant that I received the most blowing snow whenever anyone answered the call of nature. Other expeditions have resorted to cooking pot bedpans in less severe conditions, but for some reason we did not, although the undesignated latrine crept closer and closer to our doorstep. My sleeping bag was rapidly losing insulation due to the wetness of blowing snow, and this was complicated by my six-foot one-inch frame pressing tightly against both sides of the tent. I tried to make myself comfortable, as I looked enviously at Anshel who now had the insulation of my soft foam pad. The buffeted tent wall snapped my head like a prize fighter's rhythm bag—into near subconscious concussion. The single center pole of the pyramid tent shuddered and rattled in response to each blast of wind. The radio stayed stowed in my sleeping bag. I was saving the last strength of the weak batteries in case the tent failed. It would give us one final "Mayday" call, as if someone could come to our aid in this white purgatory. When sleep finally swept away my thoughts, it was to the fragrant gardens of the voluptuous redheads. During the night, I was awakened by Howard's shouts. The tunnel entrance had come untied and was flapping in the wind; if the wind shifted, the tent could be exploded like an over-inflated balloon. Quickly I retied the hatch. I lay awake for long periods of time listening to the whirling wind and possible changes in the tent's response patterns.

DAY 34 — JULY 22

Our vigil stretched into its second day. An increased brightness suggested that the clouds were mostly gone yet there was no let-up in the haunting howl of the wind which filled the Harper valley with a perpetual ground blizzard. We had lived at 15,000 feet or higher for eleven days now. The summit had receded a week into history, and we had battled storm upon storm ever since. Our bodies had been taxed greatly in climbing to the summit and under the present conditions recuperation was nonexistent. Deterioration made significant physiological and psychological inroads. The wind had long since bared our weaknesses and was now crushing our strengths. It had been more than a day since I had eaten a warm meal and the crowded tent did not afford a safe opportunity to operate a stove. I sipped at my near empty water bottle in a vain attempt to keep pace with dehydration. Soon the dark urinations of the past day ceased completely. Morale plummeted. An apathetic tangled mass of compressed humanity lay in the tent's pale blue glow, with little sleep or communication.

Finally late in the afternoon the wind calmed enough to see the mountain around us and above. Rooster-tail snow plumes were blowing from every ridge. Striated, transparent ice clouds glistened high on the peak, like angel hair against the blue-black sky. The storm seemed to be abating, and for the first time in more than a day I resumed pondering the plight of the upper group. Hopefully they were sitting out the blow in a comfortable snow cave; perhaps they would think us idiots for trying to weather it in a flimsy tent. Hopeful thinking, however, was not likely reality, and I assessed our capabilities to regroup and aid the upper party. We were low on food, nearly out of fuel, and some of our sleeping bags were damp; however, there was no frostbite or serious illness. Jerry Lewis and Anshel were weak: we could send them down the mountain, perhaps with one strong man, while two of us constructed a substantial snow cave. With an air-drop of supplies and dry sleeping bags and time to regain our strength, we could stay high as long as necessary to get to the aid of the upper party. The high winds had removed or compacted the loose snow so that climbing would be much easier now. I made a few comments about my plans, but received only blank stares from the others. I felt that Howard was silently stalking my fortitude, like a vulture waiting for my will to weaken.

Weak batteries and loose jacks plagued our first radio transmission in over 36 hours. For the most part Eielson could only hear the swishing sound made when I pressed the transmitter key.

RADIO TAPE 8:00 PM:

Gordy: "Ah, Unit Two, Unit Two, this is Eielson. KHD6990, Unit Two this is KHD6990 Eielson."

. . .

Gordy: "Ah, Unit Two, ah, I'd like you to answer the following questions by keying your transmitter. If dry sleeping bags and food are air-dropped to you at your present camp, ah, would there be any of you that would feel strong enough to go on back up? Ah, if the answer is yes, key your transmitter three times. Key your transmitter three times if the answer is yes."

[I looked toward Howard and Paul who were looking at each other. After a short pause Howard shook his head slowly negative and Paul followed. Hope sank into the pit of my stomach and surfaced as anger. "Here are two men in fairly good physical condition calmly turning their backs on the lives of others," I thought. Biting my lip, I fought an impulse to broadcast my emotions over the radio. Maybe if the weather got balmy they would yet change their minds.]

. . .

Gordy: "Ah, I didn't read that. Ah, the question Wayne wants answered, ah, if you are dropped dry sleeping bags and food at your present camp, how many of you would feel strong enough to go back up higher?"

Joe: "Ah, not over one of us at the present time."

Gordy: Ah, did I read you to say—not more than one? Ah, if the answer is yes, key your transmitter three times."

Joe: "Swish, swish, swish."

Gordy: "Okay, I read that. Ah, I read that—stand by one."

Gordy: "Ah, Wayne, ah, not over one would be strong enough to go back up if—if dry sleeping bags and food—food were air-dropped. Ah, not more than one."

Wayne: "Are any of them frostbitten or in trouble? Are any of them in, ah, in any kind of bad condition, ah, other than feeling weak?"

Gordy: "Okay, we'll check on that."

Gordy: "Ah, Unit Two, are any of your, ah, people in the—in your camp, ah, frostbitten or is there any other serious problems other than just being weak? If the answer is yes, key your transmitter three times. If it is no, key it twice."

Joe: "Swish, swish."

. . .

Gordy: "Okay, 10-4, we read that, 10-4. Stand by one."

Gordy: "Ah, the answer on that is no, Wayne. There's no serious difficulties other than. . . just being weak."

. . .

Gordy: "Ah, Joe, Wayne wants to know whether or not you feel the snow is deep enough up at the high camp for those ah, six or seven to dig in. . ."

Joe: "Swish, swish, swish."
[By now, Wayne surmised that we had decided to descend the mountain.]

. . .

Wayne: "Okay, well, that's all I can think of at the moment. Ah, you might ask them to make a contact about every, ah, ah, three hours from now on, ah, until they drop off of Karstens Ridge, if they can."
[I asked Eielson if they could have Don Sheldon signal us after his overflight of the high camp and let us know their condition. I also confirmed our observation of clearing skies with the weather forecast, and described the location of the 3 gallons of fuel at 15,500 feet.]

Gordy: "Okay, there's no chance that any of you, if you were dropped dry sleeping bags and food, could go back up. Is that correct?"

Joe: "Ah, repeat, not more than one of us would feel like going up."
[Through Eielson, Wayne asked about the condition of the supplies cached at Denali Pass. I could only advise that we had not inspected that cache.]

We began sorting through the cache to collect exposed film left by the upper party and supply ourselves with high-energy food for the descent. The others wanted to start down the ridge as soon as possible to take advantage of the calm winds; but a very cold night was falling, so we decided to wait until morning. The Mountaineer tent was nearly collapsed flat, but miraculously still in one piece. Howard and Paul decided to move into the small tent for the night and began digging it out. With the additional elbow room, we boiled up vast quantities of warm brew to fortify ourselves, and all water bottles were filled to overflowing.

At the beginning of the 11:00 PM radio contact, Howard instructed me to tell Eielson that we had sick men in the party and that is why we could not go back up to the high camp. "Howard, we both know that isn't true," I retorted, "and I won't transmit it." Jerry Lewis and Anshel were very weak, but only Lewis had eaten little and seemed to need an immediate drop in elevation. The rest of us were refreshened somewhat from our windy ordeal and were more storm weary than exhausted—our affliction was mental.

RADIO TAPE 11:00 PM:

Joe: "Ah, we're waiting until morning—waiting until morning. We have a couple of people hampered and cannot travel tonight."

. . .

[I tried to keep the radio contact short to conserve the batteries. Howard seemed to be getting increasingly frustrated and asked to speak to Eielson.]

Joe: "Ah, Howard Snyder wants to say something."

George: "Yeah, go ahead."

[I handed the radio to Howard who was standing just outside the tent. "If he is insistent on perpetrating a lie—he will have to do it himself," I thought in anger.]

Howard: "Hello, Eielson, this is Snyder. Do you read me?"

George: "Say, again."

Howard: ". . . we're really having problems here. . ."

Gordy: [to George] "Better get Wilcox to say it. His voice is a little clearer. . ."

George: "Ah, I could not read you. Ah, please say again slowly or ask Joe to give the message. We seem to read him better."

Howard: ". . .we cannot go up. . ."

Gordy: [to George] "Let Wilcox say it."

George: "I cannot read you. Please, ah, Joe's voice comes through over the interference better."

Howard: "This is Snyder. I'm having trouble with the battery pack. Having trouble with battery pack. I wanted to say that we have three people pretty sick up here. . ."

Gordy: [to George] "Have 'em—have 'em tell Wilcox to talk. We can hear his voice a lot better."

Voice at Eielson: "Ask 'em if they heard something up there."

George: "Yeah."

Gordy: [to George] "Tell 'em to have Wilcox repeat it."

George: "Please ask Joe to repeat it. His voice comes over the interference better. I still cannot read you."

Howard: ". . .having trouble with the battery pack, over."

George: "Okay, we're reading you."

Howard: "Okay, this is Snyder. . ."

Gordy: [to George] "Tell 'em to have Wilcox do it."

George: "Still could not, ah, read your message except that you said you're having trouble with the battery pack, and—I caught, ah, down the ridge, I thought—but that's all I could understand."

Howard: "Roger. . . we have three sick people—we will be moving down the ridge, over."

Gordy: [To George] "Three sick people moving down the ridge?"

George: "Are you moving—going down tonight?"

Howard: "Negative, negative—going down in the morning, over."

Gordy: [To George] "Three sick people—find out what's wrong."

George: "Ah, I read you that—you say you have three sick—three ill people moving down the ridge tomorrow."

Howard: "Roger, roger—this is why we couldn't possibly go up now. We have to get them down, over."

. . .

I was astounded by Howard's desperation to justify the desertion of the high party. He had fumbled with the radio and battery pack in the cold for more than five minutes, critically draining our weak batteries to tell Eielson something that was not only incorrect but impertinent to the rescue situation. Eielson already knew that we were descending the mountain in the morning, and they had not asked for an elaboration. Lewis and Schiff were weak. I wondered who the third sick man was supposed to be.

I began to ponder the feasibility of remaining at Camp VI alone while the others descended. Climbing alone unroped on the Harper would be a possibility as no one had fallen completely into a crevasse since the Lower Icefall of the Muldrow and I already had a trail to follow. I doubted that the others would try to force me to go down if I insisted on staying high alone.

The tent was roomier now with only three people, but noticeably colder. There was little wind, yet the temperature was probably the lowest that we had encountered. I padded my damp sleeping bag with down clothing. A sharp abdominal pain told me that my body was responding to the evening's warm meal, requiring a short trip away from the tent. Returning to my sleeping bag I noticed that my fingers were stiff. I had exposed them to the weather briefly, but they did not feel cold—just stiff. It took several minutes to fumble my sleeping bag zipper closed. Placing my hands in my crotch, I lay in the chill of the night among unsynchronized breathing and considered tomorrow's decision. In a few hours I would have to decide whether I would go down with the others or stay alone. A troubled, cold sleep finally came, without the company of redheads.

DAY 35 — JULY 23

The morning came with mild wind, the mountain visible to the summit. The others created an excited almost happy bustle as they prepared for the descent. No words were spoken of the upper party. I was immediately shocked to discover that my hands were still numb and frantically clawed out of my sleeping bag to investigate. My hands did not feel cold when touching them against warm parts of my body, neither were they discolored. They could not be frostbitten, but what was the problem? Dehydration[3] or maybe a pinched nerve during the night? Not likely that it happened to both hands. My hands felt as if I had gripped a bar for as long as possible, until overcome by fatigue; only time did not relieve the fatigue. I could use my hands, although somewhat clumsily and with a dull pain. I rolled up my sleeping bag and sat alone in the middle of the tent. "What's wrong?" I addressed the blank tent walls. Could I possibly stay here alone now? Perhaps I could go down the ridge with the others and come back up with the Mountaineering Club of Alaska Expedition which should by now be on Karstens Ridge. But that would mean a delay of at least two days, and the weather seemed good right now for a climb to high camp. The others prodded me to pack my pack several times, and then began packing it for me. I sat huddled in the middle of the tent—defeated. I had matched my will and strength against Denali's wrath—and was now but a child, humiliated before a stern master.

Howard entered the tent and tried to warm my hands. I told him that they were not cold. "I'm going to rope you up second behind me," Howard said in a tone that told me he had assumed leadership of the group. "I want a strong man there to belay," he added. Howard left and Anshel came in while I was fumbling with my crampons. He said that his toes were a little numb from the cold night.

"Will you strap my crampons on for me?" I asked, suddenly

---

3. Dehydration accelerates exposure, a condition in which the body sacrifices the warmth of its extremities in order to maintain its critical core temperature.

aware that my subsonscious had already accepted the fact that I would be going down the ridge with the others. I had joined the deserters.

Howard manned the morning radio contact with Eielson, telling them that I had frostbitten fingers. This time I was only slightly surprised by his transmission of erroneous information.

The tent was quickly packed, and I clipped into the rope. I gazed briefly at the food cache, the only thing we were leaving. Earlier in the morning I had discarded my wool pants there in favor of wearing my down insulated pants on the descent. Already the discarded pants were partially covered with drifting snow. We started down shortly before 9:00 AM. Up glacier there was lightly blowing snow, and no sign of the overdue climbers.

If frozen eyelids peered down windswept slopes, they would have seen five human forms descending slowly from the 15,000 foot camp—three in fairly good health, and a fourth still capable of upward steps. No despair can be as great as that of abandonment.

The wind of the past two days had removed a couple feet of snow, leaving our old trail exposed above the glacier surface; it broke away easily and was treacherous walking. It was apparent immediately that we would have trouble with Jerry Lewis. About every 50 feet he collapsed to the snow for a 10-15 minute rest. Halfway across the Browne Tower traverse, Howard stopped and suggested that we drop lower for possibly easier walking. Paul and I objected to taking an unknown and likely crevassed route, so we continued our unsteady course.

Jerry Lewis was tied in third on the five-man rope team, and I belayed him on the rougher sections. From the last part of the Browne Tower traverse, we could see the site of the upper camp. I carefully searched the uniform whiteness: no tents, nothing. It took us more than two hours to drop down to 14,500 feet at the top of Karstens Ridge. There among the rocks we paused to consider whether or not to give a Dexedrine pep pill to Lewis. Howard was skeptical of the medication and wanted advice from Eielson. There were no doctors readily available and, of course, the park rangers would not give any medical advice. While Howard was talking on the radio, I pondered an old imported can of Ovaltine uncovered by the high winds. It was dated 1921 and was apparently a relic of an early expedition, although the closest recorded ascent of Mount McKinley following this date was in 1932.

Jerry washed down the Dexedrine tablet and we continued the tricky descent. At the top of the Coxcomb, we clipped into our fixed line and started down the broad steep ridge that soon hid our view of the Harper. Other fixed lines from past years had been exposed in the recent winds which had removed several feet of snow. Soon we could see far down the ridge, a sight that lifted our spirits. Our 12,100 foot camp was occupied by the Mountaineering Club of Alaska Expedition. I could see individuals milling about camp, a strange sight to our month long isolation from the rest of humanity. Jerry Lewis remained weak; perhaps the Dexedrine prevented him from getting worse. He periodically collapsed precariously to the snow, which made me very thankful for the fixed line. An unchecked fall here would not stop for at least 3,000 feet. Howard's frustration and irritation seemed to increase with the increasing length of Jerry's rests.

At the Coxcomb cache I was not surprised when Howard and Paul uncovered 9-man days of precious food to take *down* the mountain. (There was already half a month of food cached below us along the 3-day route to civilization.) The weather began deteriorating rapidly, and Jerry took some coaxing to get going again. Activity in Camp V appeared more organized now. They had obviously observed the difficulty which we were having with Jerry. Perhaps they were preparing to come up to aid us.

Clouds boiled up from the valleys and the wind freshened as we continued our painful descent. Only the crest of the ridge itself cut the fog, maintaining our uninterrupted view of the 12,100 foot camp. My hands had improved with the drop in elevation and were nearly normal now. I later learned that I had probably suffered a form of chilblain, characteristic of brief exposure to severe cold.

The MCA climbers started up the ridge and met us at about the 12,500 foot level. Their leader, Bill Babcock, was the first man to greet us with overflowing energy which clashed with our subdued condition. Momentarily unable to think of anything to say which was not already obvious and remembering that the MCA Expedition had paid for half of the fixed line, I offered, "This is the fixed line which is now yours."

"Yes, we know," he replied with obvious assurance. They had leveled a platform where we stopped for a hot drink before continuing to Camp V. Jerry was relieved of his pack for this short foggy descent. On one narrow pitch the snow goggles which I had parked above my eyes fell to the snow. I reached quickly, but too late as they skidded out of sight, a man-made contribution to the Traleika Glacier. Luckily I carried a spare pair for just such a contingency. At camp we were able to relax and evaluate the enormity of the situation. The MCA group understood that they were now the best positioned rescue team for the upper party, and I assumed their willingness without asking. I told Bill about our food and fuel caches higher on the mountain. These, plus possible air-drops, would enable them to climb with few relays. Bill said that the MCA group had stored 15 days of supplies with Don Sheldon in case they got into a tight situation and needed an air-drop. These supplies could be used for the rescue operation. The weather deteriorated badly, as I prepared for a 2:00 PM radio contact. I informed Eielson that we had descended to 12,100 feet and were with the MCA group. Eielson then asked if I wanted an all-out rescue called for the upper camp.

This question was quite perplexing. Air-drops had already been cleared and according to Park Service policy these could only be authorized (except for scientific groups) in an emergency situation. Weren't we already in a rescue? Our backup, the Alaska Rescue Group, had already been notified and were likely riding their bags pending the overflight. I could not imagine them ignoring the serious findings of an overflight or waiting for a formal request in an obviously grim situation. Airplanes had not been able to fly near the mountain in over a week without risking having their wings ripped off in the turbulence. Even if they could, the mountain was not about to be stormed by paratroopers and helicopter landings would be unlikely at extreme elevations.[4] The MCA party was not only the best positioned and acclimated, but the only feasible rescue team unless another expedition was higher. And this possibility was already being checked out. I could not see how more could be accomplished by calling an all-out rescue. Perhaps a hundred people would mill around Wonder Lake for a week drinking tea and scratching their heads. A lengthy discussion with Eielson ensued, hampered by weak radio batteries. We rigged a

---

4. Under very calm conditions high altitude helicopters can land near the summit; however, calm weather did not seem likely in the immediate future — probably not before the MCA could climb to the high camp.

dipole antenna, but it did not help much. Finally I told Eielson that I would like an all-out rescue called, pending the results of Sheldon's overflight of the high camp.

Bill Babcock seemed amazed that I had not yet called an all-out rescue. Apparently the helicopter rescue of three climbers on the Winter Expedition had been very expensive (the helicopter had been brought in from Seattle), resulting in a lot of criticism from the public. "There are critics who will claim that people should not be allowed to climb mountains to just get in trouble and waste the taxpayer's money," Bill said, "but you can't worry too much about them—you might have seven stiffs up there."

I told Bill that I wasn't the least bit concerned about public reaction and repeatedly asked him what more could be done if a rescue were called. Finally he agreed that probably nothing extraordinary would happen that was not already being done. Then added that mainly it was a disposition in thinking among the powers that be, in the Park Service and ARG. To take the lid off might facilitate air support and high altitude reconnaissance flights and perhaps even involve the air force. I pondered his thoughts. Finally I decided that, if necessary to increase the tempo of the support operations, I would give the go-ahead on a rescue. The MCA climbers offered us the use of their snow shovel and ice saw to level our tent platform. Their hefty tools made ours appear like toys. In a few minutes the job was complete, and I proceeded to get better acquainted with the MCA group. The expedition was composed of mutual friends from the same mountaineering club, yet they had suffered severe internal problems. At the onset of their climb, they became disoriented on the tundra and wasted several days in the wrong valley, ending up at the precipice of Gunsight Pass,[5] instead of McGonagall Pass. Two of their original nine climbers became so upset that they left the expedition. Another called it quits after they had finally reached McGonagall Pass. He made a solo hike to Wonder Lake. The progress of the MCA had been slowed by bad weather, particularly in the nearly continuous and still prevailing storm of the last week. Organization seemed smooth now, although one man admitted in frustration that he had

---

5. The topography of the area suggests that they did not end up precisely at Gunsight Pass but rather at the top of the Carlson Creek valley.

been thinking of leaving the group and climbing to the summit alone. He felt that they had wasted too much time and had already forfeited their chances of making the top as a group.

One member of the now six-member MCA expedition was Grace Hoeman, the wife of prominent Alaskan mountaineer, Vin Hoeman, who was currently leading an international expedition on Canada's Mount Logan. She was an anesthesiologist under her professional name, Dr. Grace Jansen, and had taken charge of Jerry Lewis as soon as he arrived in camp. I entered the MCA Logan tent where Jerry was being cared for with liberal quantities of food and drink. Grace informed me that Jerry had frostbitten toes. "How bad?" I asked. "Will he need to be airlifted out?"

"No," she answered, "I have given him some Roniacol to improve circulation, and he should be able to walk out with the help of codeine. He will need medical attention once he gets out though—whirlpool treatments and so forth."

The long afternoon in Camp V passed on the back of a tortoise. It didn't seem that enough was being done toward getting aid to the high party. My compassion expected the MCA climbers to launch immediately into the swirling snowstorm with the fortitude of a John Wayne movie, yet my common sense exposed this as folly. To climb ahead of their supplies and/or air support would risk their own safety and compound the emergency. I paced the camp in restless anxiety and pondered the feasibility of going back up with the MCA group. I mentioned this prospect to Howard, as he was entering his tent. "What do you think of a couple of us going back up with the MCA group if we can get dry sleeping bags?" I asked.

"Paul and I are taking Jerry down the first thing in the morning," he answered in a tone of finality and disappeared into his tent. In reality, air-dropping dry gear on the narrow Karstens Ridge would be almost impossible. Perhaps if I could get off the mountain quickly and dry my gear, I would be able to return with an airlifted group.

The communications prospects for the MCA group were not too good. They were only equipped to talk to Radio Fairbanks, which so far they had been unable to do. It seemed greatly advisable that they be capable of communicating directly with the Park Service, where most major rescue decisions and coordinations would have to originate. I offered to loan our radio to Bill, as we could not use it anyway once we dropped below 6,500 feet. Only two or three days of routine terrain separated us from Wonder Lake. Bill gladly accepted the offer.

At the evening radio contact I told Eielson that Jerry Lewis was much better and had minor frostbite. High winds could keep Sheldon's light plane from flying for days and Eielson asked me what I thought of a high altitude reconnaissance flight by a larger plane from the Rescue Coordination Center at Elmendorf Air Force Base in Anchorage. I replied in the affirmative. I then clarified my request from the previous radio contact. I said that I wanted rescue operations to be ready to go into effect *immediately* following Sheldon's overflight of the high camp. I added that if this meant calling an all-out rescue, then I was now making that request. I also told Eielson that fresh batteries should be air-dropped to the MCA for the radio we were loaning them. Anshel had been listening to the conversation and indicated that he would like his parents notified that he was safely descending and not part of the party being rescued. He yelled to the Colorado climbers that an all-out rescue was underway and asked them if they wanted their parents notified. I transmitted that all parents of the descending party should be notified. I completed the radio contact by informing Eielson that if we hiked out before rescue operations were complete, I would personally like to be airlifted back on the mountain to assist.

I noticed that Bill Babcock's Kelty pack frame was broken and heavily lashed. "What happened to that?" I asked.

"I dropped it with a big load and it snapped," he replied.

"It must have been a hellish load," I said. "I thought that Kelty packs were indestructable. That's the first broken one I've ever seen."

The Colorado climbers and myself had identical pack frames, so I offered to switch frames with Bill to make his rescue climb less agonizing. He readily accepted and told me that I could get financial reimbursement from his wife in Anchorage. The MCA group did not seem to have any other equipment problems: one man had lost his ice axe in the McKinley River, but was resupplied with their expedition spare.

As I was retiring to the tent, Anshel drew my attention to the fiberglass rod tent sleeve which had been on the windward side during the storm. It was still firmly packed with wind-driven snow to the point of bursting, a vivid reminder to our memories. Compared to the demons who had stalked the heights, the calm snowfall of Camp V was as secure as a mother's womb. This peaceful quiet was emphasized by the ease of my own breathing in the denser air. For the first time in nearly two weeks, I tumbled into a relaxed restful sleep.

DAY 36 — JULY 24

Morning was obscured by a dense fog which insulated us in an ivory bubble. Dr. Jansen asked if she could descend the mountain with us; she was suffering from pre-menstrual headaches which were compounded by altitude and felt that she would be a liability to the rescue effort. I indicated that she could accompany us, but felt badly that the services of a doctor would not be available high on the peak. This information was given to Eielson at the 8:00 AM contact, the last transmission before turning our radio over to the MCA. I also indicated my desire to get out quickly and attend the observation flight to help ascertain knowledge of the missing men, and repeated my willingness to be airlifted back on the peak. I was surprised to learn that a bureaucratic decision had been made to wait on Sheldon and not use a larger plane at high altitude. Merry had supported the high altitude flight, but could not persuade those who make decisions. I told Eielson that the high altitude plane should be sent up *now* or as soon as possible. I also said that I thought there had already been several days in which high altitude aircraft could observe the high camp area, days in which surface turbulence would not permit a small plane to fly.

The Colorado climbers switched to their low altitude footgear, and Jerry Lewis gave some of his high altitude stuff to Babcock in case it was needed up higher. We tried to outwait the weather, but morning became noon with no relief. Finally we bade farewell and began a nasty descent in gusting snow. Only five men were left at Camp V: Bill Babcock, his younger brother, Jeff, Gayle Nienhueser, John Ireton, and Chet Hackney. They looked insignificant as the camp disappeared in the mist above us, yet were our only hope for the higher party. The Colorado climbers had started down the ridge before us, but we quickly caught up with them in the slow pace forced by Jerry's painful feet. Since we were traveling on two separate ropes, I yelled to Howard above the howl of the wind as to where and when we might rendezvous for a meal or to camp. A profane reply indicated that he was no longer interested in my opinions or suggestions, and so we continued the descent as two estranged groups operating independently. The narrowness of the trail kept us marking time in the rear on the ridge. We passed a MCA snow block cache shelter at the 11,500 foot saddle and descended in soft snow to the Muldrow.

At Camp IV, I stopped to claim my low altitude boots from the cache and carefully repacked my felt boots in their watertight bags. I anticipated needing them again, if I should be airlifted to the Harper with a rescue group. I stuck my stockinged foot into a leather boot, and grimaced with pain. Quickly I pulled my foot out to examine the obstruction; there was none. I held my toes in uncomfortable awareness. There was no mistaking the tender symptoms of frostbite, probably incurred during the last cold night at Camp VI, and until now concealed in the roominess of my high altitude footgear. With no words to the others, I forced my feet into the leather boots, strapped on my snowshoes and started hiking—letting my toes gradually adjust to their new harsh environment, as my mind blocked out the pain. On the Muldrow our old unwanded trail was noticeable only by a very slight variation in color on a uniformly smooth surface. With snowshoes the trail was quite firm. The two rope teams traveled in leapfrog fashion, passing each other at staggered rest stops. Our lassitude became obvious, as we stumbled unconcerned down pitches which had commanded our respect on the ascent. On one occasion in the Great Icefall, Anshel walked up to Grace, who was tied into the middle of the rope, to put something in her pack for her, leaving slack rope. We were in an unsafe area, and a crevasse fall by Anshel would accelerate unchecked for 50 feet, which would likely be fatal and probably catapult the entire team into the glacier's jaws. Grace recognized this danger and sternly reminded Anshel of his hazardous action. As we negotiated the Great Icefall, the weather broke, exposing Karstens Ridge—a lenticular cloud obscured the slopes above. We had passed unnoticed beyond the fierceness of the Harper Icefall.

Late in the evening we arrived at the Camp III food cache at 8,100 feet and set to rifling choice items for our continued descent. All of the fudge, nuts, and a few other readily consumable foods were stuffed in our pockets; the food bags were left at the campsite like gutted game carcasses. Without the aid of elaborate latrines, a female ropemate presented some problems. Anshel and I could simply turn our backs and pretend to be intrigued by something in the distance; however, Grace had to request formal privacy. On one such occasion before leaving Camp III, the Colorado group hiked right by, apparently not realizing the situation. Grace's indignant wrath quickly reprimanded them.

We hiked on through the night.

DAY 37 — JULY 25

A lot of melting had occurred since our last passing, requiring that we skirt to the left to negotiate the Lower Icefall. The steep, rock-blackened ice was barren and hard, requiring crampons and exhaustive caution. Rocks tumbled from Pioneer Ridge with frequent authoritative rumbles. We could see only a few yards up the foggy slope and could only hope that we would not become involved directly in nature's persistent efforts to reduce this mountain to sea level. Finally we took an overdue rest break at a meltwater stream, sitting together with our packs uphill to fend off possible falling rocks. It was with great relief that we gained the nearly flat safe glacier below the icefall. We certainly did not need snowshoes here but wore them to increase traction and out of habit. No old tracks were visible, and our present passing scarcely scratched the nearly bare ice. The soothing abundance of oxygen deceived me into thinking that I was not yet tired, while in truth my limbs wobbled from fatigue and the atrophy of forced inactivity during the past storms. Hour followed hour, as I plodded into the damp whiteout; the scraping of my Snowtreads mesmerized my mind. I was startled from my trance by Anshel's shouts.

"We're not going straight," he advised. "We're weaving all over the glacier." I took out my compass and sure enough, I was hiking 45 degrees from my intended path. We resumed again, but this time I held a compass in my hand to steady our course. At about 6:00 AM we came to a huge transverse moraine. "Could this be Mount Moraine?" I wondered. It looked totally unfamiliar. The easiest walking was near what I believed to be the center of the wide valley. If we cut to the left too soon, we might encounter surface lakes and disruptions. If we stayed in the center too long, we would risk missing McGonagall Pass altogether. We decided to stop on the moraine for a good meal and a few hours of sleep. Perhaps the fog would burn off in the heat of day. Grace had some cheese and moose sausage from the MCA food supply. It was very tasty to an appetite dulled by weeks of freeze-dried menus. Grace, on the other hand, was tired of the MCA food and quite relished our fare. The Colorado climbers came by a couple of hundred feet away, and Anshel gave them a shout. They wordlessly waved and continued hiking past us into their nineteenth hour. Three sleeping bags were crowded into the Mountaineer tent for a four-hour nap in the warming sun, before resuming our pilgrimage. Anshel had returned my foam sleeping pad which improved my rest. The world's finest mattress could not have been so comfortable.

We left our 6,100 foot moraine camp at 11:00 AM with rested strength and under lifting fog. Both sides of the dirty bare glacier were visible now as we headed directly for the pass. At about 12:30 PM we stepped onto the McGonagall Pass moraine, unroped for the last time, and began a lengthy feast in the unstable weather. I broke out the freeze-dried steaks, but this was no victory banquet to flatter our taste buds; we were now eating for survival. A dozen steaks sautéed in catsup disappeared among the three of us. The theodolite and some other items cached at the pass would have to be added to our already mountainous and soaked packs. We began mentally weighing and evaluating the various choices. To be left were all snowshoes, Walt Taylor's perlon rope which had been our lifeline on the descent, all of the equipment originally cached for recovery by other members of the expedition (except for exposed film), fuel, and all food requiring cooking. The pile of discarded supplies was enough to keep an expedition going for a week. Collectively it was valued at perhaps a thousand dollars, yet if we had to pack it out on our backs, it was worthless to us. Finally we painfully shouldered our hundred-plus pound packs in the driving rain. The pass did not appear much different from a month ago, except for the haunting absence of the laughter and anger which had echoed from its rocks. I could sense hidden personalities dipping water from the stream and standing around the old kitchen, personalities which I knew would not pass this way again. If they came down at all, it would be as frail survivors in a helicopter. I took one last look across the dingy, gray shadowed glacier where not one flow measurement wand remained, and headed down the narrow ravine. Melting snow had exposed large boulders which became more prominent and more difficult to negotiate with each step downward. I felt like an ant descending a hill of marbles—one false step under my heavy burden could snap an ankle or leg like a toothpick. We arrived at the Horse Cache with great relief and stopped to regroup. Gear which had been cached here would be left untouched. It was already late in the afternoon. We would not make Wonder Lake today.

Stepping onto the tundra was like entering a lushly living, emerald world of intoxicating fragrances—a world almost forgotten in the cobwebs of my memory. I hiked slowly along in momentary euphoria, not minding the rain on my face, the weight of my pack, or the slap of low bushes. The tundra surface was so different from the accustomed snow of the past month that I felt a little awkward, stumbling about like a sailor trying to regain his land legs. A mile below the Horse Cache we came upon a familiar blue tent, and Anshel woke Paul to tell him of our passing. The Colorado group seemed to be settled in for a much needed rest. Slowly we moved on, my rain-weighted pack forcing the lashings of the broken frame to cut deeply into my back and the tufted tundra irritating my tender toes into a stiff-locked limp. The sense of being in utopia was quickly eroding. Anshel and Grace did not seem to be in any better shape, as we three weak shadows moved into the bleak evening at barely a mile an hour pace.

At about 9:00 PM our soggy trio came to an MCA camp. Since they did not use pack horses, the MCA group had established relay camps on the tundra. The sight of the already pitched tent was persuasion enough to command a sleep stop. We had come only five and a half miles from McGonagall Pass. Small talk accompanied the warming soup, and we got to know Grace better. She had emigrated from Germany after World War II and met her current husband, Vin Hoeman, through their mutual interest in mountaineering. Grace exhibited a strong willed character, when she talked about her conflicts with the MCA leader, Bill Babcock. She related how a simulated crevasse fall in a pre-trip workout had resulted in a broken rib. Also Grace had been vocal in her disapproval of their going up the wrong valley early in the expedition and Bill had countered by citing an instance when Vin had, by mistake, climbed the wrong mountain. While discussing food recipes, Grace's headstrong disposition melted into the role of a typical suburban housewife.

Before retiring, I allowed myself my first look at my frostbitten toes. They did not seem discolored, yet a thumbnail print lingered indefinitely in dull pain. With no words to the others, I climbed into a damp sleeping bag for some rest. There was no rain fly on the tent and puddles formed on the waterproof floor to be absorbed by dozing sleeping bags. No one seemed to mind at this stage of the game.

DAY 38 — JULY 26

Early in the morning, the uncomfortable wetness exceeded our somewhat relieved fatigue, and sleep became impossible. A hurried breakfast of cheese, sausage, and candy was followed by wringing out socks and sleeping bags. Packs were once again assembled, several pounds heavier than the previous day. Grace added a large MCA shovel to her pack, and we resumed our trek at 4:00 AM. The Colorado group had not awakened us during our six hour sleep so I suspected that we were still ahead of them.

Our hiking pace was no faster than the previous evening. The misery of our plight increased with each stumbling step. The pack frame lashings again ground into my stiff back muscles. I had by now run out of distracting thoughts to occupy my mind and finally began a low moan audible only to me, and synchronized with my pace. These soon evolved into sobs, not of despair, but of resignation. Just before 8:00 AM we came to Clearwater Creek, flood water swollen in the morning light. We hiked up and down the bank looking for a likely crossing. There was none. I finally decided to try a crossing at the upper end of a small island that split the obstacle into two thundering channels. For greater mobility, I took off my wet down pants leaving only fishnet longjohns and wind pants. Cautiously I entered the foamy water and negotiated only a few yards before being suddenly swept off my feet. Quickly I stripped the pack from my shoulders, as it could easily become an anchor to drown me. Surprisingly it did not sink, and I used it as a float. Kicking and struggling, my feet occasionally hit the bottom to propel me in my intended direction. I gained the long island far downstream and walked upstream along its shore, half dragging my pack. Without pausing, I threw my pack into the second channel for a repeat performance. After what seemed like a long time, I staggered to shore and dragged my pack a few feet out of the water, before collapsing in exhaustion.

With the return of logical thinking, I analyzed our circumstances. I was a very strong swimmer, yet had barely managed the crossing. Anshel and Grace probably could not cross without the aid of a fixed line. I took from my pack the length of plastic rope which we had used on the Clearwater during our hike in. Coiling it loosely and tying a rock to one end, I tried to heave a line to Anshel on the far bank. Repeatedly I tried and repeatedly it fell yards short of Anshel's outstretched hand to be swept downstream in the swift torrent. Anshel and I stood as deep in the water as we dared, but still my throws were short and became increasingly worse in my fatigue. Anshel and Grace would have to wait for the flood to abate or else hike to the headwaters of the stream to effect a crossing. Cold, wet exposure was already slowing down my physiology— most obvious was my slurred speech and clouded thinking. Not a single dry item of insulation remained in my pack or on my person. If I recrossed the creek to wait with the others, I could not take my pack for it was now more an anchor than a float. I doubted that Anshel and Grace had any dry clothing to loan me. Besides, what about the Colorado group and Jerry's frostbitten feet? Surely they would not be able to cross the stream either. I shouted this to the others, and they agreed that I should go on alone and get help for Jerry. Grace said that Lewis would need medical attention soon and could not afford a lengthy delay waiting for the water to recede. He had probably walked on his frostbitten feet too much already. Since a horse probably could not cross the flooding stream, she suggested that I have a helicopter sent back for him; she circled her hand above her head in case I couldn't hear above the deafening roar. I signaled that I got the message and prepared to leave. My pack was dragged up the bank and sternly heaved. Nothing happened. It stayed rooted to the ground. I simply could not lift my water-soaked pack. Taking the last two packages of fudge and a package of mixed nuts, I waved to the others so that they understood that I was leaving my pack. Perhaps the helicopter would pick it up. Two dripping figures on the far bank of the creek began pitching a plastic shelter for their patient vigil, as I ascended the high bluff and began my hike to Wonder Lake. My movement soon brought renewed warmth to my body and clarity to my thinking. Exposure was held at bay only by the body heat generated from contracting muscles. Until I got to civilization, I dared not stop to rest.

Alone on the tundra, I plodded along, weaving between pothole lakes and up and down small hills, sometimes skidding down the heather of sodden slopes. For some unknown reason, I began thinking about the possibility of encountering a grizzly bear in the low brush. To be mortally wounded by a bear at the end of my ordeal seemed ironic, almost to the point of laughter. Perhaps the thoughts were precipitated by my vulnerability. I had brought nothing with me, except for my ice axe which, at present, was little more than a psychological crutch. The passage of time became a daze. At times I sensed that I was still descending a slope far behind me or already climbing a hill still ahead.

About mid-morning I topped the Turtle Hill ridge for a full view of the flooding McKinley River, and stood motionless in horrified shock. A mile and a half away was not the many channeled, braided river of my recollection, but a single blackish mile-wide devastating force, gouging the earth with abandon. Not even the soft tundra could absorb the roar of the swirling water, the rumble of tumbling boulders, and the splintering snap of logs tossed about like twigs. The sight exceeded my wildest imagination, sending waves of overt fear through me. There were no options now: to hike to the head of the river and cross on the Muldrow snout would require a 14-mile detour. I was up against the wall. I had endured all that the mountain could give me, only to be decisively defeated so close to civilization, almost within sight of the road. I do not recall traveling from the low ridge to the river bank; it seemed that my eyes never left the flood that filled the horizon like an ocean. Vainly I searched for a crossing that was not there. I stopped at the top of the river bank and stared blankly. Surely a strong, well-rested man could not cross this icy barrier and certainly not a man in my weakened condition. The shivering of exposure began to grip my body again and I wanted to cry, but there were no tears. If I had to die, why couldn't it have been high on the peak?

As I opened a package of mixed nuts, the last of my food, I thought about the *Zen Zen* story of the man eating a strawberry in the face of vicious tigers. I became acutely aware of the taste of the nuts, rolling each one about in my mouth to dissolve its salt covering and discover its form completely before crushing it into a burst of flavor. These were truly the finest nuts that I had ever tasted.

The thundering noise filled my ears and possessed my mind, until I felt a yielding of my soul, as if it had become an integral part of the black water. "Damn!" I said aloud, "If I'm going to die, it's not going to be sitting here like a sick dog. I'll go down fighting all the way to the Bering Sea." I descended the bank quickly, half falling, and waded into the beckoning water without hesitation. Its biting cold made the Clearwater seem tropical by comparison. Fifty yards from shore, the waist deep water was overwhelming and swept me afloat—the shoreline rushed by in the assumption of my new perspective. For a while I kicked along the bottom to keep my head above water and propel myself across. Eventually I could no longer touch bottom and swam weakly at the mercy of the whirlpool currents. After what, in my memory, could have been seconds or hours, I came to a submerged rock bar in only knee deep water and stood momentarily in fatigue and the pain of cold. My feet were already numb, but I was committed now to the effort and entered the next channel in the same manner. Halfway through the swim, my baggy wind pants were caught by the current like a parachute and ripped down. With the wind pants trailing from my boots, it was like swimming with my feet tied together. I could not correct the problem. My entire body was going numb now. I thrashed my arms and legs several times into the rocks of the next submerged bar, before realizing that I was across the channel. I stood more wobbly this time, with my fumbling fingers trying to pull up the sea anchor wind pants. I tried to pull them off to be completely rid of their hazard, but the ankle openings would not go over my boots. I thought of taking off my boots, but even if I could manage the laces, in the swift water I would likely lose the boots, virtually assuring that my feet would be shredded by razor sharp rocks before I could reach shore. I tried my ice axe, but it was not sharp enough to cut the nylon cloth of the wind pants. I thought of the knife which in haste had been left in the pocket of my pack. In frustration I tugged at the defiant material, with cold clumsy fingers.

Gathering the loose waistband in one hand I staggered on, the two banks of the river appearing equidistant now. The next bottomless satanic channel was the most treacherous of the lot, as I more or less collapsed into its glacier meltwater. Kicking became swimming and once again my wind pants ripped down. Finally I could no longer struggle, and my body went limp. I was solitarily concentrating on the motions of swimming, but my limbs did not respond. Pathetically I had reached the end of the line. In a gray whirl the densely shadowed overcast blended with the brackish water, until the motion stopped, and I wondered if it was all over. In semi-conscious bewilderment, I realized that I had drifted onto a rock bar and was still very much alive. I tried to stand but was too weak. For a few minutes I just lay with my head above water, coughing and spitting a heavy mucus of glacier silt and vomit. Stomach acid burned my sinuses. I could no longer feel the cold. Slowly I rose from the water. Numerous cuts and abrasions covered my arms and legs from being smashed against rocks. The knuckles of my right hand were badly lacerated, but I still held my ice axe in an iron grip. Blood forced a streamlet down the ice axe shaft and dripped into the water. Similar crimson ribbons meandered through the hair of my legs. I again pulled up my wind pants and negotiated the remaining five hundred yards of the river on trembling legs, without having to swim, and before sensing my victory.

Once on the far shore, I began to shudder recalling what I had just done and how close I had come to not making it. I gazed back at the murky mistress of death and was quite unexpectedly overcome with near audible laughter for having cheated it of a well-earned victim. Surely such triumphant arrogance in the face of death is a form of insanity. I climbed the low bank. Suddenly faintness gripped my drained body and spun the trees, sky, and water into a fuzzy kaleidoscope. I fell to one knee and endured its passing.

I regained my feet shakily and continued. My body was still numb, forcing my eyes to visually place each step. Soon I came to a shallow pond of rain water across the trail and crumbled into its soothing warmth. Gradually feeling returned to my body in tingling pricks of intense pain. My reacquaintance with reality was excruciatingly acute. I was now keenly aware of the grinding glacier silt in my boots, yet I dared not take them off until I was in the safety of the campground. I do not recall much of the hike from the McKinley River to Wonder Lake, except that I seemed to get a little stronger and repeatedly vowed to myself never to cross the river again, even if it meant leaving my pack full of expensive mountaineering gear where it lay.

Upon arriving at the campground I asked a camper to drive me to the ranger station, taking care to form each word properly in my slow speech. He apparently thought that I was a fellow camper, as I had to repeat the request before he understood clearly and graciously obliged. The calm warm interior of the vehicle further revived me during the short ride to the ranger station. Instinctively, I reached for my pack when I unloaded.

Five and a half weeks and 142 miles earlier, a young, ambitious expedition leader had sat in a small ranger cabin discussing a probable routine McKinley climb over tea and cookies. Now I seemed ages older and wiser, as I entered the cabin which had become quite spacious in the interim. Wayne Merry greeted me with a broad smile, an outstretched hand, and a hearty congratulations. I hesitated. "Congratulations for what?" I asked in puzzlement.

"For reaching the summit of McKinley," he replied in a tone of uncertainty.

Assured that he was not being facetious, I limply extended my hand and added, "Some conquest—my expedition is strung all over the mountain in at least three separate groups with no communications or mutual assistance. The high party is either in great trouble or dead." Of the original 12 man group, I was the only one who had returned all the way under my own steam and that only at a great cost, being stripped of everything except a weakened will to live, which had certainly been reduced to a fragile thread in the raging McKinley River.

Wayne's disposition quickly changed to the desperate concern which we both felt. When I ascertained the status of the rescue operations, I literally exploded at how little had been done. The high altitude overfight which I had requested days ago had not yet been approved. Sheldon had flown the previous day and Wayne had been able to contact his plane directly. It had been a fruitless flight. Due to a wave cloud obscuring the top vertical mile of the mountain Sheldon had not been able to get to 17,900 feet and had dropped[6] the supplies intended for high camp near the site of Camp VI. The MCA climbers were supposed to reach this level today. They had been slowed by deep snow and heavy packs, moving up only one camp in three days. With luck they might make high camp tomorrow. Eielson had been able to establish radio communications with part of Boyd Everett's American South Face Expedition presently camped at 16,800 feet on the South Buttress. They were low on food and unable to proceed to the upper Harper area, but they were willing to be airlifted to support the rescue effort if needed and if it was feasible. The biggest rescue coordination problem was the sluggishness of bureaucracy which had been compounded by an intermittent inability to contact park headquarters by radio. The storm had also disrupted telephone communications between park headquarters and Anchorage, and three nights earlier had washed out several sections of the road between Wonder Lake and headquarters. It seemed to require a couple of days for information to be relayed to all of the agencies responsible for decision making and often it was passed along by people completely inexperienced in mountain rescue procedures. Only today was an attempt being made between the park, Alaska Rescue Group, and the Rescue Coordination Center of the air force to formulate a combined plan of action.

Sensing my physical weakness, Wayne asked his wife to prepare some food for me. I marked the specific location of our camps and caches on various maps and photographs and corrected a few errors of fact that had inadvertently occurred during marginal radio transmissions. I also asked that a helicopter be summoned to airlift Jerry Lewis who was likely stranded with the others at the Clearwater Creek. Wayne relayed this request to headquarters. Noticing my battered right hand, Wayne asked if I needed medical attention for my frostbitten fingers. "No," I replied, "I could use some antiseptic for my lacerated knuckles, but my fingers were never frostbitten."

"But Eielson got a radio message that you had frostbitten fingers," Wayne said in recollection.

"That was Howard's opinion—not mine," I answered. Perhaps sensing resentment in the tone of my voice, Wayne asked

---

6. Parachutes are normally not used for air-drops on snow covered mountains.

how the Colorado climbers had fit into the expedition. "Not at all," I replied. Then recalling their actions at Camp VI, I added, "If anything happens to the upper party, I will never forgive them."

"Forgive who?" Wayne asked.

"Howard and Paul," I replied soberly. "They ran out on the upper group. They refused to go back up to the high camp."

"Oh!" Wayne mused in apparent disbelief, "My impression was that they were well-conditioned, cool-headed mountaineers." We studied each other's expressions for a few seconds, then Wayne returned to his desk, and I turned to the dining room for a hearty meal of soup, roast moose, milk, and cookies. My appearance and mannerisms must have been extremely barbaric. Wayne's two children stared timidly from the doorway, as I devoured the prepared feast.

Revitalized with nourishment, I joined Wayne in the office and together we resumed the task of rescue coordination — at best a critical game of guessing and supposition on the plight of Clark's party. Where could they be? Perhaps Anshel was right, and they had tumbled from the summit down the South Face to become a gnarled mass of protoplasm, an organic speck engulfed in the Kahiltna Glacier, or perhaps they were frozen at the 17,900 foot camp by icy winds that could have reached 150 miles per hour. I could not bring myself to assume that they had perished, for to do so would make our present efforts futile. I wanted to feel that I could still provide aid to the upper party. Searching and stretching my imagination, I considered the possibility that the summit party had followed the wrong wands down and descended the West Buttress by mistake—highly unlikely, but then barring complete annihilation, it was a possibility. Perhaps they were now safely camped with the Western States Expedition which did not have radio communications. Wayne shared my optimism, although he felt they were still high on the peak, dug into snow caves. "After the Winter Expedition I have a high respect for the human body's ability to survive," he offered.

At about 2:30 PM I talked to headquarters on the park radio and personally requested that a helicopter be sent to airlift Jerry Lewis. Wayne offered me the use of his basement shower and the loan of some dry clothing and shoes which his wife had assembled. I graciously accepted and started hobbling toward the basement stairs. "Are your feet frostbitten?" Wayne asked knowingly. "No,"

I lied. To admit frostbite now would preclude my going back on the mountain with a rescue. I was already acclimated for high altitude and wanted to keep this option open. I suspected that my frostbite was only minor anyway.

"Are you sure you don't have bum feet?" Wayne asked again.

"It's just glacier silt in my boots," I replied and headed for the shower. The warm throbbing water massaged my tired muscles with a music that was soothing and relaxing. This was one part of civilization that I had dearly missed; I did not even mind the sting of my numerous cuts and abrasions. Finally all of the glacier silt and dried blood was washed away, and I climbed into clean, fresh-smelling clothing. Although I had become accustomed to them, my dirty clothing must have smelled repugnantly fermented to the Merry family. When I returned to the ranger office, I was given some mail which had arrived for me during the climb.

Eielson had an afternoon contact with the Mountaineering Club of Alaska which revealed that they were at 15,000 feet and searching for Sheldon's air-drop in two feet of fresh powder snow. They asked that their supplies stored with Sheldon be air-dropped so that they could climb to 17,900 feet without having to first relay food and fuel up Karstens Ridge. After communication with both Wonder Lake and park headquarters, the request was approved with the stipulation that they should take care not to overextend themselves as bad weather could prevent an air-drop for a lengthy time.

I joined Wayne in his rounds so that I could monitor any radio communications on the mobile unit in the Park Service pickup truck. Headquarters called shortly to advise that no military helicopter was available at present and that the Alaska Rescue Group would secure one in the morning. They asked if this would be okay with Wilcox. I exploded to Wayne in profane anger. I knew that there were many commercial helicopter companies in Alaska. Sure they would charge a fee, but then, how could cost be a consideration now?

"I risked my life to come out here and get a rescue helicopter, and I'm getting goddamned tired of this dilly-dally Mickey Mouse. I want a helicopter sent right now—*today!* And I don't give a damn how much it costs!"

"Do you want Wilcox's exact words?" Wayne asked headquarters.

"Go ahead," they replied.

Wayne continued, "Wilcox's exact words are. . ." The message was loud and clear. Radios and telephones started humming in response.

The MCA contacted Eielson late in the afternoon. They still had not located Sheldon's air-drop. They asked if Eielson could get in contact with Sheldon and get a better fix on the drop. Gordy called Wonder Lake, but Wayne was unable to contact Sheldon.

RADIO TAPE 6:00 PM:

. . .

Wayne: "He's probably shut it off in the evening, but I'll give her a try tonight and then early tomorrow."

Gordy: "Okay, then we'll check with you again in the morning. . . before we contact the climbers. . ."

Wayne: "Okay."

Gordy: "Okay, is there anything else at this time, Wayne? How's Joe doing?"

Wayne: "Ah, Joe's in pretty good shape. He, ah, banged the hell out of his fingers, ah, swimming across the McKinley. . . but, ah, otherwise he's okay."

Gordy: "Ah, good show. Ah, I hope we can get the rest of 'em out in that good of shape, too. Ah, nothing further from here then. KWA702."

Wayne: "KWA701 clear."

Wayne and I returned to the ranger station to await developments on the helicopter evacuation of Jerry Lewis. It was mid-evening before we, at last, heard the unmistakable pluttering whine of a helicopter and sighted it swinging low over the tundra under the darkening overcast. It circled the area, splintering the calm, and then set down near the cabin. The cabin appeared as a humble relic, a fossil from a bygone era, contrasted to the computerized design of space age technology. The helicopter had come from Farewell, Alaska, 120 miles to the southwest, and was piloted by Pat Gray.

Following a brief discussion, Wayne boarded as a guide, and the proud power of man floated over the tundra toward the unfordable McKinley River. Little more than a half hour later, it returned and unloaded Jerry and Grace, their gear, and my pack. Weather and darkness were closing in, and I wanted the pilot to fly Jerry Lewis directly to Anchorage or somewhere where he could get to a hospital. Wayne said that the other three on the Clearwater also wanted to be airlifted out, and he indicated that they could not cross the flooding rivers, and if left, would most likely have to be rescued anyway when they ran out of food. Lewis did not seem to be in severe pain so I agreed, and a second relay was made. After the second group was safely unloaded at Wonder Lake, Wayne pumped 50 gallons of helicopter fuel, while the pilot evaluated the weather conditions. Finally, Pat elected to wait for morning, and we all retired to the ranger cabin.

Familiar faces and personalities seemed strangely different in the reflection of civilized manners. It was decided that the most expeditious way to evacuate Lewis to Anchorage would be for him to return to Farewell with the helicopter and then on to Anchorage by a fixed-wing Civil Air Patrol plane. Grace lived in Anchorage and requested to accompany Lewis, if it would not increase her portion of financial obligation for the rescue. I assured her that it wouldn't, and travel plans were finalized. Pat Gray typed out a flight voucher and I signed it. Jerry Lewis indicated that he had some travel insurance that might cover the helicopter flight.

I strung my wet gear as best I could in the basement furnace room for drying, while the new additions to the blossoming Wonder Lake community took showers. The Colorado climbers retired to a small trailer behind the cabin to spend the night, while Anshel and I drew berths in the attic. Even the low gabled ceiling seemed spacious compared to my accustomed tent shelter, and the quiet lack of flapping fabric was a new sensation. Anshel said that the Colorado climbers were upset that I had called a helicopter without their permission. I didn't respond to Anshel's statement. My thoughts were at 17,900 feet, and I lay awake far into the night studying the rafters in the dim light. It was the end of a very long day and the beginning of another. Perhaps the MCA would reach high camp today.

DAY 39 — JULY 27

Shortly before 6:00 AM I stirred briefly at the clatter of the helicopter departure and then dozed another hour. The morning was damp, but looked thin; perhaps there was good weather up above. Howard and Paul had decided to leave for Anchorage if the Power Wagon could negotiate the newly bulldozed roadbeds. Anshel indicated that there was little he could do by remaining here since he was not physically capable of going back on the mountain. He said that he would ride to park headquarters with the Colorado climbers and there catch a train to Anchorage. The three began packing.

During their morning radio contact the MCA reported that the weather was perfect and that they expected to reach the 17,900 foot camp at about 7:00 PM. They also said that Sheldon had flown over them at 4:00 AM and dropped them a note (apparently to help them locate his air-drop of July 25).

At about 10:00 AM the Power Wagon was loaded and ready to leave. I went out for an emotionless farewell. I told Howard and Paul that if Jerry's insurance did not cover the flight, and they were upset about it, that I would personally assume all of the financial obligation. No definite response was given, and the three drove off returning Wonder Lake to its former solitude. Wayne turned to me. "I told Howard and Paul that since they are already acclimated, they should be available to be airlifted back on the peak if a rescue requires it. They said that they would be staying a few days with Grace in Anchorage in case they are needed."

"I wouldn't count on their going back up," I said matter-of-factly.

Wayne and I stood looking at each other for a moment. He seemed a little less surprised by my attitude. He offered, "Grace said that she wasn't very impressed with the Colorado group either. She complimented your leadership on the descent. Anshel also commended your leadership." The conversation ended without further words. Less than an hour later we learned from park headquarters that Gary Hansen, chairman of the Alaska

Rescue Group, was to fly the mountain immediately and that Sheldon's early morning flight had spotted no activity in the high camp area.

A light rain continued through the day. I paced anxiously around the office and about the grounds, periodically descending to the furnace room to fluff damp gear and brush off dried glacier silt. Wayne caught me limping and asked again about my feet. "They're fine," I answered. Later I switched to a roomy pair of rubber boots which I had brought to Wonder Lake in an aborted plan to wear them as low altitude footgear. I moved into the trailer for what could be a wait of several days.

In the late afternoon park headquarters radioed the results of Gary Hanson's flight. He had spotted the MCA still in camp at 15,000 feet, our food cache at 16,500 feet, and six climbers just above Denali Pass. These were assumed to be members of the Western States Expedition who were unaware of the search operations. Sheldon was planning to try to drop them a note in the morning so that they could join forces with the MCA.

By the 8:00 PM radio contact, the MCA had climbed to the 16,500 foot cache where they planned to camp for the night. They had located most of Sheldon's 15,000 foot air-drop—a task which had apparently delayed the start of the day's hike. (It was later learned that the ARG had sent Sheldon some of the supplies for the July 25 air-drop packaged in white pillowcases—with long marking streamers tucked out of sight. By error the drop had been made without removing the pillowcases. The ARG had also given Sheldon three radios: one to drop to the MCA, a second to drop to the high camp, and a third to keep in his plane to assist communications. All three radios had been dropped to the MCA.)

I was disappointed that the MCA had not made the high camp yet and to distract my frustration I accompanied seasonal ranger, Dick Shields, to the campground for a campfire program. I don't remember much about the campfire except for the noticeable lack of mosquitoes, bad weather and life cycles had perhaps suppressed their multitudes. Upon learning of my climb of McKinley, some of the campers asked questions about mountaineering to which I gave cordial, but short answers. I did not disclose the true gravity of the present rescue situation.

Back at the ranger cabin, Gordy and George arrived from Eielson with the tape of Clark's summit party. I listened intently and repeatedly for clues to what might have happened—but there seemed to be none. The most surprising discovery was that John Russell apparently was not on the summit with the other five, although it was virtually certain that he had left the high camp with them. Mark named only five people as being on the summit and said: ". . . all five of us got to the summit at exactly the same time."

Another fruitless night fell in quiet gloom; the rain on the metal trailer roof matching whatever pattern or rhythm I desired. At least they had good weather up high on the mountain and a full scale rescue was now in operation.

DAY 40 — JULY 28

The MCA informed Eielson that they were proceeding to 17,900 feet under mild snow and weather conditions and expected to arrive there at about 5:00 PM. They also reported that Sheldon had not yet air-dropped the supplies which they had left with him.

In late morning Wayne was in contact with Sheldon, who was making supply air-drops a half mile down glacier from the MCA party. When asked why he was dropping below the MCA Sheldon replied, ". . .This is as high as this plane can go. . ." The MCA would have to descend to collect the drop and would probably not make it to the high camp today. Sheldon had also been unable to drop a note to the Western States Expedition. At 2:00 PM Wayne radioed park headquarters. In a tone of considerable frustration he pleaded that they should stop depending on Sheldon alone for high altitude operations. Sheldon was not getting the job done up high. Communication of ideas was also a serious problem. Wayne also strongly recommended that Major Stevens of the Rescue Coordination Center be asked to supply a C-130 aircraft to make a large air-drop near Denali Pass as soon as possible. Radios, tents, dry sleeping bags, and 180 man-days of food and fuel should be dropped. Within the hour headquarters radioed back to ask if I concurred with the large air-drop request. I was spreading my drying gear on bushes in the breaking weather when Wayne called me to the radio. Wayne and I had formulated the large air-drop plan over a period of a couple of days and I readily verified to headquarters that I wanted the drop.

I talked with Wayne about the day's depressing developments

and in particular Sheldon's low air-drop. I was perplexed: if Sheldon could not fly high on the peak, how did the ARG expect him to drop supplies at 17,900 feet? I had never met Sheldon or had any communication with him, so I asked Wayne about him.

"He's a strange guy to meet," Wayne said. "You don't know if he's a genius or crazy. He has his own ideas and is hard to talk to, but the guy *can* fly. He can put that plane where no one else can."

"Yeah," I replied, "if he's done half the things that legend makes him, he would have to be an insane genius."

I expressed to Wayne my increased irritation at the pace of the rescue operations. He nodded in agreement, then showed me several drafts of a letter which he had written resigning his position with the National Park Service. At first I felt that Wayne was letting me into a part of his private life which was none of my business. However, reading the letters gave me a subtle awareness of the bureaucratic problems that we were dealing with, not only at headquarters, but also at the Alaska Rescue Group and the Rescue Coordination Center. The situation had so frustrated Wayne's efforts to get assistance for Clark's party that he was seriously considering terminating his Park Service career. My anger cooled and we discussed what *could* be done.

I went outside to readjust my drying gear. My McKinley River clothing was completely saturated with gray silt. The photo station camera seemed to have come through the Clearwater soaking in good shape. I gazed at Denali, enshrouded in striations of dark clouds and mechanically paced about the grounds. It probably would be another day before the MCA could reach the high camp, another forever to wait. Wayne was aware of my anxiety and quoted, "They also serve who only sit and wait." There were exchanged smiles, but no laughter. It seemed that tragedy needed only final recognition as it hung above my hopes with poised purpose—like the sword of Damocles.

To kill a long afternoon I returned to the trailer and began reading a stack of recent magazines borrowed from Wayne. First to be examined was a copy of *Playboy*. The series of unclad beauties could not compare with the redheads of windswept Camp VI, so I turned to the news magazines to see what the world had been doing in my absence. I learned that a complete youth drug culture had evolved over the past year with LSD, marijuana, and flower power. Having been shielded in the involvement of expedition planning and a conservative church school, the new cult had almost completely escaped my attention. Also I discovered that a short Middle East war had been fought during the busy pre-trip Puyallup period. Finally I got to the sports magazines which, considering my mild interest in summer sports, was getting near the bottom of the stack.

RADIO TAPE 8:00 PM:

MCA: "Over, Eielson."

Gordy: "We read you faintly on that. Are any members of the seven—are any of the seven members alive?"

MCA: ". . . we found one body—one body, over."

Gordy: "I read you to say you have—you have found one body. Is that correct?"

MCA: "Roger, roger, in the tent. In the tent, over."

Gordy: "Have you seen anything of the other six?"

MCA: "Negative—negative, over."

. . .

MCA: ". . . over."

George: "Repeat please—repeat."

MCA: ". . . tomorrow, over."

George: "Please repeat again."

MCA: "We'll try for the summit tomorrow, over."

. . .

George: "Ah, repeat your sentence three times slowly, please."

MCA: "Five going to try to go to the summit tomorrow. Five going to try to go to the summit tomorrow. Five going to try to go to the summit tomorrow. . ."

Gordy: [to George] "Try for the summit tomorrow. . ."

George: "I read that as you are trying for the summit tomorrow. Is this correct?"

MCA: "Roger, roger. We will search on the way. We will search on the way, over."

. . .

Gordy: [to George] "Search on the way."

George: "You will search on the way. Okay, we read you."

Gordy: [to George] "Find out who that guy. . . is. . ."

George: "Do—is the—is the body Steve Taylor?"

MCA: "Do not know, over. Do not know, over."

George: "You do not know, okay. Ah, we will be continously monitering the radio, ah, through the day tomorrow. Ah, any time you wish to make a call—there will be someone here. Do you read?"

MCA: "Roger, roger."

. . .

MCA: ". . . a weather report—a weather report—a weather report, over."

. . .

George: "You would—do you want a weather report?"

MCA: "Roger, roger, roger."

. . .

George: "Fine, ah, what time?"

MCA: "3:00 AM—3:00 AM, over."

. . .

George: "Ah, did you say 3:00 AM?"

MCA: "Roger. . . our climb, over."

. . .

George: "Stand by one. Ah, one question—was the body at the location of the 17-9 camp?"

MCA: "Roger, in the tent. Roger, in the tent. Roger, in the tent, over."

George: "Ah, stand by one."

Gordy: "701, this is 702."

Wayne: ". . . 701."

Gordy: "Wayne, they're at the 17-9 camp right now and there's one body up there. They don't know who it is yet. Ah, ah, stand by one."

. . .

Wayne: "Okay, ah, I read that, ah, there were no. . . this again — there's only the one at the 17-9 camp. Is that right?"

Gordy: "10-4, he's right at the camp. Ah, they're still on the line right here. Do you have anything else?"

. . .

Wayne: "Okay, ask 'em to try and get identification, ah, and tomorrow, ask 'em to tend to look for breaks in the wanding pattern—that might have confused them coming down in a, ah, whiteout. And, ah, that would probably be the general vicinity where they dug in."

Gordy: "Ah, roger on that."

. . .

George: "As you go up—look for breaks in the wanding pattern. The rest may be dug in. Do you read me?"

MCA: "Roger—we read you loud and clear."

. . .

George: ". . . Ah, what are your present weather conditions?"

MCA: ". . . 25 miles per hour wind—gusting higher, over."

. . .

George: "Roger, ah, do you have other information for us at this time?"

. . .

MCA: "Not at this time. Temperature's just above zero, over."

. . .

George: ". . . If you can possibly make identification, ah, please do."

. . .

MCA: "We cannot look at him. He's decomposed greatly. . ., over."

George: "Ah, we can't read you at all. Ah, if it is not critical that we have this information right now, ah, we will try again at 3:00 AM."

. . .

Gordy: "Ah, okay—go ahead, Wayne. I think we might still have them. You caught 'em signing off. Just go ahead."

Wayne: "Okay, ask them to look for any messages that may have been left, ah, by this individual which may indicate, ah, might—might give a clue to where the others are."

. . .

George: "One additional thing, ah, look for messages that the individual you have found may have left."

MCA: "Roger, roger."

George: "That is all at this time, ah, KHD6990 Eielson clear."

MCA: "Unit Two clear."

There was a knock at the trailer door and Wayne entered. "They found one body at the 17-9 camp," he said soberly. "There's no sign of the other six." The magazine that I was reading fell to the floor and a profound grief pierced my being. "I'm sorry, Joe," Wayne added. A few moments of silence passed, then Wayne indicated that he had to get back to the radio; as he was trying to contact the superintendent. He asked that I come up to the office when I felt like it.

So the tragic mystery was ending. The venture had started innocently enough, and now a man was dead—Steve Taylor—a close and valued friend and classmate. I knew Steve better than I had known anyone else on the trip. Images raced through my mind: the date that Steve had joined the expedition; his eagerness to stay with the group under the Park Service's questioning of his experience; and long Provo nights of packaging food. Who could have foreseen this disaster? I wanted to stop time—to reverse it. I thought of Steve's parents, whom I had met briefly, and of his sister who had provided us lodging in Portland. They did not yet know that Steve was dead. I left the trailer and walked about the area in scattered and random thought, unaware of my surroundings.

Wayne was soon in contact with Superintendent George Hall, and explained the situation on the mountain. A few minutes later headquarters called back with a weather report. A front was moving in, but precipitation should not begin until the day after tomorrow. Headquarters also indicated that the large RCC (Rescue Coordination Center) air-drop was assembled and scheduled to be dropped at Denali Pass either this evening or early in the morning.

Wayne came out onto the porch, offered me a drink, and we discussed recent events. I had never been an imbiber of alcohol, yet consumed the drink with little notice as well as a generous refill. "Steve was a close friend," I said. "He had really blossomed into a strong, confident mountaineer."

"It's too bad," Wayne consoled, "that a man gets cut down just as he's coming into his prime. You probably already know," he added, "that, regardless of the circumstances, a tragedy is always accompanied by a great deal of criticism. As leader, much of that criticism will be directed toward you. There will be many questions that you will have to answer to others and to yourself. You should be prepared. If you begin blaming yourself for what has happened, you might end up on skid row or strung out on LSD."

"Thanks for the advice," I answered, "but I have no intentions of crawling into a hole of self-pity." (I had not yet begun the exhaustive soul-searching that would haunt my thoughts and dreams for years.)

Wayne had me read the *Rescue Log* which he had been keeping and initial it as to its apparent accuracy.

DAY 41 — JULY 29

At about 3:00 AM Chief Ranger, Art Hayes, called Wonder Lake and requested that I proceed to headquarters immediately to assist in coordination of the rescue and to be present when the superintendent made the inevitable phone call to Steve Taylor's parents. It was agreed that I would drive Hank Janes' van to headquarters and take with me the personal effects of the climbers, which had been left at Wonder Lake.

The MCA's 3:00 AM radio contact with Eielson indicated that they were taking three days of food with them to the summit. When asked, they said that they had found no extra sleeping bags at the 17,900 foot camp.

I loaded my nearly dry but discolored gear into the Hankmobile. Although I was fairly certain that Hank would not hike out to Wonder Lake, I still felt as if I was using someone's vehicle without his permission. I left our empty supply trailer at the ranger station, since I didn't feel that I could ford the bridgeless creeks with it in tow. Perhaps I could return for it when the road was repaired. I pulled out at 4:50 AM escorted by seasonal ranger, Dick Shields, who was driving a Park Service vehicle. The short convoy moved slowly along the badly washed road, stopped once by several strolling caribou. We passed Eielson at about 6:30 AM. The visitor center looked quietly deserted in the pale morning light, yet I knew that a radio vigil was being alertly maintained. We stopped briefly at Toklat Campground, while Dick explained Park Service firearm regulations to a group of campers, who were hiking about the grizzly bear area at Toklat Flats with a high-powered rifle at ready.

The weather was breaking, as I continued on toward park headquarters and intermittent views of the mountain were becoming more and more exposed. The rescue machinery was finally running smoothly. The mountain was under siege by the Rescue Coordination Center of the United States Air Force, the Alaska Rescue Group, Sheldon, and the Mountaineering Club of Alaska. Too late for Steve, and maybe too late for the others. I did not think that the six missing climbers were still high on the peak, for to do so would be conceding their death. Surely they had descended unnoticed and were wandering about on the tundra somewhere, tired and hungry with their route to civilization blocked by flooding rivers. I could even anticipate their greeting after finally being discovered, with someone like Mark saying with a smile, "Well, it took you guys long enough to find us." I drove on in a fatigued insomnia, created both by the recent tragic news and the delicately painful stage of my frostbitten toes, throbbing like a colossal toothache.

Wayne had offered me the use of his winter apartment at headquarters, and upon arrival I was shown to the quarters. I then reported to the superintendent's office to help coordinate the rescue efforts. I talked with George Hall for a while and agreed to write a *Narrative Report* of the last part of the expedition. He asked me if I was sure that the body at 17,900 feet was Steve Taylor. "Fairly certain," I replied.

"We need to be as certain as we can before calling his parents," George stated, "and we need to do that soon, as news reports are already out that there is a rescue in progress."

"Considering the circumstances," I answered, "I have just assumed that it is Steve, but I guess conceivably it could be any one of the seven. If the MCA gives a description of the body, I can probably make positive identification, at least as positive as we can be before viewing actual photographs." I began developing a series of questions to be relayed to the MCA. I felt that affirmative answers to a few of these questions would confirm my suspicion that the body found was Steve Taylor.

By telephone I talked with Major Stevens about the large RCC air-drop which had been made at Denali Pass during my journey to headquarters. He explained the mechanics of making such a high altitude drop and seemed understandably pleased that it had been accomplished with great accuracy. I thanked him for all of the support which the air force was giving to the rescue.

At about 3:00 PM I had a radio communication with Wayne Merry to relay information. I also informed him that according to air observations the MCA should have made the summit at about 2:00 PM. Eielson broke into the conversation and indicated that they had heard nothing from the MCA.

The afternoon passed with no word from the MCA. Finally, George Hall and I decided that Steve's parents should be notified. All of the families by now probably already knew that a rescue was underway and were likely anxiously awaiting word and fearing the worst. (I later learned that our earlier request that the families of the five expedition members who were not the object of rescue efforts be notified—was never fulfilled. My family first learned of the expedition's difficulties through the news media.) The superintendent placed the call and relayed the gloomy news, "It is my unfortunate duty to inform you that your son, Steve, is believed to be dead. . ." I talked with the Taylors for a few minutes and explained to them the apparent circumstances of the tragedy. "Are you absolutely sure it is Steve?" they asked.

I told them that no one in the rescue group knew Steve, and it was probably not possible to evacuate the body safely. "We will have to wait for another radio contact to get a description. We might even have to wait for photographs to be certain." The Taylors seemed to take the news calmly and the conversation quietly ended.

In a telephone conversation with my mother, she said that she would just as soon that I didn't go back on the mountain. I explained to her that I was acclimated, willing, and deeply obligated, but that at the present time there was already a rescue team on the mountain and no immediate plans for me to go back up. Compassionately she understood my responsibility.

I resumed work on the *Narrative Report* and later accepted an invitation to dine with the superintendent's family. The Halls were gracious hosts, and the dinner with many courses provided me with a much needed distraction from the emotional weight of the day. We spent the evening in small talk with no mention of the mountain.

RADIO TAPE 8:00 PM:
(A very weak transmission)

George: "Did you find any signs of the missing six?"

MCA: "Swish, swish, swish."

George: [to Gordy] "What does that mean?"

Gordy: [to George] "Three means yes. Ask them did they find all of the six."

George: "Did—did you find all six?"

MCA: "Swish, swish."[7]

Gordy: [To George] "Ask them how many they found."

George: "How many did you find? Ah, indicate by the number of clicks."

MCA: "Swish, swish."

Gordy: [to George] "Two. . ."

---

7. Keying the transmitter twice means "no."

George: "You found two. Are they alive?"

MCA: "Swish, swish."

. . .

George: "Could—could you make identification?"

MCA: "Swish, swish."

George: "Roger."

MCA: "Eielson, can you read me—can you read me?"

George: "Yes we read you—go ahead."

MCA: "The expedition is very tired and we wanted to—and we'll be moving down tomorrow."

George: "What is your present location?"

. . .

MCA: "Eielson, we're at 17-9, 17-9."

George: "Roger, ah, you say you're headed down tomorrow—is that correct?"

MCA: "If possible—the weather is extremely bad."

. . .

[Eielson then asked the MCA a series of prepared questions designed to ascertain the circumstances of the tragedy and the identity of the bodies.]

MCA: "We have sighted no packs. We have sighted no packs. I found one ice axe, a Stubai. . ."

. . .

George: "Roger—ah, can you give us any description or articles of clothing on the others?"

MCA: "Negative, negative—wait a minute. On the second body I found today a, ah, he, ah, he had a . . . ah, Eddie Bauer sleeping bag wrapped around him."

. . .

George: "Is it possible for you to take photographs. . ."

MCA: "Negative, negative, ah, we're planning to go out tomorrow morning if possible—they're up the hill quite a ways. Quite a—quite a walk to get there."

. . .

George: "Do you have other information for us right now?"

. . .

MCA: "Negative, the weather is socked-in in a whiteout."

. . .

George: "We would like a—to verify this on you. Is—is there any possible information or indication you might have on the location of the four missing members?"

MCA: "Negative, negative."

George: "Can you give any information at all or indication or possibility of the location of the four missing members?"

MCA: "Negative, negative."

. . .

George: ". . .You say the two bodies were just above Denali Pass. Ah, how far above?"

MCA: "Ah, they were on the east side of the pass. . ."

. . .

George: "Ah, how far from the camp. . .?"

MCA: "We can't see 'em right now, but, ah, they're visible from this camp."

. . .

George: "Roger."

. . .

MCA: "Eielson, one body. . . several hundred feet below the outcropping—the other one. . . where the ah, area starts to fall off. . ."

. . .

George: "Could you tell if they were roped or dug in?"

MCA: "Ah, they were not roped up and, ah, it looks to me as if they ah, tried to weather out the storm somewhere and the wind just blew 'em away."

. . .

[Headquarters had been monitoring the transmission via a radio patch and soon the telephone solitarily splintered the serenity at the Hall home. George picked up the phone, spoke momentarily, and hung up. He started out the door and said without looking directly at me, "Let's go. They've—found two more bodies and they're on the radio now." We almost jogged the short distance to the office and found the radio transmission still in progress. I listened in disbelief.]

George: "Could you determine whether there were any injuries—physical injuries?"

MCA: ". . . looked like they froze to death."

George: "Roger, we got that."

Gordy: [to George] "Superintendent is on—if possible we want to get any identification that they have—it's very important."

George: "Ah, if at all possible, ah, we would—we would like to have some means of identification. I realize your conditions, ah, but if this is at all possible, ah, it is—it could be quite important."

MCA: "Swish. . ."

. . .

Gordy: "They have no identification at this time Mr. Hall. . . very difficult situation. . ."

. . .

George: "That's all we have, ah, for tonight. Do you have anything further?"

MCA: "Swish, swish."

George: "Roger, ah, 8:00 AM tomorrow morning then. This is KHD6990 Eielson clear."

George Hall and I sat in the privacy of his office, so quietly solemn that I scarcely breathed. The expedition file lay on his desk. Finally we could delay our task no longer. "We have some phone calls to make," George said soberly and picked up the telephone. "Operator, I would like to place a person-to-person call to Mr. S.P. McLaughlin in Eugene, Oregon. The number is. . ." The difficult drama repeated itself six times, never becoming any easier. "It is my unfortunate responsibility to inform you that your son. . ." Some of the parents asked to talk to me, and I explained the situation as best I could. Nothing I could say was adequate for the moment. Perhaps to those with whom I spoke, but not to myself. Afterwards I paced about the building, feeling useless. Everything that I had tried to do, everything that I could think of doing, seemed hopelessly futile.

I had several late evening radio conversations with Wayne. We agreed that the best disposition of the bodies would be burial in a convenient crevasse, after photographs had been taken for identification. The ice axe which the MCA had found was near the trail far below the high camp, halfway down the upper Harper icefall. I requested that the MCA be asked to check the shallow crevasses and ice blocks on their descent in case stronger climbers had got that low and had sought shelter in the icefall. (The Rawert Expedition of 1966 had reportedly weathered a storm for 13 days in a shallow crevasse at 17,200 feet in the upper Harper icefall.) We also agreed that an aerial inspection should be made of the icefall.

Several comments had to be repeated as the transmission was intermittent, and Wayne and I were both fatiqued from lack of sleep.

Retiring to my quarters, I tried to get some rest. I had not slept for nearly two days, but my toes were aching terribly, allowing only an hour of sleep here and there. For the most part, I read magazines and listened to folk music on Wayne's stereo. I stayed in the apartment far into the next morning.

DAY 42 — JULY 30

When I finally arrived at the headquarters office, George Hall informed me that a chartered plane of newsmen had arrived from Anchorage to talk to me. He had told them that I was not available for an interview. I thanked George. I was in no mood to talk to newsmen. George also said that Bradford Washburn had called from Boston to send me his condolences. "In view of your pre-trip correspondence, Mr. Washburn wanted you to know that he did not have an 'I told you so' attitude," George added.

My request that the MCA search crevasses on their descent had been passed on to them during their 8:00 AM contact with Eielson. It was hoped that the large RCC air-drop could be consolidated at Denali Pass for use in future emergencies; however, the MCA said that they had recovered nothing from the drop. (Most of the materials had landed near the pass, except for the fuel which had been dropped by parachute. It had drifted westward, landing a ways down from the pass). They reported that the dead man at 17,900 feet was in a torn tent and that about 10 man-days of food had been found in camp. The MCA indicated that they were in a whiteout and planned to descend to their 12,100 foot camp as soon as there was a break in the weather.

In the lobby of the McKinley Park Hotel, the boldface newspaper headlines read: "ONE BODY FOUND ON MCKIN-LEY." I knew then I had lost my anonymity and soon I would be unable to avoid the inevitable questions of the world.

At 4:00 PM the MCA radioed Eielson that they were at the 15,000 foot camp and proceeding down Karstens Ridge to 12,100 feet. They had seen nothing. I was very disappointed that the MCA was not staying high on the mountain for a lengthy search. With the RCC air-drop they had enough supplies for over a month. They probably felt that there was no chance of finding anyone alive and seemed anxious to get down because of the unstable weather. I suspected that they were also spooked, not only by the worsening weather, but also by the bodies which they had found. They wanted no part of a mountain that could vent such total destruction, that could kill men, apparently dropping them in stride.

DAY 43 — JULY 31

At 8:00 AM the MCA informed Eielson that they were breaking camp at 12,100 feet to descend the mountain. The ground search was over.

Parents and relatives of the missing climbers soon began arriving at park headquarters. Hank's father, Paul Janes, came from Indiana; Dennis' parents, Mr. and Mrs. Elmer Luchterhand, and their teenage daughter came from New York; Steve's parents, Perry and Beth Taylor, came from Illinois; and Steve's sister and brother-in-law, Judy and James Goodfellow, came from Oregon. These people came to the site of the disaster, while relatives of the other lost men made frequent phone calls to the park. We all shared the common bond of tragedy, and considering the circumstances, our mutual support was greatly appreciated. There were noble moments of public strength and private moments of doubtful tears. I was uncommonly impressed by family resemblances and mannerisms. I felt especially close to Steve's mother.

The haunting question among the families and myself was that none of the three bodies had yet been positively identified. Where were the other four climbers? Were they still alive. And if they were, then some sons were not dead. Elmer Luchterhand said it best when he stated, "Normally when someone dies, the family can close around his absence—his room, his funeral and gradually accept his death. But not knowing where he died, how he died or when he died, and not being able to retrieve the bodies—it is all very unsettling." The truth of Elmer's statement was revived in my memory six months later when the mother of one of the lost climbers asked me if I thought that her son could have descended the mountain and be afflicted with amnesia—perhaps living in an Indian village.

The superintendent was graciously assuming the responsibility of hosting the bereaved families and placed himself at their disposal. I told him that I would not be convinced that all seven climbers had perished until a last aerial survey had been made of the tundra surrounding the peak. Mr. Hall assured me that I was being overly optimistic and holding out unreasonable hope. Unfortunately he was right.

Perry Taylor expressed interest in bringing Steve's body down the mountain and asked me what the chances were of landing a helicopter at 17,900 feet. He and I presumably would effect the recovery. I indicated that he was not acclimated for such a task, and the danger was far greater than the value of retrieving the body. After talking to Don Sheldon about the idea, he abandoned it.

The next day we all traveled to Eielson Visitor Center. At a site near there, which we thought would be a good place for a memorial monument, we each gathered a rock to form a small cairn. Clasping hands we stood for a moment of silence, approximating somewhat the finality of a funeral. Paul Janes said that Mount McKinley would serve as a fitting monument for Hank; no one could receive a nobler tribute to his life than the continent's highest mountain.

With the spreading news of the disaster, I was increasingly approached by curious inquisitors, some critical, some in awe, but all poorly informed. One short man with a British accent asked, "Didn't those chaps have a spade?"

"Yes," I answered, "they had a snow shovel."

"Why didn't they dig a hole?" he asked.

"I have no reason to believe they didn't," I replied. The man's puzzled look caused me to continue. "At those extreme elevations and without the means to melt snow, they eventually were forced to leave their snow caves, to try and get back to their high camp." The man seemed partially satisfied and walked away.

Another man, a member of the Western States Expedition, came up to me and shook my hand vigorously. "I want you to know that I know what you did to try and save those men, and I think you did everything humanly possible," he offered. He left me pondering his statement. Perhaps he was referring to my swim of the McKinley River, which although treacherous was not a direct effort to aid the high camp party.

A correspondent for *Time* magazine sought me out for a lengthy interview. "This may be a disaster to you," he said with a smile, "but it's going to make one hell of a good story." I stopped short. It was all I could do to keep from driving my fist with full energy into his broad grin. He quickly sobered and the conversation continued at a more moderate pace. In the end the reporter agreed to send the expedition's exposed film, which had been soaked in Clearwater Creek, to a laboratory for special processing. Hopefully some of the pictures could be salvaged.

George Hall told me that he had received a very indignant phone call from someone with the Weather Bureau in Seattle telling him that a forecast of the storm which had killed the climbers could have been obtained from them, that arrangements for forecasts could be made with their agency. George asked me what I thought of the call. I replied that before the trip, Jerry Clark had investigated the possibility of establishing a reliable source of high altitude weather information through direct forecasts, but had been unsuccessful in securing an appropriate radio receiver. An arrangement with an agency to have had such information relayed through Eielson would not always have been dependable due to our sometimes weak and intermittent communications on the mountain and disrupted telephone service to McKinley Park. We were often unable to obtain the general public weather forecasts which were broadcast over Anchorage radio stations. The Seattle Weather Bureau official was the first of a multitude of hindsighters.

A couple of days later the MCA group hiked out to Wonder Lake to conclude their expedition. Wayne taped a lengthy interview with them and upon arriving at headquarters they were interviewed again. I had them leave the borrowed radio (Unit Two) with George and Gordy at Eielson, an inadequate gift for unselfish and vigilant radio operations under the most serious of conditions. Wayne accompanied the MCA group to headquarters. The most surprising revelation was that the MCA had not photographed any of the bodies which they had found, even after repeated radio requests to do so. Their combined memory of other identifying details, such as color of clothing, was equally poor and fragmentary and no film or diaries had been recovered (except for the film that Anshel and I had collected on our descent). Under the persistent and perceptive questioning of Elmer Luchterhand, there was a clarification of some of the facts.

On the morning of July 28 the five members of the MCA group collected an air-drop from Sheldon, and then began an all day climb from their camp at 16,500 feet to the 17,900 foot camp. John Ireton and Chet Hackney found an unmarked Stubai ice axe laying on the snow near their route. It was about halfway up the upper icefall, probably at about the 17,200 foot level. John picked it up, stuck it in the snow, and left it right where he had found it. At about 17,800 feet, approxinately two hundred yards below the high camp, they found John Russell's bamboo pole still bedecked with neoprene streamers. It was stuck deeply into the snow and leaned slightly uphill. Around the base of the pole was wrapped a blue Co-op McKinley sleeping bag encased in a red Alpine Hut sleeping bag shell. Inside the sleeping bag was a pair of down booties and a pair of wool socks. Arriving at the site of the high camp, they found one body partially wrapped in the shredded remains of the Logan tent with one gloveless hand exposed. The body was in a crouched or sitting position, as if the man had been trying to steady the center pole of the tent when he died. Both hands and face were blue-green in color, swollen and cracked. Frostbite blisters on the hands were open, and his hair was matted and frozen. The dead man was frozen to the fabric and pole of the tent. The MCA did not believe that the man was in a sleeping bag, although they did not cut into the frozen jumble to verify this. The radiant heat absorption of the tent fabric had caused some thawing of the body and the odor of decomposition was strong. Dennis' snowshoes which had been used as anchors for the guys of the Logan tent remained in their half-buried position. Mark's tent was nearly buried, but still intact although snow had filtered through the zippers partially filling it. Gayle Nienhueser cut open the side and found it empty. They found about 10 man-days of food and no fuel although they did not dig around much or look in the torn Logan tent. The MCA dug in for the night near the camp. The next day they found only a few plastic wands (from a West Buttress expedition previous to our climb) remaining on the summit route. In the afternoon as John and Chet were resting near Archdeacon's Tower on their return hike from the summit, Don Sheldon in a Piper Super-Cub[8] dropped them directions and a note saying that

---

8. Apparently not the airplane that he had flown for the earlier air-drops.

he could see something, perhaps a body on the slope below them. John walked to the edge and looked, spotting an orange object several hundred feet away. On the way down to investigate they found a Wilcox-Expedition wand firmly frozen into the snow.

The object was a body clothed in orange wind pants, red or orange wind parka, and overboots. Chet saw another body three to four hundred feet lower on the slope, and they climbed down to it. The apparent route of the dead climbers was crevassed as Chet fell partially into one. The second body was wrapped in a cloth-covered Eddie Bauer sleeping bag and had blue pants. The slope was steep with ice cliffs and large crevasses at its base where it entered the Harper. Both bodies were in sitting positions with one leg extended, as if braced against the wind. The upper one was slumped forward, and the lower one was leaning backward. No ropes, packs, or ice axes were found. The bodies were on a straight line between Archdeacon's Tower and the 17,900 foot high camp.

Despite the lack of identification photographs, the MCA had functioned well as a mountaineering unit under the most morbid of conditions. Still, few people were completely satisfied with their brief stay at high elevations. "It looks to me like the MCA wanted to get off of the mountain as fast as they could," I told Wayne.

"Yeah," Wayne agreed, "it would be a shame if next year someone was found frozen in a snow cave on the Harper with a diary dated up until August 5th or something."

That night in Wayne's apartment I finally asked Wayne for some pain killer for my frostbitten toes. "I think I have some Darvon," he said, looking at me as if he had known all along that my feet were frostbitten.

The next day the last of the personal effects of the lost climbers were distributed to the parents, including items which had been left in the Hankmobile. I gave Wayne the lone pressure cooker left from the expedition, and Paul Janes gave me Hank's mountain rescue hard hat which had been left in the van. Paul prepared to drive the Hankmobile down the Alcan, while I boarded the train to Anchorage with some of the families and members of the MCA group. The Taylors loaned me the necessary money to fly to Seattle with them, and we went directly to the airport. Gary Hansen, an Anchorage architect and chairman of the Alaska Rescue Group, joined us there to talk to me about the past rescue operations.

There was good news about Jerry Lewis; he was responding well to treatment and would apparently lose only his toenails.

Soon we were airborne in modern comfort. After our flight had leveled off, Perry Taylor stood to place his coat in the overhead rack. For a moment, in the dim light of the cabin, he could have been Steve. The pilot's voice came over the intercom— our altitude was several thousand feet higher than the summit of Mount McKinley.

6

Aftermath

Cheryl met me at Seattle-Tacoma International Airport and we traveled to Puyallup for a week of resting, while I received medical attention for my frostbitten toes. I then returned to Utah visiting the Goodfellows and McLaughlins en route. I had not met Mark's parents previously, and they were cordial and friendly. Nearly all of their questions which could be answered had been answered by others before I got there.

Opportunists are ever present for possible economic windfalls as evidenced by a story related to me by the McLaughlins. Apparently early in the rescue operations, an Anchorage funeral home had phoned them and asked to be contracted to ship Mark's body to Oregon.

I soon learned that Vin Hoeman was leading a Humanitarian Climb of McKinley to identify the bodies and bury them. The six-member expedition was being sponsored by McKinley Park and contained some very experienced climbers, all McKinley veterans. Chuck Crenchaw who had climbed with Clark, Janes, and McLaughlin, was in the group as well as Dick Springgate. (Dick had spent the last few days of his 1963 McKinley ascent without a stove, melting drinking water in a canteen cup between his legs.) Also included were Ray Genet of the Winter Expedition and Ed

Boulton of the Seattle Rescue Council. The expedition was rounded out by Grace (Jansen) Hoeman who was on the climb to provide medical identification and evaluation of the victims. Unfortunately Grace was again troubled by illness and had to be flown off the mountain. I was still recuperating from frostbite and was not invited on the climb.

The search climb found very little. On the summit they found some of the school pennants which I had left plus a Purdue Outing Club patch which Hank had planned to leave there, proving that Clark's group had actually made the summit. Above Archdeacon's Tower they found three of our wands closely spaced leading toward the steep slope. Nearly six feet of new snow covered the 17,900 foot campsite which they were unable to locate. They found only the top few inches of the bamboo pole sticking above the snow level.

In mid-September, after the descent of the Humanitarian Climb, Bradford Washburn conducted a critique of the disaster in Anchorage. I was short of funds and did not attend the critique. As expected, nothing new or enlightening emerged from the conference.

Cheryl was in her first year of teaching kindergarten and I half-heartedly began graduate studies in math and physics at Brigham Young University. My fellowship in physics was complemented by a half-time teaching assistantship in mathematics. Over the year there were disruptions in the domestic tranquillity of our home, problems that finally resulted in Cheryl and I getting a divorce. I went through periods of depression because of both the climbing disaster and my family problems. Although some people seem religiously strengthened by surviving an ordeal against immense odds, I was not. I did not feel that my life had been spared for some great or noble purpose. There was little logical reason for me to be spared while my friends lay silent beneath Denali's snows.

The tragedy was equally harsh on the surviving families. Some were affected much more than I by the severe emotional trauma. The mountain soon claimed its eighth victim. Hank Janes' mother, who had been greatly distressed since the McKinley tragedy, died of a massive heart attack on September 25.

There were several tedious loose ends of the expedition which had to be officially resolved. The Green Bomb was sold to the proprietor of the Northway Junction service station where it had been abandoned, and a Park Service employee bought the equipment trailer which had been left at Wonder Lake. Graciously the Alpine Hut did not charge the expedition for the rented tents which had been destroyed on the mountain. Jerry Lewis' insurance eventually paid most of the helicopter evacuation fee. Although the other rescue operation costs were largely absorbed by government agencies, there still remained about a thousand dollars of expenses to be shared among the survivors and families. The necessary contacts to conclude expedition affairs precipitated a period of intense correspondence. Friends and relatives sought copies of pictures and documents to try to piece together the tragedy—as they diligently searched for the elusive answers that were never there. The items most often copied and distributed were the numerous slides, the pre-trip autobiographies, the *Expedition Log,* the *Radio Log* (kept at Eielson), the *Rescue Log* (kept at Wonder Lake), the post-trip *Narrative Report,* and about six hours of taped radio communications. Some families of the lost climbers became interested in establishing a memorial marker in McKinley Park, a concept which was found to be contrary to Park Service policy. The families then considered placing a marker just outside the park boundry. I recommended that seven unnamed peaks in the McKinley area be named after the dead climbers, an honor which had already been bestowed on several previous McKinley victims. This suggestion was discussed and eventually discouraged by those in authority. A hearing was held in Nanana, Alaska, in late fall for the purpose of issuing death certificates for the seven lost mountaineers.

In December I took a one-week whirlwind automobile trip to the volcanoes of Mexico with an old climbing companion, Kim Turley and another friend. They climbed Orizaba, while I waited at the climbing hut; I was ill from indiscriminate cuisine. Shortly after arriving back in Utah, Grace and Vin Hoeman came to visit. We didn't do any climbing, but it was good to see Grace again and meet her husband. Vin was a small man of high energy. He had several impressive major climbs to his credit, yet still found significance in the novelty of having reached the highest point in each of the fifty states. He had recently become chairman of the Alaska Rescue Group. Vin and I continued to correspond and seriously planned an ascent of McKinley should spring winds expose any evidence of the tragedy. Denali chose to keep her secrets.

Although my two years in graduate school were academically disoriented, I did get a great deal of satisfaction from reviving a mountaineering course which had been dormant for several years. Brigham Young University sits in the shadow of the Wasatch Mountains which have many vertical faces of barren, rotten rock, deceivingly tempting to untrained students. Several times yearly, climbing accidents had injured or killed unsuspecting hikers. The small Alpine Club could not provide the volume of training necessary, and an alpine safety class was desperately needed as an effective deterrent to naive tragedy. Steve Taylor had seen the need for such a class and would have instructed it himself. The class was the type of legacy which he would have appreciated.

During the summer of 1968 I developed a special interest in one of the coeds living near me. Helen Carey was not only beautiful (a Miss Idaho contestant), but strong and agile at mountaineering which made for some friendly competition. We hiked the fall-painted hills and shared our dreams. The relationship was solemnized in a winter marriage and celebrated with a ski resort honeymoon. My unsolidified plans for climbing in the Andes or working in Antarctica would have to wait or be reformulated to include a partner.

I became very interested in acquiring a good two-man mountain tent, and after nearly being buried on McKinley, my search was made with considerable discretion. I discovered that no retail outlet offered a tent which could meet my high standards. Finally convinced that only my own design and workmanship would be acceptable, I became a tentmaker. Bill Daily who had been a tentative member of the McKinley expedition during its organization, also became interested in the project and joined me, transforming our homes into mini-factories for a few weeks. The finished product surpassed my expectations.

Helen's progress in mountaineering was marvelous, and she was soon assisting me in the climbing class. On one late winter climb of the West Buttress of Mount Timpanogos in 1969, Helen and I met with near tragedy. We were the only two climbers in a dozen-man team able to negotiate the last few pitches of a new route, and we proceeded alone the two hundred yards to the summit, while the others waited below. We were hiking along a sawtooth ridge which

I knew to be heavily corniced. Helen was leading with 50 feet of rope between us, and I instructed her to stay well back from the edge whose lee side was a thousand-foot vertical rock wall. The stroll to the summit seemed almost routine, when suddenly there was a sharp crack like a bolt of lightning. I hesitated an instant with my senses poised. There was a rumble like a freight train as a section of snow 50 feet long and 20 feet wide fell from the ridge with Helen in the center. The near edge broke just a few feet from my cramponed boots. Instinctively I dove away from the ridge crest with my ice axe in an iron-gripped self-arrest. I was so close to the top that I felt sure Helen's fall would drag me over the edge. Strangely there was very little tension on the rope, and as the thundering avalanche quieted, I started breathing again. Then, I was really struck with fear. Why hadn't I experienced a stronger pull on the rope? Was the friction of the rope sliding over the ridge that great? Or could it have snapped? I gave the rope a tug and it slid toward me slack in my hand. "Oh God!" Images flashed through my mind of Helen riding the giant cornice to a white eternity—my wife—my love—my life. I yelled, but heard no answer. Frantically I anchored my ice axe, tied off the rope, and crawled to the fractured edge of the snow. I pulled up more rope and then heard "hello" from Helen only a few feet below me. I was instantly relieved to discover that she had been climbing the rock face and this had caused the rope to become slack. She had been calling to me, but I had not heard her from my position on the other side of the ridge. Soon she crawled up beside me, and we embraced tightly.

Helen had taken off her gloves to climb the rock, and I placed her numb hands under my armpits. "Thank you," she said almost tearfully, "for saving my life."

"Your life?" I said casually, trying to distract our thoughts from the close call. "I was tied to the other end of the rope. If you'd gone, I would have too." We sat for several minutes on the snowy ridge, laughing and embracing. The summit was so close that we could have hit it with a snowball, but it would have to wait. For today, the mountain had won.

On the descent I was engrossed in thought and spoke little to the others. Helen and I had nearly bought it on the ridge today. How many more chances could I give the mountains, before the odds caught up with me? Mountaineering had lost a great deal of luster for me. Now it seemed more like a game of Russian roulette.

We did climb Timpanogos again, the very next weekend in fact, in the enjoyable company of close friends—Bill Daily, Bruce Knudson, and Sally Gordon. At first, our ambitions were modest, but soon they blossomed into a grand traverse (hiking from civilization on one side of a mountain, over the mountain, and down to civilization on the other side).

A few weeks later I heard a news report that an avalanche on Nepal's Dhaulagiri had killed several of America's finest mountaineers including Boyd Everett and Vin Hoeman. I corresponded briefly with Grace who was very grief stricken. (Grace continued to climb, leading an all-woman ascent of Mount McKinley in 1970. The following year, while climbing in Alaska, she too was killed in an avalanche.)

In early June of 1969, Helen and I led a dozen college friends on a climb of Mount Rainier. While signing the summit register, I remembered that Steve had not signed the register on our pre-McKinley ascent. He had planned to sign it twice on his next climb of the mountain. There would be no next time for Steve. I signed his name in the register and added a paragraph of my own thoughts.

Late in the afternoon as we neared timberline, I drank from a spring and considered the day's climb; a marmot whistled through the wet fog. Somehow I had lost the excitement of mountaineering which seemed to possess me in earlier years. On this climb I had become almost bored, accepting the splendor of the mountain without gratitude and meeting her challenge without respect, walking the edge of chasms large enough to swallow a battleship with an almost casual indifference. Perhaps my adventure in mountaineering was coming to an end.

I spent the summer as a senior instructor for the Colorado Outward Bound School. Helen, also worked for the school as an instructor.

The Colorado Outward Bound School is one of a series of world-wide outdoor academies. The program is therapeutic, and its purpose is to promote a positive self-image and better self-awareness through stress and is particularly effective with school dropouts, underachievers, and people who have had a vicarious orientation toward life. A typical course consists of four weeks of rigorous mountaineering, river running, and sailing, followed by a solo (a period of several days alone in the wilderness without food—a period of introspection). Nature is an unforgiving master and exacts the internally conceived discipline born of a nonhuman adversary.

Helen and I were involved first with a course for girls, and later a course for teachers and public school administrators in coordination with the Graduate Education Department of Greeley College, Colorado.

Several Outward Bound instructors were thinking of organizing an expedition to K2, the world's second highest mountain,[1] but the McKinley tragedy was still heavy, so I passed up this opportunity. I felt a need to get away from mountaineering, at least for a while. Although I had been hired permanently and believed strongly in the principles of the Outward Bound experience, I resigned at the close of the summer.

My correspondence with the survivors and families of the McKinley expedition tapered off. For the next decade I did very little serious climbing. It was a time for reflection, contemplation, and speculation. My pondering of the McKinley tragedy continued.

---

1. Also known as Godwin Austen.

7
Analysis

A few months after the expedition Wayne Merry wrote in a magazine article: "It is inevitable that the greatest tragedy in American mountaineering history should be the subject of endless discussion and exhaustive analysis. This is desirable; an increased awareness of the hazards is bound to result. But it is easy to stray from objectivity into judgment and criticism based on guesswork, and this benefits no one. Rather than. . . analyze the strengths and weaknesses of the expedition. . . it would seem better to review, in the light of what happened, the conditions which affect any party high on McKinley. For the potential remains. . . any climber who sets foot on Mount McKinley enters the realm of enormous natural forces which no human strength can overcome, but which awareness can help to avoid."[1]

Wayne's prediction has been fulfilled many-fold, usually without the precaution which he suggests. The facts of the disaster are few and fragmentary, giving rise to a proliferation of theories based on guessed events and imagined personalities. Some analyses which I have read have been thought provoking while others have been somewhat amusing. As leader of the expedition it had been

---

1. Wayne P. Merry, "Disaster on Mount McKinley," *Summit*, December, 1967, Vol. 13, No. 10, p.8.

expected that I would present my evaluation of the facts attending the disaster, an evaluation which I have not postponed through negligence or indifference, but rather through the fitful and seemingly endless pondering of various aspects of the tragedy. I am aware that my attempt at analysis suffers many of the inadequacies and uncertainties characteristic of other accounts. Yet, I also realize that it was my responsibility throughout the expedition to ascertain continually the abilities and motivations of each climber, together with the assorted interplay of personalities. If I have an advantage, it is in the investigation of the facts from this inside point of view. In some cases it is more enlightening to consider what didn't happen before speculating on what did happen.

FACT: **Delayed summit start.** On July 17, the group descending to 15,000 feet left high camp at noon, while the summit party did not start their ascent for perhaps three hours.

REASONED   Several things could have delayed the start for
SPECULATION: the summit. First of all they were trying to locate the three quarts of drifted-under fuel, which would more than double their fuel reserves. Secondly, Steve Taylor changed his mind about trying the assault, and they were considering whether or not he should be left alone at high camp. Additional time was likely spent making Steve comfortable with food, water, and a stove. Thirdly, they were experiencing the physiological slowdown of altitude; everything they did just took longer. Lastly, they were cautious about the unstable weather. They did not want to rush off until they were certain that the clear weather was going to hold. This uncertainty was amplified by the fact that Eielson was unable to give them an updated weather forecast.

FACT: **Six, not seven, start for summit.** Clark's team radioed Eielson at 4:40 PM from just above Denali Pass that six climbers were on their way to the summit with an ETA (estimated time of arrival) of 8:00-9:00 PM.

REASONED   It was later verified by Mark McLaughlin in
SPECULATION: their summit broadcast that Steve Taylor was the
seventh man who stayed at high camp because he
did not feel well. Their ETA of 8:00-9:00 PM
suggests that they felt that they could climb to the
top without difficulty or delay.

FACT: **Climbing team asked about cornices.** At 8:00 PM
Clark's team radioed Eielson and asked the 15,000
foot camp (through Eielson) whether or not the
summit was corniced. They indicated that it was
cold, and their ETA for the summit was 45
minutes to one hour.

REASONED   Some people have supposed that Jerry Clark
SPECULATION: was looking at a large cornice which he thought to
be the summit. Other considerations make this
extremely unlikely. Clark's team was hiking in a
whiteout which persisted throughout the evening
and night. From our position at 15,000 feet it
appeared as a thin veil characteristic of the
interphase between moisture laden air and a
cooler snow surface. Otherwise, the sky was clear.
Later in the evening Jerry Clark estimated the
visibility at about 400 feet. If Jerry was seeing a
large cornice less than 400 feet away, it seems
unlikely that he would have given an estimate of
45 minutes to an hour to reach it. (By comparison,
on July 20 our feeble foray toward high camp
into a tremendous storm, covered about 1,000 feet
per hour.)

The only large cornices visible on the summit
route (short of the suspected bivouac site) were
overhanging the west side of the ridge with a
southerly direction of approach. Clark had studied
the map of the summit route in great detail as well
as looked at numerous photographs. He had a
compass and knew that the direction of approach
to the summit was almost due east. I doubt that
Jerry was actually sighting a cornice. He probably
asked about the possibility of a summit cornice,

since he suspected that they would be reaching the top in whiteout conditions, and he wanted to know whether they should use considerable caution.

FACT:

Floundering and unable to follow wands. At about 9:30 PM Clark radioed Eielson that they were unable to continue following the wands and that they were "just floundering around on the flat. . . the wands are too far apart—can't find out where they left the ridge." Jerry expressed frustration that they didn't know whether they were on the summit ridge or whether the summit ridge was supposed to be wanded.

REASONED SPECULATION:

It appears that many of the wands marking the summit route had blown out during the July 16 windstorm. From Jerry's description of being on a ridge which was flat, it seems likely that the group was on the Archdeacon's Tower ridge probing into the shallow flat snow basin separating them from the summit ridge.

FACT:

Reported cold radio batteries. At the 9:30 PM contact Clark indicated that they had "cold batteries" and that "the rest are at the camp." The next morning on the summit Jerry said that the radio batteries were still weak.

REASONED SPECULATION:

The spare radio batteries were cached at the head of the Muldrow. The only batteries which could have been left in camp were the ones in the battery pack which supplied the radio through a connecting cord. Jerry probably left the battery pack in camp to save weight, relying on the internal radio batteries for the short summit hike. These batteries were quite strong initially, but were far more difficult to keep warm as the entire radio had to be kept warm. The use of cold batteries rapidly drained their strength, resulting in poor communication.

FACT: **Radio fell silent after initial contact.** At about
                    10:45 PM Clark attempted to talk to Eielson.
                    After initial contact had been established, the
                    radio fell silent.

REASONED   Clark indicated in his summit broadcast the
SPECULATION: next day that cold batteries had likely disrupted
                    this attempted radio communication. Clark's
                    group was also probably debating whether or not
                    to bivouac and may have changed their minds
                    about informing Eielson of their plans, not
                    wanting to cause alarm.

FACT: **Bivouac reported.** At 11:30 AM on July 18, Jerry
                    Clark radioed from the summit: ". . .we ended up
                    bivouacking as a matter-of-fact. It got so fogged-in
                    that we couldn't go up or we couldn't go down."

REASONED   At face value this statement is somewhat
SPECULATION: shocking. Did Clark's team proceed to the summit
                    without taking any of the wands at high camp
                    (more than a hundred)? Did they keep hiking
                    upward, even when the route became indistinct
                    until finally they were cut off from retreat? After a
                    bivouac and with the prospect of finding the
                    descending route dim, did they yet push upward to
                    the summit? Such questions depict a bold and
                    foolish party with a summit-at-any-cost philoso-
                    phy. Not one person in Clark's group was of this
                    disposition. No stretch of the imagination can
                    picture them agreeing to such an endeavor.
                    Altitude does affect thinking, but its effect is to
                    decrease motivation, not increase the summit drive
                    unreasonably.
                        When the Mountaineering Club of Alaska
                    arrived at the 17,900 foot camp, they found only a
                    few wands. Although bundles of wands could
                    easily have been blown away, I suspect that most if
                    not all of the high camp supply was taken by
                    Clark's party. Three of their wands were later
                    sighted closely spaced above Archdeacon's Tower

leading over to the steep slope where two bodies were found. An additional wand was found on the steep slope. These wands were not placed by the July 15 summit party. Clark's party might have stumbled onto the wand cache which the first group had left on the ridge behind Archdeacon's Tower, but this seems unlikely considering their probable conditions of weather and visibility.

Examining Jerry Clark's summit statement in the light of his personality, I find that it was said in a light, almost jocular tone, with tongue-in-cheek. An accurate translation might be: ". . .we ended up bivouacking as a matter-of-fact. It got so fogged-in that we couldn't go up and we didn't want to go down." Considering the conservative nature of Clark's group, it would take the ideal combination of two factors to precipitate a bivouac en route to the summit—urgency and security. The urgency was likely evident in a combined feeling that if they returned to high camp, then they would not get another chance at the summit. Perhaps they had not found the lost fuel at 17,900 feet and knew that they could not count on the 15,000 foot group to bring them more. Also they had to feel that a bivouac would not desperately endanger them.

No sleeping bags were found by the MCA at 17,900 feet even in Mark's tent which was intact. This suggests that perhaps every member of Clark's party had a sleeping bag with him. The MCA's rather casual investigation of the high camp also revealed no snow shovels or stoves and very little food. Clark's group certainly had a snow shovel, snow saw, and probably some food and a stove as well, although it is doubtful that they took extra fuel. The food which they took likely required no cooking; the stove was intended for melting drinking water only. The weather was cool, but otherwise fairly calm. They probably decided to wait on the fog for a few hours before starting down; a wait that eventually lasted all night.

During their summit broadcast, Jerry and Mark expressed no fear or apprehension about finding their route back to high camp. I can only conclude that they had wanded the trail and felt that the descent would be straight forward and routine.

FACT: **Russell not mentioned among five on summit.** During the summit broadcast, Mark named only five climbers on the summit and indicated that "all five of us got to the summit at exactly the same time." Mark reported that Steve Taylor had been left at high camp. Mark also said of Steve: "He's probably wondering where we are at the moment." John Russell was not mentioned among the summit climbers, nor was he mentioned as being left at high camp, nor was he mentioned as being left at the bivouac site.

REASONED   It is obvious that John Russell started the ascent
SPECULATION: with Clark's party, but somewhere en route, before they reached the summit, John parted company. Had John returned to high camp on the previous afternoon or evening, then Mark's summit broadcast would have indicated that there were two men at the 17,900 foot camp. Had John left the group when they elected to bivouac, then Mark would not have offered that Steve was probably worried about the summit group, for by then, John would have informed Steve of the upper group's bivouac plans.

Some people have suggested that Russell did not hike back to the 17,900 foot camp, but rather remained at the bivouac site and waited while the others were on their summit climb. John's temperament would make this theory unlikely. (Also Mark may have reported from the summit that John had been left at the bivouac site.)

John had a decisive personality; he would not have waited alone. If he wasn't climbing upward, then he would have been hiking downward. My guess is that John parted philosophy and company with the others on the morning of July 18 and hiked back to the high camp alone. The fact that Clark's party all got to the top at the same time tends to suggest that they were climbing on one 5-man rope (probably two ropes tied together) rather than as two rope teams.

FACT: **No radio calls after leaving summit**. Even though Eielson monitored their radio almost continuously, no further calls came from Clark's party after they left the summit.

REASONED   It is unlikely that the radio batteries were so
SPECULATION: weak that Clark would have been unable to reach Eielson after properly warming them. It would have been easily possible, contrary to my initial assessment, for the radio to have been damaged beyond Jerry's ability to repair. A simple loose wire would have been difficult to mend in a high wind with cold hands and extreme fatigue. More probably, however, Jerry did not call Eielson at 8:00 PM on July 18 because he knew that they might soon be in trouble if the storm continued much longer. He was likely saving the strength of the radio batteries for a possible "Mayday" broadcast. The radio might have been swept away with the packs before Jerry had a chance to use it again.

FACT: **Russell's bamboo pole discovered below the 17,900 foot camp.** John Russell's streamered bamboo pole was found by the MCA group a couple of hundred yards below the 17,900 foot camp. It was driven into the snow two to three feet and slanted 15-20 degrees uphill into the wind.

REASONED   John had spent the better part of an afternoon
SPECULATION: at Camp VI, decorating this bamboo pole which he intended to leave on the summit. When illness

forced him to relinquish part of his pack load during his July 15 climb to high camp, John still retained his streamered "warrior's staff." The pole was fluttering in the midst of camp when we began our descent on July 17. It is extremely unlikely that John would have endured a great deal of effort and inconvenience and then not have taken the pole on his summit climb. It is almost certain that the pole left the high camp with Clark's summit party. This, of course, means that it is also very certain that someone brought it back down. This is further evidence that Russell left the summit party and hiked down alone, likely on the morning of July 18, when it was probably still possible to follow the route. The pole meant nothing to the others in Clark's party; and, of course, had they agreed to leave it on the summit for John, then they would have done just that—left it on the summit.

The high camp was not in line-of-sight with the 15,000 foot camp; however, the location of the bamboo pole was. It seems probable that the pole was placed as an attempt to signal the lower camp. It was likely placed during a period of rather clear weather; otherwise, the man placing it could not be certain that it was visible from the lower camp. Although the pole may have been placed early in the ordeal, we may not have seen it from the 15,000 foot camp nearly 2½ line-of-sight miles away, since the ground blizzard was blowing into our faces. Or if we did see it, we may have taken it to be just another wand. The winds were likely strong at the time that the pole was placed, requiring that it be slanted into the wind at an angle which probably coincided with the necessary windward lean of the man. The depth of the pole into the snow and the fact that it obviously endured extreme winds suggest that the man placing the pole was strong and had good use of his hands.

FACT: **Ice axe found at 17,200 feet and sleeping bag around bamboo pole.** The MCA group found an unmarked Stubai ice axe near the trail at about 17,200 feet and a blue Co-op McKinley sleeping bag in a red Alpine Hut shell wrapped around the base of the bamboo pole about two hundred yards below the 17,900 foot camp.

REASONED   Only Steve Taylor had the sleeping bag and
SPECULATION   shell combination described by the MCA. Both Steve and Walt had unmarked ice axes which presented a bigger investigatory problem. After a careful study of expedition slides taken earlier in the climb (including some taken on pre-trip climbs with Steve Taylor) and a close inspection of several enlarged prints, it was possible to identify the ice axe found at 17,200 feet as Steve Taylor's. The MCA indicated that the ice axe probably blew down the slope. This theory makes a little sense, if the axe was used to anchor a pack which was ripped away by the wind. Two things are bothersome however. First of all it is unlikely that an ice axe would blow along the snow. Ice axes are designed to grip the snow; they make much better anchors than sleds. Secondly, even if the axe did become airborne like a straw in the breeze, the probability that it would come to rest precisely on the trail between high camp and Camp VI is extremely small.

Others have speculated that when the summit party did not return, Steve Taylor made a solo attempt to descend to the 15,000 foot camp. Unable to follow the poorly wanded route and too weak to even hold on to his ice axe, he dropped it and climbed back to the high camp. It seems certain that Steve was very weak during his vigil at 17,900 feet. A man who has enthusiastically planned to climb McKinley for nearly a year does not elect to remain at high camp on the appointed day without due cause. It is even conceivable that during an attempted descent, he would have become too weak to hold on to his ice axe. (Considering that I instinctively held on to my ice axe during a nearly unconscious swim of the McKinley River, even though it was of no value to me, I would have to believe that a mountaineer who would abandon his ice axe on a glacier would be very weak indeed.) Here is where the relative energy requirements become boggling. Had Steve hiked to 17,200 feet, he would have been nearly a fourth of the way down to the 15,000 foot camp. At this high elevation and on a calm day, it takes about three times as long to climb upward as it does to cover the same terrain downhill; thus time-wise and energy-wise Steve would have been as close to the low camp as the high camp provided he could follow the route. If there was a strong wind down glacier, which is virtually certain, then the energy scales would tip drastically in favor of travel to the low camp. Had Steve tried to descend the mountain during the height of the storm and become so weak that he could no longer hold his ice axe, he could not have returned to high camp. It would have been impossible even for a well-acclimated strong climber. The likelihood that Steve made such an aborted trek in a brief period of relative calm is also remote. An attempt to descend would have been most likely when the high camp tent was ripped apart.

The MCA and others believed that the sleeping bag had blown out of high camp when the tent failed and just happened to be caught by the pole on the trail. The evaluation of this theory requires several considerations. First of all, the wind which destroyed the tent was certainly capable of lifting a sleeping bag high into the air on its journey downward; thus, the minute probability of aligning with the pole is further complicated by height above the surface of the snow. Secondly, even if the bag did manage to hit the pole, it most likely would not have hit it broadside exactly in the middle of the bag. While the aerodynamics of a soft spineless sleeping bag are difficult to study, one thing is rather obvious: the tapered mummy bag was asymmetric; it would not have blown down the glacier broadside. An airborne sleeping bag would likely spiral wildly down the glacier while a bag blown along the surface would probably tumble and slide. I also have to wonder why the sleeping bag was not at least partially separated from its shell. Had the bag been ripped out of the tent by surprise, its owner probably would not have had the top firmly closed; in the turbulent air currents, some separation of the bag and shell would have been expected. Lastly, the combined weight of the bag and shell was nearly eight pounds. Propelled by high velocity winds, the bag's momentum, even in an obviously inelastic collision, might have snapped the bamboo pole if it chanced to catch it. The probability that the sleeping bag escaped the grasp of a man who knew that it was essential for survival, whipped down the glacier until it came to the bamboo pole, and there came to a stop, opening calmly broadside to wrap itself snugly around the base of the pole is so infinitesimal as to stagger the imagination of a mathematician. There were enough extraordinary events associated with the tragedy without suspecting the ridiculous.

An alternative explanation of the sleeping bag is that it was placed there as a signal to the lower camp. This theory also has some problems which are difficult to explain. Why would a man place his sleeping bag around the pole for a signal when the brightly colored sleeping bag shell would have served as well, permitting him to retain use of the bag? Under dire circumstances a man may act illogically; he may blindly stumble down the mountain casting aside ropes, packs, sleeping bags, ice axes, and anything else which he presumes to slow his progress. Under such circumstances, acts of omission, failing to do essential tasks, are far more common than overt blunders. To hike from high camp down to the pole, place a sleeping bag around the pole, and then return to camp would not be an act of omission; it would have to be carefully considered, planned, and executed. Even a mind greatly affected by altitude and storm would not have purposely *expended* energy in a manner which clearly assured its own death. Struggling in the storm at 15,000 feet, I certainly would not have parted with my sleeping bag even if I had been blown down the mountain. And below Archdeacon's Tower a frozen corpse still did not relinquish its hold on a sleeping bag. There apparently had been no attempt to secure the sleeping bag to the pole, although there were tie straps on the sleeping bag shell and strips of nylon available on the pole. Whoever placed the sleeping bag around the pole probably had very poor use of his hands.

The attempts to explain the ice axe and sleeping bag suffer from the same erroneous premise: the assumption that Steve Taylor was alone at high camp throughout the ordeal. If the probability that John Russell returned to the high camp is accepted, then the facts can be explained without relying on spectacular kinematics. One of the men could have tried to descend alone from 17,900 feet, taking with him only a sleeping bag and ice axe, which were discarded en route.

FACT: **Ripped Logan tent at 17,900 feet.** The MCA group found the Logan tent at 17,900 feet blown down and ripped apart.

REASONED   The Logan tents were of a very sound
SPECULATION: construction. On a recent Antarctica expedition, they had endured winds clocked at over 100 miles per hour. The most likely time for the high camp Logan tent to have failed would have been the intense wind of July 21 and 22. At this time the wind at 15,000 feet was well over 100 miles per

hour, and the expert consensus concerning wind velocities higher on the mountain is about 150 miles per hour. Some knowledgeable people have speculated that the winds could have been as high as 200 miles per hour.

FACT: **Frozen body in Logan tent.** Partially wrapped in the blown-apart Logan tent, the MCA found one body. The hands and face were blue-green, cracked and swollen with open frostbite blisters, and the hair was matted and frozen. The body was not reclining, but in a crouched position as if holding the tent pole.

REASONED   The most obvious question is: Why did a man
SPECULATION: try to survive in a destroyed tent when a few feet away Mark's tent was standing intact? (At 15,000 feet Anshel and I wasted little time in moving to the Colorado tent when ours drifted under.) The logical answer is that a man wouldn't have stayed in the shredded tent; he would have immediately sought shelter in Mark's tent, unless, of course, he was already dead when his tent failed. The condition of the body gives a few clues as to the time of death. The clinical manifestations of severe frostbite are swelling and blisters upon thawing, followed by open blisters and great discoloration within a couple of days. These physiological reactions are the body's attempt to heal itself; a process which essentially stops at death. If the person found at high camp died before the tent blew apart on July 21 or 22, then it seems likely that he suffered extensive frostbite on or about July 19. The assumption that the body found at high camp was Steve Tayor is questionable. Steve was a student at Brigham Young University where short hair was not only the custom, but school policy. His hair was so short that it is doubtful that it could have been described as "frozen and matted." On the other

hand, John Russell's long curly locks would probably have fit this description well.

FACT: **10 man-days of food at 17,900 feet.** The MCA reported finding only 10 man-days of food at 17,900 feet.

REASONED   The high camp food had been transported in
SPECULATION: half-load bags, 10 man-days per bag. Although some food may have been eaten and some may have been taken by Clark's summit party, there should still have been 2 or 3 bags at the high camp each containing 10 man-days of food. It appears that the MCA found only one of these bags; the others were likely buried or perhaps in the tangle of the Logan tent.

FACT: **Two other bodies near 19,000 feet.** On the steep, crevassed slope below Archdeacon's Tower at an elevation of about 19,000 feet, the MCA found a Wilcox Expedition wand and two bodies. (Three closely spaced wands were later found just above Archdeacon's Tower by the Humanitarian Climb.) The bodies were 300-400 feet apart, unroped, and without ice axes or packs. The bodies were on a line between Archdeacon's Tower and the 17,900 foot camp. The MCA described the upper body: "I walked over near Archdeacon's Tower and looked down and I could see an orange object. . . he was sitting with one leg —I think it was the left leg—extended. . . kind of crouched with his head forward too, like he was trying to protect himself from the wind. . . I think his pants were orange. . . red or orange parka. . . I think he had overboots on." They described the lower body: ". . . and he looked like he had an Eddie Bauer sleeping bag—green cotton one— wrapped around him, around the upper part of his body. . . one leg extended. . . he was laying back. . . I think he had blue pants on. . . this one had a lot of snow on top of his body." Footing on the steep slope was unstable; powder snow was covered by a weak wind crust which broke off in dangerous slabs. On the entire route between high camp and the summit, the MCA reported very few wands still remaining, just a few of the plastic ones left by a previous expedition.

REASONED SPECULATION: From a well-organized group of men standing on Denali's summit on July 18 to icy corpses on the slope below Archdeacon's Tower on July 29, a great deal must have transpired, events which are forever lost to history. Logic, however, suggests a few possibilities. From 15,000 feet on July 18, the mountain became obscured with a snowstorm about noon. This was the beginning of the relentless storm which abated only briefly on July 20. The storm probably hit Clark's party before they had returned to their July 17 bivouac site on their descent from the summit. It is possible that they lost their way before returning to the bivouac site, where they had likely left their packs, sleeping bags, and snow shovel. If so, then their unprotected struggles for survival would have been short lived. The location of the two bodies and the presence of a sleeping bag suggests that Clark's party did get back to the bivouac area. The initial severity of the storm at this elevation is unknown, although the winds were likely strong enough to blow away many wands marking their route back to high camp. The diary of a member of the Western States Expedition which was dug in at 17,200 feet on the West Buttress route on this date reads ". . . wind of increased velocity observed in the evening, must have been hellish at the pass." Either the storm's suddenness obliterated the downward route or else Clark's party was detained for a few hours, perhaps by illness or injury. By evening it would have been too late to descend. It is virtually certain that the summit party was roped during their ascent. They probably unroped again at the bivouac area when weather forced them to hole up. Finding experienced mountaineers in a crevassed area unroped and without ice axes can only mean one thing: they had neither. At the second bivouac the ropes were likely stored in packs which were in turn anchored to the snow by ice axes. A tremendous wind such as the one of July 21-22 could have swept the packs away along with the ropes and ice axes. One body was partially buried which could mean that the other four climbers were also on the slope, already covered by drifting snow.

The wands found were not placed there by men expending their last reserves of life energy— men without ropes, packs, ice axes, or reason to mark their route. (A descending party normally has no reason to mark its route unless it feels that it might have to backtrack.) The wands were obviously placed earlier in the ordeal. Their close spacing indicates that they were placed in a whiteout, and the direction suggests that it may have been a compass course toward the high camp. Initially the MCA reported that the two bodies looked like they had been blown off of the mountain from higher up. The sitting position of the bodies and their alignment with respect to Archdeacon's Tower and the high camp make this theory very unlikely. From above, the upper body which was slumped forward was described as being clothed in orange. This indicates that at least the wind parka was orange. Two members of the upper party had orange wind parkas, Mark McLaughlin and Walt Taylor. The MCA's close up description indicated that they thought that the wind pants were orange and that the parka was red or orange. Only Walt had orange wind pants. The temptation to identify this body as Walt Taylor, however, is confused by several things. First of all, Walt's wind parka was a light "pumpkin" orange. It would not have been described as being "red or orange." Secondly, although Walt had overboots, I do not at any time on the climb recall seeing him wear them. Lastly, Walt was clearly the strongest of the summit climbers. It is unlikely that anyone would have managed to descend further on the mountain. Mark, on the other hand, had a dark orange wind parka with red wind pants, and he always wore overboots. The lower body is easier to identify. Only Dennis Luchterhand had a cloth covered, Eddie Bauer sleeping bag. Unless he died earlier and someone else had taken his bag, I have to assume that the lower body was Dennis Luchter-hand. Dennis did not have blue wind pants, although he did have blue down pants. His wind pants could have been lost if they had been stored in his pack during the bivouac.

With the pertinent facts evaluated, only one task remains before attempting a reconstruction of the tragedy: a detailed study of the death storm to ascertain the exact nature of the natural forces which caused the disaster.

8

Storm of Storms

A person who has spent more than a few days in an intense high altitude storm is apt to reply when quizzed later, "Hell! That was the worst damn storm ever!" I have had similar feelings; however, I have always stopped short of such a proclamation probably because of a scientific background and a belief that, after all, ultimate situations are things that happen to other people. And yet, I cannot imagine more adverse conditions than those on Mount McKinley in 1967. Information from other 1967 McKinley expeditions seems to support this assessment. The Western States Expedition was pinned down at their high camp from July 17 to July 27, waiting for the weather to permit a summit climb, and the South Face Expedition indicated on July 24 that they had already been socked-in for ten days. They finally made the summit on July 28. Boyd Everett, at that time perhaps the most experienced McKinley mountaineer, wrote of the storm: "The duration and violence of this storm seemed to be unusual even for McKinley."

It would require a lengthy study to analyze thoroughly the July 1967, Mount McKinley weather together with all of its ramifications and compare it with McKinley weather for other years and other expeditions. It suffices here to discuss in general the July 1967 McKinley area weather, and then inspect in detail and compare those aspects of the high altitude weather most relevant to the tragedy.

Upon reviewing voluminous National Weather Service data from the archives of the National Climatic Center and with the assistance of consulting meteorologist, Robert M. Kinzebach,[1] an objective weather picture began to emerge.

Both the short July 16 storm and the major storm July 18-26 moved into central Alaska fairly rapidly after first intensifying over the Bering Sea. The first storm was an occluded front, weakening (apparently) on July 15 as there was a high pressure ridge over the area. The storm developed so quickly that an early forecast would not have been likely. The second storm was an offshoot of a very deep low, north of Point Barrow. It moved in from the northwest and was diverted into the McKinley area by a strong Pacific high. Subsequently, a semistationary front developed with the deep arctic low and the strong Pacific high persisting both on the surface and aloft for the duration of the storm. High westerly winds aloft were evident in the Mount McKinley area. At the surface there was very rainy weather which continued intermittently through mid-August.

The effects of the weather at low elevations are well documented. Mount McKinley National Park keeps photo files of major road and bridge damage, files which go back at least to 1939. Although there is minor storm damage nearly every year, according to a park official: "The July 1967 storm was somewhat unusual, at least at lower elevations."

During 1967 McKinley Park recorded nearly three times its July average for rainfall. The rains accompanying the July 18-26 storm were responsible for almost all of this precipitation with nearly three-fourths of an inch more rain falling on the single day of July 24 (the day that the park roads were washed out) than is

---

1. Robert M. Kinzebach (Colonel retired, United States Air Force) has 35 years of weather forecasting and analysis experience including professional services for the United States Air Force; Pan American Airways, Alaskan Division; and the National Weather Service at Seattle-Tacoma International Airport. He has published several studies concerning Pacific Northwest stratus forecasting. Bob is a casual mountaineer and has engaged in weather activities and research studies for the preparation of a book on Northwest outdoor recreational weather. He has also published a series of aerial-photographic guide maps for Northwest mountaineers and backpackers.

normally recorded for the entire month of July.[2] This storm also caused heavy precipitation to be recorded at surrounding stations. Far to the north near the parent Point Barrow low, a Canadian research vessel was trapped and damaged three times in the Arctic Ocean by wind-driven ice (July 22-25), and finally had to be towed to port.

By mid-August the effects of mountain storms and continuing widespread rains hit the lowlands with full force. Sudden flood waters engulfed Fairbanks and the surrounding areas, requiring that 10,000 people be evacuated by helicopters and river boats. The flood reportedly caused more damage than the 1964 Good Friday earthquake, and Alaska was declared a national disaster area.

However impressive a discussion of low elevation weather anomalies may be, it is rather immaterial to the task of isolating conditions near the summit of Mount McKinley. To attempt this, the study must focus on the weather aloft for the specific time span of the tragic storm with due consideration for the irregularities caused by the mountain itself. Upper air meteorological measurements are not taken at every weather station. Fortunately, however, Mount McKinley is triangulated precisely by three stations which record weather aloft data: Anchorage is 140 miles to the south southeast; Fairbanks is 160 miles to the northeast; and McGrath is 147 miles due west. Upper air observations are made at these stations twice daily. Any extensive high-elevation weather disturbance moving through the McKinley area would almost certainly be manifested in the data from one or more of these three stations.

Although all three stations showed high altitude evidence of the July 1967 storms which hit the upper slopes of Mount McKinley, McGrath was found to be the most indicative. The western storm fronts swinging out of the Bering Sea passed directly over McGrath before striking McKinley 147 miles later with virtually no intervening obstructions to drain their punch.

---

2. McKinley Park normal July precipitation: 2.59 inches.
Precipitation July, 1967: 7.39 inches.
Precipitation July 18-26, 1967: 6.14 inches.
Precipitation July 24, 1967: 3.28 inches.

The medians of the triangle formed by Anchorage, Fairbanks, and McGrath intersect over Mount McKinley. The three smaller triangles formed have equal areas.

The McGrath weather aloft reports for various altitudes closely paralleled each other with higher elevations generally giving rise to lower temperatures, lower relative humidity, and higher, less variable winds. Weather aloft data is not collected at actual altitudes, but at constant pressure altitudes, altitudes where the air pressure has designated values. The 500 MB[3] air pressure level would normally be representative of the weather at about 18,400 feet; however, in the low pressure of storms it would drop somewhat and probably be indicative of the conditions at Denali Pass (18,200 feet) and high camp (17,900 feet). Coincidentally, 500

3. MB (millibar) is a measure of air pressure. The air pressure at sea level under standard conditions is 1,000 millibars. The 500 millibar level is halfway through the mass of the earth's atmosphere.

MB data lends itself well to study and comparison since it is the weather aloft level selected by the National Weather Service for extensive documentation. Further specific comments will be in reference to 500 MB data with the understanding that conditions encountered by Clark's party over a thousand feet higher on the peak were somewhat more extreme.

The temperature averaged 2.2 degrees Fahrenheit for the eight and one-half day storm. This mild temperature caused wet gear in the sheltered tents. However, in the exposed high winds, the wind chill was so great that it would have mattered little if the actual air temperature had been twenty degrees cooler.

The relative humidity rose sharply on the evening of July 17 which explains the whiteout encountered by Clark's summit group. For the first three days of the storm (July 18-20) the humidity was higher at night and lower during the day. For the next three days (July 21-23) it was lower in general with nights a bit lower than days. Somewhat clear weather was evident during this time although blowing snow still obscured visibility. For the remainder of the storm (July 24-26), the humidity repeated its pattern of the first part of the storm with the temperature dropping to -10°F. Snow and cloud caps were reported high on the mountain.

The single, most significant criterion for the intensity of a storm is wind velocity, since it is responsive directly to the steepness of the gradient between the high and low pressure regions which cause weather. Wind is also the primary storm threat to the high altitude mountaineer and precisely the aspect for which the July 1967 storm was most unique. A specific wind reading may occur in an uncharacteristic gust or calm; however, persistently high readings indicate general high winds aloft. Abnormally high winds were recorded over McGrath for the entire duration of the storm.

Any obstruction blocking the path of air mass movement causes disruptions, and a more imposing structure than Mount McKinley cannot be imagined. When winds hit the mountain, there are several factors which tend to increase their effective velocities. It is difficult to dissect the wind patterns on a particular peak as every mountain responds somewhat differently to varying speeds and directions of winds; however, in a simplified sense, high isolated peaks cause primarily three types of air mass disturbances near their summits.

Moving air which meets the top portion of a peak must flow either over or around it. The blocking of direct air flow creates a lower pressure on the lee side (like the suction behind a truck on a freeway) which draws the wind over the contours of the mountain. Since air moving over and around a peak must follow a curved path which is longer than the undisturbed straight path of adjoining air, it must travel faster. This is similar to the airfoil effect of the upper surface of an airplane wing. A wave is set up in the air mass and is made visible when lifted moist air causes a lenticular cloud cap.

LENTICULAR WAVE

(Sketch by Gus Swanberg)

A second type of wind amplification occurs on twin-peaked mountains if the wind is blowing through the pass formed by the summits. The air mass is squeezed, forcing a narrower stream of air flow. To maintain the same volume of air mass movement, the wind between the peaks must move faster. This funneling effect is similar to the increase in velocity caused by the narrow portion of a river channel. In scientific circles, it would be called a modified Venturi effect.

FUNNELING: Modified Venturi
(Sketch by Gus Swanberg)

The third type of disturbance is the turbulence caused by the peak as it rips the air mass like a rock in the rapids of a stream. This effect is greatest in high winds and is also the most localized and at any given time may vary drastically between two positions only a short distance apart on the same mountain. Turbulence is very evident in high winds on the lee side of ridges and passes, especially if the slope is gentle such as occurs on the Harper Glacier. It comes in pounding pulses which might destroy a tent which would otherwise withstand a particular storm.

TURBULENCE

(Sketch by Gus Swanberg)

The combination of wave action, funneling, and turbulence can cause winds high on a mountain to be 150% or even 200% of the general flow of air aloft for an area. Accordingly, our estimates of winds during the July 18-26 storm were higher than the winds aloft recorded at McGrath. This was evident even at lower elevations. On July 23 pilot Don Sheldon reported winds at 10,000 feet on the southwest side of McKinley which were 162% of the 10,000 foot McGrath readings for the same day.

Using the 500 MB winds aloft data for McGrath, it is possible to construct a wind profile graph for July 1967, as well as a speculation of probable winds which were experienced at high camp and above. (The winds were variable in direction both before and after the big storm; however, during the time span of the storm the profile accurately describes the winds directed toward the mountain.) The area under the wind profile is proportional to the volume of air which passed over McGrath at 18,000 feet. During the July 18-26, 1967 storm, more than 11,000 miles of wind blew over McGrath headed, of course, for the upper slopes of Mount McKinley.

WIND PROFILE: July 1967
McGrath, Alaska 500 MB
(18,000 feet)

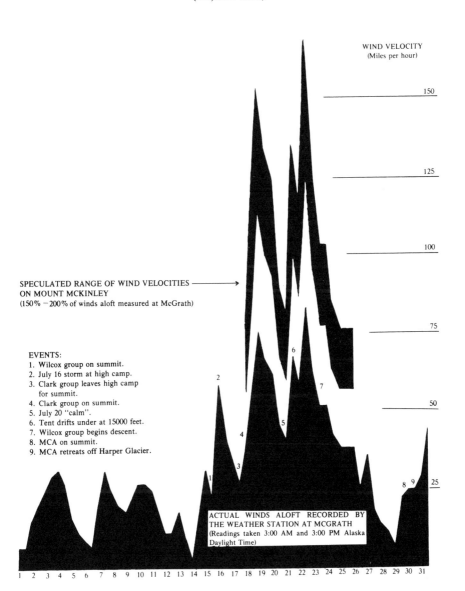

WIND VELOCITY
(Miles per hour)

SPECULATED RANGE OF WIND VELOCITIES ⟶
ON MOUNT MCKINLEY
(150% −200% of winds aloft measured at McGrath)

EVENTS:
1. Wilcox group on summit.
2. July 16 storm at high camp.
3. Clark group leaves high camp
   for summit.
4. Clark group on summit.
5. July 20 "calm".
6. Tent drifts under at 15000 feet.
7. Wilcox group begins descent.
8. MCA on summit.
9. MCA retreats off Harper Glacier.

ACTUAL WINDS ALOFT RECORDED BY
THE WEATHER STATION AT MCGRATH
(Readings taken 3:00 AM and 3:00 PM Alaska
Daylight Time)

DATES

(Artwork by Lowell Egman)

The death storm came in two prongs. The first three days exhibited southwest winds accompanied by precipitation. During this portion of the storm, the 15,000 foot camp seemed to be sheltered a bit by the South Peak. This sheltering effect would have been less at high camp and nonexistent at the extreme elevation of Clark's party. The brief calm of July 20 which we experienced at 15,000 feet is somewhat evident on the wind profile, although it was less pronounced at higher elevations. There may not have been any calm near the summit; however, some clear weather was certain. Following the calm, the mountain was hit by a sharp trough aloft, heralding the highest winds of the siege. The most significant aspect of this part of the storm was a distinct shift in wind direction to the west northwest, blowing directly into Denali Pass. There was no shelter from this wind as boiling turbulence was sucked down the Harper to smash our 15,000 foot camp. With the direct funneling of wind through Denali Pass, conditions at high camp would have been unbearable. (The terrain of the Harper Glacier is well suited for maximizing all primary magnifications of wind velocity.)

The Western States Expedition camped on the West Buttress (windward[4]) side of Denali Pass made an aborted try for the summit on July 22. Their expedition log vividly describes the magnification of wind velocity at the pass: "We were in calm weather until very close to the pass. Then we were caught up in the wind and swept through the pass. We managed to find shelter behind some rocks (where the stronger gusts were still enough to blow a man away if he were caught off guard) and reorganize. Then we had no choice but to crawl, one at a time, on hands and knees (12-point crampons and ice axe) directly into the wind."

By July 23 the winds had abated somewhat at 15,000 feet, permitting our descent from Camp VI. By afternoon, precipitation likely resumed high on the mountain.

The grim description of winds encountered by Clark's party is astounding. For a full eight and a half days, the winds probably averaged 80 to 110 miles per hour with peak gusts well above 150 miles per hour. Even during the brief July 20 "calm", it is doubtful that the climbers trapped near the summit had winds less than 50 to 60 miles per hour. The most profound characteristic of the storm

---

4. The magnification effects of funneling and turbulence are usually negligible on the windward side of a mountain until very near the crest.

was that winds were extreme day after day after day: too extreme for aircraft to venture near the peak, too extreme for rescue climbers to ascend, too extreme for Clark's group to descend.

Obviously, the July 1967 storm was tremendous. However, trying to compare it with other storms which have occurred on McKinley over the years was perplexing. Few McKinley expeditions have encountered really severe high altitude storms which means, of course, that most lofty storms on the peak have probably proceeded without first hand observations and estimates. Even had such not been the case, a researcher would have to contend with subjective influences: for, certainly a healthy climber, strong willed and motivated toward the summit, would view the severity of a particular storm differently than a climber weakened into retreat.

I reasoned that the most objective procedure would be to limit my investigation to the upper air data for Anchorage, Fairbanks, and McGrath. Still, the task of trying to surmise when the critical combinations of meteorological phenomena may have precipitated a whiteout or snowstorm on the upper slopes of McKinley was more nebulous guesswork than I cared to attempt. (Normally storms moving across the Gulf of Alaska from the south or southwest would be the most moist.) Finally, I decided to focus my research on the single aspect of winds aloft with attention to high readings which persisted for a number of days and, as far as comparison is concerned, without speculation as to how the mountain may have responded to individual storms. My study, therefore, is essentially a survey of upper air movements within the McKinley triangle formed by the three weather stations. I reviewed all of the years of 500 MB (18,000 foot) wind data available for the month of July as well as the data for other months in which summit climbs were known to have occurred. (To increase the validity of the study, a few additional climbing season months which did not have summit climbs were included.) The weather study encompassed 105 months of data spanning the years from 1946 to 1979 and was completed in 1980. There were three summit climbs prior to the commencement of these records, which apparently did not involve extensive high altitude windstorms.[5] The results of my

---

5. A near ascent in 1912 was beaten back by what was reported as a tremendous storm, although the expedition was able to retreat off of the mountain.

investigation were startling enough to provoke my disbelief and cause me to recheck the data. The evidence was undeniable. There were no July windstorms even remotely comparable to the July 1967 storm. In 33 years of July observations (about 2,000 wind measurements) McGrath did not record a single July wind velocity aloft as high as the 1967 storm (82.8 miles per hour). In fact, of the eight highest McGrath July readings over a 33 year period, four occurred during the 1967 storm. In addition, over the years only single July readings at Anchorage and Fairbanks were found to be as high as 82.8 miles per hour. Both were isolated occurrences.

At high elevations it is the length of a storm that is the real killer. A strong climber may endure a few hours or even a day or two of really hellish weather simply by digging in and waiting, perhaps not even eating or drinking. However, if such weather persists, the climber is forced to maintain his physiology: to melt drinking water[6] and consume food. The psychological drain and waning of morale becomes progressively more difficult to withstand. The simplest necessary chores are soon virtually impossible to perform. If the weather does not permit the operation of a stove or if a group is caught on a summit dash, customarily with few supplies, then the chances for survival are diminished drastically each day. An eight-day storm is certainly more than twice as threatening as a four-day storm.

When the data for all 105 months was considered (more than 19,000 wind measurements), 28 significant windstorms were identified and isolated for study. These were storms which were capable of producing continuous winds on the upper slopes of McKinley of at least 60 to 80 miles per hour[7] for four or more

---

6. Eating snow drains the body heat (and energy) greatly and is not a functional means of maintaining body moisture at high altitudes. Melting snow in water bottles within sleeping bags (as a 1963 expedition did) is also insufficient for a long siege. It drains a great deal of energy for very meager returns.

7. Weather Service readings are made in meters per second. Seventeen meters per second was used as the windstorm criterion as it corresponds to approximately 38 miles per hour, a velocity which could easily be magnified to 60 to 80 miles per hour on the mountain. To qualify as a significant windstorm, each of the twice-daily 500 MB wind readings had to be measured at 17 meters per second or higher for a minimum of four consecutive days at one or more of the three weather stations.

consecutive days. Such winds, even in otherwise clear weather, could easily blow away wands and create an immobilizing ground blizzard, trapping any climbing party that chanced to be caught.

Although several windstorms had winds as high as the July 1967 storm, in terms of duration and expanse, the death storm was in a class by itself. At eight and a half days it was 55 percent longer than the next most severe McKinley windstorm involving summit climbers: the March, 1967 storm which trapped three members of the Winter Expedition at Denali Pass. They barely survived.

There were apparently two unique features of the July 1967 storm. The southern high and northern low, both on the surface and aloft, were in more direct opposition than the other storms and for a longer period of time. This opposition channeled the air movement directly over central Alaska. Also the July 1967 storm had a very sharp trough aloft not exhibited by the other severe windstorms. The trough hit McKinley after the July 20 "calm" with high winds of unknown velocities. This brief surge of wind probably would have escaped being measured at the weather stations and could have resulted in sudden gusts as high as 200 miles per hour on the upper slopes of the mountain.

The ominous reality is so overwhelmingly compelling that its mere statement seems inadequate: Jerry Clark's summit party without the slightest doubt, encountered the most severe, high altitude windstorm in all the previous history of McKinley mountaineering. Mount McKinley's prominence as host to the most treacherous mountain weather in the world suggests a sobering conjecture: it may well be that Clark's group was caught in the most severe, high altitude windstorm in the entire history of mountaineering.

Many have been the expeditions that have fallen short of Denali's summit challenge, that have suffered decisive defeat in the face of unsubmissive weather and have been forced to beat a hasty retreat, lucky to have their lives, yet still not fully appreciating the role of fate in their survival. Time and again mountaineers have walked the edge of the chasm of oblivion; yet, death invited has not come. It is easy for such climbers to believe that their survival is due to their great mountaineering knowledge, preparation, awareness, perseverance, or intelligence. In a mountain realm where meteorological naivaté often passes unchallenged, such illusions of security continue to persist unchecked. However, the devastating potential remains, fully capable of striking suddenly and annihilating the strongest of mountaineers. Few climbers tremble at the remote prospect; yet, in 1967 the blow fell solidly and fate's assessment was the sacrifice of seven.

9
Tragedy Revisited

In an opening crevasse or tumbling icefall a decade or a century from now, Denali may yield conclusive evidence of what really happened in the disaster of 1967. Until then, we are left with only speculative theories. Any attempt to reconstruct the tragedy must necessarily sew together the known facts and personalities with a great deal of conjecture. Although straying from objectivity, such an account has significant value in enlightening future expeditions. Trying to reconstruct what happened also provides some emotional comfort to the survivors and serves as a tribute to the dead climbers.

At noon on July 17, the climbers at the high camp waved good-bye to Wilcox, Schiff, and the three Colorado men and watched them slowly begin their descent toward Camp VI at 15,000 feet. There were only two tents remaining in the high camp now, and it seemed a lot lonelier, although the majority of the expedition was still there. It would have been nice to have already made the summit and to be descending with the others, but the coveted goal still loomed above. This was their day to climb upward, to be

243

strong and unwavering, to realize a long time dream. The pleasant thoughts of accomplishment would have to wait for tomorrow. Preoccupied minds lost interest in the figures on the slopes below, and eyes were lifted to the ridges above, surveying the breaking weather and analyzing the blowing snow.

Jerry Clark quietly quizzed the condition of his men. Everyone wanted to make a try for the summit, although Steve and John seemed weak. There would be a little time to make personal decisions as they waited for the erratic weather to make its intentions known. Supply-wise, the high camp had lots of food. The fuel was low, however, so they decided to spend their weather waiting time looking for the 3 quarts of lost fuel. An hour of digging in the vicinity where the Colorado tent had been proved fruitless.

John had been unable to keep much food down at high camp, a condition which he had tried to conceal from the others. Steve was more obviously ill. He emerged from the Logan tent and weakly walked around camp. His throbbing head and faintness soon caused him to sit down. There was little point in protesting the physiological decision: Steve would be unable to accompany the others in their bid for the summit. Jerry related the situation to the other climbers. No one wanted to stay with Steve and forfeit their chance at the summit. After considerable discussion, it was reluctantly agreed to leave Steve at the high camp alone. The Logan tent was arranged with plenty of food and a filled stove to make Steve as comfortable as possible. The other men began serious preparations for their climb. In the meantime another hour had slipped by and the weather had cleared considerably.

Dennis talked to Jerry about taking his sleeping bag. Jerry was skeptical at first, but remembering that no weather forecast had been available and understanding the mountain's potential, the idea made more than a little sense. The weight of a sleeping bag would not slow a climber much and if needed it would be priceless. Soon each man was packing his sleeping bag for the assault. Dennis packed the snow shovel and Walt packed a freshly fueled stove. Jerry would carry the radio, leaving the battery pack behind. Water bottles were filled and a couple of days' rations were robbed of their quick-energy, noncookable food—food that filled the pockets of packs and wind parkas. The group had worked as rapidly as altitude would allow, but still it was 3:00 PM before the last of the six was cramponed and tied into the long climbing rope. Walt would lead, Jerry second, and the others followed at appropriate intervals. Hank would bring up the rear and wand—his accustomed responsibility.

The climbers exchanged lighthearted comments with Steve, and were off. The trudging of cramponed footsteps faded into the distance as Steve's high camp vigil began. Only the soft roar of the stove and the faint aroma of warming soup kept the loneliness at bay.

Leaving a trail of wands, the climbing men easily gained Denali Pass, quietly enjoyed the magnificent view, poked about a bit in the debris left by other expeditions, and then continued their ascent. Soon Jerry was able to raise Eielson on the radio. Snow conditions were good and the weather was clear. Everything was proceeding as planned. As they climbed higher, they encountered a few wands still standing from a previous expedition.

Occassionally eyes lifted to study the route ahead, but for the most part the team moved in a mechanical trance, each man engrossed in his own private thoughts. To escape the boredom of their slow pace some men began counting steps, breaths between steps, or watched the rope slither along the snow ahead of their feet; the rope periodically lifting in response to the tension caused by the pauses for wanding. They moved as a well-synchronized chain gang—in slow rhythmic steps. But their footsteps persisted, each one wearing away a minute segment of the peak and decreasing the distance to their goal.

Almost unnoticed a whiteout slowly formed along the snow. At first the surface merely appeared fuzzy and mittened hands repeatedly rubbed supposedly fogged goggles. Gradually the whiteout thickened and began to rise. The men stopped to study the weather and the route ahead. Aside from the mild fog there was not a cloud in the sky. No approaching storm to worry about. Certainly there was no great cause for alarm. They could safely proceed; the chill of night would likely dissipate the fog before they reached the summit.

Their unaccustomed pace and impaired vision soon confused their sense of progress until they weren't quite sure just where they were. Fortunately, enough wands remained on the route ahead that they could cautiously continue. As the 8:00 PM radio contact arrived, Jerry began to wonder if the whiteout would not dissipate. Occasionally, through the drifting fog, he could see what appeared to be a ridge ahead of them. If they were hiking as rapidly as the July 15 summit group, then they could well be approaching the summit ridge itself. Perhaps they were only an hour from the top now. Knowing that corniced ridges and summits are very dangerous in a whiteout, Jerry decided to check it out with the 15,000 foot party.

After a radio contact made brief by Jerry's conscientious conservation of the cold radio batteries, the group forced onward into the thickening fog. A half hour later they came to the ridge which they had been seeing. But was it the summit ridge? If so, then it should drop off steeply down the South Face of the mountain. It did not—or at least it did not for the short distance that they could see into the whiteout. If it wasn't the summit ridge, then there should be more wands marking the route beyond the ridge. The rope team probed into the flatness, trying to find either another wand or the steep pitches of the South Face. Finding neither, they returned to the low ridge somewhat confused. Perhaps this *was* the summit ridge. If so, then the route would turn here and the next wand would be on the ridge. Short forays both ways on the ridge were fruitless. Where were they? They might still be on the summit ridge; perhaps it just wasn't wanded. Mountaineers often do not wand distinct ridges where there is little chance of getting disoriented in a whiteout and the first group hadn't mentioned whether or not the summit ridge was wanded. An hour had gone by with no progress; time and energy were being wasted. Maybe the 15,000 foot party was listening in for a summit broadcast. Maybe Eielson could raise them. Jerry took the radio from his pack, wishing he hadn't left the easily warmed battery pack at high camp. There wasn't time to warm the radio, especially if he wanted to catch the 15,000 foot group before they turned in for the night. A short and frustrating radio communication followed. Not only was Eielson unable to contact the 15,000 foot group, but Jerry had considerable difficulty talking directly to Eielson. The effort had been useless.

The six men huddled together to confer. The wind picked up

and whispered along the ridge, making them uncomfortable. Some men felt that they were not on the summit ridge and should push across the flat to the next upslope. Others thought that they were already on the flat ridge between Farthing Horn and the main summit which would explain the absence of the steep South Face pitches. If so, then going south on the ridge for a few hundred yards would put them on the summit. Examining a topographical map in the wind and dim light did not bring about a consensus. If they weren't between the summit and Farthing Horn, then the only other possibility would be near Archdeacon's Tower. The map showed a flat area between Archdeacon's Tower and the summit ridge and perhaps a very low ridge before the flat. However, no distinct ridge was in evidence. If they were near Archdeacon's Tower, then traveling northeast a ways would bring them to the outcropping of rocks forming the tower. Skeptically they trudged first one way and then the other on the ridge for what to them seemed like a long way. There was no summit to the south and no rocks to the northeast. They were completely bewildered. Maybe they had gotten off of the summit route entirely earlier in the whiteout; yet, they had been following sparsely spaced wands to this location. It was after 10:00 PM now. They had been floundering in frustration for nearly two hours. They had spent enough energy to have climbed to the summit if they only knew where it was—if the damnable fog would just dissipate for a minute.

Jerry announced the obvious, logical, and normal decision to return to high camp. With sparse fuel reserves, this decision had a deeper meaning. Silence gripped the group of men as they realized that not getting the summit today meant not getting it at all. Had they come this far, perhaps to within a stone's throw of the top, only to be turned away? Thoughts weighed the investments of time, money, and energy against the soupy whiteness.

An opinionated discussion beset the gathered men. Caution told them to descend—they could not continue climbing and a bivouac would be too risky. The mountain would be here another year. Ambition, however, argued that they had little to lose by waiting for the weather to clear, all night if necessary. Certainly other climbers had camped at higher elevations on other mountains and a couple of expeditions had even camped on the summit of McKinley. The men had all of the gear and supplies needed for a camp except for a tent, and a snow cave would serve as well, perhaps even better. Surely their stay would depict more a camp than a bivouac. In the end ambition got the nod, with the stipulation that if the weather didn't clear, then they would move down first thing in the morning. There was no way to inform Steve of their plans. They would just have to hope that he wouldn't become so worried that he tried something rash like hiking down the mountain alone. He might be sleeping a lot and not even realize that they were overdue.

The men unroped and began preparing for the night. Two snow caves were dug on the lee (southeast) side of the low ridge, not nearly so elaborate as the one which had been dug at 12,100 feet. Each was only a couple of feet high and a tight fit for three sleeping bags. Jerry switched on the cold radio to inform Eielson of the situation. After making the preliminary call, he was unable to communicate with Eielson. Just as well. It would just alarm and upset people to know that the climbers were bivouacking. Crampons were unstrapped, packs secured, and sleeping bags fluffed. An uneasiness hovered about the resting men as they silently pondered the wisdom of their decision. The mountain patiently waited for morning.

In time, the bivouacked men awakened and pushed through the drifted snow which had partially blanketed the snow cave entrances during the night. The whiteout was persistent. Everything was as it had been the night before. Only time had changed. Depressed and beaten, the men consumed cups of warm soup and then slowly prepared for the descent. The little rest gained by the bivouac was quickly sapped by the altitude. Suddenly there was an excited proclamation. Hearts lifted as the drifting fog parted, revealing a rock outcropping along the ridge from where they stood. Momentarily the flat area next to the ridge appeared and beyond this another upslope. At last they knew where they were! They just hadn't investigated far enough the previous evening. They were on the flat ridge behind Archdeacon's Tower and the summit was across the flat and up the next slope, perhaps two hours distance. The fog closed in again. But this time it did not dampen spirits, for now they had seen too much to turn back. Without a word the decision was reached. They cached their sleeping bags and other items to lighten their packs and a compass bearing was taken to assure that they wouldn't become disoriented again.

As the others excitedly roped up, John moodily sat slumped against his pack. Being unable to replace body liquids adequately for a couple of days now, his fingers and toes were already getting numb even though well insulated. John knew that he could not afford to climb upward with the others or even remain at their present location. Frostbite would be certain. None of the others suspected how weak John really was. He had to descend, yet he did not want anyone to go back to the 17,900 foot camp with him and forfeit their summit chance. He reasoned to himself that he could safely return to the high camp alone. The route was well wanded and they had not encountered any significant crevasses. When John's failure to participate in the summit preparations required an explanation to the others, he announced his intentions. John's disclosure was met with a chorus of objections that anyone would even consider a solo hike. Knowing that his best chance of breaking away was to be decisive, John shouldered his pack, grabbed his bamboo staff, and steamed toward the nearest wand while simultaneously and unflatteringly suggesting that the others could go ahead and freeze their asses if they wanted to. The group had been caught off guard and John quickly disappeared into the fog. Shouts of protest followed him into the windy whiteness, but there was no reply. John was gone.

The high climbers were somewhat shaken by John's leaving. Wordlessly they shouldered their near-empty packs. Walt led off as the rope team set out across the flat. Soon they came to the upslope approach to the summit ridge which moderated their pace greatly. Like a file of ants they tramped onward; their inability to see their objective almost suspending them in time. Monotonously they proceeded until even the step-counters tired of their task as thoughts echoed in unison, "How much further can it be?" Finally they came to the crest of the summit ridge and began the traverse to the summit. They were actually going to make it. They had gambled with a bivouac and now it appeared that they had won a remarkable victory. Walt was so intent on staying clear of the ridge precipice that he was within a few yards of the top before he suddenly noticed the decorated hump of snow ahead and stopped short. Recognizing where he was, Walt silently coiled the rope. The next man was unaware that Walt had stopped until he found himself next to Walt, looking at the same glorious sight. The solemn victory of this moment would be shared together. This was the object of the quest which had stalked their long friendships and cemented their efforts of the last month. With their arms around each other, the five mountaineers simultaneously stepped onto the summit snow. Almost tearful embraces of gratitude followed. Jerry had carried the radio inside his parka so that it was warmed enough for a summit broadcast to Eielson. He talked a few minutes with a rather surprised Eielson and then turned the radio over to Mark. Not wishing to alarm anyone, Mark did not tell Eielson that John had left the group.

John's fatigued descent was slow and tiring. Whenever he stopped to rest, he had to desperately fight the strong urge to sleep. To fall asleep on the unprotected ridge would be an eternal sleep. A long time passed before the notch of Denali Pass arrived and another long time passed before the tents of camp came into view. Steve stirred from his sleep as John crawled into the tent. Steve was at first greatly relieved at what he thought to be the arrival of the overdue team, and then much suprised to learn that John had returned alone and that the others were still going up. A detailed discussion of the bivouac accompanied warming soup.

There was nothing to see from the enshrouded summit so Clark's group soon began a weary descent. For the first time, thoughts could properly be directed to the future: to celebration, families, girlfriends, jobs, and college. Before the team had reached the flat, the wind freshened and a heavy snow began falling. Alerted by the changing weather conditions, the party hurried to their bivouac site to pack their cached gear. They knew now that the whiteout had obscured the approach of a storm, the one thing that they had most feared. Hopefully they could get back to high camp before it became too intense, for they could not afford to spend any more time at these extreme elevations.

Blowing snow quickly erased John's footprints and tugged at the wands which marked the route down to high camp. The wands had been well placed; however, the swirling wind began working them back and forth, loosening them ever so slightly with each savage gust—by now over 70 miles per hour. First one wand succumbed, then several more. There were no ears to hear the skittering rattle as the colorful flags vanished. The lifeline to high camp had been severed.

Five men braced themselves into the gusty gale and inched downward. Walt stopped periodically to sight the next wand and then proceeded on. The route soon became difficult to follow as some wands were blown out. Finally their progress ground to a halt. Walt could not locate the next wand. Too many wands were missing. Jerry walked up next to Walt and together they squinted into the blowing snow. The rope team then retraced its steps back to the last two wands, aligned itself, and projected the direction several rope lengths into the blowing snowstorm, swinging wide arcs. No luck—no wands. They huddled to discuss the situation. A decision would have to be made—and soon. It was. They would return the short distance to the bivouac snow caves to regroup.

Once again weary limbs and lungs were called on for upward climbing. The terrain was only slightly uphill, but seemed immensely steep to their drained bodies. At last the men arrived at the now familiar bivouac site and collapsed into the snow caves, crampons and all, without even unroping. Sheltered from the wind, they regained their senses and began strategy planning to get out of their predicament. Basically they had three options. They could push down the mountain in the probable direction of the route, hoping to rediscover the wands or, by luck, make it to Denali Pass and on down to high camp. This was a possible but risky proposition especially since they would be directly exposed to the high winds which had increased to 100 miles per hour. Secondly, they could remain in the snow caves and wait out the storm. Maybe it would be of short duration. This option was also undesirable as some of the men needed an immediate drop in elevation. A third possibility would be to follow the ridge to Archdeacon's Tower and from there take a compass course toward where they calculated the high camp to be. Even if the men couldn't locate the high camp, they could get in the general vicinity and dig in again. Most importantly, this option would get them a couple of thousand feet lower on the mountain, giving them a much better chance for survival. There was only one problem. From their observation of the upper part of the mountain while at high camp they had noticed ice cliffs and crevasses at the base of the Archdeacon's Tower slope. The map confirmed these glacial disruptions. Since it had not been an intended route, no one could remember whether or not there was a safe passage through this area. To climb down the slope and then be forced to ascend again by a blocked route could critically overtax the weakest of the men. The decision was made to split the group. They would separate their long rope which was actually two ropes tied together. Two men would lead out and wand their descent. If all went well, they would be able to negotiate the disrupted area and the other three men would follow four hours behind. If not, the two men would return to the snow caves. This plan would conserve the waning energy of the weaker men.

The two route-finders roped up and began their trek. At Archdeacon's Tower, the lead man took out his compass, which had already been set at the correct bearing, and proceeded slowly down the slope. The second man followed a hundred feet behind, wanding at close intervals. In time, the slope steepened and the crevasses became more frequent until finally the route was blocked altogether by the precipice of a 30-foot ice cliff. Cautiously the two men crept to the edge and then began long traverses first one way and then another in hopes of finding a corridor to the Harper Glacier below. To their right the slope was even steeper and the ice cliff cut upward. Hiking to the left, the wind-slabbed snow repeatedly broke dangerously beneath their steps. The ice wall was seemingly endless. Another day, on another mountain, descending this obstacle would have provided little challenge to their technical skills, but altitude and wind had drained them and the others back at the snow caves were even weaker. Surely there was an easier route, if only the whiteout would lift for a minute and let them see. With great frustration, the two climbers began the arduous ascent of the slope, leaving the route wanded. Back at the snow caves the news was very disheartening to the other three. If the poor visibility continued, the party might eventually be forced to try a descent of the ice cliff; but for now they could only wait, for the tempo of the storm had increased tremendously.

The ropes were stuffed into packs which were in turn anchored by ice axes. The last of the fuel was used to melt snow and the men crawled into their sleeping bags with half-filled water bottles and assorted food items. At the 8:00 PM radio contact, Jerry could not communicate with Eielson or hear the 15,000 foot camp. He could hear Eielson faintly. There was, of course, no serious concern yet for the summit party.

At high camp, however, the story was different. John and Steve knew that the upper group should have returned by late afternoon. They would not have chosen to spend another night bivouacked in this storm. Their failure to descend could mean only one thing: they could not descend. Either there had been some sort of accident or else the summit group had gotten lost in the storm. Perhaps some of the wands had blown out. The alarmed men pondered what they could do. Both were too weak to go looking for the overdue party and there wasn't even a rope in camp. Also they had no radio with which to summon help from the 15,000 foot camp or anyone else. Anxiously, they passed the night, straining to hear the familiar sounds of a rope team entering camp.

The next morning, John crawled out of the tent to survey the situation. High on the peak the storm raged on, but at high camp and below there was only blowing snow. Looking with the wind down glacier, visibility was fairly good. John studied the thinly veiled high-wind cloud cap just above them. The situation really looked bad. The two agreed that John should go down the trail a ways and try to signal the lower camp. With his long bamboo pole and the two smoke flares belonging to Steve and himself, John slowly descended toward the top of the highest icefall. A couple of hundred yards below camp he stopped and squinted. Yes, there it was: a flicker of blue through the blowing snow. He could see the 15,000 foot camp.

John set off one orange smoke flare, but it dissipated almost instantly in the wind. He waited for a half hour. Once during a lull in the wind he thought that he could see a figure in the lower camp. He set off the second smoke flare. There was no reason for the low camp to be looking for a smoke flare. They most likely assumed that Clark's party was safely at high camp. Frustratedly John waved the bamboo pole and yelled as if someone could hear. Finally he drove the pole deep into the snow. Just maybe the lower camp would see it. Slowly he returned to high camp.

After a belated breakfast in which neither was able to eat much, Steve and John considered what to do. If the summit team had made it to the ridge above Denali Pass, then they would have been able to get as far as the pass, they reasoned. Maybe they were dug in at the pass awaiting a break in the weather to descend the flat area down to high camp. Probably some wands had blown out on this short segment of the route. John decided to gather a few of the wands remaining in camp and climb back to the pass, replacing the blown out wands en route. If the upper party was at the pass, he could lead them down.

Tired and fatigued, John began the painful trip into the lenticular cloud cap. His limbs were stiff and his hands and feet were numb from dehydration, yet his leaden legs lumbered upward. By the time he reached the pass, the wind was a high-pitched whistle. John's hands were so numb now that his ice axe hung limply from its wrist strap. He hiked a few feet up the ridge and called out. It was useless. There was no sign of Clark's party. They must have been trapped higher on the peak. John turned and stumbled back down to high camp; blinding spindrift and unbalancing gusts caused him to fall several times. When he finally got to high camp, he found that he could not unstrap his crampons or manage the tent zipper. Quickly Steve hustled John into the tent, helped him into his sleeping bag and began warming his frostbitten hands. John was shivering and his speech incoherent. Steve crawled into the bag with him to provide more warmth. Gradually he came to his senses, crying out in pain as his hands thawed. They would have to abandon the high camp as soon as John had rested enough to travel.

In the afternoon a snowstorm moved in and quickly reduced visibility to a hundred feet. Steve did not want to make an unroped descent of the poorly marked route in a whiteout so he decided to wait for morning to take John down. Maybe by then someone from the low camp would come up to investigate.

The situation in the high snow caves was getting grimmer by the hour. At midday, water bottles were empty and by evening dehydration was inviting frostbite. Morale plummeted. There were no jokes. Genuine fear entered their thoughts.

By morning the high winds had dropped lower on the mountain, lashing the high camp. For hours, Steve and John huddled in the middle of the tent trying to dampen the severe vibrations of the center pole. Shortly after noon the storm almost miraculously abated, with the winds dropping to about 20 miles per hour. Steve crawled out into the near calm, surprised to see that the top of the mountain had cleared. At last the summit climbers could come down. For an hour Steve waited and watched, but he saw no climbers on the ridges and slopes above him. Where was the summit party? Why didn't they come down? And where were the climbers from 15,000 feet? They should have come up by now.

Steve did not know that the low camp's efforts to aid the higher camp had already been turned back. Nor did he realize that even though it was clear higher on the mountain, it was not calm. The winds were still over 50 miles per hour.

High on the peak someone noticed that it was clear and crawled out. He yelled. Four other men quickly emerged from the snow and prepared for the descent. Sleeping bags were sloppily stuffed into packs and the men roped up—their numb fingers fumbling with the knots, slings, and carabiners.

Which way should they go? It didn't look like the weather would hold. Their best bet would be to descend the Archdeacon's Tower slope and find a route around the ice cliff before the fog closed in again. When they reached the top of the slope, they could see the high camp and they thought that they could see a figure standing beside the Logan tent.

The two climbers at high camp were anxious to begin their descent to the 15,000 foot camp. For one last time Steve's eyes searched the upper slopes. What was that? It looked like an orange dot on the snow below the rocks of Archdeacon's Tower. Could it be a man? Yes! It was—and there was another—and another. The summit team had started a descent directly toward high camp. From Steve's advantageous position below the ice cliff he could see that there was no apparent route through it. Steve yelled toward the upper team—waving his ice axe over his head. It was no use. There was no way to make them understand. Steve then watched in disbelief as an invisible force ominously dipped from the sky and blasted a phenomenal snow plume from Archdeacon's Tower. As the wind dropped further, he saw one man of the summit team blown from his tracks—only the rope saved him from being blown off the mountain. Blowing snow quickly engulfed the mountain and Steve could no longer see the upper team. It was too late now for Steve and John to begin their descent. Petrified, Steve re-entered the tent and tightly secured the portal.

On the slopes of Archdeacon's Tower, the ruthless wind tore at the five men as they lay prone, anchored by their ice axes. The wind had shifted to the west northwest and was pounding them full force at more than 150 miles per hour. When possible the men tried to move up, to return to the snow cave shelters. Half crawling and unable to see, they got as far as the first rocks of Archdeacon's Tower before they were forced to stop and dig in. One man dug while the other four held the rope taut to keep him on the mountain. Periodically, they switched shovelers. Beneath a weak wind slab the snow was powdery dry and poorly suited for snow caves. Once again, two caves were dug, these more crude and crowded than the first pair. Packs were secured and icy fingers fumbled with crampons and sleeping bag zippers. With great exertion and determination they had escaped the tremendous winds, but the cost for their meager shelters was high. Some hands and feet were beyond feeling and faces were blanched white with frostbite. There was no way to keep sifting snow out of sleeping bags and clothing where it gathered to be melted by body heat. It had been more than a day since the last of their liquid had been consumed and now the food was gone as well. Overspent lungs gasped the thin air and bodies shivered in desperation, a last rampart against the cold.

All day and through the night, the two men at high camp clung to the center pole, fighting to save their tent, for they had no shovel with which to dig a snow cave. The morning came without relief. In fact the sinister storm increased in intensity with the wind feeding its soul. This was a wanton wind: troubled, brooding, and thundering; contrary even to the nature of Denali, having its spiritual birth elsewhere; holding the mountain in siege, not wavering or relenting until it had claimed a precious prize. The tent lurched and yawed and tugged at its tethers. Hell's tympany pounded on the side walls in seismic waves and the center pole gyrated and vibrated violently, a frayed and fretted string plucked by the fickle finger of an enraged goddess. Gallantly, the tent held a calm bubble in a frigid hurricane, protecting the lives within by a margin as thin as its nylon fabric. The snow mist sifting into the tent clothed the two men in ghostly white. They were slowly losing their battle for life. The storm was driving them ever closer to the brink of annihilation.

The wind screamed across Archdeacon's Tower, lifting and loosening the packs. Finally one ice axe pulled free and a pack disappeared into the wind. Then another and another until the slope was swept clean.

The mountain seemed to be assaulted by a series of storms in close succession, each concealing the arrival of the next. Into the afternoon and evening, the heinous winds continued, seeking to claim the souls of the besieged mountaineers. By now, it had also reduced the 15,000 foot camp to survival status.

Jerry Clark had been considering warming the radio batteries for a "Mayday" call and finally composed his thoughts into action, crawling halfway out of the snow cave to fetch the radio from his pack. He was terrified by what he saw—or didn't see. They were gone! All of the packs—the ropes, wands, snow shovel, crampons, radio—everything! There was nothing to do but crawl back into his sleeping bag and wait, for now they had been stripped of all of their instruments of survival. Now their fate was cast to the dictums of the storm. By now others surely knew that they were trapped high on the peak. Perhaps a rescue had already begun. What did it matter. No device of technology, no power of civilization was capable of reaching through the storm. They were on their own, the terms which they had accepted at the onset of the climb.

It was the evening of July 21, although by now Steve and John at high camp and those above had lost track of time. They did not know if it was morning or evening nor did they care. Communication was now difficult, as thinking became scrambled and incoherent.

In the high camp tent, one man held the tent pole while the other tried to rest in his sleeping bag. Periodically they changed places. John was not able to grip the pole with his hands and could only wrap his arms around it and brace his body against it. The metal pole continually drained his warmth. John fortified his will by moaning softly under his breath. A few feet away, Steve privately called upon the strength of his religious rearing.

In the early morning, Steve awoke to relieve John's pole vigil. He mumbled as he struggled out of his sleeping bag and pulled on his boots, unable to tie the laces. John did not answer, so Steve tapped him on the shoulder. There was no response. Finally Steve turned John around and gasped in mortified shock; the frozen eyes of a corpse stared past him. John was dead. Confused and delirious, Steve shook the stiff body. In vain he tried to pry it from the pole. Finally accepting the reality of the present, Steve retired to the far side of the tent.

Through clouded thinking Steve planned what he must do. He would have to try to descend alone—now, while he still could. Every second of delay was bringing him closer to death. He untied the tent portal and looked out. The camp was in chaos and Mark's tent was nearly buried. Locating his pack near the doorway, Steve dragged it into the tent along with his ice axe. His hands could not manage to reclose the tent entrance. Suddenly the wind shifted and drove itself full force into the tent opening. The pressure increased immensely and Steve's ears popped. The seams stretched and strained. With a loud "crack!" the tent exploded—spilling its contents to the wind. Steve wrapped himself around his sleeping bag, but his pack was gone. He crawled out of the tangled and shredded tent and surveyed the mess. John's body was still frozen to the collapsed center pole. Needlessly, Steve spent several minutes wrapping the torn tent around John's body.

With his ice axe and sleeping bag, Steve began the descent, crouched and sliding, frequently being blown down by gusts of wind. By the time he got to the bamboo pole he could barely hang on to the bulky sleeping bag and wrapped it about the pole to rest. It was no use. He would have to leave the bag. Perhaps he could share a sleeping bag with someone when he got down to the 15,000 foot camp. Steve continued on, his ice axe hanging by its wrist strap from an almost frozen hand. Repeatedly he stumbled and fell and got up again. His gloves were now gone. He could scarcely breathe and his eyelids were freezing. He did not even notice when his ice axe slipped off of his wrist.

Each time Steve fell he imagined himself getting up immediately, yet each time was longer than the time before. By mid-morning he collapsed for the last time. Still, in his mind he saw himself rise again and continue down, but his body did not move. Wind drifted snow over the still form until only the wind remained.

By afternoon the fiendish wind had removed several feet of

snow from the slope below Archdeacon's Tower and began eroding away one of the powdery snow caves. The two men inside clawed at the snow to try to deepen their shelter, but their frozen hands made poor prehensile tools at best. It was hopeless. Crawling over to the other snow cave, the two men explained their predicament in slurred speech. They indicated that they were going to make a run for high camp. Everyone knew that the chances of reaching high camp in the high winds were very slim; however, one man crawled out to join the descending party. The two groups wished each other good luck as club-like hands clasped and faces of friendship gazed upon each other—for the last time.

Weary arms hugged flaring sleeping bags as block-like frozen feet stumbled down the steep slope. The three men did not communicate and soon became separated. There were no thoughts of crevasses or of the ice cliff below. Each man's vision was hypnotically fixed on an orange dot which was intermittently visible; nothing else mattered. They did not realize that what they were seeing was not the standing Logan tent at high camp but its shattered remains. There was no high camp.

The floundering men paused to rest more often now. One climber could only see a single man below him on the slope. Had the other man fallen into a crevasse or was there another man? Another climber turned uphill to see if his companions were following. Once turned, he could not remember what he was searching for. Perhaps he should be climbing up the slope. After a few steps upward, he turned downward again.

And so, the men stumbled on. Their senses becoming distorted as reality blended with illusion. The howling wind that had filled their ears, now seemed to enter their heads and blow within their minds. Everything appeared to be moving calmly—in slow motion. They felt as if they were floating beneath a gossamer sky, in a sea of shifting snow, floating with the wind down the glacier to the green tundra below. . . and beyond. The illusion continued, but the slowly freezing human forms moved no more.

As time ticked on, the men in the snow cave could no longer raise their limbs to knock away the snow that began drifting over the entrance to their shelter. Claustrophobia gripped them. They wanted to break out of their tomb and run down the mountain, but they could not move. After a while the desperate panic passed, and their circumstances no longer seemed to matter. Had it been hours since the others had left. . . or was it days? Wandering thoughts turned toward home, that extension of mortal birth that seems so secure when it is beyond reach. Surely at the brink of death a man's thoughts reach out to the source of his being. Surely the soul comes at last to set in the love of its rising.

White winds swept across the high slopes and raked through the derelict camp, unaware of its triumph.

PICTORIAL ODYSSEY

ALASKA

Preparation:

Steve Taylor—ice climbing.

Steve establishing a boot-axe belay.

Anshel's elaborate harness.

Approach:

The Alcan—John uses a primitive jack while Walt and Steve make repairs.

Anshel Schiff

Mount McKinley looms above Walt and Dennis: "no paper mountain."

Ascent:

2,100 feet **Day 1—June 19** Anshel Schiff

Mark fording the mile-wide McKinley River.

2,300 feet **Day 1—June 19**

After the McKinley River crossing, the vast tundra.

2,500 feet   **Day 2—June 20**   Anshel Schiff

Dennis downed in Clearwater Creek. Jerry Lewis and Walt come to his aid.

4,500 feet   Anshel Schiff

Day 3—June 21

Horse Cache—Walt departs with a load of Blazo.

Jerry Lewis above the Horse Cache, climbing toward McGonagall Pass.

5,500 feet

5,720 feet

Day 4—June 22

John at McGonagall Pass, looking up the Muldrow toward Pioneer Ridge and North Peak.

5,700 feet **Day 4—June 22** Anshel Schiff

Jerry Lewis operating the theodolite near Camp I.

5,720 feet **Day 8—June 26**

Jerry Clark, Howard, and Paul drying gear at Camp I.

5,800 feet

On the Muldrow above Camp I, a rope team skirts a glacier surface lake.

6,500 feet

At the foot of the Lower Icefall, the Camp II cache grows as North Peak breaks the clouds—South Peak to left.

6,400 feet

Walt on return from Camp II. Hanging glaciers cling to Pioneer Ridge to the right.

Howard Snyder

6,500 feet   **Day 9—June 27**

Moving to Camp II: Steve, Mark, and Jerry Lewis at Camp II as Joe approaches with a team from McGonagall Pass.

Day 10—June 28

Nearing the top of the Lower Icefall—Hank following Joe—on the mountain at last.

7,000 feet

Dennis Luchterhand

500 feet

Day 10—June 28

Back at Camp II, an impressive vanguard of clouds.

Day 11—June 29

Camp II, Walt in three feet of powder.

6,500 feet

7,900 feet **Day 13—July 1**

The expedition threading snow-covered crevasses above the Lower Icefall.

8,100 feet

Camp III—two Logan tents, the Mountaineer tent, Mark's tent, and the Colorado tent.

8,100 feet

Dennis and the Camp III "throne."

8,100 feet   **Day 16—July 4**   Dennis Luchterhand

Group photograph: Steve Taylor, Joe Wilcox, Howard Snyder, Dennis Luchterhand, Mark McLaughlin, Paul Schlichter, Jerry Clark, Jerry Lewis, Hank Janes, Anshel Schiff, John Russell, Walter Taylor.

8,700 feet

Approaching the Great Icefall. Ahead the Flatiron sits beneath Taylor Spur.

9,300 feet

The Great Icefall: "a giant game of fox and geese." Rock at upper left is Browne Tower.

Jerry Lewis crossing a snow bridge in the Great Icefall. ▶

Above the Great Icefall toward the head of the Muldrow, Karstens Ridge is left skyline, Harper Icefall in center. ▼

9,600 feet

10,500 feet

11,000 feet

The awesome Harper Icefall.

10,900 feet **Day 17—July 5**

Avalanche mist hovers over Camp IV.

11,000 feet

Snow at Camp IV.

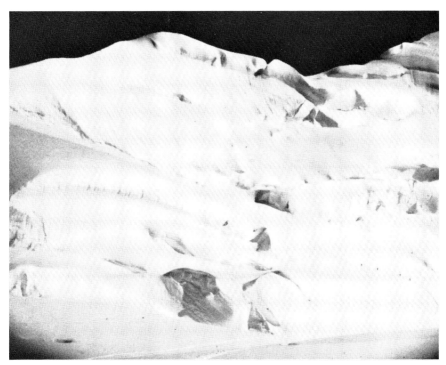

11,300 feet

Anshel Schiff

Assaulting Karstens Ridge, climbers at lower right. Camp V will be located at the ridge saddle at upper right. ▲

Day 18—July 6

A "jump ridge": Joe breaks trail up the lower Karstens Ridge while John and Walt follow. ▶

11,700 feet

Howard Snyder

12,100 feet · **Day 22—July 10** ·

From Camp V, the upper Karstens Ridge. Snow plume from Coxcomb with Browne Tower obscured. Climbing team faintly visible near base of Coxcomb.

Joe approaches a cornice just above Camp V.

12,200 feet   **Day 22—July 10**   Dennis Luchterhand

Paul, Mark, and Hank above Camp V. Mount Koven and Mount Carpé beyond.

12,300 feet

Clipped into fixed line, Joe follows Steve up a snow bulwark on Karstens Ridge.

12,400 feet

Karstens Ridge: Jerry Clark pauses for a radio contact a few feet from the Traleika chasm.

Muldrow glacier from Karstens Ridge, trail above Camp
IV faintly visible at lower
right. ▶

12,500 feet

12,700 feet

Karstens Ridge—Wind, rock, and blue ice. Coxcomb above, Browne
Tower to the left.

13,200 feet **Day 22—July 10**

Sastrugi wind slab: Paul leads a pitch of the Coxcomb.

14,500 feet **Day 23—July 11**

Entering the high realm above Karstens Ridge. Mark breaking trail near Browne Tower, summit dome at far right.

15,000 feet

Camp VI: Mark's tent, Browne Tower, and the combined Muldrow and Traleika Glaciers—two vertical miles below.

15,000 feet

Dennis tending the outdoor kitchen at Camp VI.

Cook tent with frost liner—John and Dennis.

15,000 feet **Day 26—July 14** Anshel Schiff

Walt and John checking debris after
tent fire.

15,000 feet **Day 26—July 14**

Anshel assisting Walt with burned hand
—Steve and Howard in background.

15,400 feet   **Day 27—July 15**   Anshel Schiff

Above Camp VI on the Harper: Steve follows John.

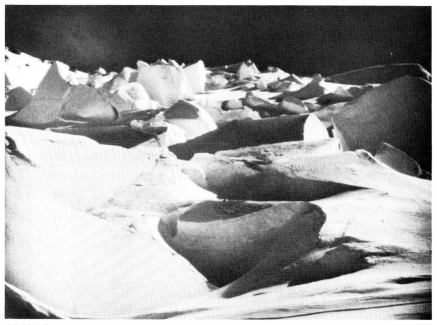

16,100 feet   Anshel Schiff

Wind polished seracs in the first icefall above Camp VI.

17,900 feet   **Day 27—July 15**   Howard Snyder

Camp VII: Joe gathers rope for summit climb. View down Harper, upper
icefall. Mount Mather upper right.

19,550 feet **Day 27—July 15**

From the ridge behind Archdeacon's Tower, view across the flat toward the summit ridge. Faintly visible at the right are the footprints and a plastic wand from a previous expedition. ▲

Day 27—July 15

◄ Joe on the summit—
Kansas State College pennant.

20,320 feet

Tragedy:

17,200 feet   **Day 40—July 28**   John Ireton

The unmarked Stubai ice axe found near the upper Harper icefall. ▲

The streamered pole and sleeping bag found 200 yards below Camp VII. ▶

17,800 feet   John Ireton

Day 40—July 28

17,900 feet   **Day 40—July 28**   John Ireton

The ruins of high camp: Mark's buried tent at left—the destroyed Logan tent at right—ice cliffs and Archdeacon's Tower above.

TRIBUTE

JERRY CLARK

HANK JANES

DENNIS LUCHTERHAND

MARK McLAUGHLIN

JOHN RUSSELL

STEVE TAYLOR

WALT TAYLOR

In climbing beyond the realm of mortality,

there is no disgrace in defeat.

In the winds of space,

there is no dishonor in death.

10
Epilogue

Being personally involved in tragic circumstances leaves an endless emptiness; yet, every day that a man wakes up, breathes and walks, life goes on. And so it was with me. The impact of an immensely unique experience gave way to the tasks of daily living.

After leaving Outward Bound in 1969, I began a restless teaching career, beginning first with a year at Ogden High School in Utah and Weber State College. Although I did little climbing, I did find time to discuss and promote outdoor education with state education officials and was an outdoor education consultant to the State of Utah Title I convention. The next year was spent teaching and coaching (cross-country and track) in Grandview, Washington where I privately incorporated the Denali Outdoor Academy.[1] However, there was impetus for only one mountaineering course in cooperation with the Grandview School District.

In the fall of 1971 Helen and I moved again, accepting positions to teach at McGrath, Alaska. Aside from its elaborate National Weather Service and Federal Aviation Administration facilities, McGrath is a modest village of about 300 people situated on the Kuskokwim River. The village was rather modern, yet isolated by a lack of roads. Conveniences we had long taken for granted were

---

1. Name later changed to: White Winds Outdoor Academy.

considered extravagant luxuries. Simplicity was the accepted mode of living.

The bush experience was both exhilarating and lonely. Helen and I quickly went native in our new environment, donning mukluks and parkas when fall came and the river froze. We butchered moose on the kitchen table and stocked our freezer for the winter. Snowmobiles were the popular means of transportation and recreation; however, we did not want to miss such an excellent opportunity to experience history, so we reverted to a sled and dog team.

Teaching in a bush school was quite hectic. Seven teachers conducted grades kindergarten through high school. At times I taught three different classes in the same room at the same time. To keep in shape and alleviate problems with my weak knees, I began a systematic jogging program of about ten miles per day and continued right through the winter. It got cold in McGrath, down to 65 below zero; although after 20 below, it was difficult to sense cooler differentiations of temperature. In the spring when it warmed up to zero, the weather really seemed balmy, and everyone ran around in their shirtsleeves.

After the spring flood and before the insects of summer, Helen and I left Alaska to spend the summer in the lower United States. We visited relatives, hiked across the Grand Canyon, and then joined Bill Daily and Bruce Knudson for a social climb of California's Mount Shasta. Helen, however, remained at the campground as she was expecting our first child in late fall. I also ran several marathon races during the summer and found the distance (twenty-six miles, three hundred and eighty five yards) a very taxing jog.

Helen and I did not return to McGrath, as we had transferred to Sand Point, a small fishing village at the near end of the Aleutian Islands. The climate was warmer than the Alaskan interior, yet it seemed much more remote—truly the end of the earth. The area is geologically very active; we could see the cone of a semi-active volcano, and earth tremors occasionally rattled the dishes in our cupboards.

These treeless islands are the birthplace of horrendous winds that often sweep across the Gulf of Alaska to lash Mount McKinley. The expected high winds did not disappoint us, and we learned to walk at an angle along the boardwalks. There must have been only a handful of days when the bay was free of whitecaps.

Teaching was as diverse as that encountered in McGrath. I was also employed in operating and maintaining a seismic station for the Lamont-Doherty Geological Observatory of Columbia University. I continued jogging and, as a dietary experiment, spent most of the year as a vegetarian.

Eventually the long autumn days of hiking the grassy bluffs and walking along the rocky beaches to watch the eagles soar down the cliffs and the gulls forage in the tide ended as we waited for the completion of Helen's pregnancy. Occasionally, there was the excitement of a few inches of snow, and almost daily there were the playful antics of a lone sea otter that frolicked in the kelp a few yards from our door.

Helen wanted me to be with her during childbirth, so I took leave of my job for a while and accompanied her to Anchorage. Earlier we had discussed the possibility of a home delivery, which would have been necessary had the baby come early, while we were still in Sand Point. After touring the sterile environment of the hospital and talking to a rather mechanical obstetrician, Helen became adamant that she wanted a home delivery. I was agreeable; however, it took a bit of persuasion to overcome the apprehensions of the friends we were staying with, Greg and Linda Brown. If something unpredictable did happen, we were only a short distance from the hospital. I began reading a stack of do-it-yourself childbirth books and kidded Helen that she couldn't go into labor until I had finished. I turned the last page at 11:00 PM on December 11 and immediately fell asleep. A few hours later, I was awakened by Helen—her labor had begun.

An elated euphoria filled the house as the Browns and I made the much planned preparations for the event. We felt confident, but were still sobered a little by doubt. What if something went wrong? Like most other people, we had long been conditioned to view childbirth as a mystery endured in muffled pain behind the swinging doors of a spotless delivery room and understood only in the low tones of masked physicians. Yet, admittedly, childbirth was older than the American Medical Association.

As the time grew closer, our nervousness was completely overshadowed by a calm feeling of responsibility. We functioned as a competent team, making Helen comfortable and maintaining her total concentration on the task before her. We were like fans at an athletic event, silently and strongly pulling for their chosen competitor. In a very real sense, this was an athletic event complete with sweat and fatigue, certainly more natural than the sedation and interruptions of a hospital delivery room. Helen responded beautifully, staying on top of each contraction with excellent control and precision breathing. Soon, I held in my hands a tiny being. Almost immediately a cry emitted, startling us with the realization that another person was present in the room. Our daughter, Amanda Jo, had arrived. Joyously, we burst into conversation and laughter. There was a round of well-deserved congratulations and a few phone calls to disbelieving relatives and friends.

Later I signed Mandy Jo's birth certificate as the "attending physician." Actually, I felt that I had done very little during the birth. Mother Nature would have proceeded had I not even been there. In retrospect, it seemed a glorious, yet simple, event and I felt privileged just to be allowed to participate. Society shields us too much, I think, from some of life's most precious experiences, and in particular has institutionalized the two most significant events in life: birth and death.

Helen and I returned to Sand Point where I resumed teaching, and she tended our child. When we later prepared to leave Alaska, it was with mixed emotions. There was the fulfillment of ending an adventure; yet an immense nostalgia tempted us to linger awhile longer in this last vast wilderness.

We next settled in the Pacific Northwest near Mount Rainier, and I began teaching courses at Renton Vocational Technical School, Green River Community College, Tacoma Community College, and Auburn High School. (John Russell was a graduate of Auburn High School.) I enjoyed several successful seasons as a track and cross-country coach at Auburn High School.

During December of 1974, Helen and I were expecting our second child and again decided to have a home delivery. We approached this birth in a much more relaxed manner. Early in the morning on the day after Christmas, we were blessed by the arrival of another precious daughter, Sarah Kasandria—much to the astonishment of her paternal grandmother who was visiting from Kansas. Few of life's joys can be compared to the birth of a child with its fresh renewal and promise of genetic immortality.

Unfortunately modern life allows us to reassess intimate feelings and needs continually and discourages the building of permanent commitments. Gradually my life was once again beset by domestic turmoil, and three years later, Helen and I were divorced. I continued teaching and have devoted the summers to parenting and casual climbing. Both daughters have taken an early interest in mountaineering. (They climbed more than halfway to the summit of Mount Rainier before Sarah had entered kindergarten.)

Over the years I have lost contact with most of the people involved in the 1967 tragedy. Anshel Schiff is still teaching at Purdue University and Howard Snyder, who has worked in various parts of Canada and Alaska, now works in Calgary. Howard occasionally climbs with Paul Schlichter. Paul and Jerry Lewis presumably still live in Colorado. Wayne Merry left the National Park Service in 1969 as a delayed consequence of the McKinley disaster. He lives at Atlin, British Columbia, and has recently completed the manuscript for a book on cold weather survival. Wayne also writes regularly for *Backpacker* magazine. Don Sheldon died of cancer in 1975, and George Hall is presently affiliated with the Alaska Historical Society.

The McKinley expedition seems like a long time ago now as it loses significance and relative importance among other life experiences. The only lingering reminders are impaired feeling and circulation in my toes. They are very sensitive to cold, and a damaged toenail takes more than a year to replace. I no longer harbor grudges or guilt toward the expedition actions of myself and others, for our errors were very much human. It is a milestone in my life to finally put the McKinley disaster to rest and turn toward the future.

Philosophically, I believe that a person's capacity to reason and experience was meant to be utilized fully. Too often in our society, wealth is preferred to knowledge, comfort to experience, and security to adventure. Yet knowledge is the most enduring wealth; comfort cannot be appreciated without a diversity of experience, occasionally reducing life to its simplest requirements; and adventure gives birth to the judgment and self-confidence of authentic security. True security resides in a person's faith in his own resourcefulness that no matter what comes, he will function to the best of his ability. A person who does not grab hold of life and squeeze out every ounce of living is forfeiting a part of his existence.

Perhaps the burning drive of the expedition mountaineer will rekindle within me. Recently the high Himalayas seem to possess a silent magnetism. I doubt that I would turn down an opportunity to climb Mount Everest. Or maybe I will build a quiet cabin on a parcel of forested land which I own near Mount Rainer. My personal running program has become rather intermittent. Occasional racing success has been largely due to the natural endurance of a high cardio-vascular efficiency with a heart rate as low as 28 beats per minute. Although I try to maintain my jogging program at a meditation level, a couple of credible goals still attract me: I would like to run 100 miles in a single day, and a total of 25,000 miles (the distance around the earth) in my lifetime.

Several years ago I acquired a forty-foot Chinese junk for some eventual ocean sailing—perhaps around the world. The reasons for such a voyage lack the intensity of an expedition and seem to be more for peace of mind than adventure. Methodically and progressively, however, preparations proceed with an occasional spark of genuine enthusiasm. Lately, I have spent a lot of time on the boat. There is a certain fascination in the rhythm of the tide, the morning mill-pond smoothness of the bay, the ballet of evening sails ghosting across the darkness of a forested ridge, and the beckoning of a scarlet sunset. The mountains and the sea are similar adversaries: each seductive in its charisma of speechless beauty; each luring the human spirit to match its unchained energy; each playing with the seeker, rewarding persistence with the aridness of undrinkable water, and caution with hidden storm. Nevertheless, each provides an element of inner truth—that essential quality of wisdom that must be earned.

I do not want to begin a voyage alone; perhaps I do not want to begin a voyage at all. And yet, as I feel the tide tug at my mooring, I can imagine a sparkling anchorage faraway where a boat can stay for a week or forever—someplace that I should be going to. As Jerry Clark's brother wrote after the tragedy: "A snug harbor is a safe place for a ship. . . but then, that's not what ships are made for."

Dr. Wolfgang Klemperer

When one has good wine,
A graceful junk
And a maiden's love,
Why envy the immortal gods?

Li T'si Po
(A.D. 705-762)

PART II: DOCUMENTATION

11
Birth of
an Expedition

The organization of the expedition as it occurred: a summary of expedition newsletters which I called M-forms,[1] a selection of pre-trip correspondence, and the written agreement with the Colorado McKinley Expedition.

M-1

November 16, 1966

TO: All members and alternates of
      Joseph F. Wilcox Mt. McKinley Expedition 1967

SUBJECT: State of the expedition at the present time (revisions will be mailed as they occur).

COST: $300.00 per person plus personal gear. The money will cover food and group gear for the expedition and transportation to and from Alaska. The first $100.00 is due on or before Dec. 1, 1966 (unless special arrangements are made with the leader). Other deposit dates will be supplied later. Revisions in necessary funds will be mailed if and when they occur.

---

1. "M" for "McKinley".

DATE: The expedition will officially begin with a two-day get acquainted workout on Mt. Rainier. (Every person will be expected to be in attendance unless arrangements are made with the leader.) The seminar will begin as soon after school as people are able to get to Washington. Members—please notify me as soon as possible of the earliest date after May 29 that you can be in Puyallup, Washington. After two days of workout, we will leave for Alaska. The entire expedition will take 5-6 weeks depending on the weather on the mountain.

MEMBERSHIP AND ORGANIZATION: The ten-man expedition will consist of two groups, a scientific group and a high climbing group. Dr. Millett, chairman of the BYU Geography Dept., is in the process of outlining some scientific experiments to be completed by the scientific group. This group will consist of approved interested climbers who would like to gain glacier experience possibly in preparation for future expeditions. This group will be responsible for supporting the high climbing group as high as the base of Karstens Ridge (11,100 feet) and for keeping the route open through the Lower and Great Icefalls. They will also operate the main base camp radio. This group will have about four members. The high climbing group will consist of ideally six climbers who have demonstrated superior climbing ability at high altitudes.

AIR SUPPORT: At present I am considering the possibility of an air-drop (or ski plane landing) at McGonagall Pass. This would shorten by about a week the time that would be spent transporting supplies across the McKinley River.

EQUIPMENT: Group equipment will be purchased by the leader. Financial statements will be mailed periodically to expedition members. After the expedition, the group equipment will be sold; and the profit, along with any money left in the account, will be distributed among the expedition members.

A detailed list of personal gear required will be supplied by December 20.

Joe Wilcox. . .

M-2

December 17, 1966
OFFICIAL PERSONAL EQUIPMENT LIST
Joseph F. Wilcox Mt. McKinley Expedition 1967

REQUIRED EQUIPMENT

1. SLEEPING BAG—1 down bag of *known* quality (at least 3 lbs. down fill).
2. SLEEPING BAG SHELL — 1 of water resistant material such as Reevair cloth with built-in insulating pad.
3. DOWN PARKA — 1 of *known* quality (fur-ruff recommended). (The Terray down parka does not offer desirable face protection and a wind-tunnel extension or fur-ruff will be required.)
4. WIND CLOTHES — 1 parka with wind-tunnel hood and 1 pair wind pants (Reevair cloth is highly recommended as wet weather will be encountered as high as 10,000 ft.). Wind clothes should *not* be water*PROOF*. If your wind clothes are not of Reevair cloth, a poncho must be taken or a raincoat for use at low elevations.
   NOTE: an adjustable strap attached to the wind-tunnel hoods affords desirable adjustment for fair weather. . .
5. UNDERWEAR — 1 suit fishnet, 1 suit cotton-wool combination or all-wool.
6. PANTS — one pair wool, 1 pair insulated (insulated underwear may be substituted for insulated outer pants).
7. WOOL SHIRT or SWEATER — 1 or 2.
8. HATS — 1 or 2 stocking caps and/or Balaclava plus face mask (49¢ at Co-op).[2]
9. MITTS — 1 pair leather or canvas with wool liners plus 1 pair down mitts (expedition model) with 2 pair nylon gloves for use inside mitts.
10. DOWN BOOTIES — 1 pair.
11. BOOTS — Lowa double boots or Korean boots or felt boots (boots must allow adequate toe room).
    NOTE: Korean boots should not be purchased from an army

---

2. Co-op is the old nickname for Recreational Equipment Incorporated.

surplus dealer as many of these boots are surplus because they have *failed* cold weather tests. Previous expeditions have had problems with Korean boots falling apart on the rough terrain between the road and McGonagall Pass. Climbers taking Korean boots will be required to take a second pair of boots to wear during the hike in. A patching kit will also be required.

High-top, two-buckle felt boots have been used quite successfully on McKinley above 10,000 feet. They are inexpensive (about $5 or $6) and can be purchased at most surplus stores (inspect them well before buying). They are as warm as Korean boots, have a stiff sole for a good crampon fit, and are much lighter than either the Korean or Lowa boots. Climbers taking felt boots must take a second pair of boots for low elevations. Two or three pairs of thick felt insoles will be required for use in the felt boots. Care must be taken not to wear felt boots and crampons without also wearing overboots (crampon rings will wear holes in bare felt rapidly).

12. CRAMPONS — of known quality. *Must fit boots.*
NOTE: Climbers taking felt boots must have crampons for *both* felt and low altitude boots.
13. OVERBOOTS — insulated overboots required regardless of boots being taken.
14. SOCKS — several pair of the combinations adequate for your personal needs.
15. TALCUM POWDER — 1 or 2 small containers.
16. SUN GOGGLES — 2 or 3 pair (1 pair with extra dark lenses). Ground glass or non-curved lenses are desirable for preventing eye strain.
17. ANTI-FOG CLOTH — 1 for use on goggles. . .
18. SUNBURN LOTION
19. OPAQUE SUNBURN CREAM — such as Glacier Cream or zinc oxide.
20. FIRST AID KIT
21. POCKET KNIFE
22. MAP — 1 topography map edited by Bradford Washburn. . . Cost is $2.00.
23. COMPASS
24. MATCHES — waterproof and plain in watertight container.
25. PERSONAL MESS GEAR — 1 cup, bowl, and spoon.

26. WATER BOTTLES — 2 quarts total volume (any denominations).
27. PACK — 1 heavy load type with adequate straps for lashing on extra gear. The quality of the pack is quite important as you will be carrying loads from 60-80 lbs. Expedition Cruiser or Expedition Kelty packs are highly recommended. If you would like to take another type pack, submit a request to me giving full details of the pack you wish to take. Top extension bar and bottom shelf bar are recommended attachments.
28. ICE AXE
29. PRUSSIK SLINGS — adequate for glacier travel (at least 3).
30. NYLON CORD — about 100' (for repairs and emergency uses).
31. NOTEBOOK AND PENCIL
32. HANDKERCHIEFS
33. WATERPROOF CARRYING BAGS—the importance of keeping gear dry cannot be over emphasized. More than one expedition has met a sad fate by underestimating this fact. Pack your gear as if anticipating getting your pack dunked in the McKinley River (more than a possibility).
34. INSECT REPELLENT
35. AVALANCHE CORDS — 1 red perlon 52' long with distance markers every 6' ($1.10 at Co-op).
36. SNOWSHOES — 1 pair trail or Alaskan trapper or other approved models (mending kit is required).
    If you do not have snowshoes and do not wish to buy any, they may be rented from several sources. Co-op rents the trail model for $2.50 a week.
37. SKI POLES — one pair (no skis will be allowed).
38. 1 ARTIFICIAL LIGHT—not much in demand at this time of year, but essential in case of emergency.
39. LIBERAL SUPPLY OF YOUR FAVORITE THROAT LOZENGES—for use while breathing high, cold, dry air. (Don't take this item lightly.)
40. THREE ALUMINUM CARABINERS
41. 1 ALUMINUM-NYLON RESCUE PULLEY
42. 1 ROLL OF ORANGE SURVEY FLAGGING
43. CHAP STICK or CAMPHOR ICE. . .

RECOMMENDED EQUIPMENT

1. Foam pad for use in addition to sleeping bag shell for extra warmth and comfort. (An air mattress is not recommended.)
2. Camera equipment
3. Candle lantern
4. Bad weather amusement (chess, checkers, cards, paperback books, etc.).
5. Mosquito head net
6. Plastic socks (especially for those taking water*proof* boots).
7. Hard hat—most serious mountaineering injuries, even on glaciers, are head injuries.
8. Tennis shoes — for wading in the McKinley River.
9. Athletic supporter. . .

M-3

December 17, 1966

TO: All members and alternates of Joseph F. Wilcox Mt. McKinley Expedition 1967

SUBJECT: State of the expedition

COST: $300.00 (no revision)
1st deposit $100.00 due on or before December 1, 1966
2nd deposit $100.00 due on or before March 1, 1967
3rd deposit $100.00 due on or before May 1, 1967

MEMBERSHIP: At present the expedition membership is complete with two alternates—you will receive an official list of expedition members by January 10, 1967.

DATE: The two-day workout on Mt. Rainier will begin at 6:00 AM, June 10, 1967, at the Paradise Ranger Station. (Eat breakfast before this time.) The expedition at McKinley Park will begin on June 15 or 16 and end about July 10-15 (depending on weather on the mountain). The expedition will disassemble at Puyallup, Wash., about July 15-20.

Those who can are encouraged to arrive before June 10 as I will be making several ascents of Rainier between Memorial Day and

June 10. (The two-day workout will not include a climb of the mountain.) I will try to arrange for some kind of lodging for those who come early.

EQUIPMENT: Form M-2 is intended to be a complete list of personal gear; however, small revisions may be added. Should you desire to deviate from the required list of equipment, you should make a written request and obtain written permission from the leader. . . Some equipment such as wind clothes, sleeping bag shell, overboots, down booties, etc., may be made by the climber at a considerable savings, but care should be taken to keep the quality high.

The recreation dept. at BYU has snowshoes which we could probably borrow; however, I am not sure that they are of good quality. I will test a few of them in January.

Several climbers have mentioned the possibility of taking skis, and being an avid skier myself I can understand their interest; however, considering the terrain and isolation of the climb, I have concluded that the glacier is no place for skis regardless of ability.

Slight changes in the required personal gear may be made for the scientific team since the weather they experience will be less severe. Although it is recommended that everyone meet the M-2 requirements, the following is a list of items which may not be required for the scientific support members:

6. Insulated pants or underwear
8. Face mask
9. Down mitts (Korean fur-back dacron mitt may be substituted if extra wool liners are taken for warmth).
13. Overboots need not be insulated.
39. Throat lozenges

Other changes must be approved.

AIR SUPPORT: I have received word from the park superintendent that in order to qualify for air support the expedition must be sponsored by a scientific institution, society foundation, or government agency. I have contacted several possible sources of backing, but have only received one reply so far. More on this later.

Should we not get air support, the nature of proposed research will be limited to that which can be done with very lightweight equipment (10-20 lbs.). . .

EQUIPMENT: If you have not already done so, send me a detailed list of the mountaineering gear you have now. I am particularly interested in gear which would fall into the "group" category which the expedition might rent.

AUTOBIOGRAPHY: In order to get everyone well acquainted before the expedition, I would like each person to write an autobiography (2-4 typewritten pages) and send 12 copies to me on or before February 1, 1967. Ditto copies are fine and each copy should have a snapshot attached (thirty for $1.50 variety are okay). I will combine the autobiographies with other information and send each climber a combined expedition autobiography.

The autobiographies need not be of thesis caliber, but very casual and sincere. They should contain such information as: age, weight, height, climbing experience, interests other than mountaineering, reasons for joining the expedition, marital status, vocation (or vocational plans), education, political views, philosophical views, interesting experiences, and any other information that would reflect your general background and personality.

FOOD: It is expected that members will be active in mountaineering this winter and spring (or at least active in skiing, snowshoeing, cold weather camping and other activities to gain additional experience and keep in good shape). In so doing, please sample a variety of freeze-dried and dehydrated foods. If you have particular likes which you wish to be included in expedition menus or particular dislikes you wish excluded, let me know before March 1. I am also interested in any recommendations you might have on group gear.

FINANCES: The first financial statement will be sent on about January 10. . .

Letter from Alaska Rescue Group.
January 9, 1967

Dear Mr. Wilcox,

A memorandum, dated November 16, 1966, and addressed to all members of the Joseph Wilcox Mount McKinley Expedition 1967, has been brought to the attention of the Alaska Rescue Group by Mr. Robert Goodwin of Anchorage, Alaska. From this memorandum we understand you have been in correspondence with the Mount McKinley National Park Service who perhaps by now have advised you of a Park Service requirement, that McKinley Expeditions should have the Alaska Rescue Group or another qualified group (subject to park approval) backing them up. We, therefore, have enclosed information on the Alaska Rescue Group in the event that you wish us to provide such a service. In any event we would be pleased to give you local assistance even if you do not require our services.

We can do the equipment check for you in Anchorage as we have the authorization from the park.

In regard to the air-drop the park can be quite adamant since it is a national ruling. If they do deny you the air-drop and if you plan to approach the mountain from Wonder Lake, horses can be used. For information on obtaining horses we suggest you write Ginny Wood, Box D, College, Alaska. Horses belonging to a friend of hers have been used in the park before. However, I do not know what the park policy is on horses.

Yours sincerely,

Marjorie Maagoe
Sec. & Treas.

Letter From American Geographical Society
January 10, 1967

Dear Mr. Wilcox:

I have gone to some length to see if it would be feasible for this society to provide the type of sponsorship which would meet the Park Service requirements for air support. Unfortunately, this is not possible at this time. Sponsorship is given only very occasionally and is almost always restricted to parties operating directly out of this society. The Board of Directors would have to give its approval and my information at this point is that they would not be willing to do so.

Please do not mistake this as indicating lack of interest. It is purely an organizational matter. We wish to encourage you in this endeavor and are very willing to assist in whatever way we can. . .

Sincerely yours,
William O. Field

M-4

January 21, 1967

PERSONNEL STATEMENT: Wilcox-McKinley Expedition 1967

Expedition Leader: Joseph F. Wilcox
Deputy Leader (Climbing Team): F. Jerry Clark
Deputy Leader (Scientific/Support Team): Anshel Schiff, PhD

PRE-EXPEDITION ORGANIZATION

Climbing Team	*Central Branch*
Malcolm B. Bourne	Daily
F. Jerry Clark	Taylor
Hank Janes	Wilcox
Dennis Luchterhand	*Northwest Branch*
Mark McLaughlin	Clark
Joseph F. Wilcox	Janes
	McLaughlin
Scientific/Support Team	*Eastern Branch*
William Dean Daily	Bourne
Anshel Schiff	Luchterhand
Stephen A. Taylor	Schiff
R. Steven Wunsch	Wunsch

. . .

M-5

January 21, 1967
FINANCIAL STATEMENT

EXPENSES. . . TOTAL TO DATE. . . $31.67
. . .
DEPOSITS. . . TOTAL TO DATE. . . $1000.00

M-6

January 21, 1967

TO: All members and alternates of the
    Wilcox-McKinley Expedition 1967

SUBJECT: State of the expedition

FINANCES: The first financial statement (M-5) is enclosed. Most expenses so far have been for secretarial supplies. I have approved expense accounts for Jerry Clark, who is investigating sources of radio equipment, and Malcolm Bourne, who is studying the possibility that a travel-lecture film could help finance the expedition (ex post facto). These accounts are conservative, covering correspondence materials, 5¢ / mile traveling, and other minor expenses. My wife, Cheryl, is acting as expedition secretary. . . The use of ditto carbons will result in a substantial savings over Xerox reproductions. Airmail communication on all expedition matters is necessary because the members are widely scattered geographically. A carbon copy of all expedition correspondence will be kept on file.

AIR SUPPORT: Because of the late date of organization of the scientific prospectus, it is not possible to obtain the type of sponsorship that would qualify the expedition for air support. There is a possibility that pack horses can be used. According to the Alaska Rescue Group, horses have been used on the north side before. I am checking with the Park Service about this possibility.

SCIENTIFIC EXPERIMENTS:[3] Proposed research includes a theodolite survey of flow and ablation rates on the Muldrow and Traleika Glaciers and the combined glaciers near McGonagall Pass. The establishment of survey and photographic stations which could be reoccupied in future years is also planned for the Harper Glacier just above the icefall at about 15,000 feet if time permits. (I understand this would be the first such work done on the Harper.) The experiments will be fully sanctioned by the American Geographical Society and the Foundation for Glacier Research.

---

3. Also planned but not listed here was Bill Daily's research on sodium glow in the atmosphere.

However, support will be limited to loan of equipment, film, and other small items.

EXPEDITION ORGANIZATION: (subject to revisions) The scientific group will spend 2-4 days establishing the necessary rods on the glaciers near McGonagall Pass and establishing a few photo stations. The climbing group, being several days ahead of the scientific group, will establish glacier rods on the Harper as soon as they reach that elevation. This will also serve as an acclimation period. When the scientific team arrives, they will acclimate for a few days while serving as a support team to the climbing team's summit assault. The climbing team, upon returning to the lower Harper, will support a summit assault by the scientific team. (Changes in personnel between the two groups may take place depending on acclimation rates.) The scientific team will resurvey the Harper, providing ten days have elapsed since the rods were set, while the climbing team descends the mountain. A resurvey of the lower area will be conducted by both groups.

EQUIPMENT: With the probability of everyone going high, the M-2 equipment list will be required of everyone. If you have not already done so, do not buy snowshoes for the expedition. Dennis Luchterhand has sent me some information on a new type of synthetic snowshoe called Snowtreads. They are made of polypropylene resins with nylon bindings and they weigh only 1 lb. each. The cost is $15 and they come with a 1 year replacement guarantee. I will contact the company regarding a possible discount for the expedition. On the second page of the M-2 form please add:

44. SIGNAL MIRROR
45. DAY-NIGHT FLARE
46. PLASTIC-COATED CARD OF STANDARD
    GROUND-TO-AIR SIGNALS

These three items will be furnished from group funds to each person at the start of the climb.

The purpose of the survey flagging (item #42) is for general marking in areas where wands should be conserved, such as a trail through a forested or bushy area. It also would be very helpful in laying out ground-to-air signals should an emergency arise.

Equipment recommendations: refer to M-2
18. Neo A-Fil with digalloyl tri-oleate
19. A-Fil sun cream with titanium dioxide

43. A-Fil sun stick

The A-Fil products have been highly recommended by previous expeditions (also by Jerry and Mark). Plastic tubes are considered better than metal ones. If you have problems getting crampons large enough to fit over all of your footgear, consider lengthening a pair by taking them apart in the middle and inserting a piece of metal. All arrangements must be thoroughly tested before the expedition.

For those who wear glasses, clip-on Kalichrome lenses by Bausch and Lomb are recommended for use during whiteouts. These lenses might be obtainable in sunglass or goggle form for those who don't wear glasses.

PRE-PLANNING: The Northwest Branch is working on wands and will most likely be making the expedition tents. Mark has made his own tent and the design and construction are very good.

The Central Branch will be doing the food packaging and all expedition correspondence.

The Eastern Branch is so spread out, it is unlikely that a cooperative effort can be made by that group. Malcolm is investigating movie possibilities. Dennis is testing the Snowtreads. He will check their effectiveness on steep slopes and possible alterations or attachments that could improve their traction.

We have connections for possible large discounts at Ski Hut in Berkeley, Alp Sport in Boulder, and Gerry in Boulder. Requests on personal gear discounts should be limited to that to be used on the expedition.

Jerry Clark works for a company that rents a long distance telephone line, and he can call anywhere in the far western states free of charge. This is a great help in communication between the Northwest and Central Branches.

Your recommendations and ideas on food and equipment are welcome. At present we are weighing the advantages and disadvantages of various kinds of stoves. Feel free to air your views. . .

FORMS:[4] M-87a . . . and M-87b. . . must be completed and returned to me by March 1, 1967 . . . Form M-87a should accurately reflect your experience and confidence in mountain-

---

4. Park Service forms: M-87a is a climbing experience form and M-87b is a medical form.

eering. If you are coming early (before June 10) to climb Mt. Rainier, include this as a *planned* climb on your M-87a form. . .

Jerry Clark is allergic to onions.

Letter from Steve Wunsch

Dear Joe,

I appreciate your offering me a position on the support team for the McKinley expedition next summer, but I'm afraid I'd better turn it down. This decision is not so much the result of having only made the support team, for I realize that the chances are now good that they will also reach the summit, but there have been some rather painful changes in my family situation since I applied for the climb, for which it would be better if my plans for next summer were more flexible. I'm sorry for the inconvenience I've caused you in getting the team together, and I wish you and the party all the luck in the world on the climb. I'm sorry I can't be with you.

Sincerely,

Steve Wunsch

January 31, 1967

Dear Expedition Member,

Enclosed is an agreement for the Alaska Rescue Group to act as the support party for our expedition. This form must be signed by every member of the expedition. . .

Sincerely,

Joseph F. Wilcox

Letter from Ginny Wood
February 4, 1967

Dear Joe:

Regarding your request for information about horses to be used to pack supplies to McGonagall Pass—

There is a packer located at Lignite, Alaska (this is on the Alaska Railroad about 20 miles north of the McKinley Park Station). Name: Berle Mercer. I have helped him pack climber's gear to the Muldrow at Oastler Pass just below McGonagall for a group climbing Deception, Tatum, and Brooks. You can write to him direct—Berle Mercer, Mercer Ranch, Lignite, Alaska. . .

Sincerely,

Ginny Hill Wood

Letter from Dennis Luchterhand
February 7, 1967

Dear Joe,

Got the Snowtreads for $6.50 plus postage. They're very cooperative and promptly responded when I mentioned I was testing them for a McK trip. I presume we could all get them for that rate if we let them advertise with our trip. We finally had snow, and this morning at −10°F I took the things out for a good test. The snowshoes are about 3/4 the surface area of the standard "bearpaw," but are more elongated. The binding is very handy, built with Kelty type fastener (the kind of buckle and strap Kelty uses for waist strap), and the snowshoes can be put on with heavily mittened hands. In deep powder snow, like all snowshoes they sink in a fair ways. On partially crusted deep snow (the kind I always associate with windblown mountain snow) they do beautifully and will well support my 175 lbs. plus heavy pack. Again like all snowshoes the traction for uphill work is poor, and I will experiment further with parachute cord and/or sisal and this problem should be licked. Surprisingly the traction is excellent for going downhill steeply forwards. On hard-packed sidewalks there is absolutely no traction, but again cord binding around the edges should solve this. I was raised on long trail model snowshoes and these have up-pointing toes like skis—Snowtreads are flat like bearpaws, and I caught a toe a couple times this morning and landed on my nose, but I imagine a little practice would give one a new set of habits—after all people have been using bearpaws for centuries. The "living hinge" is the only thing I have reservations about. You may have seen such a hinge on plastic card file boxes for 3″ x 5″ index cards in the bookstores. The hinge looks hardly thicker than heavy aluminum foil, and being ignorant about the new plastics I can only be very skeptical about their durability. I have a chemistry professor who says these hinges will take anything, and I gave them a good wrenching a couple times this morning with no ill effects at all—so maybe they're all they're claimed to be.

Perhaps you should get a pair (at the price you can't lose much!) and see what you think of the hinge. What is so bloody fabulous about the things is that they weigh nothing at all—by far the most enjoyable snowshoeing I've done in that respect. I also did some hopping around on boulders, again with no ill effects—at −10° no less. So except for the hinge I think they're ideal for our use. Perhaps we could get 2 extra pair for emergencies at the hinge (2 pair would allow for 4 breakages and I don't think we'd have that many). I'm very much for them.

With respect to snowshoeing in general on any type shoes: with a strap going around the heel to hold the foot forward, that strap tends to fall down under the heel when the foot is rammed forward as in going downhill (i.e. the entire return from the summit) on the snowshoes. You need a loop or an eye for that strap to go through at the back of the boot and this loop should be fastened securely to the boot. I will experiment with epoxy glue fastening loops to the back of my Korean and felt boots.

Used the Korean boots for the first time this morn also (they're marked as army rejects) and was just amazed by their insulation ability with one light pair of socks. Wore the felt ones 2 weeks ago, and with enough socks in to keep warm, the largest size made were almost too small for my size 14 feet. The combination of these Korean boots and the light Snowtreads; I did not get (for the first time in years) any rubbing (which has always led to blisters—even with the felt boots and trail snowshoes last week) across the toes where the front hold-down strap goes across to hold on the snowshoe.

So, my vote is for taking these Snowtreads for the trip, and also having a pair or two extra in case of hinge failure. Somebody else ought to give them a try before we take any on the trip though; maybe others can find other bigger flaws.

Dennis. . .

M-7

February 12, 1967

TO: All members and alternates of
    Wilcox-McKinley Expedition 1967

PERSONNEL: Steve Wunsch has dropped from the expedition. . . This leaves the expedition with 9 active members. . . Should you know of someone qualified to fill the vacancy on the scientific/support team have him contact me immediately. . . By March 1 we will be making formal application to McKinley Park and ARG: the membership will be frozen at this time. . .

FOOD: I have negotiated a 20 percent discount on packaged freeze-dried and dehydrated foods with Perma-Pak in Salt Lake. We can also get some things in bulk rate which amounts to about a 75 percent discount.

HORSES: The park has approved the use of pack horses and I have written to the packer. The cost may be high, but it will be a great advantage to get the gear into McGonagall Pass. . .

SNOWTREADS: Dennis has inspected and tested the Snowtreads with favorable results (a copy of his letter is enclosed). We can get them for $6.50 a pair plus postage for the expedition. You can order them from:

Sportsman Products Inc. . .

Be sure to specify what expedition they are for. Those of you who have trail snowshoes (large model), please let me know as we will need to take a couple pair along for breaking trail in deep powder. I am ordering 2 pairs of Snowtreads to serve as spares for the expedition.

EQUIPMENT: Requests for discounts from Gerry or Alpine Hut should be directed to Hank Janes. These must be a combined order with March 15 being the deadline. Mark has negotiated a 10 percent group-wise discount with Holubar; March 15 is the deadline for contacting Mark. Requests for Ski Hut and Alp Sport discounts should be directed to Dwight Cotton (March 15 deadline). Kelty has agreed to add a large back pocket to any Kelty pack going on the expedition. The pocket is larger than the one on the expedition model and will cost about $5. If interested, contact

Jerry Clark before March 15. (I am still highly recommending expedition model packs.)

Those of you who plan to take Lowa boots should consider the advantages of a second pair of inner boots or boots to wear at the wet lower elevations. Most problems with Lowas have been loss of insulation due to dampness.

WHEELER PEAK: We had a great time in Nevada during semester break—I have enclosed a report of the trip. While the conditions may seem (and perhaps are) exaggerated, it would be very difficult to convince us that the report is not factual. The climb was good "weather" training for McKinley. . . even got a little frostbite. We have received an undue amount of publicity including a TV interview.

RADIO: We will most likely be using citizens band walkie-talkies for intercamp communication. Should you know where any such units can be borrowed or rented, please notify Jerry Clark as soon as possible. (Include make, model, and channel.)

Joe

Letter from Jerry Clark
February 15, 1967

Dear Joe,

. . . Re: Stoves. Optimus looks like the best so far, particularly if we can end up with a lighter case for the beast. At least for base camp we might profitably use the 2 burner model since we could be getting 2 burners on one heavy tank—The 2 burner model is described on the instruction sheet with the stove I sent you yesterday.

Re: boots. It looks like Korean thermals might be better, weight-wise, than I had thought. I think it should be possible to glue leather strips on the boots to protect them from wear by snowshoe/crampon straps. Pliobond cement (like we're using to fasten the wand flags) would probably do the job. One problem I've encountered with thermals in the past is that they tend to rub a lot at the tops; I'll work on that, particularly if I decide to take thermals.

Do you have any specs on the felt boots yet? I saw a model

which looked like an improvement over the ones I'd used about 10 years ago last month. I wonder how much they weigh, for instance. These could probably be reinforced with leather, too. Do you know of any with a sole which isn't flat?

Re: crampons. We're considering making crampons less hard on boots by coating the parts in contact with boot sides with the soft polyethylene material used for dipping handles on tools. Also thinking of ways to take up extra side room when a large pair of crampons is used on smaller boots. Hopefully, we can end up with 1 pair of crampons which will fit lower altitude boots well and also fit high altitude boots. . .

Jerry Clark

Letter to Jerry Clark from Anshel Schiff

I have received your card and assume my package crossed in the mail. I would like to have more poop on route, number of camps above base, and tentage. I seem to recall your mentioning use of 4, 2-man tents. I take a rather dim view of this approach; it would prove inflexible at best and disastrous at worst. I would assume that high altitude work would be done by 2-man ropes. This would require scheduling beyond what I think is possible. It leaves little room for miscalculation. I do not think that I would look forward to spending 2 or more days with 4 people in a 2-man tent sitting out some bad weather. I would suggest at least one commercial 2-man tent (reasonably sure that it would not be blown apart) and a homemade 2-man tent. The one I had in mind would be about 5-1/2 lbs. with poles. This would provide flexibility and should it go with 4 people in camp, the commercial tent could still hold 4 in a pinch. As far as my choice, 4-man McKinley Ski Hut with discount sounds good for intermediate camps. Co-op Mt. McKinley is fairly light. While I do not like the thought of the smell, oiliness, and priming problems of a kerosene stove, the added safety from fire and toxic fumes may be worthwhile.

As for boots, I think the statistics speak for themselves. From Park Service bulletin, 0% Milt. Kor., 33% "Civilian" Kor., 7% with insulated double boots were frostbitten and hospitalized! (I would like to know what a "Civilian" Korean Boot is. Does it include rejected Milt. Kor.?)

Looking for word on Mark's tent pattern?

Anshel

Letter from Dennis Luchterhand
February 17, 1967

Dear Joe,

Being a *purist* I'm much against horses being taken on our trip at any point!! — especially if it's going to raise the cost. THEY SMELL!!

. . . Your climb sounds neater than Hell!

. . . If it helps in your car planning in any way, I am fairly sure I will want to stay in Alaska after the trip and come back to the lower 48 on my own steam (i.e. hitch-hike).

Things sound real thumbs-up!! Every so often I get so excited about the trip I just quit work on my thesis for a day!!. . .

Dennis Luchterhand

(I wrote Dennis a lightly humorous letter explaining the need for Sherpas on Everest and horses on McKinley. Also explained that a real purist would not use automobiles and roads.)

Letter from Berle Mercer
February 19, 1967

Dear Joe:

Thank you for your letter of February 7.

Present schedules of mine for the coming season will permit me to pack your gear leaving Wonder Lake on June 16. I would expect to arrive at Camp Denali, just out of the park north of Wonder Lake, on the afternoon of the 14th or early the morning of the 15th. If you have your gear there by the afternoon of the 15th, that will allow it to be partially sorted and grouped for faster packing and an earlier getaway on the morning of the 16th.

The snowfall has been very heavy this winter; however, I do believe that we can get your gear at least as far as the fork of Cache

Creek where one branch goes to Oastler Pass and the other to McGonagall Pass. The trip in could vary from 1-1/2 to 3 days depending upon snow conditions in the deep ravines causing paths to be shoveled for the horses or wide detours. I feel by then not many such conditions will exist.

As to price, it will be 30¢ (thirty cents) per pound for the gear of yours that we pack in on horses. . . I will greatly appreciate anything you can do to help get other packing lined up for me while in the Wonder Lake area. I will not pack for any climber earlier than the dates I have quoted for you.

Either a 50% of the total anticipated charge or $150 deposit is required to reserve dates. . .

Sincerely yours.

Berle E. Mercer

Letter to Park Service
February 20, 1967

Dear Sir:

Thank you for your recent letter concerning pack horses. . . Has anyone ever stayed overnight on the summit? If so could you supply me with names and addresses? I would like to contact them concerning specific problems they might have had.

Upon transporting a large quantity of expedition food through Canada, will we be required to pay a duty?

Sincerely,

Joseph F. Wilcox

Note from Dennis Luchterhand

Joe—

Thanks for the funny letter on mountaineering purity!! (Horses) and up with Sherpas!!! I hadn't worked on that aspect—the Himalayan expeditions would never work without them (Sherpas). So now you've destroyed a night's sleep—and it would be the night before I leave to start walking out to meet you guys!!

Dennis. . .

Letter from Malcolm Bourne
February 23, 1967

Dear Joe,

. . .I haven't done as much skiing as I would like but have gotten in some ice diving for National Geographic, snowmobiling, and a little hiking in the snow. I am now starting a conditioning program so should be able to run all over McKinley by June.

Several things are in the air so please excuse the delay in expedition info from me.

Equipment and clothes seem to be out of the renting market so large purchase orders will have to be sent in a few weeks.

The freeze-dried bacon bars are very good and the meat bars the most unpalatable dog food on the market (even cavers can't eat them). We have tried all the foods that Gerry sells and have found them all good with the exception of the meat bar.

Ken Williams, my roommate, is planning on making a 35MM film of Alaska this summer covering 8^+ months on the winter, summer, and hunting aspects of Alaska. The film will also have underwater shots and he wants me to film part of the climbing expedition in 35MM for inclusion in this big film. He plans on air-dropping film to me on the expedition (assuming everything materializes) so this may be a sideline to take advantage of if it goes. He has collected most of the crew and funds for this filming expedition at present and the prospects look good. . .

Malcolm

Letter from Mark McLaughlin
February 27, 1967

Dear Joe,

As you know, Jerry is in Mass. for 3 weeks, so I have lost the use of the phone. This letter is to tell you that of the 4 people that we told of the trip (with the thought of them joining) 2 have responded in the affirmative. John Porter and John Russell. They will both write to you soon, very soon, so that if you want 2 more members for this expedition, it is possible. John P. is president of the University of O Alpine Club and John R. is a freshman, but he is, I think, 23. Anyway, they both think they can raise the long green, soon, and both have read my information which you have sent out. You will hear more from them soon.

My medical will be late. I apologize, I forgot to get an appointment to have it done; soon, maybe not today, but soon!!

I have trail snowshoes, a gift from another friend who couldn't go, and after watching 130 pounds of Mary Holland break up Hank's Snowtreads, I think that I will take the heavy old wooden long, but! reliable trail snowshoes. Jerry isn't happy with the Snowtreads, and neither is Hank. How on skis? Have not received my tent poles from the Apline Gut [Hut] yet but soon, maybe not today, but soon!! Am planning to push back the Holubar order until about the end of March. Anshel has already sent in his request for Holubar stuff.

Such is about all from the
M2 faction of the Northwest (and still Growing) faction
of the J.F.W. 67 Mt. McK. Expd. & S.S.

Letter from McKinley Park
February 27, 1967

Dear Mr. Wilcox:

In 1960, members of the Meiji University Alaska Expedition spent the night of May 14 on the summit of Mount McKinley. The temperature at that time was –35°F. The leader of that expedition was:

Takeichi Katano. . .

Dr. Bradford Washburn may also have spent a night on the summit during one of his extended trips on the mountain. His address may be found in our M-87 information sheet, which you have.

Problems involved in spending the night on the summit should differ from normal high altitude camping problems only in intensity. There is adequate room on top, but no shelter from winds unless snow conditions allow you to dig in; an arduous process at that altitude. Temperatures will undoubtedly be low. It will probably be very hard to get much sleep even if the weather is perfect, as the physiological effects of altitude are usually severe. Generally, we would advise against spending the night on the summit unless the weather is perfect and a forecast obtained by radio is favorable.

You had better contact Canadian Customs directly for information on bringing large stocks of expedition rations through the country.

I would suggest that you submit your individual application forms as early as possible, so that if any members are not deemed qualified for the summit party, their commitment will not have been so great and personnel adjustments may be more easily made.

Thanks for the miscellaneous information you sent along. We enjoyed it.

Sincerely yours,

Wayne P. Merry
Acting Chief Ranger

Note from Dennis Luchterhand

Joe—

Jerry Clark wrote me a brief note: "We tried and broke Snowtreads—" and says no more about it. Hope he wrote you more than that—we should decide before everyone buys them if we want them on Mac. Hope all is going well—they are here.

Dennis Luchterhand

Letter from Alaska Rescue Group
February 28, 1967

Dear Mr. Wilcox,

We are glad to hear that the park approved the horses.

Just wanted to let you know that the Winter Mt. McKinley Expedition is using Snowtreads and we can let you know how they worked for them when they get back to Anchorage. They are presently waiting good weather for the final climb to the summit and I believe they are camped about the 17,000 foot level.

Yours sincerely,

Mrs. Marjorie Maagoe
Sec. ARG

Letters from Anshel Schiff

Dear Joe,

Communication with Clark and Mark indicates their disappointment with Snowtreads. They are talking of Snowtreads and skis. My own view is regular snowshoes if Snowtreads prove inadequate. . .

I understand that I am going to get stove and picket problems. I think I should be able to resolve weight of stove. I am not sure what picket problem is. . .

Anshel

March 6, 1967

Dear Joe,

. . . I still do not have boots. I would like Korean. I will have to hold off on crampons until I get boots. What do you think about holding off on crampons until I get out to Washington? Fitting through mail seems to be more trouble than it is worth.

I do not have snowshoes yet. It seems that Snowtreads have come into disfavor. I would prefer not buying a pair of [snow] shoes.

I have not been able to find pair of goggles with flat lenses. If you know of something locally, you might get me a pair with a couple sets of lenses.

When do you anticipate that I will get these things? I hope to make several things and would like stuff by mid-April or sooner.

Anshel

P.S. Still do not have stove. How many stoves will have to be modified?

Dear Joe,

Received your letter and have more questions. I am also sending a copy of this to Clark for his comments. . .

Pickets: Design specification "sturdy design" leaves something to be desired. I realize that you probably cannot be more specific. I will give you some of my thoughts and would be interested in your comments. . .

¼" Goldline. The "fixed" line of this stuff would be like a rubberband—strong but springy. This would not provide the handrail that is required. If one does fall, it would be limited if he could hang on or if he was clipped in but it would provide no support to regain balance. For this job, strength is not that important nor is energy absorbing ability. I think other types of rope would be better and cheaper. . .

Picket must be strong enough to be driven into ground.[5] And they must not "cut" their way out of slope. This would be a function of the snow. Hard snow would require a strong picket for driving but it would not cut out. Soft snow could be put in easily but it would require a large projected area so that it would not pull out sideways. . .

I have some ideas for stove but I will need to have stove to see if they will work. Sample of material is enclosed. . .

A few questions on equipment. . .

Korean boots: do you know where I can get a pair of 11w? How many pairs of stockings are usually worn with this type boot? How do you identify real Milt. Korean? I have seen two pair locally, one with air valves and the other without. . .

Insulated overboots: Are these used with Korean type boots? Should they breathe or be waterproof?

Anshel

M-8

March 7, 1967
WILCOX-MCKINLEY EXPEDITION 1967 — MENUS

While the menus are reasonably specific, they are not final. What we eventually take with us will be governed by the availability

---

5. On mountains, snow and glacier surfaces are sometimes referred to as "ground."

of individual items and your reactions to these sheets. There will be no changes once we pack the food. If you dislike something or would like to see something added, please make suggestions as soon as possible.

For calorie and food references I have used the menu list for the 1964 Mountaineer McKinley Expedition, log of Swarthmore Denali Trip—1966, the appendix of *Freedom of the Hills,* [6] and the *Better Homes and Gardens Cook Book.* Dr. Paul Sondrup has checked the menus for general balance and overall calorie content. The menus have more solid and bulky foods than most expeditions. This should be a contributing factor in group morale and keeping regular. The liquid content will be over 1 gallon per day.

The quantities are listed for one man. The average weight of each man-day of food will be 37.7 ounces [7] (about 2⅓ pounds). Average calories per man-day is 4505, 119 cal/oz.

The meals will be packed in 2-man-day bags allowing considerable flexability of menus within one day. No exchanges between day bags should be made. Each bag will be labeled as to what menus are enclosed and where not indicated by menus specific flavors will be listed. Cooking instructions will be on individual items. Saccharin Kool-Aid serves no useful purpose; it is just a weightless way to kill snowmelt taste.

Among food items that were vetoed for general use as a result of allergies or extreme dislikes are:

onions
Tang
leeks
garlic   No one seems to like all flavors of Instant
pineapple   Breakfast, and there is no flavor that
coconut   everyone likes. All flavors will be used and
pemmican   people should avoid taking a day bag with a
meat bar   flavor they dislike or else they can trade with
bananas   someone.
Kippers
raisins

---

6. Complete title: *Mountaineering • Freedom of the Hills.*
7. Nearly all measures are in dehydrated form.

Both groups (scientific and climbing) will have a food bag with salt, pepper, catsup, Tang, onion flakes, Kippers, raisins, soups, cooking oil (for fried foods), etc.

The amount of coffee, Pream, teas, and Postum packed will depend on how many people express an interest in having it and how frequently. In making out the menu, I realize the impossibility of satisfying everyone, yet there must be a certain amount of standardization of menus.

BREAKFAST

Average weight 13.0 oz.   Average calories 1492   Cal/oz. 115

BREAKFAST A	CALORIES	OUNCES
Carnation Instant Breakfast		
with instant whole milk	280	2.5
Logan Bread	500	4.0
honey-peanut butter	180	1.2
applesauce with cinnamon	195	2.0
Wyler's lemonade (1 qt.)	220	2.0
½ Wilson Bacon Bar	300	1.5
(vitamin & mineral pill)	---	---
Total	1675	13.2
BREAKFAST B		
Instant Breakfast with milk	280	2.5
strawberries ½ cup sweetened	120	1.5
fruit cake (1 piece)	330	3.0
grape drink (1 qt.)	220	2.0
honey-peanut butter	180	1.2
½ pack Knorr soup	100	1.0
bacon chips	300	1.5
(vitamin & mineral pill)	---	---
Total	1530	12.7
BREAKFAST C		
Instant Breakfast with milk	280	2.5
dry cereal (wheat)	350	4.0
½ cup milk	75	.7
sugar	157	1.7
strawberries ½ cup	30	.5
bacon chips	300	1.5
(vitamin & mineral pill)	---	---

		CALORIES	OUNCES
fruit punch (1 qt.)		220	2.0
	Total	1412	12.9
BREAKFAST D			
Instant Breakfast with milk		280	2.5
½ Star Lite Ranch Style Breakfast:			5.5
egg		110	
pork sausage		100	
fried potatoes		200	
fruit cake		330	3.0
honey-peanut butter		180	1.2
raspberry drink (1 qt.)		220	2.0
(vitamin & mineral pill)		---	---
	Total	1420	14.2
BREAKFAST E			
Instant Breakfast with milk		280	2.5
Jell-O (hot or cold)		160	1.5
fruit cocktail (½ cup)		100	1.0
½ cup milk		75	.7
½ Wilson Bacon Bar		300	1.5
oatmeal		220	2.0
sugar		67	.6
lemonade (1 qt.)		220	2.0
(vitamin & mineral pill)		---	---
	Total	1422	11.8

LUNCH

Average weight 9.7 oz.	**Average calories 1288**	Cal/oz. 133

LUNCH A		CALORIES	OUNCES
candy bar(s)		300	2.2
Triscuits		375	3.0
peanut butter cups		250	2.0
cheese		200	2.0
cashews		180	1.0
saccharin Kool-Aid (2 qt.)		---	---
vitamin C pill (500 mg)		---	---
	Total	1305	10.2
LUNCH B			
fudge		500	4.0
potato chips (probably crushed)		200	1.2

		CALORIES	OUNCES
saccharin Kool-Aid (2 qt.)		---	---
vitamin C pill (500 mg)		---	---
cheese		200	2.0
pecans		180	1.0
cookies		190	1.5
	Total	1270	9.7
LUNCH C			
fudge		500	4.0
Cheez-Its		275	2.2
saccharin Kool-Aid (2 qt.)		---	---
Life Savers		150	1.0
peanuts		180	1.0
cookies		190	1.5
vitamin C pill (500 mg)		---	---
	Total	1295	9.7
LUNCH D			
fudge		500	4.0
Puffed Wheat Nuts (or Corn Nuts)		150	1.0
mixed nuts		230	1.3
Life Savers		150	1.0
peanut butter cups		250	2.0
saccharin Kool-Aid (2 qt.)		---	---
vitamin C pill (500 mg)		---	---
	Total	1280	9.3

DINNER

Average weight 15.0 oz.   Average calories 1725   Cal/oz. 115

DINNER A		CALORIES	OUNCES
beef steak (Star Lite)		320	3.0
½ cup peas		60	.5
macaroni and cheese		437	4.25
grape Jell-O		160	1.5
Bacon Thins		175	1.5
lemonade (1 qt.)		220	2.0
cocoa (Swiss Miss) with milk		220	2.0
nuts		180	1.0
bouillon cube		---	---
	Total	1772	15.75

DINNER B	CALORIES	OUNCES
gravy and sliced beef	300	2.5
Triscuits	313	2.5
mashed potatoes (instant)	200	2.0
margarine	208	1.0
cherry drink (1 qt.)	220	2.0
sliced peaches	200	2.0
cocoa	220	2.0
jam	82	.5
bouillon cube	---	---
Total	1743	14.5
DINNER C		
tuna	250	3.5
½ cup corn	85	.5
rice with bouillon	200	2.0
strawberry Jell-O	160	1.5
Fruit Galaxy	100	1.0
grape drink (1 qt.)	220	2.0
Logan Bread	500	4.0
margarine	104	.5
bouillon cube	---	---
fudge	125	1.0
Total	1744	16.0
DINNER D		
chili with beans	600	5.5
Triscuits	375	3.0
hamburger	210	2.0
instant pudding (choc.)	230	2.0
lemonade (1 qt.)	220	2.0
tomato crystals	50	.5
bouillon cube	---	---
Total	1685	15.0
DINNER E		
½ Chicken Stew Dinner	550	5.0
½ cup green beans	75	.5
strawberry drink (1 qt.)	220	2.0
Triscuits	313	2.5
fruit punch Jell-O	160	1.5
fudge	188	1.5
honey-peanut butter	180	1.2

		CALORIES	OUNCES
bouillon cube		---	---
	Total	1686	14.2
DINNER F			
½ Beef Stew Dinner		600	5.5
½ cup peas		60	.5
mashed potatoes (instant)		200	2.0
Yukon Biscuits		300	2.5
drink (1 qt.)		220	2.0
Jell-O		160	1.5
margarine		208	1.0
bouillon cube		---	---
	Total	1748	15.0
DINNER G			
½ Star Lite Pork Chop Dinner			5.0
2 pork chops		250	
fried potatoes		200	
applesauce		150	
salad blend (contains onions)		30	.5
drink (1 qt.)		220	2.0
instant pudding (butterscotch)		230	2.0
cocoa		220	2.0
nuts		180	1.0
fruit cake		220	2.0
bouillon cube		---	---
	Total	1700	14.5

M-9

March 8, 1967

WILCOX-MCKINLEY EXPEDITION

DEADLINE: The deadline for submitting equipment requests to the various people has been extended to APRIL 1. This is so that group gear can be included in the orders.

FOOD: A preliminary menu is enclosed (M-8). Food costs will amount to about $1200.00 for six weeks or about $1000.00 for five weeks.

HORSES: I am very much in favor of using horses and will contract them unless I receive a great amount of objection from the majority of the members. The cost will be 30¢/lb. to pack gear into

McGonagall. This will shorten the expedition to 5 weeks, requiring $200 less in food. If we contract 1200 pounds leaving each of us with about 50 pound packs, it would cost $360. (Only $160 "excess cost" considering the food savings.) Horses will also enable the two groups to be organized in a desirable way for activities on the mountain.

TENTS: A decision on the tents will be made on about March 20. I have been checking into commercial tents, and it appears that with a moderate discount, we can buy tents as cheaply as we can make them. Tents which impress me at the present time are the Alpine Hut Logan, Gerry Himalayan, and Alpine Hut Mountaineer. Should we buy tents, the cost would be about $450 for a Logan, Gerry, and two Mountaineers. The scientific team would use a Logan and Mark's tent. The climbing team would use a Gerry and two Mountaineer tents which could be connected into one long tent. . .

SNOWTREADS: I have tried the Snowtreads and am favorably impressed. They were excellent under a 280-pound load, 185 pounds of me with a 95-pound pack (a Kelty full of sand). An engineering friend and I managed to break a pair by applying 4,000 inch-pounds of torque for 1 minute to the binding in its most vulnerable position. (Larger torques for shorter periods of time caused no adverse effects.) The break occurred above the hinge. The hinge didn't exhibit stress marks. It is unlikely that such a stress would result from normal use. By wearing a Snowtread on one foot and a trail snowshoe on the other, I was able to make a good comparison. The Snowtreads, being smaller, sank in more, but their light weight, better traction, and much greater agility compensated for this fact. I feel that they are superior to other types of snowshoes in everything but deep powder. I do not anticipate a great amount of deep powder on McKinley, but plan to construct an aluminum mesh attachment which will make them more effective for such conditions.

In testing the Snowtreads, three of us purposely tried to tear them up—heavy packs, climbing trees, jumping on boulders from as high as 6 feet, etc., with no luck. Such conditions would have ruined a pair of wooden snowshoes. I can confidently say that their **general design and construction is excellent; however, being** molded, weak points may be present. Jerry, Mark, and Hank are somewhat disillusioned by the fact that a 130-pound girl broke a pair in Oregon, and they do not recommend them. I do recommend them, but strongly suggest that all pairs to go on the trip be tested rigorously for possible flaws. It cannot be overemphasized that snowshoes are part of the "personal" gear and everyone has their own ideas as to what constitutes a good pair. My discussion of Snowtreads is meant to be enlightening but not compelling. I do urge everyone to try a pair before making a decision as to what they will take.

TRANSPORTATION: Present plans are to take two cars and one trailer to Alaska. I plan to take my car, a 1954 Ford (not much to look at, but mechanically sound). I have not yet lined up a second car. If you have a car which you would consider taking, please let me know. My current thinking is to allow $50 general wear and tear on each car (to be paid at the end of the expedition) plus one-half of the repair expenses to be paid by the expedition. . . All gas and oil costs will come out of expedition funds. An extra $25 allowance will be given to my car since I will be pulling the trailer and transporting most of the expedition food and gear from Utah. If you would like to use your car, it must be in excellent condition at the beginning of the trip including very good tires and spare, complete tune-up and inspection, etc. The Alcan, although long, is not as bad as legend makes it so there shouldn't be any over-concern about taking one's car.

PERSONNEL: Bill Daily has a lung condition and has dropped out of the expedition. . . The vacant positions on the support team have been filled by:

Walter W. Taylor. . .   John Russell. . .

Bloomington, Indiana. . .   Eugene, Oregon. . .

Letter from Walt Taylor

Joe,

Enjoyed reading your Wheeler Peak ascent. Thanks for sending the clippings. I've enclosed the climbing experience forms. The medical forms are being delayed by some minor lab tests.

re: probable arrival date at Mt. Rainier.

I have a final exam scheduled for the afternoon of June 6.
I'll try to get an earlier time.

re: possible group equipment.
. . .
I also have access to Boyd Everett's *The Organization of an Alaskan Expedition* which was written for a seminar at the Harvard Mountaineering Club. It's quite detailed, well written, and enlighteningly opinionated. Perhaps you're already familiar with it. If not, I could probably send it out or write you his opinions of specific problems. . .

Walt Taylor

P.S. Is Dwight Cotton still handling the Ski Hut discount requests?

Note from Anshel Schiff

Dear Joe,
. . . I have a Kelty frame and a bag that I have made. It is same size as regular Kelty bag (not expedition). However, I am adding extra pockets. I think it is well constructed and should be adequate. Clark has seen it and you can get his opinion.

I have often heard it suggested that a small wisk broom is good for removing snow before entering tent; I did not see it mentioned on your list.

Anshel

Note from Malcolm Bourne

Dear Joe,
Sorry for the delay in getting this information to you. I am at present fighting to be able to go on the expedition with my boss, school, and the army. I should know the final outcome within two weeks.

On filming costs, this is how they break down for a 35 and a 40 minute 16MM films and how to figure costs: . . .

Malcolm B. Bourne

Letter from Anshel Schiff

Boo

I have received letters from both Joe and Jerry. I will condense and make comments on each. I am enclosing a copy of Joe's letter to Jerry. In that Jerry's letter was 9 pages I am afraid Joe, you will have to figure out Jerry's questions from my answers. I hope no one feels slighted with this method of reply. . .

If you are taking 2500′ of fixed line, 15 pickets would seem to be too few to me. 20 pickets seems too few to me!. . .

Notching bottom of picket would improve holding power. This could be extended to give some barb action. If there is sufficient snow to require removal and resetting of picket, barbs may be more trouble than they improve safety. . .

Sectioned pickets would provide another spot that could cause trouble. I think a couple different size pickets could be taken.

I would be in favor of a driving tool. It could also be used to drive OUT pickets. . .

Spring vacation starts March 25 and ends April 3 (7:30). Looks like I will be going on Appalachian trip. This will probably be a good start for getting in shape. . .

I think some of these things can be tried in Washington and dumped if they do not work. I do not know what type of shop facilities are available for making modifications. . .

Anshel

Note from Hank Janes

Dear Joe,

Here is the scoop on Alpine Hut:. . . the manager of the Portland store talked to his boss in Seattle about the possibility of us testing their Logan tent. The boss says they have already been tested on four expeditions (including the recent one to the Antarctic)—so to make it short, his answer was no. They will rent Logans to us for $60 or sell us the tent with frost liner at $200, less 20% . . .

Hank

Note from Dennis Luchterhand

Joe—

M-8 and M-9 look good. Re: menus—*all* sound very good. I'd like to see more Logan Bread—the stuff's a good lift—maybe a bunch in each group's food bag with the salt, pepper, Tang—Things are going well.

Dennis L.

Letters from Jerry Clark

Joe—

. . . Still no good leads on Mark's old girl friend lost in Baja California. That's become almost a tragedy of stupid errors. It's unbelievable! Not only didn't they tell anyone exactly what their plans were—a search party helicopter landed on the summit found an undated entry with no additional information there either. They haven't been seen since February 5. It's hard to stay optimistic when 65-100 searchers can't seem to turn up much. Mark's not particularly a happy guy. . .

If you haven't been to Boston yet, don't bother. I think it's more exasperating than Chicago to drive through! Bet it's exciting living here—one could be lost hundreds of ways just going between two familiar places! Lots of historical stuff around though.

Smile!

Jerry

March 13, 1967

Dear Joe,

Re: Skis. Anshel (at least up until Jan.) hasn't used climbing skis or done any ski mountaineering. I'm 99.99% sure his opinion of ski mountaineering is purely intuitive. Would appreciate your checking local ski mountaineers. . . I'd. . . like to get a chance to compare heavy pack on skis vs. heavy pack on Snowtreads/trail shoes. I plan to do so. . .

Re: Snowtreads. Glad to hear they've worked out better for you —perhaps we had a "lemon." I really like the weight aspect and think I can come up with a much-improved binding arrangement to eliminate some of the twisting I found objectionable on traverses, uneven surfaces, and in soft snow. I'm amazed you didn't find them small for the loads; you must have had much firmer snow than that we tried them in.

Re: Walt Taylor. Glad he's available and you're impressed. Hope he's assimilated useful medical knowledge. He should be good for morale too. . .

Re: Pickets, etc. 2500′ of rope and 15 pickets does seem like a lot of rope between—I've suggested Anshel check polyethlene rope—seems to me (though I'm not sure) that it stretches less than nylon. It is harder to grip, though. . .

Planning on tests and modifications just before the trip seems very ill-advised. I think we should make every effort to reduce the last minute panic. We'll be glad to test pickets and connecting methods — lots of snow and ice available. . .

Hope the above is coherent and reasonably inoffensive. I've got a lot on my mind and I'm in a rotten mood.

("Excellent" skiing in New Hampshire would be "fair" in Utah—but it's good diversion.)

. . .

Food Thoughts:

. . . It seems desirable to me to add calories to the (nominal) "lunch". . .

Saccharin-flavored drinks—I find these particularly unappealing when hungry. For me, the weight of the packages even seems excessive!. . .

Breakfast D. Sounds sort of greasy for use at extreme altitude. . .

Jell-O: Mark and I are quite fond of hot Jell-O. We're also philosophically disposed to its use because of the protein and sugar content. I would drink it morning and night if available. . .

Would appreciate VERY much having the peanut butter and honey separate. (I like both, but not the combination) I hope other candy will be retained in meals with peanut butter cups so I can trade mine off. . .

Potato chips. How about substituting shoestring potatoes or other types of crackers? (Lunch B) Somehow potato chip CRUMBS seem an unnecessary frustration. . .

I'm in *favor* of retaining cold cereal in Breakfast C and putting some into Breakfast E unless others object. . .

I'm a little apprehensive about high fat content in many dinners. . .

Jerry

Letter to Berle Mercer
March 14, 1967

Dear Berle,
Find enclosed an expedition check for $150 to reserve your packing services for June 17. . .

Joseph F. Wilcox

Note from Hank Janes

Dear Joe:
It just occurred to me that we perhaps should color code our personal equipment to avoid confusion during and after the expedition—or at least mark our own stuff in some way. At the present time my stuff is marked red—Jerry's equipment is marked blue—Mark's is red and yellow combined, I think. . .

Regarding the proposed arrangements with the packer: I vote yes—sounds good!

Hank

Letter from Mark McLaughlin
March 16, 1967

Dear Joe,
Comments on M-8 and M-9.
Would be in favor of the horses. Sounds like a good idea—also if this means possibily a little more gear (scientific type) think that is good. . .

Sure would rather see lots of Wyler's lemonade and Jell-O to drink—personally guarantee to drink 1 pk. of lemonade per day. . .

The bacon bar needs to be in something.

Split pea soup with bacon bar—good for dinner.

Don't care for any tea, Tang, Pream, or Postum. Would prefer lemonade (Wyler's) everyday. . .

Life Savers NO! Sours, yes.

How about some pepperoni or jerky for lunch?

Puffed Corn Nuts are for the ravens.

Fudge is good!. . .

Dinners are too complicated—too much mess and cooking. Two pots are enough. . .

What does the butter (margarine) come in—melt proof?

What are "Yukon Biscuits?". . .

Jell-O—Green Death (lime) is best flavor. . .

I like your packaging suggestions. Suggest army surplus plastic bags from Co-op. . .

Jerry will be back "soon." Talk to you then.

Mark

Letter from Malcolm Bourne
March 20, 1967

Dear Joe,

This is the letter stating my decision to leave the McKinley expedition. I really regret to do this but under the present circumstances it becomes a necessity due to finances, army obligations, my present job and future plans.

The army summer camp extends through June 10 with the possible penalty of a trip to Viet Nam for leaving the unit.

Job Corps refused to grant a leave of absence and those willing to help out on this problem are unable to obtain satisfactory results. To quit means no possibility of returning to Job Corps later at McCoy.

In order to return to school the summer session is a necessity at LaCrosse and not yet known at Platteville. . .

I wish to thank you very much to have invited me to join your group and for all I have learned being associated with this expedition.

THE BEST OF LUCK TO YOU ALL.

Sincerely,

Malcolm B. Bourne

Letter from Anshel Schiff
March 20, 1967

Dear Joe,

Menus look good. A couple of comments. It is hard to tell from menu but I think hot Jell-O is good just about any time. I would like to see more of it in the morning. It seems to stick to one's ribs better. . .

I would like as much info about scientific equipment and plans as you have. . .

I think your estimates for car cost are unreasonable and inadequate to tell the truth; I question the use of a car as old as yours. (I must say that I have not been on Alcan Highway and stories I have heard are no doubt exaggerated.) I think asking anyone to use a reasonably new car for a straight $50 would be unreasonable. . .

Now to the picket problem. . . Figures for the smaller diameters can be improved by plugging with wooden dowl. This would not add much weight or cost and we may get by with 1" diameter. My earlier estimate on cost was probably way off. I will try to get better figures. I will run test with "stuffed" pickets and let you know how they look. The problem here is finding a dowl that fits. . .

. . . Does toe of Korean thermal boot (with overboots) fit through toe of Snowtreads?

Anshel. . .

Note from Dennis Luchterhand
April 8, 1967

Dear Joe—

Jerry Clark's putting up a convincing fight against Snowtreads —guess I may get a pair of trails. . . Thesis will get done but it will be tight. . .

Dennis

Letter from McKinley Park
April 12, 1967

Dear Mr. Wilcox:

We have received your application material for a McKinley climb, and are in the process of evaluating it. Several questions have arisen.

1. Mr. Russell's application material is too brief to evaluate properly. I am sending a new blank to him for completion.

2. Mr. Stephen A. Taylor's experience appears limited to one climb, plus several planned climbs. We do not feel that his experience is adequate for an expedition which is equivalent in most ways and more difficult in some than expeditions to the Andes or the Himalaya. We would recommend that he postpone his McKinley plans until he has gained considerably more experience.

. . . The only other expedition which plans tentatively to climb the Muldrow route in mid-June is the Colorado Mount McKinley Expedition, led by

Mr. Howard Snyder. . .
Boulder, Colorado. . .

You might be interested in combining certain functions with his party such as sharing fixed ropes rather than carrying two, and perhaps combining forces for the pack string to McGonagall Pass. We urge you to coordinate with them on radio communications. If you both carry radios on the same frequency, your mutual strength and safety will be vastly greater. Incidentally, the Colorado group is composed of only four members at this time.

You are apparently planning to "warm up" on Mount Rainier en route to Alaska. This is an excellent idea. You should make it a point to spend half a day or so being sure that all members are proficient at various types of crevasse rescue. It is the rule for members of McKinley expeditions to drop into hidden crevasses while packing up the glaciers, especially in June. You should expect this and be fully prepared for it.

As soon as we have finished evaluating your application material, we will contact you.

Sincerely yours,

Arthur J. Hayes,
Chief Park Ranger

Letter to McKinley Park
April 18, 1967

Dear Sir:

Thank you for your letter of April 12. I did not carefully review the climbing applications before forwarding them to you. Upon examining them today, I find that John Russell's application is quite brief and Steve Taylor has understated his experience and ability to the point of being misleading.

John Russell moved to a new address last week; I have requested him to complete another application should you be unable to contact him at his old address. I have also had Steve Taylor complete a more realistic application which I have enclosed. . .

Should you feel that any member(s) of the expedition are not qualified for the trip, we will make any changes necessary to meet the required standards.

I will contact the Colorado group concerning cooperation on the mountain.

Sincerely,

Joseph F. Wilcox

Letter to Howard Snyder
April 18, 1967

Dear Howard:

. . . I understand from the Park Service that you also will be on the Muldrow in June. It might be of benefit to both of our groups to coordinate some of our efforts. We plan to take 1500 ft. of fixed rope[8]. . . and 15 pickets for Karstens Ridge. If you wish to use our pickets and fixed rope we would require that you pay for ⅓ of the cost. . .

We have contracted pack horses from Wonder Lake to McGonagall Pass. If your group would like packing service contact:

Berle Mercer. . .
Lignite, Alaska. . .

8. Revised quantity—our original plans were to take 2500 feet of fixed line.

He is charging us 30¢ per pound and I'm sure that cost would be the same for your group.

It would be advantageous if our groups had radio contact on the mountain. We are renting radio equipment from Fairbanks and plan to use smaller commercial units for intercamp communication. What are your radio plans?

According to the Park Service you, at present, have only four climbers. Should you have problems getting cleared because of your small group, you might consider joining our group. However, I can make no commitments without reviewing your group's climbing experience. Any such action would have to be initiated within the next two weeks. I have enclosed some information to acquaint you with our group. . .

Joseph F. Wilcox

Letter from Mark McLaughlin

Dear Trip Leader:

Got your extravaganza on Mt. Nebo—Mary resents being replaced as the female equipment tester, but since we haven't got anymore Snowtreadless to break up, our equipment testing has come to a screeching halt.

There is a place here that teflons pots and pans, about $3.50 to $4.50, depending on the size of the pot. Thought it might be a good investment to have this done to the pressure cookers and to one small pan in each cook group. Takes about 3-4 weeks to have done so would appreciate an answer soon. . . How soon will we get our stuff from Trailwise? How soon will you let us know what the Park Service wants to know about our skiing?

Met an old friend of yours last weekend skiing: Chuck Crenchaw, from Seattle, who remembers you from your summer at Rainier. He is going on a climb with us in two weeks; I met him on Rainier Memorial Day '65 and later in the summer of '65.

Jerry supports my stand on teflon! DOWN with peanut butter cups!! Looks like that is about all from here. Looking for another progress report. . . Anshel still wants to know exactly what the science program will consist of.

Thanx

M^2 & fjc

of the NW Faction of the

Joseph F. Wilcox Mem. Mt. McK. Expd. & S.s.p. (1967)

Letter from Jerry Clark to Communications Equipment and Service Company in Fairbanks, Alaska

. . . We would appreciate knowing frequencies (and modulation type) on which local weather forecasts are regularly broadcast so that we can construct a small portable receiver. . .

Sincerely,

F. Jerry Clark, Radio Officer
Wilcox '67 McKinley Expedition

M-10

GROUP GEAR

5 collapsible plastic bottles 1 gal. each
2 six-quart, 10 1/4" x 5" deep kettles
5 Optimus 111B stoves
6 plastic funnels
5 pot grippers
fuel (white gas) 35 gallons
*tents (2 Alpine Hut Mountaineers, 2 Alpine Hut Logans,
   1 homemade)
4 large sponges
2 wisk brooms (plastic)
4 large spoons
4 wire whips
8 tube tents 2-man (4 bright blue, 4 orange)
2 pack scales (80# range)
pots 5 sets
10 orange smoke bombs (daytime)
10 highway flares (night)
400 wands
snow shovels (2 large, 2 small)
2 spatulas
1 4-quart pressure cooker
2 5-quart pressure cookers with extra gaskets and pressure valves
5 120 foot climbing ropes
2 piton hammers
25 ice screws

20 assorted pitons
1500 feet ¼" Goldline for fixed line
15 pickets (for fixed rope)
1 pair adjustable crampons
300 feet parachute cord
2 10' x 10' black plastic melt tarps
* 21,000 ft. altimeter; 16,000 ft. altimeter
3 extra pairs Snowtreads
2 ice saws
1 max. min. thermometer -30°F to 130°F
2 thermometers -50°F to 120°F
* anemometer 0-150 mph range
* precipitation gauge
* hygrometer
* barometer
12 pot cleaners
1000 waterproof matches
1 extra tent pole for Logan tent
2 log books
5 fiberboard hot pads
2 first aid kits (extensive)
2 repair kits
30 rolls toilet tissue

* These items were latter modified or discarded from the group gear list. A small wind gage and a 16,000 foot altimeter were taken. For fixed line we took polypropylene water ski tow rope rather than Goldline. One (rather than two) Alpine Hut Mountaineer tent was taken. There were also a few other minor changes.

M-11

April 22, 1967

TRANSPORTATION: It has been suggested by several members that my estimates for car stipends are too low. Since no one has offered the use of his car, I am inclined to agree. I am initiating the following proposal with hopes of better response.

Passenger car $100.00
Passenger car pulling trailer $150.00

The stipends will be paid in advance (about May 15) along with $25 allowance for a pre-trip tune-up. The expedition will pay expenses and all repair costs up to $100. Fifty percent of all repair expenses over $100 will be covered by expedition funds. At the beginning of the trip, the car will be expected to be in excellent repair and insurance sufficient to cover liability and injury claims must be carried.

FOOD: Note following revisions to M-8:

All drinks except Tang will be Perma-Pak.

The drink for Breakfast A will be grape.

The drink for Breakfast E will be cherry.

The drink for Breakfast B will be strawberry.

Saccharin Kool-Aid will not be taken.[9]

The drink for all dinners will be lemonade.

The applesauce in Breakfast A will be exchanged with the strawberries in Breakfast B.

Days 21 to 40 will be considered high altitude menus.

For high elevations 1 quart of lemonade per person extra will be packed in the day bags.

Honey and peanut butter will be packaged separately.

Dry cereal in Breakfast C will be assorted.

Strawberries in Breakfasts B & C will be 1 cup per person [sweetened].

Jell-O in Breakfast E will be orange.

Oatmeal will be replaced at high elevations by Familia.

Candy bars in Lunch A will be chocolate and honey-nut bars at low elevation; mint and rum fudge at high elevations.

Potato chips in Lunch B will be replaced by shoestring potatoes.

Peanut butter cups in Lunch D will be replaced by caramels.[10]

Life Savers in Lunch D Will be Sours.

Puffed Wheat Nuts will be replaced by Bacon Thins.[11]

At high altitudes nuts will be replaced by Sours in the lunches.

---

9. Saccharin Kool-Aid was replaced by one quart of Perma-Pak drink in each lunch.

10. Peanut butter cups in Lunch A were also replaced by caramels.

11. Puffed Wheat Nuts were 1.0 ounces (150 calories) and Bacon Thins were 1.5 ounces (175 calories).

The nuts in Dinner A will be mixed nuts [1.3 ounces,
   230 calories]

A small G.I. can opener will be included in the day bag when
   needed.

Tuna for high elevations will be vacuum packed.

Pudding in Dinner D will be butterscotch.

Jell-O in Dinner E will be strawberry.

Jell-O in Dinner F will be black cherry.

Dinner G has been completely replaced:

DINNER G (new)	CALORIES	OUNCES
cherry Jell-O	160	1.5
Knorr soup (pea)	100	1.0
Logan Bread	500	4.0
Instant Breakfast	280	2.5
lemonade (1 qt.)	220	2.0
fudge[1][2]	375	3.0
bouillon cube	---	---
Total	1635	14.0

. . .

HORSES: I have received confirmation that our pack horses
are reserved for June 17. . .

FINANCES: The estimated cost has been revised from $300.00
per person to $365.00 per person. . .

The last $65.00 will be due on June 1. If the increase in cost will
work a great hardship on you, let me know immediately. We might
be able to work something out like the use of your gasoline credit
card, etc.

P.S. We have nearly all of the food and have begun packaging
it.

---

12. Later, the fudge quantity for all menus was standardized at 4.0
ounces (500 calories) for ease in packaging.

   Triscuit quantities were likewise standardized at 3.0 ounces
(375 calories).

   Sugar in Breakfast C was reduced to .7 ounces (67 calories).

Letter from Walt Taylor to Jerry Clark

. . . Thanks for your time and counsel on the Kelty. I sent my
standard bag off to K.I. this morning. It looked rather small to
handle McKinley gear but $27.50 looked larger. I'll expect to lose
$27 worth of gear what from falling off my pack frame. What do
you think of this trip so far? Do you know anymore about your
compatriots? At the risk of appearing foolish allow me to voice
some heretical opinion. To whit, wouldn't you rather try a more
difficult route or a different untried mountain and fail than
succeed on the Muldroon(?) Glacier route? That's why I ask you
what you know about the group's general climbing abilities. I tend
to think we're underselling ourselves or overrating Alaskan mtns.
due to their altitude and height. In talking with a boy here who
climbed Mt. Logan two years ago with Boyd Everett (climber-leader
of McKinley, Logan, and Elias; planning now for K2 expedition)
I've inherited the disenchanting impression even if simpleminded
that unless a route involves some interesting 4-5 Class climbing you
wind up with a month's good winter camping experience and an
enlarged sympathetic consciousness for a pack mule. Not that
that's so all awful. I want to just stomp around on those great
expanses of snow and get up high enough that the valleys turn to
clouds, and I want to see 9 of us workeatlaughsleeptogetherfor-
amonth. But Jerr, if it's going to be nearly all 30° uphill trudging
for 3-4 weeks couldn't we at least take skis? There have got to be
some good safe, un-crevasse-like slopes up there. One of those
mornings you're going to wake up and poke your head out of the
tent and for as far as you can see there'll be 3' of fresh powder,
maybe 4 and the relative safety of snowshoes is going to be small
balm for a hopelessly wounded ski-soul. What about shortie skis?
What about if three or four of us skied roped together about 40'
apart? I'd appreciate it if you'd burn this when you're thru reading
it. This is the kind of letter that makes history after we lose two
horses and one man in the McKinley River, another man in a
crevasse, and two more are lost and buried in a 110 mph howling
blizzard, not to mention various and sundry fingers and toes. I
mention these views to you because perhaps you know better. I'm
not understimating the more obvious dangers such as crevasses,
frostbite, avalanches, the McKinley River crossing. I'm not really in

a serious position to evaluate them except thru the opinions of others gone before. But as you will have noticed, those risks are comparatively the same whether your route or objective is Class 2 or 5, and the ignominy of an accident on what should have been an easy route compounds with the degree of easiness. Another heresy: Is this group going to be largely governed by vote or one man rule? (Doubtless with this last question I've brought to your mind infamous visions of Taylor veering off and up the mtn. heedless of responsibility, wisdom, friendship; "To thine own self be true and thou canst lead an entire party in three directions." —Anon.) But I've mellowed since then. I've lost nearly all of my adolescent courage, and I've been the responsible person too many times to look with favor on un-group concern. But I trust you've thoroughly discussed decision procedures with Joe and I'd like to know while I'm still wearing oxfords rather than Korean boots.

(Later in the evening) Reading this over I'm sufficiently abashed to tone down its tone. I'm aware that one doesn't suggest plan changes when one is on a rather probationary visa. I'm actually just probing to see if I'm all wet or several of us are relatively wet. I'm having a hard time rationalizing why McKinley? Aside from its obvious recognizable conversational value and its being the highest in N. America, McKinley stands small compared to the thrill of some of the virtually untouched mountains nearby. Or what about the South Direct route? It's yet to be done. And what a sweet summit embrace there'd be if we made it; and if we didn't it would have been a try worth the expense and the effort and the inevitable risks. Are you reading this? Does this ring anything or not? The Mt. Rainier Guide Service offers to get interested parties to McKinley's summit for $1600. Is that what we're going to be doing only cheaper? I don't know. Perhaps our party is a lot weaker than I've guessed. As hi-altitude leader I expect you're pretty much aware of our capabilities at least on paper. But when are you or I or Joe or any of the others going to get another crack at Alaska? I'm asking you whether we're going up there so we can all say we climbed McKinley or whether we're going up there because there's a great climb there we want to try. I realize this subsumes a grossly armchairian view of our present plans and resounds hollowly like the Appalachian rock climber come to the Tetons, but I wonder if we're not putting the mountain in front of the climb. Feel free to curse softly. And if around June 25 or so I blanch at the sight of McKinley's gaping Muldrow Glacier and refuse to leave my tent, I would appreciate it if you would hand me this letter thru the tent portal. Let me know what you think. If you're eager and apprehensive, that'll be good enough for me. In any case I'm anxious to see the snow and the size of 20,000 vertical feet, and I've never even been thru Washington or northwest Canada.

What kind of shoes are you planning to wear up to the snow?

Is there skiing on Rainier the second week in June?

How is your job panning out?

Did you get my gear list in time?

Thanks again for all your help with Mr. Kelty and the specifications. If you know of any particularly morbid stories of what has happened to climbers on the Muldrow Glacier route, I'd be glad to have the fear of the mountain put into me before I get there so as I may adjust to it.

Walter

Letter from Mark McLaughlin and Jerry Clark

Dear Joe:

Still looking for a few answers to some questions. Would like to know about the teflon for the pressure cookers and pots as we need some 4 to 5 weeks for this service. What is the outcome of the skis? What does the Park Service need to know about our background as skiers?

We (Jerry and I and 2 friends) skied about 25 miles across the McKenzie Pass last weekend. Sat. morn at 8 AM until about 2 on Sun. afternoon, with time out for camp in the snow. There is about 8 to 10 feet of snow most places on the pass, and it was a good trip, though we were sure glad we weren't on snowshoes, or on Snowtreadless, as we were in from 2 to 7 inches most of the time. After dinner the vote from here is again for one pot, simple meals as cooking sure is a drag, and the mess is more than we hope to face for weeks on end.

Also have another friend who has driven the Alcan Highway 3 times. Please advise us again how long you plan to allow for this trip, as he (another Gerry Clark) doesn't think that we can do it in

72 hours. Him and his wife took 10 days of about 8 to 10 hour days, and a lot of the road has a 40 mph speed limit on it and a lot of that which doesn't have a posted limit has a practical limit on it, also about 40 mph.

Another suggestion (especially if we have to go to Fairbanks for radios) is that we plan to buy our Blazo up there, rather than take some 35 gal. 200# of gas with us. How on that? Though he does suggest that if we plan to travel straight through, that we take extra gas as a lot of places close up at night. Please note that 3,000 miles in 72 hours is 41.666 mph—not bad if we don't eat, sleep, drink, or piss. . .

When does Russell get his felt boots? Clark wants to see them—

Thanx

Mark & Jerry

(A return letter to Mark facetiously indicated that a *four* day Alcan drive would be about 30 miles per hour, possible on a bicycle.)

Note from Anshel Schiff
Dear Joe,

. . .After hearing the various plans for snow travel footgear, I think skis would have many advantages. My own view has thus changed and I am now in favor of skis. This assumes that the skis are to be used as snowshoes and not for skiing. Downhill skiing being banished.

Anshel

Note from Hank Janes
Joe:

I may be interested in taking my car — Dodge Van. . .
Also, please keep me in mind for the credit card arrangement. No word on the tents yet. . .

Hank

M-12

SUPPLEMENTARY FOOD
Each group will have a food bag of:
2 doz. packages Carnation cocoa
25 quarts Perma-Pak drink:
    5 raspberry
    5 grape
    5 cherry
    5 tropical fruit
    5 strawberry
2 quarts dry Tang
5 packages of sliced peaches
9 lbs. margarine
40 packages assorted Jell-O
1 lb. catsup (individual servings)
1 doz. boxes of raisins
1 doz. packages of beef jerky
6 cans Kipper Snacks
2 lbs. assorted hard candy
10 packages assorted Knorr soup
5 packages chocolate pudding
5 packages vanilla pudding
2 lbs. salt in individual servings
1 small can pepper
1 small can nutmeg
1 small can cinnamon
500 waterproof matches
6 pot cleaners (3 Tuffy, 3 spun wool)
1 lb. extra sugar

SURVIVAL FOOD PER PERSON
8 oz. Tex-Schmeltz
3 packages Swiss Ovosport
2 boxes Familia
4 ½ oz. Nu-V food bar

(Later 40 pounds of cheese were added to the expedition's supplementary food. Other changes were minor.)

M-13

MENU ITINERARY

DAY	DINNER	BREAKFAST	LUNCH
1	A	D	A
2	B	B	B
3	C	C	C
4	D	D	D
5	E	E	A
6	F	A	B
7	G	C	C
8	A	B	D
9	B	D	A
10	C	E	B
11	D	A	C
12	B	B	D
13	F	C	A
14	G	D	B
15	A	E	C
16	B	A	D
17	C	B	A
18	D	C	B
19	E	D	C
20	F	E	D
21	G	A	A
22	A	B	B
23	C	D	C
24	D	E	D
25	E	A	A
26	F	B	B
27	G	C	C
28	C	E	D
29	D	A	A
30	E	B	B
31	F	C	C
32	G	E	D
33	E	A	A
34	F	B	B

DAY	DINNER	BREAKFAST	LUNCH
35	G	C	C
36	E	E	D
37	G	A	A
38	E	B	B
39	G	C	C
40	E	E	D

EMERGENCY FOOD

Cached at McGonagall Pass

1	A	A	A
2	F	B	B
3	C	C	C
4	B	D	D

Cached on Muldrow Glacier (about 8,500 ft.)

1	B	E	A
2	D	A	B

Cached at base of Karstens Ridge

1	A	C	C
2	C	D	D

MENU FREQUENCY

DINNER	DAYS
A	6
B	6
C	7
D	6
E	8
F	7
G	8

BREAKFAST	DAYS
A	10
B	10
C	10
D	8
E	10

LUNCH	DAYS
A	12
B	12
C	12
D	12

(With consideration for menu frequency and high altitude adjustments, our finalized rations—not including supplementary and emergency food—weighed an average of 2.64 pounds per man-day and contained an average of 4998 calories. Usable protein averaged about 105 grams per man-day.)

M-14

MIND AND BODY

TO PREPARE THE BODY:

It is expected that everyone report to the expedition in superior physical condition. The very best conditioning for carrying a heavy pack long distances is to carry a pack long distances. When such is not convenient, several activities will serve as a substitute.

A. *Running*, with emphasis on distance, develops endurance and lung capacity. By June a two-mile run should not overly tire you.

B. *Swimming*, with emphasis on distance, is better than running [unsubstantiated]. Besides developing better endurance, it also coordinates breathing (a necessary function in using the rest step).

C. *Weight lifting*, with emphasis on developing the upper body, increases general strength (for self-arrests), prepares body for carrying heavy loads, expands lungs, and coordinates breathing. If weights are not available, push-ups are very good.

There are other exercises and combinations of exercises which may serve just as well; the above should, however, provide a guideline for conditioning.

Although good conditioning will contribute to better performance on the mountain, it will not significantly increase acclimation rate. An athlete in rigorous training increases his blood volume equivalent to a rise in elevation of only 3,000 feet. There is some evidence that continued training during the trip, especially on inactive bad weather days, will aid acclimation.

TO PREPARE THE MIND:

It has been said that when the planning and organization is complete and the expedition begins, its fate is already determined. Bad weather and hard luck stories for failures are usually a cover-up for poor preparation.

It is much easier to contemplate what you would do in an adverse situation now when you have days and even weeks, than to make a snap decision on the mountain where seconds are important. We will devote a lot of time at Rainier and during the trip to Alaska discussing possible situations that may arise.

To aid in your mental preparation, it is helpful to read a considerable amount of mountaineering literature. The following is a list of required and recommended reading material:

Required Reading

1. *Frostbite* by Bradford Washburn. To memorize this pamphlet would not be over-preparation.

2. *The ABC of Avalanche Safety* by E.R. LaChapelle.

3. *The Mountain World* 1956-1957 edition (pages 55-81).

4. *Freedom of the Hills* by the Mountaineers (chapters concerned with snow and ice climbing).

5. McKinley trip logs of Seattle Mountaineers (1964) and Swarthmore Denali (1966). I have copies which you may read during the trip to Alaska.

Recommended Reading

1. *Americans on Everest* by Ullman.

2. *Freedom of the Hills* (entire book).

3. *Mountain Rescue Techniques* by Wastl Mariner.

4. *Mount McKinley and the Alaska Range in Literature* see M-87.

Any other literature on mountaineering is recommended. Also review first aid manuals and renew training if necessary.

M-15

May 1, 1967

[FINANCIAL STATEMENT]

EXPENSES. . . Total to Date . . . $2,035.79
. . .

DEPOSITS. . . Total to Date . . . $2,050.00

M-16

May 1, 1967

COPY OF INVOICE FROM RECREATIONAL EQUIPMENT, INC. (CO-OP)

. . . Total Paid $321.04

M-17

May 2, 1967

RESEARCH PROSPECTUS

. . .

OBJECTIVES:

(1) To increase the understanding of glacier movements and the merging of large glaciers by surface flow measurements of the Muldrow and Traleika Glaciers. (2) To study the mechanics of high elevation icefalls by surface flow measurements of the Harper Glacier near the top of the Harper Icefall. (3) To promote long range studies by the establishment, occupation, and marking of photo-theodolite stations. . .

EXPENSES:
. . .
Total $125.00

Letter from Sportsmen Products, Inc.

Dear Mr. Wilcox;

. . . During the last month and a half we have had a limited number of Snowtreads returned with the same defect in the hinge area. We have been reworking the mold and will be using a new improved plastic that is not only stronger but will go down to lower temperatures. . .

We would very much like to have you test several of the new pairs of Snowtreads if we can have them ready in time.

We also hope to have a new lightweight compact cook stove within the next two weeks. If we are successful in acquiring this item, we would also like for you to test this item also. . .

Very truly yours,

Jesse T. Hull, President
Sportsmen Products, Inc.

(We declined the offer to test stoves as we wanted stoves of proven quality and performance.)

Letter from Mark McLaughlin
May 2, 1967

Dear Joe,

. . . We climbed Mt. Hood Sunday and skied off in a whiteout, what a mess—as one of the girls didn't have much skiing experience. Got in after dark, and home at 3:45 AM Monday—drag, drag, drag!!!. . .

How on pitons and ice screws—Jerry and I have lots of both, and I think 20 pitons is about 10 too many—

Jer and I going to MRSCO conference this weekend. Sorry we missed your call. Please put what you can into writing, as my mother's notes leave something to be desired.

See you soon.

Mark

P.S. Had a good talk with Chuck Crenchaw this weekend as he came down and climbed Hood with us.

Letter from Jerry Clark

Dear Joe,

Enclosed is a copy of a letter from Heath Co. I interpret it as mildly negative. However, it probably is worth following up. . .

Have news from the U.S. Weather Bureau on weather observation info broadcast at $\frac{1}{2}$-hour intervals. Think we should plan on a receiver to pick up same. Would require a transistor broadcast receiver—pocket size and a special converter. . .

Have heard from the Alaska (Fairbanks) Communications Service and the Park Service. . .

Communications are far from definite, but now we have info necessary to "move ahead with vigor." I'm doing so. . .

Even using citizens band gear we probably would have to be line-of-sight to Wonder Lake. . .

Had a jolly good slog up Hood last weekend. . .

Hank's usual employer who runs a summer camp for rich kids might like to buy good citizens band walkie-talkies after we're through with them. . .

Am "enjoying" a 3-day conference on computers in Palo Alto—

Jerry. . .

Letter from Heath Company to Jerry Clark

Dear Mr. Clark:

. . . If we were to loan you 4 GRS-65 CB transceivers, what type of public endorsement do you have in mind? We assume this to mean that you would allow a photograph and your name to appear in one of our ads proclaiming the merits of this equipment under rugged conditions.

. . . In general, we will not participate in any activities which will not result in some sort of coverage by the news media unless there is some other unique advertising benefit to be derived. . .

Very truly yours,

C.A. Robertson. . .

M-18

May 6, 1967

MERGER: I have just completed a semi-merger of our group with the Colorado Mount McKinley Expedition. The Park Service seems dissatisfied with our group being split into two rather small groups and with the Colorado group being so small. The merger is an agreement that our groups will climb and camp together for maximum safety and strength. We will, however, retain separate logistics and leadership. It is hoped that this organization will greatly facilitate a prompt clearance by the Park Service.

The Colorado group will meet us for a workout at Rainier and travel to Alaska with us. They do not plan to use pack horses which will put them five to six days behind us. We will be spending several days with the scientific experiments near McGonagall Pass and will be in the area when the Colorado group arrives (although most or all of our supplies will have already been moved to Camp II above Gunsight Pass). At this time we will combine our groups. At times during the trip, the climbing group may be ahead of the scientific team which will be climbing with the Colorado group, but the separation will most likely be one day's hike. (The groups will be *required* to stay well within the range of our 5-mile intercamp radio units.) The Colorado group will assist in some phases of the scientific research.

RADIO: Both groups will be able to operate with the amount of radio equipment originally planned for our group alone. The Colorado Expedition will pay an amount proportional to the number of men in their group (about ⅓ of the cost). This will save us about $100.

FIXED ROPE: The Mountaineering Club of Alaska Expedition will be climbing the Muldrow beginning about July 1 and have requested that we leave our fixed rope and pickets on Karstens Ridge for their use. They have agreed to pay us one half of the fixed rope cost for this service. We will split the remaining cost with the Colorado group cutting our cost to one fourth. . .

PACKS: Cotton now has a dealership for Mountain Master packs, they may furnish us with Expedition Mountain Masters (about five of them) for testing on McKinley. If you are interested in using one, let me know immediately. Preference will be given to those who do not have expedition packs.

M-19

MEDICAL SUPPLIES

200 tablets	Gelucil (W/C)
50 tablets	Dextro-Amphetamine (pep pills)
200 tablets	Ascriptin (aspirin with Gelucil)
200 tablets	salt tablets with Dextrose
1 pint	Phisohex surgical soap
2 tubes	Neo-Polycin ointment
3 tubes	Desenex ointment for athlete's foot
3 tubes	Pontacaine ophthalmic ointment
4 tubes	Neo-Cortef ophthalmic ointment
100 tablets	Nembutal 100 mg size (sleeping pills)
50 tablets	Dimetapp allergy pills
1 pint	Donnagel PG for diarrhea
100 tablets	V-Cillin K antibiotic
100 tablets	Sumycin Tetracycline antibiotic 250 mg size
100 capsules	Darvon Compound 65

50 tablets	AP Codeine 32 mg size
12 vials	Demerol 1 cc size
30 tablets	Senokot for mild constipation
30 tablets	Ex-Lax for constipation
100 tablets	Hinkle's Pills for extreme constipation
200 tablets	Halazone water purification tablets
8 ounces	Lubriderm lotion
2 ounces	Benzoin
2 packages	Vaseline gauze packing for severe nose bleed
100	Band Aids ¾" x 3"
60 yards	tape—assorted sizes
50	gauze pads 2" x 2" (individually wrapped)
50	gauze pads 4" x 4" (individually wrapped)
2 each	Ace bandages, 6", 4", and 3"
6 packs	Steri-Strips surgical closing tape 3 1/4" x 3 1/8"
24	safety pins—large
56	butterfly bandages, 40 large, 10 medium, 6 small
2	fever thermometers
1 can	adhesive felt (Moleskin) 1/8"
12	disposable plastic syringes (individually wrapped)
13	cotton swabs (individually wrapped)
30	alcohol pads (individually wrapped)
30	tongue depressers
2 pair	bandage scissors (small)
10	single edged razor blades
1 pack	needles (assorted)
2 pair	tweezers (blunt end)
2 books	*Frostbite* by Bradford Washburn
2 books	*Mountaineering Medicine*

All items have been packaged in plastic containers and divided as nearly as possible into two first aid kits each weighing about three pounds. All items are labeled as to specific uses.

M-20

RAINIER AGENDA
June 10-11, 1967

. . .

SATURDAY JUNE 10:

. . .

11:00-12:00 Self-arrests in rope teams—simulate crevasse falls, etc., by letting one man run down hill held by two others in self-arrests (free-for-all). . .

2:00-3:00 Travel to practice area on Nisqually Glacier—general discussion on glacier travel. . .

4:30-5:30 Making camp on glacier, checking out and marking area. . .

7:30-8:30 Orientation on first aid kit. . .

8:30-9:30 General discussion of mountain first aid. . .

9:30-5:30 Sleep—general dreams about mountaineering.

SUNDAY JUNE 11:

. . .

8:00-8:30 Fixed rope pickets and their use. . .

8:30-9:00 Communication orientation. . .

10:00-11:30 Prussiking from crevasse—begin by being lowered in with full pack, snowshoes, etc. Prussiker will be required to get over the lip of crevasse without help. . .

11:30-12:30 Simple pulley rescue. . .

1:30-2:30 Rappelling into crevasses. . .

2:30-4:00 4th and 5th Class ice climbing. . .

Most phases of the workout will be group interchange with everyone making comments and suggestions. . .

M-21

GROUP GEAR FROM SKI HUT. . .   Grand Total $134.90

M-22

PERMA-PAK SUPPLIES. . .   Grand Total $800.39

Letter from Jerry Clark

Dear Joe,

Please look over the enclosed copy of a ponderous letter to Howard Snyder. It includes answers to his questions and shop talk about communications. . . It also includes expression of the local anxiety about climbing mountains by moving cities and forming overly restrictive alliances. In short, Mark and I are highly skeptical of the plans to climb and camp together if taken *literally!!!* It looks like we're all asking for hard feelings, extra delays, and the physically extreme difficulty of establishing massive high camps if we (really) try to all camp together. In fact, depending on the capriciousness of weather and acclimatization we might be fortunate indeed to occupy the highest camp with more than 2 or 3 people at a time. A 9-man summit dash seems aesthetically unpleasing as well as extravagant logistically. It's POSSIBLE of course to have base camp at the saddle between summits and put 13 people there, but it seems highly questionable to expect to do so.

It seems more practical to plan to keep in rather frequent touch between expeditions and perhaps even arrange to share certain high equipment (such as tents, cook gear, and maybe even trade around sleeping bags if this proves desirable). But tying the two expeditions together physically doesn't seem desirable from either their or our standpoints. It is most unlikely that separate logistics and leadership can result in an always favorable mutual rate up and back down the mountain. I feel it is more than mere possibility that an overly restrictive arrangement could break down miserably on the mountain.

I presume we are prepared to let them establish routes, place our pickets and flags, etc., should it happen that they make much faster progress than we do. This is entirely possible since as a small party they may be traveling lighter and may find their interest in science less than anticipated. . .

In short, we're pleading for careful planning and each party's understanding the capabilities and plans of the other VERY WELL. We're also pleading for an "out" other than violent disagreement during the trip—

Received a trial 1½" x 5' picket from Anshel for testing.

Holubar order received and being distributed.

Pots off to California to be teflon coated. Should be back in a couple of weeks. $40.75

Am a little concerned that we seem to be getting a harder time from the Park Service than 4 of us did a few years ago. I hope we are not getting the reputation of being a bunch of clods as far as NPS is concerned. My opinion is that we have a rather strong party and that our only likely difficulties may lie in weather and the possibility that we may be over-equipped and traveling heavy. . .

I personally think that depending on the quality of the snow it could take me up to twice as long to negotiate a given distance uphill on snowshoes as on skis if I could do it at all on snowshoes. I hope this explains a little why I (and Mark and Hank) are so anxious to use skis. . .

We recently spent much time helping John Russell figure out how he could stay in the expedition. He mainly has financial problems. He also has had some understandable misgivings about the general organization of the trip and lack of specifics about what was the science/support role. He also was a bit dismayed by the Park Service's rough time about his application. He is an excellent rock climber and really has an impressive general mountaineering background—definitely not a novice.

The four of us went to a mountain rescue conference and simulated rescue last weekend. Friday we're all going to visit. . . Norm Benton who just got back from the most recent Randall expedition—this time an international jaunt in the Yukon—

We know things are getting hectic. We're trying to restrict ourselves to mild panics here. Keep us all posted as much as possible.

Sincerely,

Jerry. . .

P.P.S. Bike trailer hitch still in design stages.

Letter from Jerry Clark to Howard Snyder

Dear Howard,

. . . Frankly, I'm amazed that the Park Service is giving you and Joe a difficult time about party size considering the number of people on the mountain. Best we climb this year, next year there may be a highway to the upper icefall!. . . Even the most finely organized expeditions have been unsuccessful in putting large numbers of people at high camps—it's very difficult and not economical with respect to effort necessary to establish a massive camp versus a smaller one which can be used several times by small sub-teams.

As I see it, our (Wilcox) two team arrangement is rather flexible. Further, considering separate logistics and organizational background between your party and our (Wilcox) group, it seems unlikely to me that trying to remain physically at the same location on the mountain at all times will prove workable. "Climbing and camping together" is a difficult to define concept; does it mean camping within a radius of 10 feet or a mile: Does it mean leaving camp within 10 minutes of the same time and staying within shouting distance or making sure that everyone is accounted for at the end of the day?

I really think the Park Service would be satisfied if our two expeditions had an agreement to look out for each other, keep in communications advising of current plans in some detail, come to each other's aid, and advise the Park Service of emergencies. I don't think the Park Service will insist on our camping side by side all the time or staying a couple rope lengths apart in groups of 5 to 9 people. Should we become parties to such restricting arrangements, we're all kidding ourselves (Park Service included). I hope it will not be necessary to perpetrate such a hoax. . .

Please do not interpret them [my opinions] as aloofness: we're really quite friendly and feel contact and coordination between the expeditions is a desirable thing. But we'd like arrangements to provide the best possible balance between helpfulness and restrictiveness. . .

Jerry

Note from Hank Janes

Dear Joe,

Can only get one wrench-plier from Alpine Gut — suggest you order 2nd pair direct from Gerry. (I've tried all 4 Gut stores.) Looks like the rest of the order will be filled OK. . .

Hank

Letter from Howard Snyder
. . .
9 May 1967

Dear Joe:

Enclosed are the climbing applications which we submitted to McKinley Park. They are the only copies we have, so please return them when you are through with them. I am also returning the mimeographed information which you sent us, since you might have use for the copies. Please keep in touch with us regarding any new developments.

Yours truly,

Howard Snyder

P.S. You might wish to advise your group to install keeper strings on their mitts. Lost mitts can sure spell trouble. On the back of this letter is a copy of the letter which I sent to the Park Service.

M-23

EXPEDITION OBJECTIVES:
1. To have a safe, enjoyable summer of mountaineering
2. To reach the summit of Mt. McKinley
3. To carry out routine scientific research
4. Some members of the expedition have expressed a desire to add a little variety to the trip by climbing both peaks, spending a day on the summit, or other similar activities. Such activities would depend upon perfect weather with a favorable forecast and the strength of the party high on the mountain. They cannot, at this time, be considered major objectives.

EXPEDITION REGULATIONS:

1. Members of the expedition will be roped while crossing the McKinley River.

2. . . . we will purify all drinking water between Wonder Lake and McGonagall Pass. . .

3. Pack loads will be divided equally according to the amount of group gear and supplies carried. A person carrying heavier personal gear normally will carry a heavier pack.

4. Everyone will be roped up and have prussik slings tied to their climbing rope while traveling on the glacier.

5. Some type of hand covering will be worn at all times while traveling on the glacier. These may be removed in warm weather when not traveling.

6. Slack rope must not be allowed to accumulate within a rope team while traveling. There will be a tendency for slack rope to develop when switchbacking or traveling downhill. . .

7. As a route is established between camps, it will be wanded and remain wanded until all loads have been carried up. Only to avoid obstacles that develop later should the route be changed. Rope teams must travel within sight and earshot of each other. Bad weather will require close traveling; however, overlapping of rope teams or traveling side by side must be avoided.

8. Skis may not be used on the first rope team to establish a route.

9. Use of skis without skins or any type of downhill skiing will not be allowed.

10. Fixed ropes must be used where provided.

11. All campsites will be carefully checked out and the boundary of the safe area heavily wanded before unroping, pitching tents, etc.

12. Under no circumstances should anyone go outside this wanded area unroped.

13. Above McGonagall Pass the first aid kits should never be within 300 feet of each other. Never on the same rope team or in the same tent.

14. . . . .Rope teams will be determined by ability and function. . .

15. On inactive days above 12,000 feet a half hour of vigorous exercise (shoveling snow, etc.) is recommended every 12 hours.

16. Survival food rations, first aid kit, and smoke flares, must be carried at all times when traveling.

17. Avalanche cord must be worn when requested by the leader or deputy leaders.

18. Fuel must be stored in a supply tent (tube tent) separate from the sleeping tents.

19. Smoking in tent with any type of fuel (i.e. unlit stove) will be prohibited, either smoker or stove must be removed from tent.

20. I do not know the Park Service policy concerning alcoholic drinks. In any event, amounts sufficient to cause intoxication will not be permitted.[13]

21. In exposed campsites we will construct alternate shelters such as snow caves or block huts. During windy weather, gear within the tent should be kept compact to minimize loss should the tent fail.

22. Although the Muldrow route is considered a standard route, it should not be underestimated. Any route on McKinley must be considered a major undertaking because of the isolation, altitude, weather, and general mountain dangers. We do not plan to run up the mountain or in any way try to prove ourselves as superhuman climbers. If you have inclinations for technical climbing or climbing around in heavily crevassed areas, I suggest that you satisfy these in a more accessable area such as the Rainier workout. While climbing you should always keep a good margin of energy for emergencies. The length of the climbing day will vary depending on weather, area of travel, and the weight of the pack loads. . .

All of these regulations should appear obvious to you. I am sending them to you as a matter of formality. I may have left off some important aspects which will be assumed on the climb. . .

Note from Anshel Schiff

Dear Joe,

I have mailed a picket and a modified stove to Clark for evaluation. . . My own opinion on the stove is *NOT* to make modifications. The weight saving is about 1#/stove. However, the modified stove can be damaged relatively easily. I think that a

---

13. There was no smoking or drinking on the trip.

reflector added to modified stove should be added to standard stoves. . .

I would like a detailed description of proposed research. . .

Anshel

Letter from McKinley Park
May 10, 1967

Dear Mr. Wilcox:

We have received supplementary information from Mr. Russell and Mr. Steve Taylor on their qualifications, and have been in contact with the Alaska Rescue Group. After careful consideration, we have concluded that although your party is marginal, we will approve your expedition subject to certain conditions, which are as follows:

1. You will be required to carry a radio capable of reaching an outside station. . .
2. If you split your party as previously planned, we feel it essential for safety that one of the two most experienced members accompany each team, and that team strength be fairly equally divided. . .
3. It appears essential that your less experienced members receive several days of intensive training on your proposed Rainier stop, concentrating on crevasse rescue, belays, self-arrest, etc. You should by no means forego this.

We should explain that we do feel that a disproportionately large segment of your party has inappropriate experience. Only your careful planning, organization, training program, scheduled Rainier climb, and the agreement of the ARG to stand by for you enable us to approve your expedition. . .

Regarding the use of skis, we feel it advisable for the entire party to use snowshoes. The glacier is usually in bad condition for skiing during June and July. It is likely that they would be practical only for a short stretch on the upper Muldrow and on sections of the Harper. There is also a strong tendency to split the party on the downhill relays, which could result in problems under some circumstances. And, as you mentioned, it takes an exceptionally expert ski mountaineer to function safely in crevassed areas. . .

We congratulate you on a fine job of planning and organizing, and wish you the very best of luck with the remainder of your preparations and on your climb.

Sincerely yours,

Arthur J. Hayes
Chief Park Ranger

Panic-Gram

To: Hank

From: Jerry

Please advise Anshel as soon as possible or earlier how many of what size pickets are appropriate for the tents!!!. . .

We 3 are going to see Jack Henry in Albany who has climbed McKinley. He is going to show us slides, fill us in on history of the mountain and climbs and routes. He is a writer. You want to go?. . .

Jerry. . .

P.S. Want to attend a wand party?

Panic-Gram

To: Anshel

From: Jerry and Mark

Received the stove. Concur on your observation that the modification is not very sturdy. In fact, my stove looks like it was run over by a Mack truck! What happened? Received with extreme bend in the tank-to-burner connection so that the burner now comes out from the tank at about a 75° angle rather than perpendicularly. Also has beastly large dent in the gas tank plus another dent in the male threads of the pump (pump still seems operative). As mentioned in your letter, there is no hole in the side of the beasty for the flame control shaft. Am a little disheartened that my shiney new stove has depreciated more in a month and a half than my Svea has in 8 years! Looks like there was a casualty before assembly last time—The post office also managed to destructively test the masonite board bottom—it arrived less two corners! We're also of the opinion that the whole operation is a little flimsy to be carting around, stumbling over, etc. Too much depends on being able to melt water, cook, (pop corn), etc. We concur fully that the other stoves are better off modified only to the extent of adding reflectors if that seems desirable. *Please return my case.* Would prefer to de-modify. 'Twas a noble effort though!

Also received picket. . . As you know, the pickets will be left on the mountain for a 3rd party.

Re: crampons. My own preference is for 12 points. Perhaps that's because I like to be able to sprint up the slopes. As you observed they do also contribute to crawling out of crevasses, should that ever be necessary. Other people are dead-set against the toe points because they claim that you're "certain" to break both ankles whenever you fall, go into a self-arrest and inadvertantly catch the toe points. My own opinion is that such opinion is a gross exaggeration. But there are very good ice-scramblers who swear by—and very good scramblers who swear at the toe points. I happen to like them and have found them helpful on steep slopes. . . Haven't been able to find the plastic tool handle dip to coat the sides of the crampons for boot protection. . .

Re: skis. We three are still very anxious to take them. . .

Hank is getting the Alpine Hut stuff now. Seems to be a shortage of Reevair material. There will be lots of baggy orange clothing on the trip.

Joe says the T-wise stuff was supposed to be shipped two weeks ago; not received yet. He's starting to panic. (We are too.)

Mark is still trying to get a pair of Japanese climbing thongs with Vibram soles. Do you know of a source?

NPS is apparently giving us and the Colo. group a hard time. We've been approved for more than 2 weeks by the Alaska Rescue Group, but NPS maintains their silent vigil. How would you like to climb Logan?? Walter has expressed an interest in things more glamorous than the Muldroon Glacier. Perhaps we all will feel that way out of necessity soon. Be not as dismayed about plans to join forces with the Colo. group as we northwestern rabble-rousers were. Party leader Snyder concurs with the thought that climbing together should be liberally interpreted (same mountain, same year, mostly same route; we'll probably want to keep in contact and smile at each other every now and then).

Sorry about tardy reply. Have been busy making lists of things to panic over.

Jerry. . .

P.S. — In view of 11:30 PM call from Hank on letter from NPS to Joe (no info received here yet)—

Suggest you don't plan on skis for McKinley, tentatively.

Suggest you consider the possibility of changing destinations as no longer mere jest.

You'll probably receive more info than we have before you get this letter, but it appears that NPS is requiring reorganization of the party, limitation on skiing, and who knows what else—

I find all that more than just a little amazing. . .

P.P.S.. . . Suppose Jake and Carl would like company on Mt. Robson?

Note from Dennis Luchterhand

Dear Joe:

I have reservations on Northwest Airlines. . . June 6. . .

I'd like very much to get in a summit run on Rainier before leaving for McK.

Can't wait to get going!!

Note from Walt Taylor

Dear Joe,

I got the impression from Chief Park Ranger Hayes' letter that it is thanks to your ". . . fine job of planning and organizing. . ." that we have secured McKinley go-ahead. I wanted to write and express my congratulations also.

Yours truly. . .

Letter to Bradford Washburn:
May 12, 1967

Dear Dr. Washburn:

I will be leading a nine-man expedition on Mount McKinley this June. It appears that we will receive considerable publicity from area newspapers and TV stations to the extent that they may send men to Alaska to cover the expedition. They seem excited by the fact that we may put a camp on the summit, climb both summits simultaneously, or put a camp on each summit. According to the Park Service, some climbers spent the night on the summit in 1960. To the best of your knowledge.

1. Has anyone else spent the night on the summit?
2. Has any group climbed both peaks simultaneously?
3. Has anyone camped on the north summit?
4. Has anyone camped on both summits simultaneously?

Your help will be greatly appreciated. I do not want my group to claim a "first" unless it is, indeed, a "first." Please reply soon, because the news media are anxious to start releases.

Sincerely,
Joseph F. Wilcox

Letter from Roy Gibson

Dear Joe:

Things didn't work out as I hoped for your expedition. My general manager will not approve the expense of our filming a documentary. So we'll have to cancel any plans we had suggested to you.

I'm sorry the project did not work out. I'm sure it would have been interesting for us and for our viewers.

Sincerely,

Roy B. Gibson
News Director

Letter from Mark McLaughlin

Dear Joe:

Got the Trailwise stuff today, thanx for everything, sure looks good, and my K2 boots fit real well, sure do think I will like them.

You are about to get some thoughts on science and publicity from Jerry and John and here is from me. We talked to Jack Henry, MRSCO Rescue Chairman last Thursday night. He climbed McKinley in '61. We are against things which make it less likely for us to get to the top—I didn't say camp. I said get, and I think this movie mess and some of this science is going to do just that.

Every day we aren't packing stuff for the summit is one less chance that we will make it. One day doing science or any other damn thing is 450# less we move up one camp. Would you believe science comes last!!!!!!?? If we don't have any movies or any reporters, it is better than OK with me. Let's not blow a good chance for getting to the summit by messing around with some other items. It will be tough enough I am sure.

Thanx. . .

A couple of more thoughts—

Gas—been getting any lately??—35 gallons????? How did you decide on 35 gal.? Jack Henry—McKinley '61, 8 men, 40 days, said 15 was more than enough so suggest that unless you know a different reason, we reduce our plans to 20 or 25 gallons. . .

Probe poles. 10 to 12 foot bamboo probe poles, we are getting seem to be much more efficient for probing for crevasses and as markers. . .

'Bout all the rabble rousing I can do—

Mark

You going to send $40.75 for pots? Soon.

Letter from John Russell

Joe,

. . . The photo stations seem to be rather desirable but the glacier movements on such a micro time basis seem to be of questionable value. I would be pissed off if we did not complete our climbing goals because of a lack of time which we would have had but for the making of these "glacier studies."

Rock climbing is as close as I come to having a religious experience. . .

Reference M-17—Colorado group. . . This would be poor logistics if not pure folly to have two groups with separate leadership climbing side by side. This might even lead to secondary safety and social problems.

Reference M-14. I was not sure whether to laugh or to cry when I saw this letter. Who the hell hasn't read *Freedom of the Hills* or its equivalent more than a year ago. If there is such a person among us, please tell me; for I should not want to climb on his rope. . .

I would like to try a Mountain Bastard back breaker[14] please ship as soon as possible.

Publicity — the only excuse for putting up with the prostitution of Mother Nature is the sharing of the blood money. I would not climb with the camera carrying pimps unless we got a big enough cut to be able to call the trip a job as opposed to a retreat from TV.

May the peace which passes all understanding find you and remain with you forever and ever.

John Russell

Letter from Jerry Clark

Dear Joe,

I'm sure it's an understatement to say that you've probably noticed time is getting short. There are some very important matters which don't seem adequately pinned down (you've probably noticed that too). I have procrastinated at writing hoping for amplification of the Park Service letter advising of tentative approval and hoping for more information on "co-ordinating" with the Colorado group and on the super-colossal publicity program. I must assume I am reasonably well informed as to the status of things.

So, I feel compelled to speak my mind on several subjects, since, as I see it far reaching re-evaluations are in order, redistribution of "team" membership seems likely, and important commitments must be made by us and others practically immediately.

SCIENCE:. . . I am concerned about the real value of this information. It has been established that the Muldrow is subject to

_____

14. John is referring to the Mountain Master backpacks which Dwight Cotton had offered to loan to the expedition (M-18).

violent changes in velocity. . . As it is, it appears that all we will be able to say is that at point X (marked on the map) the glacier surface was moving at a rate of about N feet/day in June and July of 1967. While that may be sufficiently interesting to give one pause for contemplation about when the trash dumped in a crevasse *might* show up down below (assuming continued flow and ablation rates), it is hardly of great value to science other than as satisfaction of a curiosity. . .

I would personally be just as happy completely eliminating the surface movement studies. . . I am concerned that the science program may be much an artifact of an earlier attempt to get status as a scientific party; . . . I will, of course, bow to a majority opinion. . .

Photography is *slightly* different. Accurate mountain photographs can collect much more information briefly than people with fieldbooks. . .

I could enthusiastically support the photographing of glaciers — but on the way DOWN from the glacier. Let us not kid ourselves, we all want to climb McKinley if possible.

PARK SERVICE LETTER: Upon reading the copy you sent I was first mad. "What kind of dudes do they think we are? They obviously have their heads on backwards." Etc. I reflected on the exotic, but limited, ice experience of some of the gang. I talked to 2 previous McKinley climbers. I listened to tales of 10-day storms, documented with photographs. I reflected on the experience with snowshoes of some of the group (we might have to use them a lot). I reflected on some of my concern about untried items of equipment (tents, for instance). I took due account of some of the obvious confusion of NPS about such things as our intention to ski down the mountainside when we were interested in skiing up, about the feasibility of maintaining scheduled radio communication (there are long stretches of route where we can't communicate with anyone anywhere topographic studies have indicated). I tempered my indignation. It is likely they have underestimated us. Yet they are in a (better) position to know the past history of the mountain and how it has treated climbers than we are—perhaps we have at times underestimated POTENTIAL difficulty. Other climbers who have been there have repeatedly made the point that the mountain is big enough, and potentially bad enough, to LET climbers get up it, rather than being conquered. Caught in a week-or-so storm, would our split-up party fare well? How far should we REALLY split up? Shouldn't we be cognizant of the time-honored practice of not placing people in a camp overnight until they have sufficient equipment and food to survive MANY days of really bad conditions? Shouldn't we consider carefully how many man-days of portering are necessary to get camps high on the mountain? Shouldn't we *expect* a certain amount of impossible weather as a safety factor?

I think some of our thoughts are a trifle ambitious. I have heard only one person state that he would not be very disappointed if he missed the summit. I think perhaps he wasn't or isn't still serious.

SUMMIT CAMPING: Should we all end up at Denali Pass with lots of time to spare (due to good fortune and the whimsical weather gods) and should we feel like setting up camps on the summits—by all means, lets! But, I feel that *planning* to do so, announcing our intentions—is more than just a little presumptuous. It's potentially hazardous to safety and morale. The inertia and pride involved in *planning* to do so and having members of the press on location (McKinley Park) will put our backs against the wall. We'll feel we have to do it. We'll feel that way individually and collectively until we're exhausted and/or overextended if it comes to that (and the mountain is not always cooperative, we have it on good authority). I estimate that it could easily take 5 extra PARTY days of effort (in good weather, yet) to haul enough stuff to the summits (maybe only 1 summit) to be relatively sure it was a SAFE camp, secure against the elements. That's 5 days more than putting the camp at Denali Pass. That's 5 good days. Some of us will be in relatively good shape. Others will be like the VERY experienced climber we talked with last week who reflected that merely climbing up to the summit left him so exhausted and oxygen-starved that on the descent he observed that he could care less if his ropemate fell—further, that he wasn't bothered by his realization at the time—(He is coleader of a forthcoming African expedition.) He went on to mention that others on his McKinley expedition expressed similar recollections of their alertness on the summit!!. . .

PUBLICITY: John has mentioned his distaste for the hoopla of a TV documentary. I don't mind *being* a hero, but it grates against my personality a little to proclaim that I *expect* to be one. This is also an important component of the summit camping problem. The TV and news people are interested in *news*, be it real or manufactured. Imagine the newsworthiness of a RESCUE! (shudder) "Hey, anyone heard from the Wilcox gang in the last few days?" "Gosh, they might be in trouble—" If we tell them we really intend to put 2 camps on the summits, set up a lemonade stand, or track satellites—it will get reported. This makes us actors playing roles to various degrees rather than merely enjoying the climb for our individual private reasons. With the news media proclaiming our intentions to heroically camp in the howling gales on the summits of the highest mountain in North America, we will have little choice but to make it an all out endurance hike. . . What if the weather doesn't cooperate? (It has defeated exceptional parties.) Would it be FUN being reduced to more a climbing machine than necessary: 'Every day in every way I will try to work a little harder' (paraphrased from *Animal Farm*)? Would it be universally FUN throughout the party?. . .

I feel publicity should not be allowed to snowball. I feel we should carefully point out that intentions to camp on the summit are PURELY TENTATIVE or perhaps state that we are no longer seriously considering it. This way, we wouldn't HAVE to try. And if we did it, the glory would be as sweet.

To the extent the publicity originated from an attempt to get Heath Company to loan us radios—There has been no reply from Heath Company. In view of Park Service directives about redistributing the party. . . and in view of increased awareness of what the mountain CAN be like—and in view of the staggering amount of gear we must lug step by (sinking-in) step up the hill. Toning down the bravado of the publicity seems definitely in order!

Let's get most of our publicity after the fact rather than before. It's good politics. And it's good for the spleen. And for the soul. . .

Summary: I propose the following:. . .

DE-EMPHASIZE publicity. Make it clear that there is only a relatively remote possibility that we will play pack mule to the summits. . .
Plan to count on our summit camps only when we're at Denali Pass and we're warm, fat, and sassy. . .

Technical, non-philosophical drivel follows. It's VITAL THOUGH. Do read on—

Keep smiling!. . .

Sooooo—

It looks like I'm going to need some money in the very near future! Upon making a decision on walkie-talkies I'll order by phone or night letter from New York with delivery by air parcel post. . .

DO I NEED TO TAKE OUT A LOAN?????. . .

Jerry

Letter from Dennis Luchterhand

Dear Joe—

Jerry has sent me a copy of his long letter to you. . . He speaks very well for me both on matters that had been bothering me for a time, as well as on matters I had no idea of. . . The camping on the summit (a project I hadn't been aware of) should be something we should try only after everyone who wants the summit has been there—a game to play AFTER the summit. . . Let's keep any publicity to a minimum—we all have a big enough motive—the summit—without needing any exterior publicity pushes setting goals for us that are physically more dangerous than the summit (or psychologically pushing us into dangerous positions). Personally I am only interested in the climb and the welfare of our party—for myself I want NO publicity. With regard to the merging of the 2 parties—us and the Colorado group—all is well and good if it is in the interest of safety for us. Two leaders just won't work though, and I agree with Jerry that we should only be serving as backup parties for each other—no physical merging of the parties can function without a major revision of leadership which wouldn't work.

Perhaps the barrage of letters Jerry has most likely precipitated is being depressing—I CERTAINLY HOPE NOT, JOE. I'm feeling rather guilty for not getting involved in the details earlier, and from what I can tell, you and the group out there are doing a damn good job. I can hardly sit still these days long enough to get any of the final school work done—I'm so excited. It'll be a good climb despite all the little haggling that is so inevitable when a group of people get together on an adventure as big as this. Even if we don't make the summit it will be a darn good trip.

See you soon

Berg Heil
Dennis. . .

Letter from Bradford Washburn
May 17, 1967
. . .
Dear Mr. Wilcox:

We have received your extraordinary letter regarding the plans for your record-breaking efforts this year on Mt. McKinley. I have answered hundreds of queries about McKinley over a long period of time, but never before have I been faced with the problem of answering one quite like this. In fact, I am amazed that the National Park Service would grant a permit for such a weird undertaking.

A Japanese party spent a very comfortable night on top of the South Peak and another party climbed both peaks of McKinley in the same day. In fact, the 1942 Army Expedition and our 1947 expedition lived comfortably for literally weeks above 15,000 feet and could easily have spent a week or more on top of either or both of the peaks if we had had the slightest inclination to do so—or any conceivable practical reason for it. After all, climbers have spent week after week on Everest, K 2, Nanga Parbat, and scores of other Himalayan giants far in excess of McKinley's altitude, packing heavy loads and climbing difficult rock and ice simply for the sheer love of it—not just sleeping their way into headlines!

For your information, according to our records, McKinley has not yet been climbed blindfold or backwards, nor has any party of nine persons yet fallen simultaneously into the same crevasse. We hope that you may wish to rise to one of these compelling challenges.

Very truly yours,

Bradford Washburn, Director
Museum of Science and Hayden Planetarium

M-25

SCHEDULE: . . . My mailing address between May 28 and June 10 will be:

. . .

If you order something at the last minute you can have it sent to the above Puyallup address if you wish.

FINANCES: As expected finances will be rather close. Some people have not yet made their May 1st deposit. . .

COORDINATION WITH COLORADO GROUP: The Colorado Mt. McKinely Expedition will be at Rainier on the 9th, 10th, and 11th. I have invited them to join our workout, but at present they plan to climb on the 10th and 11th. . . NOTE: I have rescheduled the packing date for June 18.[15] This will give us five full days to travel to Alaska. Park Service check-out will probably be the afternoon of the 17th. The scientific work scheduled for the McGonagall Pass area will not take more than 2 days. . . Should it become necessary to split our group at any time, Jerry Clark and I will be in separate groups and the groups will be fairly equal in climbing strength. . .

EMERGENCY NOTIFICATION: (form M-24) . . . must be completed and sent to my Puyallup address. . .

LEADERSHIP: Some members have expressed a desire to know how the expedition will function on the mountain. I do not believe that an expedition can operate smoothly with military discipline nor can it operate well with no more leadership than a Sunday school picnic. As the leader, I feel that I have primary responsibility for the safety of the group and the success of the trip (whether this responsibility exists in reality could well be a topic for debate). I will reserve the right to have the last word when group safety is concerned (how the group is split up, campsites, where to install fixed rope, and when alternate shelters should be constructed) and in matters of general objectives (when to make a summit assault, whether or not to climb both summits, or if necessary when to descend without reaching the summit). If you agree with my decisions, you may call it a democracy; if you don't,

---

15. The estimate of our supplies to be packed in by the horses had grown from 1200 pounds to nearly a ton.

you may have other names for my leadership. In nearly all cases decisions can be made by group agreement. The expedition is composed of climbers with many different backgrounds, and I can envision situations when any one person will know more about the problem involved than the rest of the group. If a person has more experience than I in a particular area, I usually respect his opinion. I have asked for and/or received suggestions from every member of the expedition, most of which I have accepted readily. I plan to make even better use of the group's combined experience when we are in closer contact. The Northwest gang has a good indication as to how the expedition will be run since they have been in close contact with me throughout the planning stages—and I might add, a great help. They may swear to (or at) the fact that I have often changed my opinion when presented with convincing concrete evidence on some matters. Leadership is very much involved in the personality of the person doing the leading, something very difficult to convey in a form letter. Now that I've completely avoided the question, let's go on to another topic.

PUBLICITY: . . . While talking to a Salt Lake editor, I mentioned that with agreeable weather we might climb both peaks or spend some time on the summit or some similar activity. He asked me if these things had been done on McKinley before. Not knowing myself I wrote Bradford Washburn, explaining to him that I did not want any inaccurate information printed. He somehow got the impression that we are only climbing the mountain for publicity. His reply began by classifying us as a weird group and ended by suggesting that we all fall in a crevasse. I'm sure you will want to read it, I'll have a copy in Washington. He makes some amazing generalizations considering the very little he knows about our group.

EQUIPMENT: Wide-mouth water bottles are recommended; John Russell swears by metal canteens; Anshel Schiff suggests warning whistles.

Note from Anshel Schiff to Jerry Clark

Dear Jerry,

I have now reached panic stage. I hope to leave in a little over a week and finishing up semester and things for trip looks hopeless. . . I will make about 5 sets of fins to slip over picket to increase traverse projection. . . try and make a picket driver. . .

Anshel

Letter from **McKinley Park**
May 22, 1967

Dear Mr. Wilcox:
. . . You had inquired earlier about parties who had spent the night on the summit. . . on the off chance that you had hoped for more information on conditions on the summit, we are enclosing an extra copy of Vin Hoeman's report of their climb which includes a short stay on the summit. . .

Sincerely yours,

Arthur J. Hayes
Chief Park Ranger

Letter from Ray Heller
May 24, 1967

Dear Joe:

We are mailing today, under separate cover, by airmail, two flags from the Neodesha High School for your expedition. These flags were made by the girls in the home economics department.

The students are very interested in your trip as well as in the possibilities of the Neodesha school flag flying atop Mount McKinley. . .

Sincerely yours,

Ray E. Heller
Superintendent

Letter from Jerry Clark (sent to Puyallup)

Dear Joe,

. . . I have purchased an excellent high-powered CB walkie-talkie for the primary outside communications. I am tentatively planning to retain personal title to the unit unless the expedition wants to own it. Value including battery pack and special antenna and crystals for 3 channels is about $131. If I retain title, I definitely want it insured. I am expecting the expedition to pay for the difference in resale price and original cost—we have an offer of $75 for the transceiver, ? for accessories.

Re: Heath radios—only 3 of the 4 seem to work completely; I doubt that I can repair the other in the limited time. So it looks like we can have only a total of 3 units for our expedition and 1 for the Colo. gang. I have constructed pocket battery packs for the Heath radios (3); but we may also have to keep the transceivers themselves warm—2 of the 3 did not work correctly when cooled to 5°F at 1 AM this morning—it may be a simple adjustment matter and it may not be—"Research continues"—but I can't spend much more time on the radio problem and still be ready myself come Friday. *If* the 4th Heath radio can be fixed easily, I tentatively have it scheduled for leaving with the Park Service 'just in case' they mosey out in the field or fly around looking for us. We on the mountain can get along without it I think. (Lafayette radio OK at 5°F.). . .

Re: . . . Snowtreadmills, Inc. This is a real mess. I think some people won't want them now—Russell for practically certain. I'll look at them and make up my mind whether to take them or trail shoes. I wasn't impressed with the way Treadmill bindings dis-functioned, but in-the-field repairs and modifications seem unlikely. How we'll ever make sense of the various orders and money which have been sent to the company, I don't know—here's hoping. Too bad the company couldn't have told us what was going on earlier. Russell has written twice, I have written twice, Russell tried to call them (no listing), etc. Russell cancelled his order by mail and I changed my order from 2 pair to 1 pair by mail—Talked to Walt Sunday night; he was concerned that he had heard nothing and was hoping to be able to pick up trail shoes in Seattle. He probably won't get the letter since he's leaving Bloomington this afternoon—He's planning to meet us at the campground late Friday night, by the way. . .

Hank and I will be up LATE! (Friday).

Mark is trying to get to Rainier for a climb with friends (if he can get things done).

Anshel may be in Washington already looking for you. (A couple days ago he was thinking of flying out and camping at the equipment house.)

Walter is trying to get some Demerol tablets and Darvon Compound (free)—too bad we didn't know he can get drugs from supply houses free before we bought lots!. . .

Jerry

P.S.—Alpine Hut could not get my altimeter. That leaves only Mark's 16,000′ one unless we want to take my 12 oz. aircraft model. That's too bad; we've found altimeters helpful locating camps and creating warm feelings of known locations in whiteouts.

Letter from Sportsmen Products, Inc.

Wilcox-McKinley Expedition:

Mr. Howard Snyder of the Colorado group—Mt. McKinley Expedition came into our office yesterday. He will pick up the Snowtreads for the expedition use on Tuesday, June 6, 1967, and bring them with him to your meeting place for the expedition.

Our apologies for not sending you information sooner, but we were waiting for the new improved Snowtreads to be ready for your use. The new Snowtreads are being made of a new low-temperature high-impact material and we did want you to have them instead of the older model for your expedition.

We are sending along 13 pairs with Mr. Snyder so that you will have enough for each member of the expedition and also some extras.

The best of luck to you for a successful expedition.

Sincerely,

Jesse T. Hull,
President

EXPEDITION AGREEMENT

In view of the fact that the Colorado McKinley Expedition has lost a member and cannot be considered an expedition, the following agreements have been reached regarding their complete merger into the Wilcox-McKinley Expedition:

1. Members of the Colorado McKinley Expedition will now be considered members of the Wilcox-McKinley Expedition.
2. The Colorado group will, of course, camp with, travel with, and be under the same leadership as the rest of the Wilcox-McKinley Expedition.
3. Separation of gear, tents, food, etc. will be retained when convenient due to differences in equipment and food types and preferences. Such food and equipment can be interchanged when necessary for group planning and safety.
4. The responsibility for rescues and subsequent costs will rest equally among the twelve members of the Wilcox-McKinley Expedition regardless of the personnel and circumstances leading to such a situation (i.e. 1/12 of the cost per man).
5. The expedition will not assume medical and/or hospitalization expenses in excess of first aid kit supplies.
6. Expenses for pickets and fixed ropes shall be split in the following fashion: Alaskan group ½; Wilcox group ¼; Colorado group ¼ .[16]
7. Radio costs will be divided among all members of the expedition (Wilcox and Colorado) on an equal basis (i.e. 1/12 per man).
8. The expedition will assume responsibility for damage to group gear (i.e. tents, stoves, pots, and other items used cooperatively).
9. With the exception of items 4, 6, 7, 8 above, expedition expenses will not be shared between the Wilcox and Colorado groups.
10. The expedition will not assume responsibility for damage to personal gear, the liability for such damage being a

---

16. Arithmetic would suggest that the cost should have been split: Wilcox group 3/8, Colorado group 1/8. However, an adjustment was made as the Wilcox group was paying to have the pickets and line packed in by the horses. The Wilcox group was also supplying all of the wands for the expedition.

responsibility of the individual or individuals causing the damage.

11. Radio refunds after the expedition will be given to the Colorado group on a 1/12 of total refund per man basis.

Signed:

Joseph F. Wilcox   Howard Snyder

12
Climbing Resumes

Pre-McKinley mountaineering experience of expedition members, compiled primarily from their applications to Mount McKinley National Park.

JERRY CLARK

Year	Mountain	Route	Responsibility
1957	Grand Teton	Grand Teton Glacier (Direct)	Leader
1958	Owen (Tetons)	Koven	Leader
	Grand Teton	Grand Teton Glacier (Direct)	Leader
1959	Haggerman's	Northeast (snow)	Leader
	Grand Teton	Grand Teton Glacier (Direct)	Shared Leadership
1960	Grand Teton	Exum	Leader
1961	Medicine Box (Wyoming)	Diane Wall	Leader
	Grand Teton	Grand Teton Glacier (Direct)	Shared Leadership
1962	Symmetry Spire	Durrance Ridge	Shared Leadership
	Pinnacle Peak (Wyoming)	Southwest (2nd ascent)	Shared Leadership
1963	Grand Teton	Exum	Leader
	Middle Teton	Dike	Shared Leadership
	Moran (Wyoming)	Skillet Glacier	Shared Leadership
	Oldenburg (Antarctica)	North (1st ascent)	Shared Leadership

Year	Mountain	Route	Responsibility
1964	Haggerman's	Snowmass Glacier	Leader
	Gannett (Wyoming)	Thumb Basin - 2 Glaciers	Shared Leadership
	Oliver (New Zealand)	Sealy Ridge	Leader
1965	Owen (Tetons)	Koven	Leader
	Pingora (Wyoming)	Regular	Leader
	Grand Teton	Grand Teton Glacier (Direct)	Shared Leadership
1966	Mount Rainier	Nisqually Icefall	Alternate Rope Leader
	Jefferson (Oregon)	Jefferson Park Glacier	Shared Leadership
	North Sister (Oregon)	Villand Glacier	Rope Leader
	Spire (Oregon)	(Class 6: 1st ascent)	Alternate Rope Leader
	Mount Adams (Washington)	North Side	Shared Leadership
1967	Mount Hood (Oregon)	?	Shared Leadership

General: Thirteen years climbing and instructing experience; two seasons (6 months) mobile field glaciological experience in Antarctica: approximately 2,000 miles over-snow traverse, skiing, climbing; climbing and ice safety instructor, United States Antarctica Research Program; Mountan Leader: Purdue Outing Club, University of Oregon Alpine Club, University of Wisconsin Hoofers Mountaineers, Obsidians (Eugene, Oregon); Member: Obsidian Rescue Team.

HANK JANES

Year	Mountain	Route	Responsibility
1963	Shadow Peak (Tetons)	Southeast Face (1st ascent)	Shared Leadership
	Longs Peak (Colorado)	Window Route	Leader
1965	Mount Hood (Oregon)	left ridge next to Eliot Glacier	Shared Leadership
	Capital Peak (Colorado)	Capital-Daly Ridge	Leader
	Mount Sneffles (Colorado)	Northeast Face	Leader
	Longs Peak (Colorado)	Notch Couloir	Leader
	Longs Peak (Colorado)	Little Notch	Leader
1966	Mount Adams (Washington)	Lyman Glacier	Shared Leadership
	Three Fingered Jack (Oregon)	East Ridge	Alternate Rope Leader
	Longs Peak (Colorado)	East Face	Leader
	Longs Peak (Colorado)	Keiners	Leader
	Crestone Needle (Colorado)	East Face	Leader
	Mount Rainier	Ingraham Glacier (partial ascent)	Member
	Mount St. Helens (Washington)	Dogs Head Route	Leader
1967	Mount Hood (Oregon)	?	Shared Leadership

General: Climbed many of Colorado's 14,000 + foot peaks; extensive winter camping and ski mountaineering, temperatures as low as —40°F; experienced in technical ice climbing; member MRSCO, Mountain Rescue and Safety Council of Oregon.

JERRY LEWIS

Year	Mountain	Route	Responsibility
1964	Navajo (Colorado)	Navajo Glacier	Member
	Longs Peak (Colorado)	West Couloir	Member
	Snowmass (Colorado)	Snowmass Snowfield	Member
1965	Boulder Flatirons	(two roped climbs of 700 feet)	Leader
1966	Longs Peak (Colorado)	North Face - Southwest Face (traverse)	Alternate Rope Leader

General: Camped on Libyan Desert (1958-1960); cold weather camping in wilderness areas of Greenland (1962); completed rock climbing course (1965); ice climbing on frozen Boulder Falls; snow technique practice on Longs Peak and St. Mary's Glacier, and simulated crevasse rescue practice above Loveland Pass (1966); snowshoeing above 10,000 feet, about 20 miles each winter (1965-1966); several winter camping trips above 10,000 feet (1966-1967); ice climbing on Boulder Canyon ice flows (1967); year-round heavy labor above 8,000 feet; miscellaneous climbs in Colorado: Greys, Torreys, North Arapahoe, South Arapahoe, Apache, Belford, Oxford, Laplanta, Alice, Democrat, Humbolt, Hallet's, Neva.

DENNIS LUCHTERHAND

Year	Mountain	Route	Responsibility
1962	East Lester Peak (Wyoming)	(traverse)	Member
	Middle Lester Peak (Wyoming)	(traverse)	Member
	West Lester Peak (Wyoming)	(traverse)	Member
	Ellington Peak (Wyoming)	West Side	Member
	Jackson Peak (Wyoming)	West Side	Member
1963	Ice Point (Tetons)	North Ridge	Shared Leadership
	Mount St. John (Tetons)	South Couloirs	Leader
	Disappointment Peak (Tetons)	East	Leader
	Teewinot Peak (Tetons)	Teton Glacier	Leader
	Cloudveil Dome (Tetons)	Northeast	Shared Leadership
1964	Buck Mountain (Tetons)	East	Leader
	Rockchuck Peak (Tetons)	summit of ridge ENE	Leader
	Gannett Peak (Wyoming)	South	Leader
	Mount Helen (Wyoming)	West	Leader
	Mount Sacajawea (Wyoming)	East Spur	Leader
	Winifred Peak (Wyoming)	East	Leader
	Fremont Peak (Wyoming)	West	Leader

Year	Mountain	Route	Responsibility
1965	Wilde Freiger (Austria)	?	Member
	Gross Venediger (Austria)	?	Rope Leader
	Rainer Horn (Austria)	?	Rope Leader
	Schwarze Wand (Austria)	?	Rope Leader
	Hohen Zaun (Austria)	?	Rope Leader
	Kristall Wand (Austria)	?	Rope Leader
1967	Mount Rainier	Ingraham Glacier	Member

General: Full Mountain Leader, University of Wisconsin Hoofers Mountaineers; two weeks each January snowshoeing, backpacking, and winter camping in the vicinity of Lake Superior; pre-McKinley snow, glacier, and crevasse practice at the Rainier workout (1967).

MARK MCLAUGHLIN

Year	Mountain	Route	Responsibility
1963	Mount Olympus (Washington)	?	Alternate Rope Leader
	Middle Olympus (Washington)	?	Alternate Rope Leader
1964	Old Man Rock (Oregon)	? (1st ascent)	Alternate Rope Leader
	Mount Rainier	Ingraham Glacier	Member
	Mount Washington	Southeast Spur	Leader
1965	Three Fingered Jack (Oregon)	Regular (winter)	Shared Leadership
	Mount Rainier	Ingraham Glacier	Rope Leader
	Mount Rainier	Disappointment Cleaver	Shared Leadership
	Mount Washington	Southeast Spur	Leader
	Mount Jefferson (Oregon)	East Face	Leader
	Mount St. Helens (Washington)	Forsyth Glacier	Alternate Rope Leader
1966	Mount Rainier	Nisqually Icefall	Shared Leadership
	Three Fingered Jack (Oregon)	West Face Direct (1st ascent)	Shared Leadership
	Mount Washington	West Face	Alternate Rope Leader
	Mount Jefferson (Oregon)	Jefferson Park Glacier	Rope Leader
	Mount Adams (Washington)	North Side	Shared Leadership
	Mount Washington	Southeast Spur	Leader

Year	Mountain	Route	Responsibility
1967	Mount Rainier	Ingraham Glacier	Shared Leadership
	Mount Hood (Oregon)	?	Shared Leadership

General: Cross-country skiing; downhill skiing; two 1-week trips in the Olympic Mountains; archaeological survey of the coast of Katmai National Monument, Alaska (summer 1964); Eugene Unit Leader for MRSCO, Mountain Rescue and Safety Council of Oregon; Mountan Leader: University of Oregon Alpine Club; Climbing Committee Chairman: Obsidians (Eugene, Oregon); pre-McKinley snow, glacier, and crevasse practice at the Rainier workout.

JOHN RUSSELL

Year	Mountain	Route	Responsibility
?	Mount St. Helens (Washington)	?	Shared Leadership
?	Mount Adams (Washington)	Mazama Glacier	Shared Leadership
?	Mount Rainier	Emmons-Winthrop Glacier	Rope Leader
?	Mount Baker (Washington)	North Face	Shared Leadership
?	Mount Shuksan (Washington)	Northeast Face	Shared Leadership
?	Mount Hood (Oregon)	?	Shared Leadership
?	Old Man Rock	? (2nd ascent)	Shared Leadership
?	Mount Whitney (California)	?	Solo
?	Pillars of Hercules	?	Leader
?	Mount Yoran	West Ridge	Leader
?	The Tooth	?	Leader

General: Carried loads of 100 pounds to 10,000 feet and 75 pounds to 14,500 feet; assisted in six mountain rescue operations and led one; pre-McKinley snow, glacier, and crevasse practice at the Rainier workout.

ANSHEL SCHIFF

Year	Mountain	Route	Responsibility
1955	Grand Teton	Exum	Client
1962	Tahquitz Rock	?	Member
	Finger Tip Traverse	?	Leader
1965	Pingora (Wyoming)	Regular	Member

General: Backpacking and scrambling in the mountains of western United States each summer (1955-1966); camping at high exposed sites when subjected to physical fatique; completed Sierra Club rock and snow climbing school (1962); rock climbing at Devil's Lake, Wisconsin, and Mississippi Palisades, Illinois; partial ascent of Mount Rainier (1967); pre-McKinley snow, glacier, and crevasse practice at the Rainier workout.

PAUL SCHLICHTER

Year	Mountain	Route	Responsibility
1962	Longs Peak (Colorado)	?(night climb)	Member
1963	Longs Peak (Colorado)	North Face (winter)	Member
1965	Middle Teton	Southwest Couloir	Alternate Rope Leader
1966	Orizaba (Mexico)	Jamapa Tongue of Gran Glacier Norte	Member
	Popocatepetl (Mexico)	North Face	Shared Leadership
	Ixtacihuatl (Mexico)	South Ridge	Member

General: Five additional climbs of Longs Peak; led five climbs of other 14,000+ foot peaks; United States Air Force 1-week survival training (1963); Army Mountain Troops 3-day climbing school at Fort Carson, Colorado (1963); Army Mountain Troops climbing instructor at Fort Carson, Colorado (1965); United States Air Force 4-week survival training (1966).

HOWARD SNYDER

Year	Mountain	Route	Responsibility
1964	Matterhorn (Europe)	Hörnli Ridge	Member
	Monte Rosa (Europe)	West Ridge	Member
	Mont Blanc (Europe)	Gouter	Shared Leadership
	Grande Aiguilles de Triolet (Europe)	West Face (traverse)	Member
	Petit Aiguilles de Triolet (Europe)	North Face	Member
	Mönch (Europe)	Southeast Ridge	Shared Leadership
	Jungfrau (Europe)	Southeast Ridge	Leader
	Eiger	West Face	Member
1966	Mount Brazeau (Canada)	MacLeod-Valad-Brazeau (traverse)	Leader
	Mount Charlton (Canada)	North Face (Charlton Glacier)	Leader
	Mount Unwin (Canada)	North Face (Charlton Glacier)	Leader
	Orizaba (Mexico)	Jamapa Tongue of Gran Glacier Norte	Leader
	Popocatepetl (Mexico)	North Face	Leader
	Ixtacihuatl (Mexico)	South Ridge	Leader

General: Led 24 climbs of Longs Peak via all faces, during all months of the year (one night climb), in conjunction with as many as three 13,000+ foot peaks in one day; climbs of 13 other Colorado 14,000+ foot peaks (three in winter); climbs in Italian Dolomites (1964); climbs in Tetons (1965); winter climbing on 14,000+ foot peaks in subzero cold and full gale force winds (1962-1967); ice climbing on frozen Boulder Falls (1964-1966); winter camping; more than 100 miles of snowshoeing experience; traverse of 18 glaciers during the course of climbs; served as Climbing Leader (paid position) for Colorado Mountain Club Canadian Outing (1966).

STEVE TAYLOR

Year	Mountain	Route	Responsibility
1966	Mount Timpanogos (Utah)	West Ridge - Couloir (winter)	Member
1967	Mount Nebo (Utah)	Cedar Ridge (winter)	Alternate Rope Leader
	Mount Timpanogos (Utah)	West Ridge - Couloir (winter)	Leader
	Mount Rainier	Nisqually Icefall (traverse)	Member

General: Experience in building snow caves; completed mountain rescue techniques class; member of Brigham Young University Rescue Team, participation in several rescues including helicopter hover airlifts; completed outdoor survival class; first aid training; ice climbing experience including leading 6th Class; past Vice-president, Brigham Young University Alpine Club; instructor, BYU Alpine Club winter mountaineering school; pre-McKinley snow, glacier, and crevasse practice at the Rainier workout.

WALTER TAYLOR

Year	Mountain	Route	Responsibility
1958	Haggerman's Peak (Colorado)	?	Alternate Rope Leader
1960	Disappointment Peak (Tetons)	?	Alternate Rope Leader
	Mount Owen (Tetons)	?	Alternate Rope Leader
	Grand Teton	Grand Teton Glacier	Alternate Rope Leader
1961	Capitol Peak (Colorado)	?	Leader
1962	Disappointment Peak (Tetons)	Southwest Face	Shared Leadership
	Middle Teton	?	Shared Leadership
	Grand Teton	Grand Teton Glacier	Shared Leadership
	Pinnacle Peak (Wyoming)	? (1st ascent)	Shared Leadership
1963	Lincoln Gulch Split Rock (Colorado)	South Face	Shared Leadership
1965	Capitol Peak (Colorado)	Southwest Face	Shared Leadership
	Snowmass Peak (Colorado)	Southwest Face	Leader

General: Technical climbing instructor for 3 summers at the Ashcrofter Mountaineering School near Aspen, Colorado; extensive work with Colorado spring snow conditions at 11,000-14,000 feet; extensive winter camping experience; advanced skier including one winter in Aspen, Colorado, pre-McKinley snow, glacier, and crevasse practice at the Rainier workout.

JOE WILCOX

Year	Mountain	Route	Responsibility
1959	Tooth of Time (New Mexico)	Regular	Member
	Clear Creek Mountain (New Mexico)	Regular	Member
1960	Tooth of Time (New Mexico)	Regular	Leader
1961	Tooth of Time (New Mexico)	Regular	Leader
	Clear Creek Mountain (New Mexico)	Regular	Leader
	Baldy (New Mexico)	Direct	Leader
	Baldy (New Mexico)	Direct (traverse)	Leader
	Touch Me Not (New Mexico)	(night traverse)	Leader
1962	Clear Creek Mountain (New Mexico)	Regular	Leader
	Baldy (New Mexico)	Direct	Leader
	Wheeler Peak (New Mexico)	Direct (traverse of cirque peaks)	Shared Leadership
1963	Mount Rainier	Emmons Glacier	Leader
1964	Mount St. Helens (Washington)	Dogs Head	Leader
	Mount Adams (Washington)	South Side Route	Leader
	Mount Hood (Oregon)	South Side	Leader
	Mount Olympus (Washington)	Ho River - Blue Glacier (48 hours round trip)	Leader
	Mount Rainier	Fuhrer Finger	Shared Leadership

Year	Mountain	Route	Responsibility
1965	Mount Timpanogos (Utah)	West Ridge - Couloir (1st ascent)	Leader
	Mount Rainier	Gibralter	Leader
	Mount Rainier	Disappointment Cleaver	Leader
	Mount Rainier	Fuhrer Finger	Leader
	Mount Rainier	Disappointment Cleaver	Commercial Guide
1966	Mount Timpanogos (Utah)	West Ridge - Couloir (winter)	Leader
	Mount Rainier	Disappointment Cleaver	Leader
1967	Wheeler Peak (Nevada)	Direct (1st midwinter ascent)	Leader
	Mount Nebo (Utah)	Cedar Ridge (winter)	Leader
	Mount Rainier	Nisqually Icefall (traverse)	Leader

General: Ranger mountain guide at Philmont Scout Ranch, New Mexico (1960-1962) - more than 50 ascents above 10,000 feet (mostly rock scrambling); Mount Rainier National Park Rescue Team rope leader (1963-1965); snow, glacier, and crevasse training (1963-1965); experience in leading 5th and 6th Class rock and ice climbs; extensive experience in route-finding under dense whiteout conditions; participation in many rescue operations (leading several) including helicopter hover airlifts; technical advisor to the Brigham Young University Rescue Team; Mountain Leader and Winter Mountaineering Leader, Brigham Young University Alpine Club; extensive first aid training including the administration of intravenous plasma expander (dextran); snowshoeing; winter camping; advanced skier; mountaineering in subzero temperatures and high winds; more than 3,000 miles of alpine hiking; more than 500 days of camping; group leader for a project forest fire, Mount Rainier National Park (1965); pre-McKinley snow, glacier, and crevasse practice at the Rainier workout.

13
Route-Finding

LOCATIONS ON ROUTE	ELEVATION GAIN	MILE-AGE	ROUTE-FINDING LEAD
Wonder Lake Campground — Clearwater Creek	300 feet	10	-------
Campground — McKinley River	-100 feet	3½	Wilcox
McKinley River Crossing	00 feet	1	McLaughlin
McKinley River — Turtle Hill	1000 feet	2½	W. Taylor
Turtle Hill — Clearwater Creek	-600 feet	3	W. Taylor
Clearwater Creek — Horse Cache	2000 feet	8	Russell
Horse Cache — Camp I (McGonagall Pass)	1220 feet	2	W. Taylor
Camp I — Camp II	780 feet	4½	Clark
Camp II — Camp III	1600 feet	3½	Wilcox
Camp III — Camp IV	2900 feet	3½	-------
Camp III — Flatiron Cache (10,200 feet)	2100 feet	2½	Wilcox
Flatiron Cache (10,200 feet) — Camp IV	800 feet	1	Luchterhand
Camp IV — Camp V	1100 feet	1	-------
Camp IV — Trail (11,300 feet)	300 feet	¼	Wilcox
Trail (11,300 feet) — Trail (11,400 feet)	100 feet	1/8	Russell
Trail (11,400 feet) — Cache (11,500 feet)	100 feet	1/8	W. Taylor
Cache (11,500 feet) — Camp V	600 feet	½	Wilcox

Camp V — Camp VI			
Camp V (12,700 feet) — Trail	2900 feet	1½	------
Trail (12,700 feet) — Trail (13,100 feet)	600 feet	¼	Wilcox
Trail (13,100 feet) — Trail (13,300 feet)	400 feet	1/8	Luchterhand
Trail (13,300 feet) — Cache (14,500 feet)	200 feet	1/8	Schlichter
Cache (14,500 feet) — Camp VI	1200 feet	½	Russell
	500 feet	½	McLaughlin
Camp VI — Camp VII			
Camp VI — Trail (16,000 feet)	2900 feet	2½	------
Trail (16,000 feet) — Cache (16,500 feet)	1000 feet	1	Wilcox
Cache (16,500 feet) — Camp VII	500 feet	½	Clark
	1400 feet	1	Snyder
Camp VII — South Peak	2420 feet	2	Snyder

DESCENT

	ELEVATION LOSS	MILEAGE
South Peak — Camp VII	−2420 feet	2
Camp VII — Camp VI	−2900 feet	2½
Camp VI — Cache (15,500 feet) — Return to Camp VI	±500 feet	1½
Camp VI — Camp V	−2900 feet	1½
Camp V —Moraine (6,100 feet)	−6000 feet	10¼
Moraine (6,100 feet) — MCA Camp (2,800 feet)	−3300 feet	7¾
MCA Camp — Wonder Lake Campground (omit Turtle Hill)	−600 feet	13½
	Total —18120 feet	Total 39

Summary of Route-Finding Leads

CLIMBER	ELEVATION GAIN	MILEAGE
Joe Wilcox	6100 feet	11 ½
* Howard Snyder	3820 feet	3
John Russell	3300 feet	8 5/8
Walt Taylor	1720 feet	7 5/8
Jerry Clark	1280 feet	5
Dennis Luchterhand	1200 feet	1 1/8
Mark McLaughlin	500 feet	1 ½
Paul Schlichter	200 feet	1/8
	**Total 18120 feet	**Total 38 ½

*Howard also led 800 vertical feet (1 ½ miles) above Camp II which was not used as an ascent route because of avalanche hazard.

**Including supply relays each expedition member required about 100 miles and 35,000 vertical feet of climbing to reach the summit. During the expedition I spent 38 days on the mountain and traveled on foot a total of approximately142 miles.

14
Radio Log

Excerpts from the KHD6990 *Radio Log* kept at Eielson Visitor Center by seasonal rangers, Gordon Haber and George Perkins.

DAY 13[1] — JULY 1, 8:30 PM:

"Two camps, 8,000' and 6,500' (below Lower Icefall)"

DAY 14 — JULY 2, 8:05 PM:

". . . requested info as to whether or not there was a CB station in Fairbanks which might be continuously monitoring a particular channel in case of emergencies; plan to work on both a night and day schedule; talked with both Jerry Clark and Hank Janes; Janes requested that a postcard be sent to his employer notifying him that he would be 1-2 weeks late for job; all in excellent spirits."

DAY 15 — JULY 3, 8:05 PM:

". . . entire group in excellent spirits. . . very large avalanche this morning up above them; had them all apprehensive for a few moments. . . The entire group is planning on wearing Bermuda

---

1. Thirteenth day of expedition.

shorts when they reach the top. . .25° virtually no wind, soupy white snow and light fog with bluish-gray sky overhead; the only sign of wildlife they've seen up on the glacier is some raven tracks of a raven which has been following for several days. . ."

DAY 16 — JULY 4:

"No contact"

Day 17 — JULY 5, 9:30 AM:

"Upper camp at base of K's Ridge;[2] will work on route up to crest today; temperature 10 degrees last night; 1-1½' of powder snow above Flatiron. . . plastic shoes[3] breaking but easily repairable. . ."

8:00 PM: "Talked with lower camp. . .   Plan to move lower camp to base of ridge tomorrow. . .   K's has 3' of powder snow."

DAY 18 — JULY 6, 8:05 PM:

"All at camp at 11,000'; trail broken from here to next camp at 12,100'. . . 4½' of soft snow on K's Ridge; present temp. 12°; virtually no wind; snowing below 11,000'"

DAY 19 — JULY 7:

"Returned late and missed schedule; no contact."

DAY 20 — JULY 8, 9:30 AM:

"Upper camp on K's Ridge; lower camp at base; snowing. . . requested general weather forecasts."

8:00 PM: "Reception poor because transmitting from inside tent; temp. 16°; winds 30-40 mph."

DAY 21 — JULY 9, 8:05 PM:

"Main camp now at 12,100' on K's Ridge. . . setting up fixed line and making slow progress; snow conditions very soft and

2. Karstens Ridge
3. Snowtreads

shoulder deep in places. . . present temp. at main camp 16°; breezy 30 mph wind. . . requested info as to status of climbers coming up behind /MCA/. . ."

DAY 22 — JULY 10, 8:00 PM:

"Carrying loads on Coxcomb; sighted small sparrow-like birds/rosy finches?/; morale apparently high but look forward to radio transmissions because they're tired of looking at same faces/ Hank Janes talking/; asked that. . . barometer readings and tendencies be given/current reading: 30.35/."

DAY 23 — JULY 11:

"No contact."

DAY 24 — JULY 12, 8:00 PM:

"Baro. 30.28, -0.07 in 48 hours; upper camp at 15,000'. . . camp visible from Eielson all day; lower party plan to reach upper camp at midnight; times for climb (15,000') vary from 5-12 hours; temp. 2° last night; winds low; plan to start trail to Denali Pass tomorrow; estimate two days to reach it."

DAY 25 — JULY 13, 8:00 PM:

". . . temp. last night 8° . . .no serious altitude effects. . . diet quite varied; tuna-rice, fruit, Instant Breakfast, crackers, much candy, fudge, etc.; eating well with no cravings for unobtainable foods. . . winds light/ Eielson baro.: 30.25, –0.03/."

DAY 26 — JULY 14, 8:00 PM: [4]

". . . baro. 30.35, +0.10; communications somewhat broken by interference and antenna difficulty. . . Unit One at 17,900'; temp. 9°; little or no wind. . . temp. at 15,000' camp 26°; Logan tent burned down at 15,000'; 1 man burned (Walter Taylor). . . adequate 1st aid with antibiotics administered."

---

4. Beginning with this contact Eielson tape-recorded portions of the radio transmissions.

DAY 27 — JULY 15, 8:30 AM:

"Relayed weather info up; high camp tired (17,900'); decided to rest and see how weather changes; one man with slight altitude symptoms; team from lower camp will go up to high camp today with wands and food."

10:50 AM: "Will make attempt for South Peak. . . Joe, Howard, Jerry Lewis, and Paul Schlichter will make south summit try; Jerry Clark and. . . McLaughlin may make try for North Peak; present temp. at 17,900' camp 23°; not much clouds; lots of sun; steady wind gusting occasionally to 20 mph; snow conditions good; breaking through 4-5" with crampons. . ."

1:55 PM: "At 15,800'; clouds, big cirrus, 35,000'. . . going to 17,900' camp today; will rest there for 8 hours then start to summit. . . W. Taylor's burned hand fine, blister going down; / Wilcox at 18,700'/: 500' per hour climbing rate; 4 hours to summit; very slight S. wind. . . Dennis sick yesterday, resting today. . ."

4:25 PM: "At 19,550' behind Archdeacon's Tower; temp. 15°; minor headaches and altitude symptoms; but only minor; no problems; will reach summit 6:30-7:00 PM."

5:05 PM: "At 19,700'/Wilcox/; 'air mighty thin—could use a couple of bottles of oxygen'; will reach summit in about 1½ hours from now; ever since Denali Pass they've seen tracks in the snow, probably from China Lake climbers; /Unit Two / : presently at 16,500'; have been on trail for five hours. . ."

6:10 PM: "Units One and Two/on tape/."

6:30 PM: "Unit One on summit / on tape/."

. . .

DAY 29 — JULY 17, 8:20 AM:

"All at 17,900' weathered in; wind not bad—20-30 mph, but very cloudy and poor visibility (less than 200'); 4 or 5 from 17,900' camp to go down to 15,000' camp this AM (including 1 of 8 who have not yet reached peak—altitude sickness), remaining 7 will make a try for summit today if possible. . ."

9:30 AM: "Snowing and blowing steady at 20 mph; gusting to 40 mph."

11:05 AM: "Weather clearing slightly; some blue sky visible; possible summit try this afternoon. . . 5 will start down to camp at 15,000'; present temp. at 17,900' 25° but feels much colder due to wind; will maintain 8:00 PM radio schedule with both units."

4:40 PM: "6 ón way to south summit; ETA: 8-9 PM: just above Denali Pass now; will call again at 7:30 PM."

Evening: "On tape"

DAY 30 — JULY 18, 11:30 AM:

"Unit One on summit / on tape /."

8:05 PM: "Unit Two (Wilcox) at 15,000'; will wait here for others to bring 17,900' camp down; presently in a raging snowstorm; much snow coming down and 50 mph winds; moderate temp.; no contact with Unit One; Wilcox thinks Unit One probably back down to 17,900' but cannot communicate because of bad weather; says weather conditions much worse higher up. . ."

. . .

DAY 32 — JULY 20, 9:00 AM:

"Request for weather; no word from high camp."

Late AM: "Snow and wind conditions bad. . . 4 hours to travel ¾ mile toward high camp. If no contact with high camp by 8:00 PM, requested flight by ARG to:

> determine number of people at 17,900'
> drop radio
> drop white gas

High camp has five to six days' food;[5] little or no fuel."

4:00 PM: "Further data for possible flight relayed;[6] request for tape of last contact with high camp summit party to be transmitted."

8:00 PM: ". . ./on tape /."

DAY 33 — JULY 21, 7:45 AM:

"Reception by Unit Two poor; winds up to 65 mph; may build snow caves at 15,000'; estimate winds up to 80 mph at high camp."

DAY 34 — JULY 22:

"Beginning with 7/22, all transmissions are taped."

---

5. Including the 16,500 foot cache. (Only 2-3 days of the high camp food was thought to be left.)

6. From Unit Two, through Eielson, to Wayne Merry at Wonder Lake.

15

Rescue Log

A summary of the *Rescue Log* kept by District Ranger Wayne Merry at Wonder Lake Ranger Station.

. . .

DAY 32[1] — JULY 20, Noon:

" 'Unit Two' (Wilcox) called from 15,000' camp expressing concern for men at upper camp. He said that the upper camp was either very low or completely out of fuel. He said that they had about 5-6 days' rations there. He felt that some of the members at the high camp were weak when they started the climb, and that the bivouac had not helped. He requested an overflight to drop fuel, radio, and count men at upper camp. He reported high winds, temp. near zero, and alternating spells of clear weather and snowstorm at 15,000'. He asked that a definite request for an overflight be transmitted to the ARG if there was no contact with the upper group by 8:00 PM. . ."

4:00 PM: "Merry talked with Wilcox[2] to get more facts on the situation. Wilcox did not have any reason to believe the men were caught out above the camp, but had probably returned to camp at

---

1. Thirty-second day of expedition.
2. Relayed through Eielson.

384

17,900' after the summit climb. He said that he thought that the party had 2 days' rations[3] and sleeping bags for half the members *with them* when they bivouacked. The wanding interval from camp to summit was 150-200'. The party had carried compasses. . .

"Regarding conditions at the upper camp, he said that the camp was a tent camp, dug in about 2' at 17,900' and about ⅓ of the way across the glacier from the N. Peak side. . . believed them to be out of fuel.

"Regarding conditions at the 15,000' camp, he said that it was a tent camp, that there were 5 men there . . . that three of them felt strong and would move up when possible. . . They had previously tried to climb to the higher camp. . . 4 hours to go ¾ mile and estimated it would take 24 hours to reach the high camp if weather permitted a climb. . . the upper team had planned to pack the camp down to 15,000' immediately after the climb, and that their continued absence indicated that they were weak or in difficulty. He said that at their camp (15,000') they had approx. 10 days' rations for the five men, and did not appear to be concerned about their own welfare. He was asked about radio batteries, however, and did ask that some size AA Penlite alkaline batteries be dropped on the same overflight.

"Wilcox was told that under present conditions, his team was the best hope for assistance for the upper party if assistance was needed, as they were nearby, acclimatized, equipped, and feeling strong. He understood this and planned to move up as soon as weather permitted. He was told that the ARG had been alerted, and asked if he understood that they would probably be billed for the flight, as there was no certainty that an emergency existed. He replied with a 'Roger.' He was asked if he wanted to have Sheldon chartered if the ARG could not fly, and again replied 'Roger.' He was then told that a 'go-ahead' on the flight would be transmitted to ARG as requested, at 8:00 PM, if the upper camp had not been heard from."

8:00 PM: ". . .He[4] was again reminded that his team was closest, and should move out when possible. He was told the go-ahead for the air-drop would be made immediately, and radios,

---

3. Each expedition member always carried about 1 day of emergency rations requiring no cooking. The summit party probably carried additional food.
4. Wilcox.

fuel, and batteries dropped as requested *if possible*. A 7:45 AM radio check was arranged. All information was relayed to Art Hayes,[5] who contacted Gary Hansen. . ."[6]

DAY 33 — JULY 21, 7:45 AM:

"Contact with Wilcox at Eielson. No new information, except that weather was much worse. Winds estimated at steady 50, gusting to 65. Wilcox estimated that winds were higher above. They were still unable to move, but considered building a snow cave. A new radio contact was arranged for 2:00 PM. Wilcox's radio batteries may have weakend, as he could not read Eielson clearly."

9:45 AM: "Smith (Wonder Lake) rec'd word from Art Hayes that arrangements were being made for an overflight and drop with a Turbo-prop Beaver, as Sheldon's plane could not fly effectively under present conditions. Plans had been made to drop both CB and Voice Commander radios, as well as fuel, food and batteries."

2:00 PM: "No contact with Wilcox party."

2:45 PM: "Merry radioed Hayes, giving preparatory info on accommodations at Wonder Lake area if a major operation should be based here, as follows:

> Can accommodate 10 men at station if they bring sleeping bags—mattresses here for that many. Should bring own food and cooking pots.
> Could shelter 25 more if needed, if they bring all sleeping, cooking & messing gear.
> Camp Denali[7] can provide full accommodations for 18 until Monday night, at $20/day, but will be full after that. Also can shelter 6 or 8 with own sleeping gear, and feed them if needed—these indefinitely.
> Quigley cabin can probably shelter 10 men with own gear & food, if a base must be set up there for the airstrip.[8] Art should get in contact with Mrs. Nordale in

---

5. Chief Park Ranger.

6. Alaska Rescue Group Chairman.

7. The road does not end at Wonder Lake but continues for a few miles beyond the park boundary. Camp Denali is a private wilderness resort just beyond the park boundary.

8. Kantishna airstrip is outside the park boundary and about 6 miles from Wonder Lake.

Fairbanks if this will be needed. Also a tin shack at the strip can shelter 2.

The campground can serve as base for any ground troops which may arrive.

By way of preparation, the word was also passed to Hayes that:

> The Kantishna strip was 1750' long and was 32 miles from the 17,900' camp. The Wonder Lake RS was 28 miles from same.[9]

If a large operation was anticipated out here, we would need a large supply of 80/87 aircraft fuel, as there was none here, and the hotel[10] supply is limited. The Turbo-Beaver might not burn this fuel, and this should be checked. We would probably need the Handy-Talkies and several portable sets for installation at airstrip, C. Denali, etc. and these should be made ready. The superintendent should probably designate a press officer.

He was also informed that Merry was making a further list of needed materials which would be transmitted if it developed that a rescue was needed and would be based at Wonder Lake.

"Hayes replied that there was no new word from ARG. During the afternoon, Merry radioed HQ to reiterate the importance of fuel in the proposed drop, and was assured by Hayes that the full message had been transmitted to Hansen."

4:00 PM: Hayes called Merry and reported that Hansen had packed for drop at 17,900' the requested fuel, some batteries, and two types of radios, both CB and Voice Commander. Also some food. Radios and batteries were also packed for the 15,000' camp. It had developed that the Turbo-Beaver was not available (or the pilot was not) and that the packages were now being taken to Talkeetna, where Sheldon felt he could get up to that level with a break in the weather. He planned a flight in the morning if weather permitted, and was in radio contact with commercial liners to watch weather at high elevations. . ."

---

9. These distances are for air travel. Hiking distance from Wonder Lake to Camp VII was about 35.5 miles.
10. McKinley Park Hotel near headquarters.

8:00 PM: "No contact with climbers. High winds continue at Wonder Lake.

"During the evening, Merry was called by Reyer.[11] Word was sent to Hayes concerning possible needs at Wonder Lake in case a major operation was based here. . .''

DAY 34 — JULY 22, 8:00 AM:

"Eielson still has no contact with Wilcox. Raining at Wonder Lake, but winds down. Clouds at 3-4,000', moving fairly fast from SW."

8:10 AM: "Contact with Reyer at HQ. Weather bad there also. No new word on flight. Reyer requested to ask Hayes to have Sheldon check locations of MCA and Western States groups when and if he flew, as Western States group just might be dug in at 17,200' on West Buttress, and be able to drop over Denali Pass easily if needed. . . Reyer asked for weather conditions, and will also try to get a forecast from Weather Bureau."[12]

9:00 AM: "Reyer reports on weather conditions. . .

"Forecast—continuing the same today, possibly breaking somewhat tomorrow. . . Sheldon had been checking weather, said ceiling was 6,000' at Talkeetna but appeared to be 4,000' on mountain. He is not flying. . .

"It appears that there is little to do now except plan for the break in the weather. It is likely that the upper party is now low on food."

11:30 AM: "Found that channel 7 (3411.5)[13] is operable, despite assurance that the antenna was not tuned for it. Talked with Roberta Sheldon 5 x 5 at WEX6 Talkeetna, and arranged for her to phone HQ when Don is to fly the mountain so that this station can monitor 3411.5 at that time."

4:30 PM: "Clouds breaking, ceiling sometimes to about 12,000' on McKinley. Wind moderate and gusty on ground, apparently high aloft.

---

11. A park official at headquarters.

12. Old name for the National Weather Service.

13. The frequency of Don Sheldon's radio. His radio call letters were WEX6.

"Merry called Reyer, requested him to phone Sheldon and:
1. Ask him if he knew the position of the WSE.[14]
2. Ask him to look for them if he flew, and drop them a note or call them on Voice Commander radio to inform of situation, & ask them to arrange daily schedule with Radio Anchorage until the situation is clarified.

"Reyer was also asked to call Bob Hansen, Communications Engineering, and have him:
1. Call Radio Fairbanks to pass the word to the MCA crew of the present situation, and ask them to set up a daily schedule until clarified. (The MCA crew, now probably at base of Karstens Ridge, had planned to call Radio FBX at 8:00 AM and PM on Sundays.)"

7:00 PM: "Called Reyer (blind)[15] requesting that George[16] be asked about installing his 100-watt linear amplifier at Eielson during this emergency."

8:30 PM: "Mountain partly clear to summit—snow plumes and blowing snow from ridges obscure Harper Glacier.

"Wilcox makes contact with Eielson. Says lower camp is in shambles, equipment is wet, men are weak, all now in one tent. (Presumably the other is destroyed.) Says mountain is clear now, wind is gusting to 15, temp. about 0°. . . They plan to leave immediately for lower elevation. Questioned, he says that only one of them would feel strong enough to go *up*, and only *if* dry sleeping bag could be dropped. Says that they will take tent, leaving none at 15,000'. . . they will descend as far as possible tonight. Plan to leave 5 days' food[17] at 15,000', but no fuel. . . He estimates 3 days' food[18] left at upper camp at this time. He says that snow conditions at 17,900' were such (when he was there last) that he felt the upper group might have been able to dig in. Said that his group had seen some crates cached at Denali Pass, but did not know

---

14. Western States Expedition.
15. Wayne could not hear Reyer's radio transmission and could only hope that the message got through.
16. George Robinson. His 5-watt radio was already on loan to Eielson for communication with our expedition.
17. 5 days of food for the 7 high climbers. 35 man-days of food altogether. (Arithmetic would suggest that only 33 man-days of food remained at 15,000 feet, however, we had eaten less than full rations during the storm.)
18. Including the 16,500 foot cache.

contents. . .

"Wilcox said that the upper camp did not know that there was no fuel at lower camp, and that upper camp did not know of cache at 15,500'. This info, plus info on no tentage and food supply at 15,000', was to be relayed by Reyer to Sheldon, for possible note drop or radio transmission to upper team.

"Wilcox said that aside from being weak, there were no injuries or sickness in their group.

"The above information was immediately relayed to Reyer, for transmission to Sheldon, Hansen, and Hayes. Reyer phoned Sheldon's home, but Sheldon was in Anchorage and would return about 11:00 PM. Merry suggested that he call Hansen and Hayes with this info—possibly Sheldon would be in contact with Hansen in Anchorage. Also suggested that Hansen again consider the Turbo-Beaver if a pilot were now available.

"CB and park radios and Eielson, W. Lake, and HQ will continue to be monitored all night."

11:15 PM: "Wilcox has not moved. . . Will remain in place tonight. . . Did not appear worried (about own condition) but sounded in low spirits. . ."

DAY 35 — JULY 23, 8:00 AM:

"Contact with Wilcox[19] indicates that 2 of lower party are very weak and Wilcox has frostbitten fingers. They will descend to Muldrow. Felt no assistance would be needed. . ."

8:15 AM: "Reyer reports that he has been in contact with Sheldon, who is preparing to take off, but is doubtful of chances of getting through because of turbulence. Says Sheldon is very upset with Wilcox abandoning upper group, and thinks he just wants publicity. Reyer says he couldn't make Sheldon understand the proposed signals for the climbers.

"Information from 8:00 contact passed to Reyer. Merry urged that a larger plane—RCC unit if necessary—be asked to fly over the mountain to spot upper party, as condition of lower group indicated that more serious trouble could easily exist higher. Suggested Reyer ask Hayes to call Hansen, as it appeared that Sheldon might not be effective.

---

19. Howard Snyder handled this radio contact with Eielson.

"Wonder Lake and Eielson weather was relayed to Reyer for his use in getting a weather forecast."

10:00 AM: "Reyer reports that Sheldon should be flying, asks if I can monitor. Says supt. has been informed of situation, wishes to give Sheldon a chance before calling on other agency. Will monitor 3411.5 for a while. About 9:30, spotted trail in snow leading to top of Karstens Ridge from 15,000' level through brief break in clouds."

11:00 AM: "Wilcox[20] radioed that it took two hours for them to reach the 14,500' level from their 15,000' camp, and says that Jerry Lewis is extremely fatigued. Want advice on whether to use Dexedrine. Merry replied that advice could not be given from this source as the situation was not known here, and there was no physician here — they would have to use own judgment. They also report that they can see the area of the high camp and see no tents or activity. They agreed to next contact at 2:00 PM. Advice was passed to Eielson that they should watch Lewis closely for signs of personality changes or other indications of lowered general body temperature; if so to dig in, and warm him up. However, they had signed off. Requested Eielson to pass this info at next contact, also check on their general condition and location."

11:15 AM: "Information passed to Reyer. Supt. standing by, is in favor of high altitude flight. Merry urged such a flight, including drop of dry sleeping bags to lower team if possible."

11:20 AM: "Merry called Roberta Sheldon on 3411.5, passed information on condition of lower party and their observation of upper camp. She said Sheldon was presently flying scientific personnel into 10,000' level for S. Face Exp., was planning to return to strip down plane and make flight to high Wilcox camp. Arranged for me to monitor 3411.5 at 1:00 PM to talk to Sheldon. Also informed Roberta we would probably arrange for a high altitude overflight."

11:30 AM: "Relayed above info to Reyer. He says Hansen wishes to know if Wilcox wants to definitely call a rescue. Will check this on next contact. Superintendent informed and standing by. Merry again urged high altitude RCC overflight, equipped with drop sled."

Noon: "Lenticular cloud forming rapidly over peak."

---

20. Howard Snyder handled this radio contact with Eielson.

12:40 PM: "Merry called HQ to inform that flying weather around mountain was deteriorating rapidly, and suggested that if supt. agreed to high altitude flight, it should be immediate. Reyer reported that a decision had been made to wait on Sheldon's flight before calling other aircraft, and that Hansen felt WSE and MCA groups were best hope—Sheldon hopefully could locate these."

1:00 PM: "Radio contact with Sheldon, via Roberta at WEX6. He says he is just returning from a flight to land two doctors on the mountain for the S. Face group—had to land them at 7,400' rather than 10,000' because of winds. He plans to fly up to make drop if possible as soon as he gets back. Says winds of 60 knots[21] at 10,000' and probably higher above, but will try drop if he can. Asked him if he knew location of WSE, and he indicated that they were somewhere above 10,200' Asked if WEX6 was in contact with S. Face group, and Roberta indicated that they were not— probably radio not hooked up right. Arranged further radio contact at 3:00 PM."

1:15 PM: "Passed on above to Reyer & had long discussion of best approach. He or Hayes had been in contact with Hansen, who wished to use Sheldon rather than larger craft, as did Hayes. Reyer also asked clarification of some details for benefit of supt. . . . which were passed on."

. . .

2:30 PM: "Local interference from possible mobile units. . . Merry requested Perkins to broadcast blind, asking units in McKinley Park to keep air clear as possible for emergency on mountain. . ."

3:00 PM: "KWA701[22] contacted WEX6. Sheldon did not fly —too much wind. Will try in a couple of hours or maybe tomorrow. Roberta to call park when he flies. Requested her to tell Don [Sheldon] to try to locate and inform WSE if he could. . .

3:10 PM: "Passed on above to Reyer. Reyer says decision has been made to wait for Don to fly rather than call in larger aircraft. Merry requested his recommendation be passed on to Art that an

---

21. 69 miles per hour.
22. The radio call letters for Wonder Lake were KWA701.
    The radio call letters for Eielson Visitor Center were KWA702.
    The radio call letters for McKinley Park Headquarters were KWA700.

RCC plane make a run if it appears at all feasible, rather than waiting on Sheldon's limited small-craft capability. Sheldon excellent for close-in support if conditions right, but larger craft could supply a look from a few thousand feet above the mountain under conditions when Sheldon could not fly—what we need most is a *look* to see what the story is at 17,900'—if materials are simultaneously ready to drop, so much the better. Also checked to be sure that RCC was alerted to possible need for observation craft and Hueys.[23]

"Weather now entirely obscuring mountain—any chance of flying anything is probably gone for today."

4:45 PM: "Eielson reports contact with Wilcox,[24] who has made good progress and has reached the 12,100' camp of the MCA group. Lewis has improved . . . All 5 members of the Wilcox group will stay at the 12,100' camp tonight . . . Wilcox wishes to wait out Sheldon's reconnaissance. . . before making a decision about all-out rescue. MCA group estimated 4 days. . . to reach upper campsite. . . Wilcox was having transmission problems. . ."

8:00 PM: "Radio contact between Eielson and Wilcox. Reports that all are recovering rapidly, planning to descend tomorrow, need no assistance. Plan to be at McGonagall in 1 day, Wonder Lake in 2. Said they would like to go back up via helicopter if their assistance needed. They are leaving radio with MCA group, and would like to have a drop of 20 batteries (AA alkaline) to that group. They will still be all together tomorrow at 8:00 AM for the last contact. Wilcox wishes to wait for calling the rescue until Sheldon has flown, however, he emphasizes that rescue should be ready to go immediately if flight shows trouble. The MCA group said they wished to be taken higher by helicopter if it should prove necessary, and Wilcox asked that an RCC plane be called if Sheldon could not fly.

". . . All of the MCA group is at 12,100'. . . Present weather is no wind, temp. in 20's, snow falling, no visibility.

"Wilcox asked that the relatives of the 5 lower be called collect to inform they were coming down and OK. Schiff esp. insistent on this. (During the night heavy rains washed out the road between HQ and Wonder Lake.)"

---

23. Large helicopters.
24. Contact with climbers had occurred at 2:00 PM.

DAY 36 — JULY 24, 8:00 AM:

"Poor contact with Wilcox. He indicates that the lower 5 would be descending today, taking with them Dr. Grace Jansen, who is apparently having difficulty of some sort. Wilcox asked Merry's opinion on calling a rescue—replied that first requisite was probably some sort of observation to determine location and condition of team, but that all rescue personnel were alerted for action. Wilcox also asked if Merry thought a large plane could fly at high altitude for observation purposes. Replied that this had been strongly recommended, but decision was not mine to make. Wilcox commented that there had been days when high altitude observation would have been practical when small craft could not fly, and he would like the use of a large plane if conditions were right. . ."

9:00 AM: "Above word relayed to HQ: also information from last night's contact. Lost contact with HQ during last part of message—did not relay Wilcox's comments on high altitude craft. Will relay as soon as contact established. 702 tried and failed. (Contact made shortly after—HQ could read, confirmed by keying 3 times.)"

3:00 PM: "Contact with WEX6—Sheldon unable to fly. . ."

6:15 PM: "Haber reports contact with part of Everett expedition at 15,800'[25] on S. Buttress while trying to get contact with MCA group. They say they just had a storm and are now down to 5 days' food. Will try another contact at 9:00 PM."

8:00 PM: ". . . Wilcox left at noon. . . MCA is *NOT* yet in contact with FBX. Planning to try for Browne Tower tomorrow. There are now 4-5' of fresh snow, they are sinking in almost that far. They say that they are in *fair* condition. Haber's opinion was that they were primar. interested in helping the other party at this point, rather than being enthusiastic about a summit try. . ."

DAY 37 — JULY 25, 8:00 AM:

"MCA group reports weather at 12,100'—no wind, clear, with very high clouds. . . Report that Wilcox. . . has two weak people

---

25. Boyd Everett's South Face group in contact with Eielson was at 16,800 feet on the South Buttress as later verified by their expedition log.

(including Dr. Jansen). . . MCA will attempt to get to Browne Tower today, conditions good. . .

"Eielson also had faint contact with S. Buttress party—they are continuing up. . . with 5 days' rations remaining, but will be available for helicopter pick-up and rescue operation if required."

8:30 AM: "No news concerning operation from HQ. Radio reception excellent."

8:45 AM: "Merry attempted to reach HQ to be sure weather from MCA group was relayed to Sheldon *immediately* & Sheldon urged to fly before weather came in. Was unable to get response from HQ, so called Sheldon direct on 3411.5. Relayed weather, asked him to fly as soon as possible as it appeared more clouds coming from west. Reception spotty, but he replied that he was loaded and would fly immediately, anticipated being in N. Face McKinley area in 1 hr. 30 minutes in 4642U.[26] I told him I would monitor 3411.5 at that time. He asked why party at 12,100' did not go up and look—replied that they estimated it would take 4 days of good conditions."

8:50 AM: "Again attempted to reach HQ — no contact. Sent above info blind."

9:25 AM: "Ditto. Asked 702 to try to relay. (702 very clear.) No contact."

10:05 AM: "Switched to 3411.5. Heard unidentified station on McKinley calling WEX6 asking when Sheldon would arrive. Roberta answered 1-13 hrs. (????)."

10:45 AM: "Read message from 42U to WEX6 — indicated he was northbound and weather looked promising."

10:50 AM: "Contact with WEX6 and 42U—Sheldon at 8,000' in the clear, approaching to 10,000' level West Buttress to check on WSE location, then to Harper Glacier via East Buttress approach (winds more favorable). Has excellent contact with WEX6 and can hear 701 well, but is coming in faintly here."

11:15 AM: "Contact with Sheldon in 42U. Sheldon observes MCA group at about 12,500', going up fast. Reports standing wave cloud covering mountain from 15,000' to 25,000'. He observes no fresh tracks around 15,000' camp. He asked to drop gear to MCA group. I replied negative. He suggested dropping gear at 15,000',

---

26. Apparently Sheldon's airplane numbers.

replied OK but should probably hold radios to drop higher in case of being able to see higher crew tomorrow. He replied he felt (insisted!) he should drop all at 15,000', as Hansen could get him more radios if needed. Replied OK—drop all gear. He dropped all gear approximately ¼ mile west of 15,000' camp, all on trail or within 100' of it (drop at 11:40). Asked him about WSE party—he replied he thinks they are at 7,400 foot[27] level, but will check and report back in 20 minutes. Reports mountain socking in from wave cloud. Says he will now proceed to check location of WSE group and then down to 7,400' level to ferry scientific equipment of Drs. to 10,000' for S. Face Expedition.

"Immediately passed on word to Hayes to relay to Hansen. Also summed up situation and asked for sharper operation, possibly higher overflights in good weather, decision on rescue operation."

5:00 PM: "Fading contact with Hayes—asked news of rescue arrangements. He said that he had called Hansen but that Hansen was not available, and had called someone else in the ARG. Broken and fading transmission (covered partly by KWB346 Anchorage). I though he said that RCC craft were being arranged for. Also heard him say phone communications from HQ were tied up. I told him I would call (or try to call) WEX6 to ask Sheldon to inform Hansen of situation. Communication broke off. Attempted WEX6—no contact."

5:30 PM (approx.): "Contact with Eielson by MCA group. At Browne Tower. . . asked if there was food in the air-drop. . . They asked if OK to use materials in drop. Replied certainly — anything to get them to upper party sooner. Asked if they might have a drop later if needed. Reply affirmative. Informed them of five days' food for five men at 15,000' camp,[28] as reported by Wilcox. Requested them to reach Radio FBX as soon as they could get contact, and arrange phone patch with Hansen or Crews,[29] etc. to inform of details, as communication appeared to be unreliable down here. Asked them to move fast as possible. . . Tried repeatedly to call 700 or WEX6 Talkeetna, to find out about food in drop—also to ask that RCC be contacted and asked to start orbiting plane with

---

27. According to the WSE log they were at 17,200' on July 25, 1967.

28. Perhaps an error in communications. I later corrected this to 5 days for 7 men.

29. ARG officials.

drop sled over mountain looking for break in weather, starting early tomorrow. Apparently communication is broken down—I will ask them to start orbiting and will take the responsibility for the request, if they cannot get through to get it confirmed by chief ranger or superintendent."

8:00 PM: "Radio contact between Eielson and MCA group—one way only—Eielson spoke and MCA keyed yes or no. Passed on basic info about drops, requested they establish radio contact when possible with ARG. . ."

9:30 PM: "After repeated attempts to get through to HQ or WEX6, Merry asked Celia Hunter[30] to try to reach ARG members (gave numbers of Hansen, Crews, Maagoe) via HAM radio, to ask them to request an RCC craft orbiting McKinley with drop sled, to look for activity at 17,900'. . . Asked them to try to get this early in AM to take advantage of any possible good early weather. Asked them to call supt. or chief ranger to confirm authority—if they could not be reached, Merry would be responsible for request if this was acceptable. (Note: she called. . . for some time but was unable to raise anyone.)"

DAY 38 — JULY 26, 8:00 AM:

"Relayed above to HQ—was informed that no contact had been made with RCC or ARG—that it would 'be taken care of at this end.' Checked with supt.—he says he is informed of situation. Also relayed weather to HQ."

8:45 AM: "Hayes called 701 to ask what the disposition and position of the 7 men at 17,900' had been, especially, had they made the top? This information was passed on."

9:00 AM: "Hayes called to ask what weather conditions had been on summit on the 18th."

10:15 AM: "Merry back in office, called Hall for summary of NPS's[31] efforts and thoughts on a rescue. Hall reports ARG Council in meeting, with all of the information on the condition of the climbers known to date. NPS opinion of the conditions: 1.) Sheldon flying low reconnaissance is the most effective means of discovering the climbers' conditions; 2.) the MCA group should be

---

30. Affiliated with Camp Denali.
31. National Park Service.

in the area in 24 to 48 hours. Under the present weather conditions, neither Sheldon nor the helicopters could reach there before the MCA group does. Due to an oversight, the party coming up the south side[32] has no radio antenna, and are therefore not of use. We cannot tell what the conditions are at 17,900' because the reconnaissance run by Sheldon did not reach that high. The following has been accomplished: 1.) Sheldon has dropped equipment at 15,000', and 2.) the Rescue Council has to determine whether a rescue can be made, and then, whether one is needed. The NPS can only coordinate. The important problems are to identify their (the top climbers') location, and then, to arrange a pick-up if necessary. (This was good news, as up to this point it appeared at this station that the only action taken so far had been to ask Sheldon for an observation and drop flight, and it appeared that this mission was taking a back seat to other flights—e.g. to the South Face group. At this point I remarked on the effectiveness of the C-130's. Was asked to sit tight pending further decisions.)

"Hall mentioned possibility of reason for delay being attempt on N. Peak. . . He is very concerned about the safety of these 7 men. If the need arises, just about any sized airplane equipped for water landing could land on Wonder Lake. Kantishna airstrip is inaccessible at the moment."

Noon: "Wilcox arrived from mountain. Left McGonagall yesterday, had to actually swim Clearwater Cr. and 3 channels of McKinley River. Left pack this side of Clearwater. Tired and cold, somewhat skinned up from floating logs[33] in McKinley, but seems OK. He reports the following information which was not available before:

"On the 16th, a windstorm hit the 17,900' camp and 3 quarts fuel lost. If these have been found, things could be better. When he left there on the 17th, the party had 2 qts. This should have lasted perhaps 2 days.

"Taylor did not appear to be seriously ill when he left. Symptoms were typical of a fairly normal altitude reaction. Some of the others appeared to be just as sick. Wilcox did not feel that the

---

32. Reference is apparently to the main group of the South Face Expedition.
33. Error: injuries were incurred from rocks.

bivouac should have seriously hurt the party, nor that it is likely that they were unable to get back; however, he said there was a *very* slight and unlikely possibility that they might have followed the wrong wands down and got onto the West Buttress.

"Regarding the radio owned by the upper party, he reports that Clark is a good radio technician, had worked on and altered the sets previously. . . They also had a battery pack plus batteries. He consequently feels that the radio somehow became lost. . .

"There are, at this time, 5 days' food for 7 men left at the 15,000' campsite, but that is all. There *is*, however, contrary to a previous report, a cache of food at 16,500', marked with snowshoes.[34] Twenty man-days there, no fuel. The fuel cache at 15,500' is 3—rather than 2—gallons, in a 5-gal. can dug into an ice hump.

"All food in the Wilcox camps is about 50% of type requiring cooking.[35]

"Wilcox says that since the first possible emergency call on the 20th, there have been no days that a light plane could have flown effectively; but that there were clear spells on most of the days when observations from high altitude aircraft would have been feasible.

"Concerning the lower group, (of which he was a part) they are as follows:

"Snyder, Schlichter, and Lewis, are (or were left yesterday)

---

34. The 16,500 foot cache was marked with Snowtreads and wands. In previous communications I had always included this cache with my estimates of the high camp food supply.

35. This statement needs some clarification. Inspection of M-8, M-11 and M-13, and realizing that the food in question was high altitude within days 31-40, reveals that only about 15.5 percent of the cached food by calories (17.1 percent by weight) was designed to be cooked or heated and perhaps all of it could be effectively ingested without any use of fuel. Clarifying this fact, however, is not meant to discredit concern for fuel to melt snow. About 44.2 percent of the cached food by calories (48.9 percent by weight) was designed to utilize water for mixing or reconstitution, and at high elevation maintaining enough body moisture is certainly as constricting a parameter as feeding the body furnace. Dehydration is a subtle and effective killer at extreme altitudes.

camped about 1 mile this side of McGonagall Pass.[36] Lewis is in great pain from frostbitten toes and can proceed only with difficulty. Dr. Jansen says that he should not walk on the feet any more than absolutely necessary, and that he should wait for a horse or airlift. However, Wilcox said that they would probably continue to work this way in case transportation was not available. Wilcox requested a helicopter for Lewis. (This was relayed to Supt. Hall at HQ.)

"Dr. Jansen and Anshel Schiff were left camped on the south side of the Clearwater, intending to wait until the water receded. Both parties had adequate food."

3:00 PM: "Eielson contact with MCA group. . . report about 2′ of powder snow, and cannot find Sheldon's drop. . .

"They indicated that they would carry 4 days' supplies with them to the 17,900′ level.

"Babcock requested that their party be dropped the 15 days' supplies which had been left for emergency in Sheldon's hanger. They wished them dropped to them at the 17,900′ level, weather permitting, but understood that this could not be counted on. Merry relayed request to HQ while MCA stood by for reply. After considerable discussion, permission for the drop was granted. It was stressed in the reply to the climbers that they should not extend themselves to the point of possibly compounding an emergency, and that they could not count on the drop. The MCA group further requested information on the capability of rescue helicopters in case there were people at 17,900′ incapable of moving. HQ said they would try to get this info and pass it on (Hall). (No info received.)"

4:00 PM: "Word received from HQ that a helicopter had been arranged for by the RCC, that it would come to Wonder Lake and pick up Merry for a guide, then go to pick up Lewis. Possible destinations were discussed (Hall). . . "

4:30 PM: "Questions and arrangements with the RCC indicated that a military plane might not be available.[37] Wilcox indicated that a commercial craft would be acceptable and would

---

36. One mile this side of the Horse Cache—3 miles this side of McGonagall Pass.

37. That night.

be paid for, and requested that it be dispatched that night rather than the next day, even if costs were higher. (Price of $125/hr., min. 3 hr. was quoted to him.)"

5:00 PM: "HQ advises that helicopter may have to come in morning,[38] and requested information on rotor clearance. Replied that there is no problem with rotor clearance on Cache or Clearwater Creeks—adequate landing spots available (Hayes)."

6:15 PM, 7:00 PM, 7:25 PM: "Contacts with HQ re helicopter arrangements for Lewis pick-up and destination."

8:00 PM: "Contact with MCA. . .[39] They will try to reach high camp (17,900') by tomorrow. Also wished a better fix on the Sheldon air-drop at 15,000'."

8:30 PM (approx.): "Hiller 12E helicopter, with pilot Pat Gray, landed at W. Lake. Merry accompanied him to guide. Found all remaining members of lower party at Clearwater Creek. All elected to be ferried to Wonder Lake, as Clearwater was too high to ford, and they felt they would rather pay and be lifted out than wait and possibly run out of food or have to be picked up later. Pilot determined to remain at W. Lake the night, as weather was closing and darkness setting in. All personnel put up at station. Helicopter departed next morning."

DAY 39 — JULY 27, 5:55 AM:

"Helicopter departed Wonder Lake for Farewell with Dr. Jansen and Jerry Lewis aboard."

8:00 AM: "Eielson contact with MCA group. They anticipate reaching 17,900' by 7:00 PM. Report no wind, perfect visibility. Apparently team is functioning well. Sheldon flew this morning, dropped note, no equipment.

"HQ contact: Hall requests that the part of lower party which is coming out stop at HQ to make a written statement. Word passed to Snyder & Schlichter."

9:30 AM: "Hayes reports that Sheldon flew at 4:00 AM, saw MCA party and dropped note, but saw no activity around 18,000'

---

38. Apparently there was a question as to whether the evacuation could be completed before dark.

39. The radio contact was scheduled for (and probably occurred) at 5:00 PM.

level. Hansen is also flying in a Turbo-prop plane. (Some confusion here—original interpretation was that *Hansen* was currently airborne and he saw no activity.) Reported Sheldon as saying that MCA had apparently found his previous drop—there were tracks all over the area and he could see one of the gas cans."

10:00 AM: "Snyder, Schlichter, and Schiff departed for HQ in Lewis' pickup."

10:50 AM: "Passed on info from 9:30 HQ contact to Eielson. Corrected by call from Hayes; *Sheldon* reports no activity at 18,000', and Hansen due to fly mountain at 11:00 AM in Turbo-Beaver. Also mentioned that Sheldon reports that some of the dropped gear was in white pillowcases and might be hard to spot."

11:40 AM: "Message from Farewell (G. Jansen) that she had left her jacket & billfold here. (Found jacket with $19, but no billfold. Will continue to search.) Also informed Hayes that there was a faint possibility of the missing party having become confused in whiteout and following wrong wands down on West Buttress side, and that this should be passed on to the search planes for consideration. Hayes replied 'We have discussed that,' and indicated search craft were searching other sides of the mountain also."

2:05 PM: "Weather appears deteriorating, with somewhat increased winds from the NW, thickening cloud layer.

"Called HQ, relayed message on Jansen's billfold. Checked road conditions—Paxson road open, but Riley Cr. one lane only, appears sturdy. Hall knew of no news on the search operation. (Hayes called back shortly after, getting details of above. No news.)"

6:55 PM: "Report from Hayes on observations of flight this morning: Hansen spotted two men at 15,000' on Harper—possibly MCA group which had not yet moved out of camp. Saw cache at 16,500' (?) covered with black 'paper.'[40] At Denali Pass, saw 6 men in two ropes of three, but could not tell if they were moving up or down. Felt these were probably the Western States Expedition, going up. Then, flew down Kahiltna, past Windy Corner, and to

---

40. No black paper covering existed at the 16,500' cache. The cache may have been covered by a black plastic melt tarp. An uncovered food cache would also have looked very dark from the air.

the 'base camp where he[41] usually lands,' where he saw 3 men, assumed to be doctors working with the S. Face group.

"Sheldon will make the drop to the MCA group tonight. He will also try to drop a note to the Western States group, asking them to join up with the MCA team to search.

"We were requested to pass the word to the MCA tonight to try to tie up with the Western States group in order to make a search of the area, and to tell them that the Western States group would be dropped a note with details. They estimate that the WSE will be in the Denali Pass to Archdeacon's Tower area. We should also tell them that there will be a drop to them tonight. . . drop with message to WSE in morn.

"Hayes requested that information from the 8:00 PM contact be relayed to him through Reyer.

"KWA702 copied the transmission, and will relay."

8:15 PM: "Contact with Eielson—MCA party calling in, but radio trouble reduces them to clicking for *yes* and *no*. The MCA party is now at 16,500' at the cache. Will camp tonight. They plan to be at[42] 5:00 PM tomorrow. . .

"Eielson passed on the message above.

"Supt. Hall monitored the conversations.

"Haber & Perkins to come to Wonder Lake tonight, bringing recordings of previous communications."

9:15 PM: "Wilcox, Haber, Perkins, Shields . . . Merry went over all tapes taken of party on summit, reviewed maps, discussed possibilities of where the missing team might be. Wilcox mentioned that the area leading down from Denali Pass was flat and was very sparsely wanded, with half-size wands.[43] It is possible that the summit party got down to Denali Pass, could not see the way from there, and rather than taking a chance on missing the camp, decided to dig in. If this were the case they would not have been able to dig in effectively in the shallow snow at the pass, so would likely have followed their tracks back uphill for a short distance to a point where they could have dug in the lee (east side of the pass). Winds came up shortly after this, and did not abate at *lower* levels for about 5 days; it is possible that they did not abate at all, or only

---

41. Sheldon.
42. At the 17,900 foot camp.
43. If this area had not been re-wanded by Clark's party.

moderately, at Denali Pass. If the party were weak, they would probably not be able to stand against high winds, and would elect to stay put hoping that a lower team would come to their aid, or that their absence would trigger an air-drop. This would leave one man at 17,900', weak but well supplied with food and sleeping bags."

DAY 40 — JULY 28, 8:00 AM:

"Eielson radio contact with MCA group. They are at 16,500', planning to move all five men to 17,900' tonight. They got the new batteries from Sheldon's drop of 7-25, so contact is better. They report there was no Voice Commander in that drop, but that there are 3 of the small ARG radios. They say that Sheldon did *not* drop last night as anticipated. They report having a total of 10 days' food and fuel at their present location, including all drops and caches. The snow there is variable, apparently alternately soft and windswept, the present wind is 15-20 mph.

"They were informed by Eielson that they might not have communication from 17,900', as it was not direct line-of-sight, that Sheldon had been informed of their request for a drop of 15 days' food and fuel.

"Next contact at 5:00 PM."

1:55 PM: "(. . . transmitted to Hayes at HQ. . . He was asked to record the material. . .) . . .

"Was in radio contact with Sheldon at 11:05. He said that he was dropping the last of a load of MCA gear at the *14,300' level*[44] (his words). I asked him if he could save some of it for a higher drop—that MCA was expecting a drop at 17,900'. . . His reply as close as I can remember: 'Listen, I'm dropping this stuff here. This is as high as this plane can go. . . They are only about a half a mile up the glacier.' . . .

"The altitudes quoted cannot be accurate. This would put the drop below Browne Tower. . . *If* the party is descending for it from their location at 16,500'. . . it would mean . . . that they will lose all the ground they gained yesterday. . .

"I heard Roberta pass on a message to Don from Gary Hansen

---

44. From the probable location of the MCA group it appears that Sheldon's drop was at about 16,400 feet.

regarding contacting the Gerhard[45] party and asking them to search. She also said, '. . . but you can't get that high, can you?'. . .

"I have the following suggestions for whomever is planning the operation:

"1. Stop depending on Sheldon alone for high altitude operations or critical communications. His aircraft has limited capability and communications of ideas are a serious problem. He is not getting the job done up high. Use him for low altitude.

"2. Since it is quite possible that there will soon be from 5 to 11 searchers and possibly 7 victims near Denali Pass. . . I recommend that the Rescue Coordination Center, Major Stephens, be asked to supply a rescue-type plane such as a C-130 or C-118 and that they make a large air-drop of supplies just east of the pass. The snow is usually hard and windswept for about 200 yards east of the pass, and the material should not become buried and lost if no one is there to receive the drop. . .

"Since there may be as many as 18 men there, and they may be caught at any time by bad weather it seems a minimum drop would be 180 man-days of food and fuel. This would allow for 10 days for the maximum crew. However, there should be an allowance for loss of units or breakage from the drop on hard snow.

"In addition. . . I would suggest about a dozen dry sleeping bags. (Grace Jansen reports that those of the MCA group are quite wet, and those of the missing party may be wet or lost.)

"Also a reliable long-range or ground-air radio—and preferably two.

"Heavy duty tents—enough for 18 men. . . .

"The above would be a minimum drop, considering circumstances as they stand now. . .

"I recognize that this suggestion was not requested, but wish to have it considered by those responsible for the operation. . .

"Hayes received and indicated this would be discussed."

2:45 PM: "Supt. Hall called to see if the above recommendations had been made in consultation with Wilcox. (Indicated that Hansen was on the phone.) Merry replied that they had grown out of discussions with Wilcox, and would immediately ask Wilcox to

---

45. Western States Expedition—Paul Gerhard, leader.

read the message over for his thoughts. Wilcox read over the above and concurred. Merry reported this to Hall. Hayes asked again the details of the materials desired for the drop. Merry asked if part of the message had not been taped, and which should be re-read. Hall requested that only the items for drop be reiterated. This was done, and reasons for each briefly repeated."

2:55 PM: "Hayes called Merry to ask when we wished the drop to be made. Reply was that it probably should be as soon as possible, in case the weather changed again, but that whoever was doing the rescue planning probably had all the facts and would be in a position to make the decision. Hayes asked to talk to Wilcox, asked him if he was definitely calling for this drop. Reply was yes. Hayes asked that, if the drop was made, if it would not be two days before the climbers reached it. Wilcox said it should be tonight if they were going up. Hayes said he understood they were going down. Merry clarified—quoted Sheldon as saying the group was descending to pick it [Sheldon's air-drop] up; also suggested that the RCC establish radio contact with the MCA to ask *them* where they would want it dropped. . . Also that possibly a T-33 could drop the small radios as they had done during the winter operation."

8:05 PM: "Eielson has a faint contact with MCA group. They have found one body in a tent at the 17,900′ camp. There was no sign of the other six. The MCA group had retrieved Sheldon's air-drop of today. They strongly emphasized that they wanted a weather report at their 3:00 AM contact. Indicated that they did not wish a sooner contact as they had to get some sleep. (They would have put in a very strenuous day and it would be essential that they get rest if they were to avoid incapacitating fatigue and possibly altitude sickness the next day.) Planned for the next contact at 3:00 AM when they planned to start for the summit area to search. Said they did not need the proposed air-drop. Merry suggested that they look for a dug-in party near any appreciable interval in the wands."

8:26 PM: "Reached Supt. Hall after several attempts, and relayed above information. Also recommended that the air-drop be made regardless, as it was possible that there were dug-in survivors near Denali Pass and the operation might turn out to be unexpectedly long. Reply was to the effect that it would. Hall checked to be sure we meant 'body' indicated man was dead.

"Shortly afterward, Supt. Hall called with a weather forecast from FAA:[46] 3,000′ to 3,500′ and up obscured starting tomorrow—front moving in. No precipitation tomorrow, light precipitation next day. There was no prediction on winds.

"About this time Merry suggested to HQ that an RCC plane (slow) orbit the peak with an experienced mountaineering spotter aboard, observing closely the route from Denali Pass to the summit for some sign of a bivouacked party. Also passed on the information that the summit party probably had a snow shovel (according to Wilcox) and thus could have dug in well: (HQ asked why they would have dug a hole, and the reason for the construction of snow caves was briefly explained.)

"About this time HQ passed on the information that the. . . (RCC) was probably dropping the requested material about this time. Shortly after, received info that there was a delay, and that they felt that there might be a problem hitting the Denali Pass area as it was in shadow at this time. Advised that there was usually a great deal of light that high at this time of day and of year, but that air force knew its own capability best."

9:15 PM: "Discussed possible moving of CB radio at Eielson for better line-of-sight reception. Reyer tried to reach Robinson for information, but he was not available. The idea was abandoned when a map made by Jerry Clark was produced by Wilcox, which showed line-of-sight was available from most of summit ridge above Denali Pass. . ."

9:20 PM: "Hall reports that the . . .weather report suggests a cloud layer to 7,000′, possibly clear above (Maj. Stephens, RCC). Reports also that arrangements for drop are possibly hampered by shadow."

11:30 PM: "Merry called Eielson to have them ask MCA how many sleeping bags remained at the 17,900′ camp. (This would perhaps give some indication of the actions and survival chances of the missing party.) Also asked them to check how many days' food the MCA group had with them."

DAY 41 — JULY 29, 12:01 AM:

"Merry called Eielson, requesting them to tell MCA group

---

46. Federal Aviation Administration.

during next contact about the apparent line-of-sight conditions between Eielson and the summit ridge starting about ¼ mile above Denali Pass. (This had been plotted on a map by Jerry Clark of the Wilcox expedition, and Wilcox has a copy here, as well as one in the file at HQ.)[47]

"Between midnight and the 3:00 AM MCA contact, Merry, Perkins, and Haber worked out. . . carefully edited messages in priority of importance, in case contact was faint. Also worked out a series of 'click' signals for responses by MCA if they could only be heard at carrier level."

2:58 AM: "Hayes relays word from Hansen that an air-drop will be made between 7:30 and 8:00 AM, on the east side of Denali Pass. He also wishes Wilcox to come to HQ as soon as possible. (Arrangements were immediately made to have Wilcox drive in Hank Janes' van, taking with him all personal effects the climbers left at the Wonder Lake Station. Dick Shields convoyed him in the 4-wheel drive carryall to get him past the bad washout.)"

3:12 AM: "Eielson contact with MCA indicated that the group had 10 days' total supplies at 17,900′, that they would take 3 days' supplies to the summit, that they had found *no* sleeping bags at the camp except the one with the dead man. (This could indicate that all the missing 6 carried bags, and this would considerably increase their chance of surviving this long. However, as the MCA was able to converse only with carrier clicks, it was not determined if the tents at 17,900′ might have been torn and the bags possibly blown away.) They also indicated via clicks that all 5 were going to the summit area, that they were in good condition. They were informed that they would be monitored 24 hours, told of the line-of-sight potential above Denali Pass, given a weather report, told about the materials the summit party probably had with them, and asked to check carefully as possible for dug-in party in lee of summit ridge. By click signals, they indicated all was received."

3:20 AM: "Merry called Hayes to relay the following comments and suggestions:. . .

1. Very careful aerial observation flights tomorrow, especially along the east side of the crest from Denali Pass to the summit. . . . They should also observe carefully:

---

47. Jerry Clark had left the second copy at Eielson.

(a) The entire upper Harper basin above the upper icefall.

(b) The West Buttress route, entire.

(c) The glacier to the N. of the West Buttress.

"Each was a possible route if the party became confused in a whiteout and descended without finding the wands. There were also other, less likely possibilities. (As Wilcox indicated that each man was equipped with a map and compass, it still seems unlikely that they would descend the wrong route, even following the wands put in by W. Buttress parties, for example.)

2. In case there should be survivors, I suggest:

(a) That ARG affiliated Drs. be contacted for advice re possible medication drops. They are Dr. Rodman Wilson and Dr. George Wichman. . .

(b) That several large size medical division chemical heating pads be available for drop from any of the covering aircraft. . .

(c) That the army Hueys, or other high altitude choppers be alerted to a possible 18,000' pick-up attempt. . .

(d) That some ajkas,[48] sleds, or toboggans be readied for drop in case rescue choppers are not able to effect pick-up at 17,900' or above, and survivors must be sledded down.

(e) That some walk-around O_2 bottles be ready for drop in case rescue team exertion results in pulmonary edema. . . [49]

"Hayes said. . . Hansen and Crews will probably be spotting. Said all areas I had mentioned were being covered."

4:30 AM: "Merry asked Eielson to ask MCA during next contact how many tents were found at 17,900', and if only one, what color, (orange or red). Also asked that they take photos of the deceased for identification purposes."

4:50 AM: "Wilcox departed for HQ."

7:40 AM: "Hayes reports that he had called the RCC to inform them that no sleeping bags had been found in camp. He said that they were dropping all the requested items soon and would search carefully. He asked that any other information received from the MCA be passed on to HQ as soon as possible; also asked if Wilcox was en route."

---

48. Short, narrow, dish-like evacuation sled, made of metal and without runners.

49. Critical lung affliction sometimes precipitated by prolonged exertion at high elevations.

8:33 AM: "Haber reports seeing search planes—apparently Turbo-Beaver—making repeated passes near the summit."

8:37 AM: "Supt. Hall called to ask the frequency of the Wonder Lake radio."

9:00 AM: "Hayes asked what frequency I could monitor in case aircraft wanted to contact. Replied 3411.5, but could only monitor one or the other. (Shields called, suggested we could monitor 3237[50] on car radio and 3411.5 on main set. Good idea—relayed to HQ.)"

9:25 AM: "Hayes asked if we had gotten a physical description of the dead man from MCA. C-130 completed its drops and was headed back to base. Western States Expedition was headed down at 12,000'. Eielson reported seeing the plane make about 6 passes, and said further that no physical description had yet been obtained."

Noon: "Hayes said RCC wants to recover the 2 radios and batteries dropped. The drop was located ½ hour behind and 2 hours behind the party at the time of the drop, and was either near or on their trail. These sets communicate with FAA Talkeetna, and are UHF Guard on 243.0 megacycles. Also he wanted to know the names of the five MCA group members remaining."

3:00 PM: "Hayes asked that the MCA group be told that the tents and white gas were packaged together and went over the lip of Denali Pass, but are recoverable. *Be sure to cache any gear not used* in standing Denali Pass cache. Joe Wilcox then asked the following series of questions, to be passed on to the MCA group:

Which tent was the body found in? Orange or red?

Was the sleeping bag a Co-op McKinley?

Was the sleeping bag shell a red Alpine Hut shell?

Was the body over 6' long?

Was the body thin?

Was the body wearing blue wool **air force pants?**

Was the victim wearing beige down underwear?

Were there any articles, such as pack, boots, water bottle, etc., near, bearing the initials S.A.T.?

Was a red Expedition Cruiser pack and frame in camp?

Was an Alpine Hut 'Polar' down parka, red, in camp?

---

50. McKinley Park frequency.

Was there a large pair of K[51] boots in camp?

Was there an Alpine Hut pullover, red, wind parka and orange
  wind pants in camp?"
. . .

8:05 PM: "Eielson reports contact with the MCA. The contact
was rushed because of whiteout conditions. They reported finding 2
more bodies. . . but no traces of the other 4 members of the party.
These two were. . . 19,000' . . . not roped, and visible from the
camp location. 700 asked for positive identification. . . one body
was wrapped in what appeared to be an Eddie Bauer sleeping bag;
that Don Sheldon had spotted one body from the air; that all
indications pointed toward them having been blown off of some
higher point; that the radios were still packed in tin cans; that the
ARG radios were cached at 15,000'. . . "

10:10 PM: "The conditions were reported changing, weather
turning bad. . . Stubai ice axe found at base of the upper Harper
icefall[52]. . . bodies. . . several hundred feet below the outcropping[53]. . . There were no outward physical injuries. MCA group. . .
was asked to: photograph all bodies; consider the *possibility* of
the axe. . . indicating the presence of other climbers in the area,
possibly the missing 4 had managed to reach this crevassed area
and had found shelter."

10:30 PM: "701 called **headquarters** to check: Was there news
from Sheldon or Hansen re sightings? What about the disposition
of the bodies? In order not to endanger the rescuers, I suggest
burial in any convenient crevasse *if possible*. Wilcox was asked if
he can account for the Stubai ice axe. . . he replied that about 3
members of the upper group had Stubais. I asked for weather
forecast, including winds aloft for tomorrow."

10:45 PM: "Checked HQ. . . and got the following: Sheldon
had spotted one body partially buried, and had dropped a map of
its location to the MCA. About 3 of the party had Stubai axes. Joe
feels this indicated some strong members got lower. I asked him to
tell Art or the **superintendent** that I suggest an air reconnaissance

---

51. Error: "K" means "Korean" boots. I had asked if K2 boots were
in camp.

52. The ice axe was found halfway up the upper icefall at about the
17,200 foot level as later verified by maps and a photograph.

53. It was later learned that the rock outcropping referred to was
Archdeacon's Tower.

—probably by Sheldon—of the crevasses atop that icefall and on the edge of it in line with the ice axe location. Also, I asked him to check with the supt. for disposition of the bodies, and recommended burial in crevasses after photos had been taken, *but only if this is possible, and not too hazardous.* Evacuation would be hazardous. Wilcox concurred with this opinion. Asked for weather report for tomorrow, including winds aloft, for 8:00 AM contact."

11:10 PM: "Called headquarters to ask Wilcox about considering the chance that strong men did get back to camp, picked up bags and food, and went down. . . (Turned out that I was talking to John Trent.)"

DAY 42 — JULY 30, 8:05 AM:

"Weather report: at 18,000′, wind 220°,[54] 25-30 knots,[55] changing to WNW 30-35.[56] Heavy turbulence for light aircraft, worsening later this evening. Mountain will be obscured for 72 hours, with brief periods of clearing. There is moisture-laden air at 18,000′."

8:35 AM: "KWA350 FBX (USGS) called 700 to inform this station that they have a phone link with. . . AFB, and were monitoring our frequency."

9:00 AM: "Contact with MCA. . . The winds were upwards of 30 knots.[57] If they were to move today, they could reach 12,100′ cache. Their physical condition was good. They read all info, recovered no material from the drop. . . There were 12 man-days of food left at camp.[58] The tent was torn badly, and the bags and packs could have blown away. They were told to search the area, and this they confirmed. . . They don't have the AF radios, but they did reach the summit."

9:30 PM: "Presently setting up camp at 12,100′, tired but OK. They requested a weather forecast for winds and conditions up to

---

54. Approximately southwest winds.
55. 28.8 - 34.5 miles per hour.
56. 34.5 - 40.3 miles per hour.
57. 34.5 miles per hour.
58. By Clark's party. This was an error in communications: the radio tape verifies that the MCA had indicated that 10 man-days of food had been found in high camp.

12,000'. They were also asked (question originated with Hansen) whether they would consider returning to the 17,900' camp for further search after resting up at lower elevations, to which they replied, negative."

DAY 43 — JULY 31, 8:00 AM:

"Breaking camp at 12,100', transmission short, all were OK."

"The log will be closed at this point, as it appears certain that there will be no further involvement of this station in any search or rescue activities which have the slightest chance of being effective. . ."

16
Wake of Disaster

A selection of post-expedition documentation and correspondence.

Time
August 11, 1967

ALASKA

Denali Strikes Back

To the twelve eager mountaineers who struck out last month to climb Mount McKinley, North America's highest peak, the adventure did not seem too formidable. Since the first assault on McKinley in 1903, only four climbers had died on its slopes, while more than 100 people have attained the summit. Thanks in part to the National Park Service, which firmly winnows some 300 applications a year, at least half a dozen expeditions annually make a safe and often successful try to ascend Denali—The Great One—as Yukon Indians call the mountain.

Even so, it is no weekend hacker's jaunt. Though McKinley does not pose the classic technical challenges of the great Himalayan and Andean peaks, it is nonetheless known for the worst mountain weather in the world. Soaring 20,320 ft. into the subarctic sky, McKinley is exposed to 150 mph winds that batter the mountain's upper reaches with sledge-hammer blows and are even more fierce than McKinley's 72-below-zero cold. [1]

Mindful of McKinley's menace, expedition leader Joseph F. Wilcox, 24, encamped his dozen climbers 18,000 ft. high between McKinley's North and South Peaks. After Wilcox and his assault team scaled the peak, he set out with four weary companions on the long trek down. Seven others, including the expedition's strongest mountaineers, opted to assault the pinnacle.

The high party had radioed that it had reached its goal when the mountain's most fearsome weather struck. Searing snow and seismic gales tore at them, and when Wilcox and his band, stumbling down to a prearranged meeting site at 15,000 ft., waited two days without further contact with the higher party, an attempt to turn back was thwarted by the storm. After four more days, with supplies low, Wilcox and his group were in dire peril themselves until a party from the Mountaineering Club of Alaska came to their aid. After a harrowing nighttime descent, Wilcox swam four icy streams to reach the Wonder Lake Ranger Station, which sent a helicopter back to rescue his four companions.

Still lost on McKinley's slopes were the expedition's seven other members. Early last week, with the storm finally abating, rescue pilot Don Sheldon spotted a body near the 18,000 ft. camp; [2] two more were sighted later. By week's end officials abandoned hope of saving the four other missing men. In one savage thrust, Mount McKinley had almost doubled its total recorded toll.

Blaming serious tactical blunders and "fiendish" weather for what he calls U.S. mountaineering's worst disaster, expert alpinist Bradford Washburn added: "It's amazing more people haven't been killed on McKinley when you consider 400 are killed in the Alps every summer."

Letter from Anshel Schiff
August 20, 1967

Dear Joe,

I was glad to hear that you are at last back home again. Your in-laws probably gave you the scoop on things from the time I left

---

1. The temperature on the mountain was about zero; however, the wind chill was extreme.

2. Error: Sheldon sighted a body at about the 19,000' level.

you to my arrival in Wash. I called Mrs. McLaughlin while my plane was stopped in Portland. I have also called or seen Clark's mother, Mr. & Mrs. Janes & Walt's folks. I have not been able to reach Steve's folks although I have tried several times. Mr. Janes found several rolls of film in the truck[3] (one of Hank's, Mark's & Dennis' & 2 of Clark's). We will do some redistributing so that parents get pictures of their son & then return rest. . .

My feet lost their feeling but they are now approaching normality. I had difficulty sleeping for 1st week & ½ but now that I am getting into old routine of things again that has improved. While the trip will leave its scars on each of us, the loss on the mountain was tragic enough and I hope the scars that remain will not impair the future.

I have spent more than one sleepless night trying to figure out what might have happened. While in the material sense it does no good to attribute blame, I think it would provide no little peace of mind to know what really happened, in particular it would be interesting to know if the flags (75 to 150) that we brought up on the 15th (from the cache) were used. From my recollection of the summit tape, Clark said that they could not go up or *down* (on 17th) due to whiteout conditions. It would thus seem that some flags were blown away on the storm of the 16th & that in any case the route was not re-flagged. While the above may be true it may not be the cause of the trouble for even if the route down was marked, they may have bivouacked since they were so close to the summit. Since they went up after the bivouac rather than down they must have been in pretty good shape. Both Clark & Walt had very good heads & I do not think they would take any undue risks. I believe that only if a diary is found will we be able to piece things together; for, bad winds or lost route could have caused a bivouac or a fall. I heard Vin was to lead another group to conduct a ground search. . .

Drop me a line when you have the inclination.

Anshel. . .

---

3. Hank's van.

Note from Jerry Lewis
August 28, 1967

Joe,

Feet are coming along fairly well.

Bone bruises giving me the most trouble.

Talked with insurance man and there will be some delay due to waiting for insurance forms to come back from Anchorage.

I'm not at all sure just how much the insurance will cover. Doubt good coverage (flights) when more than one passenger listed but will see.

Hope everything is going well with you.

Jerry

Letter from Mrs. Harold B. Taylor
August 29, 1967

Joe Wilcox,

. . . Dr. Schiff was here one evening but now he's gone to Tetons rock climbing he said. Let us hear from you if there's anything of importance. Sometime we'll understand *why* of all this tragedy—maybe. We'd like to meet you & your wife. We're having a memorial for Walter Sept. 17—2 PM, Federated Church—W. Lafayette. . .

Letter from George Hall
August 29, 1967

Dear Joe:

. . . Your thoughts on the memorial are appreciated and will be taken into full consideration when this is worked out. . .

We are planning to hold the critique meeting on September 14 and 15, and Dr. Washburn will be present at that time. I am hopeful that the present climbing group will be available at that time. We are restraining publicity on this meeting so as to prevent spectacularisms from creeping into our talks. I don't know if you might be able to return for such meetings, but they will be held in Anchorage at a location not yet determined. . .

Sincerely,

George A. Hall
Superintendent

Letter from Perry Taylor
September 1, 1967

Dear Joe:

Thank you for the money order and your nice letter. We had a very nice service for Steve in Pittsburgh after the one in Provo.

There are a few things perhaps you can help me with and I would appreciate it very much. . .

Also, we were notified by Gary Hansen that the group with Vin spent two days on the top of the mountain and it had snowed about six feet and nothing was found except 6 inches of the pole sticking up. I would like to know anything you have picked up in the way of additional information on this subject.

You will no doubt get the Park Service official report on the accident and I may not. When you do, will you let me know and I will then request a copy. . .

Regards,

Perry Y. Taylor. . .

Letter from Mr. and Mrs. Harold Taylor
September 4, 1967

Dear Mr. Wilcox,

Harold & I would like a copy of the autobiographies that the first 9 fellows submitted to you previous to your meeting at Mt. Rainier. I read them hastily one time but now we're trying to piece together your group. Have had a letter from Mr. Jerry Lewis. We've talked to Mr. & Mrs. Janes and Dr. Schiff has been in our home 1 evening. We know so little about the group. I really think we're just hoping to reconcile ourselves if we can grab on to fragments of everything. I believe you were the only married fellow & your wife a school teacher?? I too, am an elementary 5th grade tchr. & start again Sept. 6.

I wrote to you at your Provo address that I had found in a letter that Jerry Clark had given to Walter. Sometime we'd like to meet you and hope you could come to Indiana soon. Talked to Mrs. Clark last PM. A news report said they had found 4 bodies—a flattened tent etc. but so far no follow-up and a telephone call to McKinley did not agree with this radio report. We've read newspaper reports from all around. We are so grateful for your *Narrative Report.*

The Taylors

[P.S.] Any expense we need to know about let us know. Also a bk. Walt had on National Parks we would like to locate it, esp. McKinley Park—we know so little. Also we're interested in buying slides if available.

Time
LETTERS
September 8, 1967

What Before Why

Sir: In reading "Denali Strikes Back" [Aug. 11], I was amazed that Bradford Washburn blamed "serious tactical blunders" for the mountaineering disaster. This statement seems to indicate that the expedition made some mistakes that most mountaineers would routinely avoid and that these errors were largely responsible for the tragedy. In talking with Mr. Washburn, I find that he had only sketchy information and did not at first understand why the expedition split into two groups. He certainly did not mean to imply that the tactics were responsible for the tragedy.

It is difficult to determine why the disaster happened without knowing first what happened. At the present time no one knows what happened—it may well be that no one will ever know. The summit team was very strong and equipped much better than most groups. They had the combined experience of climbing on every continent of the world[4] and their leader was a cool-headed veteran of two Antarctica expeditions. I find their loss only a little short of unbelievable. It is interesting to note that all fatal accidents on Mount McKinley have involved very experienced climbers. Mountaineers should be aware that infrequent situations do occur

---

4. Possible error—this statement may be true as several members of the summit team were well traveled, however, the only information I have is that recorded in their autobiographies and climbing resumes.

that probably no one can cope with. To suggest that this recent disaster could have been foreseen would not only discredit the victims but also be unfair to future expeditions.

Joseph F. Wilcox
Leader

Wilcox-McKinley Expedition
Provo, Utah

Letter from Norm Benton
September 12, 1967
Creswell, Oregon

Dear Joe,

I was certainly sorry to learn of the tragedy on your expedition. I know it shocked you as it did the many friends of the fellows lost on the mountain, and especially their families. About a month before you left for Alaska, 4 or 5 of these fellows came to my home to talk over equipment & other details. I already knew Mark & Jerry. I believe John Russell and Hank Janes were two of the others, but I am not sure about the fifth one.

I thought a lot of Mark, and also of Jerry. They both were well thought of by those who knew them, and will be sorely missed in this area.

Newspaper accounts have left many questions unanswered, and we in this area just do not know much of the details, not just of what happened to the seven, but also of what happened before that, what caused the party separation & etc.

I am wondering if you might find the time, sometime, to give me an account of what took place on your expedition, especially high on the mountain, but also your earlier experiences. I know that such an account would be of interest to me, and I am sure it would be to many of my friends who also knew Mark (and also Jerry's friends). . .

Sincerely,

Norm

Letter from Paul Janes
September 12, 1967. . .

Dear Joe,

I have learned from Mr. Hall at Mt. McKinley National Park that you have returned to Utah, and I hope all goes well for you in the months and years ahead. All of the parents of the climbers who lost their lives feel, I am sure, that you did everything possible to insure their safety, and that the disaster was not your responsibility, in any sense.

My wife and I enjoyed reading the letter you wrote to *Time* . . . and, of course, we support your position 100 percent.

I understand that you took a good many photos during the expedition, and I would like to have some prints of some of the best of them, particularly those in which Hank is shown. I am enclosing a check for $10 to cover the cost of the prints. Thanks in advance for your cooperation.

With kind personal regards,

Cordially,

Paul N. Janes. . .

Letter from Harold Taylor
September 13, 1967

Dear Joe,

. . . We are indeed grateful for the excellent leadership that you gave to this tremendous team of mountain climbers. We read your response in. . . *Time*. . . with interest and certainly with approval.

If you get additional information that you feel would be important to us, please call our home collect. Also, if you could supply us with pictures that we can have duplicated and returned to you, we would be most grateful. If there are other materials that involve cost, please let us know and we will reimburse you in full for all expenses. We are having a memorial service for Walter in our local church this Sunday at two o'clock PM. We attended a memorial service for Jerry Clark about two weeks ago.

Best wishes to you.

Very truly yours,

Harold B. Taylor

Letter from S.P. McLaughlin
September 17, 1967

Dear Joe,
  . . . Talked to Crenchaw in Seattle a week or so ago, and Galen McBee, a friend and climbing fellow of Mark's talked to Boulton regarding what they found on the last climb. Both reported absolutely nothing except five to ten feet of snow and terrible weather up and down. While the park officials etc., etc., by this time have probably held their critique at Anchorage, we, like you, doubt that anything new will come out of this meeting except perhaps a formal statement regarding the disaster. Maybe I should say "official statement." However, some official statement may be necessary as the court in Alaska is going to have to issue the equivalent of death certificates even though no bodies have been recovered.
  Read your reply to the editors of *Time* and it was very well done. It is too bad that when such a disaster happens, be it climbing, fire, wreck, or what have you, there is always some "expert" sounding off with an opinion as to exactly what happened and why it happened, when if he would look back or perhaps review the background of those involved, he would perhaps learn to shut up. I suppose though we will have such "expert" opinions with us all the time. I'm glad that you answered as the answer should have been from a mountaineer and not from a plain reader of *Time* such as myself. . .
  Again may we say that what happened has happened and we sincerely hope that as time goes on only the pleasant moments of the expedition will remain. And like we have told our other two climbers, keep climbing and good luck. If you get out this way again, stop in, you and your family are welcome.

                                        S.P. McLaughlin

Letter from Vin Hoeman
September 18, 1967

Dear Joe,
  . . . We flew out from Logan the last day of July and I heard

there'd been an accident on Mt. McKinley, but was assured my wife was OK before I hitched a ride to Anchorage. 2 Aug. Gary Hansen and I chartered a plane to fly low through Denali Pass looking for possible survivors now that the storm had ended. We saw objects, but nothing moved.

Babcock with the remainder of the MCA party got back out with their tale of dead men sitting on the slopes, but no identifications and so many mysteries. By 6 Aug. I had organized my thoughts and decided to lead a Humanitarian Climb to learn what we could and bury those poor guys. However, it takes time to find qualified climbers, arrange equipment and supplies, and wait for the weather to fly in—Sheldon finally got us to 9,800' Kahiltna Pass late 19 Aug. Five of us reached Denali Pass 26 Aug. and Ray Genet and I immediately went down to the 17,900' camp area, but only 2" or 3" of the bamboo pole with blue-black strips of cloth attached protruded. Was this pole in camp when you left? When Babcock got there it was 200 yards below camp with Stephen's. . . sleeping bag wrapped around it. Attempting to estimate the 200 yards in the right direction and probe seemed useless.

Next day we went to the summit, 4 of us, having to battle deep soft snow all the way. Uncovered big Neodesha flag and Brigham Young pennant I guess you left there the 15th of July, also 2 Kansas pennants? A wand that we found on top was also represented by 3 like it at close intervals on W. side of Archdeacon's Tower leading over to the steep. . . slope, the flags a red screen-size mesh material . . . stapled around back of the garden-stake bamboo wands, 2 staples to each. Were these the wands they would have had with them? Genet and I went down over this steep slope below the rocks where the one body had been found sitting and on down below, but could locate nothing on that slope.

. . . If an overflight in the spring shows winds have bared anything, I'll take another party up.

. . . I see you're an ex-Philmonter, I was there myself on what they called a Wagon Train in 1951. . .

Sincerely,

J. Vin Hoeman

[P.S.] My wife Grace sends her best regards. My thanks to you for letting her accompany you down.

Letter from Helen Bellows (Hank's Mother)
September 20, 1967
Indianapolis, Indiana

Dear Mr. Wilcox—Joe,

Your letter and the "logs" which you sent were so greatly appreciated by my family and me. We know you did everything possible, and hope you are alright now.

I am enclosing a check for $48.00 for the pictures (the slides). ... The doctor for whom I work, Dr. J. H. Doran, was a classmate of Dr. Jack Clark, Jerry's brother. He has been interested in the things Hank did for a long time.

I am in need of some further information concerning Hank. A form which I must return to an insurance co. needs to know what Dr. he saw for a physical before leaving on this climb. I doubt if you have that information but if by chance you do, could you send me his name. . . We have not had a memorial service yet for Hank, but plan to have it on Oct. 14th. We would be pleased to have you attend if possible. You can let me know.

Very sincerely,

Helen Bellows

From Walt Taylor's *Memoriam*

BIOGRAPHY

Walter W. Taylor was born November 21, 1942 in West Lafayette, Indiana.

He attended Morton Elementary School and West Lafayette Junior High School. Here he was the recipient of the Optimist Citizenship Award, chosen by his fellow students as their outstanding citizen. He then entered the West Lafayette High School where he was elected to the National Honor Society and served as president of the Student Council. He was a member of the football, track, and wrestling teams, serving as captain of the latter.

From 1960 to 1964, Walter attended Purdue University, being listed among the honor students during his undergraduate days. He was a member of the Sigma Chi fraternity.

In the fall of 1964, he entered the Indiana University Medical School. He was one of twenty-four students who were chosen to work on the MD degree and PhD degree simultaneously. He would have completed his graduate study in the spring of 1968.

Walter was a member of the Federated Church of West Lafayette and was active in the church school and youth program. He had been active in the Boy Scouts, being one of the youngest lads ever to achieve the rating of Eagle Scout in this area.

He is survived by his parents, Mr. and Mrs. Harold B. Taylor, John Taylor of St. Paul, and Karl Taylor, a graduate student at Cornell University. . .

Letter from Alice Clark
September 21, 1967

Dear Mr. Wilcox,

Thank you for sending the expedition report. I'm sure you spent many hours preparing it. We do appreciate so very much all you have done to help us understand what happened at the mountain.

I'm sure this has been a most trying time for you and all of us. I want you to know how much we thank you for all you and all the men did to find our boys.

I have been so grief stricken I just couldn't write to anyone.

We had a memorial service for Jerry Aug. 20th and one was held for Walter Taylor last Sunday which we attended. . .

Thank you again, and may we all find the strength to go forward in life again.

Sincerely,

Alice Clark

P.S. Jack and I are flying to Eugene, Oregon Sept. 28th to pack Jerry's things.

Note from Paul Janes
September 26, 1967

Dear Joe,

Just a note to let you know that Hank's mother, Mrs. Helen Bellows, died of a heart attack in Indianapolis at midnight Sept. 25.

She had been greatly upset since the Mt. McKinley disaster occurred.

Hope all is well with you.

Cordially,

Paul N. Janes. . .

Letter from John B. Russell
September 27, 1967

Dear Mr. Wilcox,

If it's not too late. . . I would like to order 2 copies. . . of the group picture. I'm sure you feel as badly about this tragedy as we do, but please don't let it get you down. We know you did your best, and that's all anyone can do.

Yours,

John B. Russell

P.S. Would appreciate it if you could label the group. Check enclosed.

Letter from Nancy Clark Strong
September 28, 1967

Dear Joe,

I am the sister of Jerry Clark. When I was home in Syracuse this weekend I learned from my brother Jack and Mother that you had offered to make an 11″ x 14″ color print of the climbing group. If it would be at all possible I would like to buy one of these prints. . .

I want to thank you for the letter that you wrote to *Time*. Bradford Washburn's comment had deeply distressed my mother, and it was good of you to clarify his remarks.

I also want to thank you for the lengthy report, which Jack copied for me. It has helped straighten out some things in all of our minds.

I know that all this has been extremely hard on you, and our thoughts have been with you. Sometimes I think that death is much harder on the living than those who actually experience it—The past two months have been a literal hell for our family, and I'm sure we are no exception. Attempts to be objective about the fact that everything changes, that nothing is permanent in our material world, somehow never seems to quite make up for a personal loss.

I know that Jerry was not afraid of death—we had talked of it—and I am thankful that he was in a surrounding that he loved, doing what he loved — when it came. He was a complex individual and to have died just an ordinary petty death somehow, to me, would have been less than fitting. I realize that I am writing this with the admiration and love of a "little sister". . .

Walt, who was a close friend, and Hank, who used to visit us often, were also fine young men. Although I didn't personally know the other four, I feel equally grieved at their loss, because I know they wouldn't have been there unless they were made of pretty special stuff. Their loss will be etched into the hearts of all of us, but I'm sure that being mountaineers they were prepared to meet the unexpected and probably wouldn't have been so torn up about their ending as we are. . .

Thank you again, Joe, for your stability and thoughtfulness to all the boys' families. And I especially thank you, and everyone concerned, for making every rescue effort possible.

Very sincerely,

Nancy Clark Strong

Letter from Anshel Schiff
October 9, 1967

Dear Joe & Cheryl,
    . . . While I am personally opposed to a monument this should have little weight on any decisions. However, I think many of those lost would share my opinion. I think that it is inappropriate that anything should be instituted which would be opposed by and not in the spirit of our lost friends.

I assume you are as pressed for time as I. Steve's folks came down to campus and I was able to show them my pictures. They are very nice people. I have also shown slides to Hank's dad and Walt's folks. I understand that Hank's mother (his folks are divorced) died of a heart attack last week.

I have not yet received the list of major expedition expenses. . . but I assume you are quite busy. . .

Was ice axe that was found at 17,000' definitely Steve's?[5]

Cheryl, how do you like your teaching? I would imagine that the 1st semester is a lot of work.

Hoping to hear from you soon.

Anshel. . .

Note from Beth and Perry Taylor
October 22, 1967

Dear Joe,

. . . We are going down to Lafayette, Indiana on the 3rd for the memorial of Hank Janes. This was delayed account his mother died. . .

There is some possibility that we will be in Salt Lake next weekend and if you are available we may get to see more of the pictures then.

Regards,

Beth and Perry Taylor

Letter to George Hall
November 5, 1967

. . . The more I think about it the more I regret having initiated the idea of a memorial. A much more appropriate idea would be to name (or re-name) features of the mountain or route after the seven. As you know this procedure has a precedent in the case of Koven and Carpé. Although most of the major features of the mountain already have names there are many unnamed peaks and spurs which although small are rugged and fitting. I am referring specifically to peaks along Pioneer Ridge, the spur off of Carpé, the

---

5. The location of the ice axe was probably about 17,200 feet.

Silverthrone area, and the ridge between the Traleika and its West Fork. The latter area would provide seven peaks in a small area. Although not along our route these peaks were visible from high on the mountain and were quite impressive.

Besides being more fitting this idea would eliminate the necessity of a man-made memorial and all the resulting controversy. I would be happy to draft a formal proposal and work through the necessary channels if this idea proves more acceptable than the "memorial." I would appreciate hearing your views.

Sincerely,

Joe

Letter from Ann Crosby

Mr. Joe Wilcox,

I have been very close to Hank Janes. I worked with him at camp for 2 years, and saw him during the winter, as often as vacations would allow. Last spring I went out to Portland, met Mark and Jerry, and climbed several times with all of them. They are the most magnificent people, and I loved Hank very much. I applied to school in Portland, planning to be there with Hank this year. Well, I will be there anyway — that has to be done; I will be living with Lee Ryker and his wife for a while. My address as I know it now, will be in care of them.

There are several specific reasons for which I wrote you. I visited Mr. Janes just last week, and while I was there, I read your *Narrative Report* of the McKinley climb. I would very much like to have a copy of that report. Mr. Janes also mentioned that a six hour tape of the entire trip was available, and would be sent to him. Can you arrange to send me a copy of that tape? If it would mean an undue expense to you, I would certainly be happy to pay you for the tape. Perhaps I don't need the entire six hours—I don't really know exactly what type of thing is on it. But any mention of Hank, or himself speaking, is very important to me. Perhaps you can help me decide on this. The last, and perhaps most precious thing, is those films of the climb. I really want to have a copy. Can you get them for me? Again, I will be very happy to pay you for all this — this material is priceless.

And the last thing is indefinable—but if there is anything you know that would mean a lot to me—about Hank, what he said, what he did, I would really, really appreciate it if you would pass it on to me. And if, in the future, if anything comes up, anything develops, that is related to all this, and to Hank, I would really like to know about it. The radio has been a merciless messenger to me; personal communication is so much kinder.

Thank you very much.

Sincerely,

Ann Crosby. . .

Letter from Harold B. Taylor
November 8, 1967
. . .
Dear Joe,

. . . The Perry Taylors were down to a memorial that was held for Hank Janes last Friday and stayed overnight with us. They brought the books and other materials that you sent out that belonged to Walter. . .

Very truly yours,

Harold B. Taylor

Letter from Vin Hoeman
November 15, 1967
Dear Joe,

. . . The Institute of Arctic Biology at College (for whom I work on occasion) has gotten interested in the shelter-cabin-lab idea for the top of West Buttress at 17,300', so, by May volunteers (?) may be erecting some kind of permanent building there, but I would think late April-early May would be the best time for an investigation climb. If we work it in with the recovery of cabin material air-drop, I'm sure we can get flights to and from 9,800' paid for by the park and/or IAB. We haven't the time to participate in actual construction. . . We have cancelled our plans for the San Francisco American Alpine Club meeting and now plan to Christmas in Utah (23-27 Dec.) en route to Ecuador. If you are back from Mexico and not otherwise occupied we might get together during that time for a one or two-day climb. . .

Our trip to Chimborazo will be partially employment, since I've talked the Institute of Arctic Biology into hiring me to bring back some mice of the genus *Phyllotis* that I noted in the refuge at 16,000′ two years ago, in order to start a test colony of high altitude genetic rodents here in Alaska for eventual testing in altitude chamber and possibly at the lab mentioned above. . .

Grace and I attempted first ascent of Resurrection Peaks down near Seward last weekend but were blizzarded off on Sunday. Not much snow here yet though. . .

Sincerely yours,

Vin
J. Vin Hoeman

Letter from Harvard University
University Health Services
November 24, 1967

. . .

Dear Mr. Wilcox:

I would greatly appreciate having your version of the incident that occurred on Mt. McKinley this summer when some climbers were killed. I enclose two copies of our report form and hope you will be good enough to complete them for me. As you know we report the accidents and, at times, an analysis of the accident. The purpose of our report is to try to educate the mountaineering community concerning the possible hazards so that we can all enjoy the mountains more safely.

Your assistance in this will be greatly appreciated. I am also writing to the National Park and others who may have additional information on this accident.

Sincerely yours,

B.G. Ferris, Jr.

Benjamin G. Ferris, Jr., MD
Chairman, Safety Committee
American Alpine Club

December 2, 1967

To the parents and survivors of the Mt. McKinley expedition:
. . . I have the slides and pictures packaged and ready to send. I have written a story to go with the slides—hope you enjoy it.

As you may know, the expedition had an agreement with the Alaska Rescue Group for rescue services. I have enclosed a copy of our agreement. ARG incurred $970.70 in expenses while rendering rescue services to the expedition:

 $25.70   phone calls
$495.00   search flying and air-drops by Sheldon
$450.00   overflights by Alaska Aeronautical

Each member of the expedition would normally be responsible for 1/12 or $80.90 of this expense. ARG will most likely be contacting you about this expense and your contributions should be made directly to them. (I understand they plan to send you copies of invoices and itemized lists.). . .

If anything is uncovered in the spring, there may be another search climb. If finances work out for me, I plan to be on that climb.

Sincerely,

Joe

[EXPEDITION TOTALS OF DEPOSITS & EXPENSES]
. . .
[TOTAL DEPOSITS] $3701.85
TOTAL EXPENSES $5183.19

Letter from Norm Benton
December 14, 1967

Dear Joe,
Thank you very much for sending me the log, the *Narrative,* and the letter giving details of the McKinley tragedy. It certainly filled in many of the details leading up to the "accident."

I have had this report "on the go" most of the time since it arrived, with many people interested in it. I believe it has been duplicated twice, once in Eugene, and once by the Randalls in Seattle. I took it up to them when I visited them over the Veterans

Day weekend, when our expedition to Mt. Kobe (AJJEX) was honored at the AAC banquet (Cascade Section). I saw an expedition movie then, and it is very good.

Sincerely,

Norm Benton

Note from Paul Schlichter
November 25, 1967

Dear Joe,
My parents have been forwarding all of your letters and I've also kept in contact with Jerry Lewis and Howard. Now that the situation is getting untangled the bills are cropping up. . .

I've been in pilot training for three months now and although the odds are not as bad as they were on McKinley, we lose about one pilot a month. . .

Paul. . .

Letter from Vin Hoeman
November 29, 1967
Anchorage

Dear Joe,
. . . That's practically unbelievable that the MCA party. . . would leave a diary they found in a cache that's gone forever! I only wish Grace had gone up with them for certainly they are not representative of MCA as a whole (see 1961 AAC Accident Report re Crews' MCA party and John Day accident) . . . agree that the Taylors' gift should go toward covering ARG expenses and I *know* MCA directors will comply, whereupon I will so inform the Taylors. . .

No, I do not think it's a good idea to try to name geographic features after those guys. I'm chairman of our MCA committee on geog. names and we've named a lot of features but our number one rule is to name no feature after any person living or dead, a good rule I think and I'd have opposed Mts. Carpé, Koven and Thayer Basin if they'd been proposed in my time. We're currently opposing (successfully) an attempt to name a peak on the Kahiltna after Batkin.[6] I've written to Jack Clark who seems to be chief memorializer suggesting a hilltop overlooking Kantishna and Wonder Lake but outside park boundary as memorial site that can be expanded into a climbers' cemetery if necessary in future, an out of the way spot tourists won't get to but those who wish to and know can. Arr. SLC airport 21:45 hrs. 23rd. Will call to arrange for trip 26th.

Yrs.,

Vin

Letter from Wayne Merry
December 11, 1967

Dear Joe,

Nice to hear from you! I had thought of writing to see how things were going, but thought I would let things heal a while before recalling any trauma!

All well here. My future plans still uncertain, but several good alternatives loom, some with NPS, some not.

My article on the accident will come soon in *Summit.* You will find it non-controversial. It is a straight, brief narrative of events with a theoretical reconstruction of the actual tragedy. No analysis, no judgments. Object: to increase awareness of the tremendous potential of the mountain and the inadequacy of even qualified climbers if caught by the storms up high. I'll follow with another describing various problems peculiar to the mountain. Same object. . .

Was at the annual AAC meeting in Berkeley, and saw Chas. Crenchaw. He said he had climbed with McLaughlin & Clark & that they were very good. Also knew you, and figured you were a good man. He was on the Hoeman climb.

Hope you have a good Xmas season, Joe. Maybe see you next spring.

Best,

Wayne

---

6. The climber who died in a crevasse fall during the Winter Expedition, 1967.

Letter from Jack Clark
December 27, 1967

Dear Joe,

Thanks for the picture and the news letter. I especially appreciated your very sensitive comments at the end of the letter. I feel that we were indeed fortunate to have one of your sensitivity and sense of values in charge of the climb. I am sure that with you on the scene that everything possible was done. I am sure that you have periods of doubt when you feel that you should have done more, but I am equally confident that everything possible was done. I would encourage you to go on from where you are now. One cannot go back and do over those things which are done. Think it over carefully before deciding to go back next summer. What would it really accomplish? If you found the men, wouldn't the sense of loss be even greater for you? If you found nothing, wouldn't the sense of emptiness be even greater? Of course, we and you want to know what happened. It's only natural, but couldn't someone else do the job just as well and spare you the heartache? You owe no obligation to the men to return. You did the very best anyone could. You've suffered as great a sense of loss as any of us. You've already gone beyond the duty one could expect from a friend and a leader. Also with the strain of the situation, one should ask himself if this might not impair his physical and mental functioning at a time that full efficiency is imperative. I am sure that this could not help but be a great strain on your wife also if you returned. I am sure that you will decide for yourself what you will do, but I would encourage you to keep the above in mind when thinking over the situation. Also, I have always felt that climbing should be a joy and a high experience. I don't see how your return to McKinley to search for your friends could be this. . .

Sincerely,

Jack

Letter from Beth and Perry Taylor
January 6, 1968

Dear Joe and Cheryl,

. . . Have you had a visit from Vin Hoeman yet? If so we would like to hear about it. Also is there any more about an early climb next spring?

We have not heard anything from Alaska since they promised to give us a report on the hearing held on Dec. 6.[7] Also we have not heard anything from anyone about the critique that was held earlier. Also they have not sent the transcript of the radio contacts after your log entries were taken over by the tape. If you know anything about any of this information we would like to hear about it.

We spent Christmas with Judy in Portland. Otherwise we are busy with our school and work. We would like to hear from you.

Regards,

Beth and Perry Taylor. . .

[P.S.] While in New York recently, we had a short visit with the Luchterhands. They are well and have had no more contact with the Park Service than we have had.

Letter from George Hall
February 27, 1968

To: The parents of the Wilcox-McKinley group
From: Superintendent, Mount McKinley National Park

Following the tragedy on Mount McKinley last summer, several parents discussed with me the possibility of erecting some kind of memorial marker to commemorate the boys. It appeared at that moment that this might be within the regulations governing such matters. I regret to have to advise you that this has been discouraged completely. . .

To the extent I may have personally built up hopes and

---

7. A hearing apparently held to issue death certificates.

expectations in this matter, you have my most sincere apology. I have come to the belief, in the past months, that a dynamic memorial should be sought—a memorial that will cause them to be remembered for their vibrant quest for high adventure and life. A simple marker in an unobtrusive point in the park would not adequately meet this need.

If I can assist in any way in the future, please contact me.

Sincerely,

George A. Hall

Note from Jerry Lewis

Dear Joe,

Ins. came through ($540). Enclosed is your share $90 plus the $20 I owe you. Also will you send Anshel's to him—I don't seem to have his address.

All others will be sent a full proportion of the return. . .

Sorry for the delay.

Jerry

Letter from Anshel Schiff
June 5, 1968

Dear Joe,

Not too much new here. The semester has just finished so I have a little free time now.

I spoke to Janes & he said that he had just settled Hank's estate. . .

He is going to drive Hank's truck out,[8] sell it there & fly back. His wife is also going.

I also spoke to Walt's folks. They are also going out at the end of July for a week. They said Steve's folks & the Luchterhands will be out there sometime during summer.

I will be working at school this summer but will spend a month in the mountains; some time in the Tetons & I think a week in the Sierras. . .

Anshel

---

8. To Mount McKinley National Park.

Letter from Vin Hoeman
June 21, 1968

Dear Joe,

In May a party of three ARG members were the first to reach the top of McKinley this year. I did not go on the trip, and since nothing was found of the lost party, had not told you about it yet, though I had been informing the other families and survivors in the process of billing them for rescue operation expenses. . .

Yours,

Vin Hoeman

Note from S.P. McLaughlin
September 30, 1968

Dear Joe,

Sorry about the delay in reply to yours of August 29th on the expedition settlement. We have had a rather hectic schedule going ourselves and the days have slipped by. . .

Sorry to learn you have had your own personal problems and I'm sure that we all realize that you have had a real burden in closing out the expedition affairs.

If your route someday comes close to our house, be assured you are welcome, and may your future course be in the sunshine of good luck and happiness.

S.P. McLaughlin

Note from Mrs. Alice Clark
September 23, 1968

Dear Joe,

Thank you for the fine report about the McKinley slides. I did not get the group of slides when you offered them. However, if your offer is still available and not too much trouble. . .

I want to thank you for all of the effort you have put into all the letters that you have had to send to all of us. I'm sorry to hear of your divorce. I hope this was not a result of the climb last year. . .

Sincerely,

Mrs. Alice Clark

Letter from Vin Hoeman
October 14, 1968

Dear Joe,

Good to hear from you and sorry to hear the summer has been a troubled one. We managed to stay out of the high mountains in spite of 3 Japanese killed in an avalanche on the border peak of Mt. Vancouver and another lone Japanese soloing Mt. Sanford. Grace and I had a particularly pleasant trip to the Brooks Range making the first ascent of Mt. Igikpak. 8,510', the highest mountain in NW Alaska, and a fantastic granite tower rock climb at the summit. . .

Sincerely yours,

Vin

[P.S.] Snowing like mad here today, Grace sends best regards, she often uses your fudge recipe.

Letter from Vin Hoeman
February 20, 1969

Dear Joe & Helen,

Thanks for the letter and invitation to the Cascades, unfortunately we're planning to go after Kimball again 7-16 March and hope to head for the Himalaya in May which will about take up the time we have free. . .

Grace is fine and joins me in wishing you both the best.

Yours,

Vin

Letter from Anshel Schiff
May 4, 1969

Dear Joe,

I have been meaning to write for months but have been putting it off.

First—congratulations. Your announcement was something of a surprise since I did not know you & Cheryl had broken up.

I suppose that you have already heard but Vin Hoeman has been killed in Nepal along with 4 other U.S. climbers & 2 Sherpas. An avalanche took all but 1 in a party as they were attempting to cross a crevasse. As yet I have no details—I assume that the next *Summit* will have more. Boyd Everett was one of those who was lost.

As for my recent history nothing too exciting. I am still at Purdue being kept pretty busy. I have been doing a fair amount of traveling but this is usually to meetings & little time is available for exploration. If you have not already finished your formal education when do you think you will be starting to work for a living?

I hope to head to California about midsummer & would like to stop by & say hello. . .

Anshel

Letter from Wayne Merry (ten years after the McKinley tragedy)
September 8, 1977
Atlin, British Columbia

Dear Joe,

. . . During the tremendous frustration of being unable to convince anyone at park headquarters that there simply had to be something wrong on the mountain, I became convinced that I would have to leave the National Park Service. However, I thought that if I could obtain the chief ranger job I could do some good, and so applied for it as a last-ditch measure. Much to my surprise, I got the position. I accepted with reservations, but in the following year found that I was unable to accomplish anything of substance within the bureaucracy and so resigned in April of 1969 after ten years of service.

At this point I went to Yosemite National Park and was employed by the Yosemite Park and Curry Company to start a mountaineering school and guide service, which I did. It rapidly became the largest such operation on the west coast, and as well as guiding, it offered instruction in all levels of rock climbing, snow and ice climbing, snow camping, minimum impact backpacking, summer and winter survival, and all levels of cross-country skiing. The guides were also heavily involved in technical mountain rescue.

After five years of that, it appeared that Yosemite Mountaineering had reached its logical limits of quality growth under the constraints of park environment and corporate ownership, and the old urge to "live north" reasserted itself. In December of 1974, I bought a big truck and moved my home and family here to Atlin, which is a superb little gold rush town, very remote, quiet and beautiful. I'm a "Landed Immigrant" in Canada, meaning a United States citizen, but fully accepted for permanent residence. I'm doing a lot of magazine writing and running wilderness trips, am the local fire chief and lead the local historical society— busy as hell with community stuff. Cindy is teaching school and also mighty busy. It is a good life. . .

Best,

Wayne Merry

17

Classification
of Windstorms

A Comparative Study of Windstorms on Mount McKinley[1]

In terms of duration of high winds, the July 18-26, 1967 storm appeared to be the most severe documented by the 105 months of Weather Service data. There is a temptation to be content with this general assessment and not delve into the actual comparison of specific windstorms; for, to reduce a list of wind readings to concise windstorms with ranked numerical handles involves enough arbitration to arouse the cautious curiosity of meteorologists. I can well understand why I have not encountered similar expositions. However, to avoid an attempt at numerical analysis for fear of

---

1. The study spans 105 months of mountain climbing seasons. The months surveyed covered all months in which summit climbs are known to have occurred, from 1946 to 1979 plus additional months during the spring and summer seasons. (Dates for Mount McKinley summit climbs through 1970 were obtained from *A Tourist Guide to Mount McKinley* by Bradford Washburn. Information on recent summit climbs was obtained directly from Mount McKinley National Park. There were three summit climbs prior to Weather Service records.) The results of this weather study are fully supported by consulting meteorologist, Robert M. Kinzebach. The study was also favorably reviewed by the National Weather Service stations at Anchorage, Fairbanks, and McGrath, and by the National Oceanic and Atmospheric Administration. The National Climatic Center has archived the weather study in its research library.

criticism would be forsaking a commitment to investigate the tragedy thoroughly as well as an opportunity to increase the awareness of future McKinley mountaineers.

A system of grading windstorms seems very appropiate for Mount McKinley where weather is often the primary challenge and always the supreme adversary. If my method of grading windstorms does not survive the skeptical scrutiny of time and experience, then perhaps it will, at least, serve to motivate others to develop a more representative system. The basic premise of the system was that it permit the grading of a windstorm entirely from the objective winds aloft data recorded at the triangulating weather stations of Anchorage, Fairbanks, and McGrath,[2] and that it also be explicit enough to be understood by persons untrained in sophisticated mathematics.

The first criterion was to establish parameters to identify specific windstorms and isolate them as individual entities. I reasoned that perhaps the lowest wind velocities capable of blowing away wands and whipping up an immobilizing ground blizzard would be 60 to 80 miles per hour. General winds aloft of about 40 miles per hour could potentially cause such conditions on the mountain and could, even in otherwise clear weather, conceivably trap a climbing team and not permit them to descend. Weather Service wind readings are recorded in meters per second rather than miles per hour.[3] Seventeen meters per second is approximately 38 miles per hour so this was the lowest reading permitted in the identification of a windstorm. As soon as a single twice-daily wind reading was not measured at this level or above, the windstorm was considered ended. To be of grave threat to a group of well-prepared mountaineers, a storm must continue for several days. So for this study I considered significant (life threatening) only those storms which persisted for at least four full days with every wind reading 38 miles per hour or above. The station where the storm was most evident (greatest number of consecutive high winds aloft readings) was termed the Primary Verifying Station. If another station also recorded four or more consecutive, high wind

---

2. The study was limited to the 500 MB (18,000 foot) winds aloft data collected at each weather station twice daily.

3. 1 meter per second is equal to 2.2369 miles per hour.

days during the same time period, it was termed a Verifying Station. If another station recorded four or more days of high winds in the same time span, but not four or more *consecutive* days, then it was termed a Supporting Station. The direction of the storm was considered to be the average wind direction at the Primary Verifying Station. The grading of windstorms was accomplished in two steps:

Step I—The extent or Volume Index was computed by multiplying the average wind velocity by the length of the storm in days. The Volume Index figure for a particular storm represents the area under its wind profile graph and is directly proportional to the amount of air (wind) which moved over the station at the measured elevation. The Volume Index for the July 18-26, 1967 storm was 460. If this figure is multiplied by 24 (the number of hours in each day), it reveals that over 11,000 miles of wind passed over McGrath during the storm.

Step II—A windstorm which is verified at only one station and is not evident in the data of other stations cannot statistically be viewed with the same respect as storms which are more widely recorded. A single station storm causes some wonder as to whether it may have lost some of its punch by the time it reached the mountain. On the other hand, a "grand slam" windstorm verified at all three stations virtually guarantees high winds on McKinley. The Volume Index of widely recorded storms was adjusted by an Expanse Factor. The Volume Index was increased 25% for each additional Verifying Station and 10% for each additional Supporting Station. The Volume Index of single station storms with winds perpendicular to the direction of Mount McKinley was reduced by 25%. The adjusted Volume Index is termed the Severity Index. The grading of a windstorm results directly from the Severity Index. A Severity Index of 100-199 is a Class 1 windstorm; 200-299 is a Class 2 windstorm; and so forth. For the July 1967 storm, McGrath was the Primary Verifying Station, Fairbanks was a Verifying Station, and Anchorage was a Supporting Station. The Volume Index was increased by 35% to give a Severity Index of 621, a Class 6 windstorm. A total of twenty-eight significant windstorms were graded in this manner. According to the criteria of this study, the smallest Severity Index for a significant windstorm is 114 (Class 1). There is, of course, no upper limit.

A SURVEY OF SIGNIFICANT WINDSTORMS ON MOUNT McKINLEY
(Study Covers 105 Selected Months)

RANK	DATES	LENGTH (DAYS)	VELOCITY[1] AVER.	PEAK	VOLUME INDEX	DIRECTION	VERIFYING[2] STATION(S)	SUPPORTING STATION(S)	EXPANSE FACTOR	SEVERITY INDEX	CLASS
*1	67 July 18-26	8½	54.1	82.8	460	W	M F	A	+35%	621	6
2	69 June 5-14	9	54.9	96.2	494	S	A	F M	+20%	593	5
3	68 May 8-15	7½	59.8	87.2	449	W	F A		+25%	561	5
*4	67 Mar 1-6	5½	71.0	100.7	391	SW	M A	/	+25%	489	4
5	71 Aug 5-10	6	58.9	71.6	353	W	A M	/	+25%	441	4
6	67 Mar 19-24	5½	57.8	85.0	318	N	A F	M	+35%	429	4
7	75 April 13-17	4½	59.2	87.2	266	SW	M A F	/	+50%	399	3
8	76 April 24-29	5½	44.9	53.7	247	S	M A F	/	+50%	371	3
*9	71 July 11-15	4½	59.4	78.3	267	W	F M	/	+25%	334	3
10	72 Sept 19-24	5½	53.1	73.8	292	NW	A	F	+10%	321	3
11	72 June 11-16	5½	47.2	73.8	260	SE	A	M	+10%	286	2
12	71 July 25-29	5	55.0	67.1	275	SW	A	/	0%	275	2
13	75 May 9-13	5	53.0	67.1	265	SE	A	/	0%	265	2
14	67 Aug 10-14	4	65.4	96.2	262	W	F	/	0%	262	2
15	70 Mar 31-Ap 4	4½	57.9	71.6	261	SW	A	/	0%	261	2
16	71 April 10-13	4	64.6	76.1	258	SW	A	/	0%	258	2
17	74 Aug 26-30	4	63.8	89.5	255	SW	A	/	0%	255	2
18	72 Sept 25-29	4½	50.0	69.3	225	W	M	F	+10%	248	2
19	71 Sept 25-29	4	61.8	76.1	247	W	M	/	0%	247	2
20	75 Sept 21-25	4½	52.9	67.1	238	SW	F	/	0%	238	2
21	74 Sept 19-23	4½	49.0	60.4	221	SW	A	/	0%	221	2
22	58 July 12-16	4	49.5	67.1	198	SW	A	/	0%	198	1
23	79 Aug 24-28	4	48.7	71.6	195	SW	M	/	0%	195	1
24	74 July 4-7	4	47.8	60.4	191	W	F	/	0%	191	1
25	72 July 17-21	4	57.6	73.8	230	W	A	/	-25%	173	1
26	67 May 12-16	4	56.2	76.1	225	NW	F	/	-25%	169	1
27	66 July 10-14	4½	45.2	64.9	203	S	M	/	-25%	152	1
28	74 Jun 27-July 1	4	48.1	58.2	192	NW	F	/	-25%	144	1

Months Surveyed

February:	1967
March:	1967
April:	1952; 1970-1976
May:	1952; 1954; 1960-1963; 1967-1979
June:	1947; 1952; 1959-1960; 1962-1964; 1966-1979
July:	1946-1979 (McGrath 1947-1979)
August:	1952; 1954; 1967-1968; 1970-1979
September:	1970-1976

1. Miles Per Hour
2. A: Anchorage   F: Fairbanks   M: McGrath
First station listed for each storm is its Primary Verifying Station

*Summit Climbers Involved
(The Park Service discontinued keeping records of summit climb dates after 1975)

This grading system does not profess sufficient discernment to claim that the storm ranked 14th with a Severity Index of 262 was actually more severe than the storm ranked 15th with a Severity Index of 261. It is valid, however, to conclude that a Class 3 windstorm (for example) was more severe than any Class 1 windstorm.

While this study may enlighten future climbers as to the intensity and frequency of severe windstorms on McKinley, it is only academically amusing in the quest to predict such storms— for the severity of a windstorm is measured *after* it occurs. (It requires 6 to 8 months for Weather Service data to be archived for public access.) The detailed and exhaustive analysis of Alaskan weather with the purpose of identifying the precise conditions which precipitate significant windstorms on McKinley would be an invaluable asset to expeditions. Such a project is, however, beyond the scope of this study and will be reserved for another time or perhaps relegated to those more skilled in meteorology. While my study has been far too brief to make predictive claims with confidence, there are a few observations worth mentioning. Alaskan storm systems usually swing out of the Aleutian Islands and across the Gulf of Alaska to enter the mainland from the southwest. As expected, Anchorage was the most frequent Primary Verifying Station for significant windstorms. It is also well known that a high pressure ridge in the Gulf of Alaska or North Pacific will force the storm track northward. Such a situation would normally cause a westerly flow of air over central Alaska compared to the more traditional southwest winds. My survey indicates that western windstorms were as common as southwestern windstorms and in general about 23% more severe—in fact three of the top five windstorms were western storms. This seems to suggest that the pushing of storm centers northward may tend to increase their intensity and duration.[4] I reviewed the National Weather Service sea-level and 500 MB (18,000 foot) Synoptic Weather Maps (weather charts) for a number of the windstorms in my study.

---

4. Bradford Washburn reports in *A Tourist Guide to Mount McKinley* (page 17) that a diverted storm hit the mountain from the west during early July of his 1951 ascent. Although this storm was not long enough to be classified as a significant windstorm, its frontal passage did register 87 miles per hour at the expedition's 13,000 foot camp (measured by a three-cup anemometer).

As suspected, the most severe (western) storms were character-ized by a persistent high pressure ridge to the south, both on the surface and aloft. Arctic lows were also present although somewhat randomly situated. The fourth ranked windstorm was also pushed northward by a strong high and had its Primary Verifying Station at McGrath. The unique aspects of the July 1967 storm were the more direct opposition of the southern high and northern low, and the passage of a sharp trough aloft, not evident in any of the other severe windstorms.

It would be well for Mount McKinley expeditions to take more than a casual interest in the development of storms accompanied by strong Pacific highs and deep arctic lows, and the approach of a trough aloft should be warning enough to dig in immediately until it passes. In practice it would probably be difficult for an expedition to monitor western storms as they apparently develop rapidly, and the pertinent data would have to be obtained directly from the Weather Service. It is also not known how often predisposed conditions actually produce significant windstorms.

High winds striking Denali Pass from the West Buttress side are apparently sometimes "born" right at the pass, based on observations made by climbers during the first and fourth ranked windstorms.[5] Climbers caught by such a windstorm in the vicinity of Denali Pass may escape being trapped if they can force a descent down a few hundred feet of the West Buttress route. If a team has adequate supplies, however, it is probably still more advisable to dig in.

The problem with presenting advice is that there are sure to be notable exceptions. Certainly, western windstorms are not the only ones to beware of on Mount McKinley. My survey identified significant windstorms from every direction except east and northeast. The 2nd ranked storm was a southern windstorm. This storm center was initially permitted its normal path across the Gulf of Alaska; however, it was there stalled for nine days by a high

---

5. In the July 1967 storm, the Western States Expedition experienced an extreme increase in winds at Denali Pass. In March 1967, members of the Winter Expedition, trying to reach three of their climbers trapped at Denali Pass by the fourth ranked windstorm, also reported a fantastic increase in wind velocity as they approached the pass from the West Buttress side.

pressure ridge in northern Canada. A review of the weather charts for the various directions of windstorms produces a confusion of seemingly unrelated phenomena which would require a lengthy study to sort out.

Ironically, some of the clearest climbing season summit weather occurs just before southwestern storms. According to experienced Alaskan meteorologist, Ted Fathauer, such storms are often preceded by about twelve hours of downward moving air which dissipates any existing cloud caps and whiteouts completely—until the updrafts announcing the storm's arrival.

According to my study the probability of a significant windstorm occurring in a principal climbing season month is as follows:

May	16%	(Winds aloft are a little higher during the
June	14%	winter months and significant windstorms
July	21%	are likely more frequent then. My study gives
August	29%	probabilities of significant windstorms as
		50% for April and 71% for September.)

With the exception of 1967, July windstorms were the mildest. The windiest year was 1967 with windstorms ranking 1st, 4th, 6th, 14th and 26th. Mount McKinley National Park discontinued keeping records of summit climb dates after 1975 (due to the increased number of climbers). However, prior to 1976 there were 166 days of summit climbs known to have occurred during the months covered by this survey.[6] It was not surprising that significant windstorms and summit climbs were almost entirely mutually exclusive. There were a few summit climbs immediately preceding and succeeding some of the milder windstorms with the climbing parties probably pinned down at their high camps during the storms. In 1966 the Rawert Expedition climbed the North Peak and then were immoblized by a lengthy storm, part of which was a Class 1 windstorm. They finally had to descend without making the South Peak. Over the years other expeditions have likely been aborted short of their goal by tremendous

---

6. On a few dates Weather Service data was incomplete (wind measurements not reported by a station). Five summit days lacked complete Weather Service (McGrath) data: July 12, 1952; July 14, 1952; July 12, 1953; June 29, 1960; July 17, 1975.

windstorms. Although windstorms are the most dangerous aspect of high altitude weather, they obviously are not the only meteorological threat. A number of expeditions have probably been turned back by persistent snowy whiteouts, intense cold, continuous deep snow, or unstable avalanche-prone slopes.

The record of summit climbs seems to support the criteria of this study—that the upper reaches of Mount McKinley usually cannot be climbed whenever one or more of the stations (Anchorage, Fairbanks, and McGrath) measures winds aloft of at least 38 miles per hour. Historically, this seems to have been the minimum 18,000 foot wind velocity which has essentially prohibited summit ascents. Of the 166 summit days only 8 climbs occurred when at least one of the weather stations recorded winds aloft of 38 miles per hour or more for both summit day readings.

A summit climb was made on May 14-15, 1960 and another on June 22, 1971 when there were strong eastern winds over Anchorage (40.3 mph and 43.6 mph). The summit was reached on August 13, 1954 when there were southern winds over Fairbanks (43.6 mph), and again on June 29-30, 1968 with western winds over Fairbanks (53.7 mph). Another summit climb occurred on May 25, 1963 with eastern winds over McGrath (48.1 mph). For all five of these climbs, the winds were very brief and limited to one station. Only the May 25, 1963 winds were in a direction aligned with Mount McKinley. It is doubtful that the other four summit-climb winds hit the mountain with full force.

Three summit climbs did, however, occur *during* significant windstorms. On July 14, 1971 two German climbers, part of an expedition led by Ray Genet,[7] bulled their way to the summit on the last evening of a Class 3 windstorm (the storm ended abruptly the next morning). There are no specific weather observations available from this summit climb; however, the existence of high winds and their subsequent moderation are verified in the diary of one of the climbers at high camp. Father Abele wrote on July 14:

---

7. Ray Genet made the first winter ascent of Mount McKinley in 1967 and was also a member of the Humanitarian Climb. Genet then spent the next twelve years operating a guide service on McKinley and climbing the mountain dozens of times—by far more than any other person. In October of 1979, after a successful summit climb of Mount Everest, Ray Genet (age 48) died during a high bivouac.

"Twice during last night we had to get up to repair the tent that was starting to come apart from the blizzard. We had to remove a section of the center pole and tie off a large hole torn by the wind. Later, the sides began to rip where portions of it had frozen solidly to the hard snow drifts and could not yield with the wind. . . Late in the day the storm began to ease a bit. . . still bothered by the wind, but by this time it had become tolerable. . . From the emergency radio we had a weather report: Winds aloft on the mountain are estimated at eighty knots. . ."

Ray Genet led a portion of the party to the summit on July 18. He indicated that he had considerable difficulty following the wands left by the July 14 climbers and at one point nearly stepped off of the South Face of the mountain.

The other two windstorm summit climbs occurred in 1967 with severe complications:

On March 1, 1967 Ray Genet, Art Davidson, and Dave Johnston, after making the first winter ascent of Mount McKinley, were trapped at Denali Pass (a bivouac camp) during their descent by a tremendous Class 4 windstorm. The men quickly lost their packs and other gear to the horrendous winds and were reduced to near helplessness. Only Dave and Ray had enough use of their hands to construct a snow shelter for the three to huddle within. This was a particularly fierce storm as it had the highest winds[8] of all storms in my survey and the cooler temperatures of winter (McGrath 18,000 foot average: −20.2°F). The climbers were blessed only in the short duration of high winds (5½ days) and in the southwest direction of the winds. They survived because they had sleeping bags, a stove, and eventually found additional

8. This storm ranked 4th in my study and had the highest average and peak wind readings. While average wind readings are indicative, the actual peak wind velocity of a storm is usually of short duration and not likely to appear in the twice-daily weather station winds aloft data. A sharp trough aloft would normally be expected to produce the most extreme instantaneous winds. Of the Synoptic Weather Maps reviewed, such a trough was evident only for the July 1967 storm.

food and fuel in caches which previous groups had abandoned. Even so, they barely survived. When they finally started down, Dave had to fasten the crampons of the other two climbers and suffered severe enough frostbite himself to later lose some toes (Art also lost a toe). Had the storm lasted a few days longer or had the low over northeastern Siberia shifted to the east to allow a west or northwest wind to blow directly into Denali Pass, then the saga might have ended differently. But the three men did survive and in so doing probably endured the most severe high altitude windstorm of any mountaineers who "lived to tell about it."

In July 1967 another windstorm summit climb occurred with the outcome only too well known. The superiority of the July 1967 windstorm is even more awesome when it is realized that it lacked only one wind reading of being a "grand slam" storm. The Anchorage winds aloft reading for 3:00 AM [9] July 24 was 35.8 miles per hour. Had this measurement been just 2.2 miles per hour higher, then Anchorage would have been the third Verifying Station giving the windstorm a Severity Index of 690. Also Clark's party was trapped closer to the summit than to high camp, more than a thousand feet higher on the mountain than Denali Pass. At the summit the July 1967 storm *was* a grand slam windstorm.

In recent years Mount McKinley has been climbed so often that an ascent is generally viewed as "no big deal." Yet, occasionally an expedition becomes tangled in a web of weather and brushes shoulders with death, indelibly impressing them with Denali's full potential for destruction. In 1977 Jeff Babcock, member of the 1967 Mountaineering Club of Alaska Expedition, led a group of eight experienced mountaineers on a 68-day grand traverse of Mount McKinley. After climbing to the summit, they were caught at 17,200 feet on the West Buttress by a severe storm. They lost

---

9. The twice-daily weather station wind readings are made at 00 and 12 Greenwich Civil Time. 00 corresponds to 3:00 PM Alaska Daylight (summer) Time on the previous day. For example, 00 G.C.T. July 20 is 3:00 PM Alaska Daylight Time July 19. 12 G.C.T. corresponds to 3:00 AM of the same day (no date change). Times for Alaska Standard (winter) Time are 2:00 PM and 2:00 AM.

their tents and most of their gear in the high winds, but managed to crawl along a fixed line to a small, weakly constructed, two-man igloo. There the eight cramped men waited, without food. Fortunately, the storm ended in three days, permitting their safe descent. While trapped by the storm, the men talked about the parallels between the 1967 tragedy and what might happen to them if the storm didn't end soon or if their frail shelter collapsed. A lengthy windstorm might have claimed eight lives.

With the great increase in number of climbing parties over the last decade, the statistical probability that the onset of a significant windstorm (May through August) will catch *some* expedition on its summit day has risen from about 3 percent to more than 20 percent. The probability that a *particular* expedition will encounter the onset of a significant windstorm during its summit day remains about constant, less than 1/3 percent. In practice these probabilities are likely lowered somewhat due to the forewarning of worsening weather and/or adverse forecasts. A realistically calculated guess would be that one summit party in about 400 to 500 successful expeditions can expect to be caught and trapped by a significant windstorm for at least four full days.

Over the years Class 6 windstorms may occur occasionally on Mount McKinley during the winter, and I believe that it is only a matter of time before another Class 6 windstorm transpires in the midst of a climbing season.

18

In Defense
of the Dead

Whenever a disaster occurs, there are those both capable and willing to explain publicly the causes; they are motivated by a sense of responsibility toward future expeditions, and perhaps a supreme belief that if men died, then blunders and errors of judgment must have occurred. It is easy for someone who did not personally know the climbers involved to dismiss the disaster as resulting from the foolish actions of a group of inexperienced and poorly organized men who probably panicked at the first sign of adversity. All kinds of speculations, regardless of their sketchy foundations, seemed to find their way into print.

One of the more bizarre criticisms was offered by a store clerk whose only contact with the expedition was when he sold Walt Taylor a pair of down pants just before we left for Alaska. The clerk suggested that the expedition was picking up equipment which they should have had weeks earlier, evidence of a "lack of organization" which possibly caused the tragedy. (Perhaps the clerk had never attempted to buy specialized expedition gear in Indiana.) It is strange how minor irregularities, many of which occur in the most ideal of expeditions, are magnified in the light of tragedy into trumpets of peril and prophets of doom. However unfair and ignorant these speculations appear, it should be remembered that they are, for the most part, the expression of man's need to reassure his faith in his ability of self-preservation. (The same internal mechanism that makes it difficult to conceive of our own death makes it difficult to conceive of a force capable of pronouncing such judgment.) Before the expedition, certainly I had not been innocent of venturing such uneducated opinions and even after the tragedy I found myself momentarily agreeing with a member of the Mountaineering Club of Alaska group who said: "If I had been caught in that storm, I would have survived."

However, I was soon sobered by the fact that some men who were as physically strong as I, did not survive. This intense experience has certainly changed my point of view and respect for natural forces. Needless to say, I have since been very prudent in venturing judgmental opinions of other mountaineering tragedies. And so this attitude has been echoed among climbing groups in various corners of the country. Not one person who had known and climbed with a member of Clark's summit party before the trip has come forward to suggest that their acquaintance was capable of blunderous judgment or of being panicked by a sudden storm.

To say that the upper party was unprepared for the conditions which they faced is an understatement, for quite obviously they did not survive. However, to meticulously dissect personalities and identify possible hidden meanings in prior events with overzealous hindsight in an effort to extract clues which would place blame for the tragedy seems to presume a divine providence which I am not willing to assume. A fairer assessment, in the absence of absolute knowledge, is to compare the actions of the lost climbers with that which seems common or normal among other expeditions. For the haunting question which addresses itself more to the future than the past is whether anyone could have endured the conditions which overcame Jerry Clark's summit party.

CRITICISM: Some people have offered that the expedition was poorly organized.

EVALUATION: The exhaustive pre-trip organization speaks for itself without apology or further elaboration. During the expedition our progress seemed a little slow, and understandably so, since we were somewhat over-equipped and over-supplied. (Our food supplies were about 50 percent greater than that·taken by most groups.) Yet, even considering these factors together with the foul weather and deep snow, we still managed to make our first summit assault on the 27th day of the expedition. I have access to two other Muldrow expedition logs: the Seattle Mountaineers Expedition of 1964 reached the summit on the 25th day, and the Swarthmore Denali Trip of 1966 summited on the 32nd day.[1] It takes a considerable amount of cooperation and organized teamwork for an expedition to climb to the summit of Mount McKinley. Some groups have had their leadership dissolve in disappointment while they were still low on the peak. Certainly abnormal disorganization was not manifested in our expedition's ability to function during the climb.

CRITICISM: Equipment was abused and poorly cared for during the climb.

EVALUATION: To the best of my knowledge all members of the expedition maintained meticulous care of their personal gear. However, as with most situations where a number of people collaborate, the use of group gear exhibited divergent opinions and attitudes. To some people the actions of one or two others may have been construed to be mistreatment. However, it is significant that no item of equipment other than the burned Logan tent was deemed inoperable during the trip. The tent fire itself was definitely an uncommon type of accident, yet similar things have occurred on other expeditions. On one expedition a pressure

---

1. The Seattle Mountaineers Expedition (a group of 21 people, 15 of whom reached the summit) had an air-drop at McGonagall Pass. The Swarthmore Denali Trip (a group of 4 people, 3 of whom reached the summit) packed all of their gear from Wonder Lake.

cooker blew up, and on another all of the stoves were lost when a pack tumbled down the mountain. On perhaps the most organized of mountaineering treks, the American Mount Everest Expedition of 1963, an exploding stove fire nearly spelled disaster for two high camp climbers on the morning of their summit bid.[2] Broken packs, lost ice axes and accidentally knocking over precious water seem also to be rather common expedition misfortunes. Some groups have apparently even escaped astounding blunders such as hiking unroped on glaciers or leaving their wands cached at the base of the mountain. Whether or not slight misuses of equipment occurred during the climb likely had little bearing on the circumstances of the devastating storm.

CRITICISM: The party was composed of men who had not previously climbed together: a mail-order expedition.

EVALUATION: In totality the group was perhaps one of the oddest expeditions ever assembled. It consisted of a nucleus of six men centered around Jerry Clark. Mark, Hank, Dennis, Anshel, and Walt had all climbed extensively with Jerry, although not all of them had climbed with each other. Steve Taylor and I had climbed with each other, but not with anyone else in the group. John Russell was a climber of independent experience who was added to the expedition late in the organization. In addition, the Colorado climbers constituted an awkward appendage. It might be said that we had a conglomerate expedition with a mail-order leader. Throughout most of the trip, surprisingly little friction resulted from our composite composition. The clash of alienated personalities did,

---

2. James Ramsey Ullman, *Americans on Everest* (New York: Lippincott, 1964), pp. 244-245.

however, hinder the 15,000 foot camp's efforts to aid the besieged upper party. Few expeditions are composed only of men who have climbed extensively with each other. Usually one person, perhaps the leader, knows nearly everyone fairly well. More common than not, some person in the original group has a relative or previous climbing companion who is eventually adopted into what must appear to him to be a party of strangers. When the lost summit party is considered separately,[3] it is obvious that their composition was not abnormal. Jerry Clark, the leader, not only knew and had climbed with every one of his men, but he had years ago been the original mountaineering instructor for most of them. He was also a close personal friend to each climber. More favorable cohesion within a group would be unrealistic to expect. Jerry Clark's quiet leadership was the cement of cooperation, while Walt's active diplomacy constituted the catalyst. Even the most ideal group can fall apart under extreme stress, and if something befell Jerry or Walt, or their mutual respect faltered, then the party would have been adversely affected, although it is unlikely that complete panic would have resulted.

CRITICISM: The expedition members were inexperienced.

EVALUATION: This criticism stems primarily from the Park Service's initial discouragement of Steve Taylor's application and to their subsequent conditional approval of the expedition. In reviewing the autobiographies and climbing resumes, it is tempting to contend that the members of the expedition had excellent experience. However, it must be remembered that nearly everyone who is permitted to climb McKinley has a great deal of experience and what may appear to the layman or

---

3. John Russell is not included in comments about Clark's summit party, as John most likely returned to high camp.

novice climber to be extensive experience may be only minimal when matched against the rigors of an expedition. A couple of men who joined the expedition, when the scientific group was still a separate entity, had sparse experience. However, they were not with Clark's summit party, and their relative inexperience could not have been a factor in the tragedy. The men who accompanied Jerry Clark were some of the most experienced climbers in our expedition and certainly compared well to other expeditions. While I would not term the combined experience of Clark's party extraordinary, it was certainly above average considering our route and objectives. (The 1967 park climbing regulations would permit 25% novice climbers on the Muldrow route.)

Pondering the expedition as a whole, I find that some climbers with relatively little pre-trip experience eventually emerged as towers of physical strength and common sense. But this is not too surprising considering the magnitude of our undertaking. Few of us had more than a couple of sub-week conquests over our less experienced comrades, an edge which was quickly leveled by Denali's insistent tutorship. I can only suspect that the same is true for most of those who challenge this vast realm. The mountain hones its own men; there are no trivial or uneventful paths to the top of the continent and no novice boots tread the summit snows. I am not suggesting that pre-trip experience is unimportant, but I do submit that with a background knowledge, understanding, and practice of basic mountaineering techniques, realistic awareness and immediate responsiveness immensely supersedes that which may have been endured on numerous lesser peaks.

CRITICISM: The climbers in Clark's party were weak and ill.

EVALUATION: Everyone is weakened by altitude. Studies by the

Institute of Arctic Biology and the opinions of knowledgeable mountaineers indicate that high on McKinley a climber's physical and mental faculties are reduced as much as 50 percent even if he senses no overt symptoms of altitude. Under such conditions, the extent of the weakening and a climber's realization of its effects are the important ingredients for safety. Altitude illness is much easier to identify since it usually results in headaches, nausea, faintness, loss of appetite, and sometimes vomiting. Dennis Luchterhand was the only member of Clark's summit party who had actually been ill, and his illness was relatively brief. Dennis became nauseous during our hike to high camp on July 14 and later vomited. He did, however, recover quickly and was able to eat well and assume other camp chores such as shoveling snow.

Some climbers experience quite severe altitude symptoms on McKinley, such as chronic vomiting, prolonged periods of inability to eat, inability to carry their own pack, and even vomiting blood. A few of these people even manage to reach the summit. It is the rare expedition which doesn't have at least one climber who experiences difficulty in acclimation. To facilitate weakened climbers some Muldrow parties establish an intermediate Harper Glacier camp at about 16,500 feet. Our expedition fared about average in acclimation, although we did not find it necessary to establish a 16,500 foot camp. Every man in Clark's summit party was able to carry a full load high on the mountain, climbing from 15,000 feet to 17,900 feet in one day. (By comparison the Mountaineering Club of Alaska took a full day to climb from 16,500 feet to 17,900 feet.)[4] Although

4. The MCA spent a portion of that day collecting an air-drop. A comparison of climbing rates is made here in a very general sense as weather and snow conditions are major factors which are difficult to ascertain.

Mark, Jerry, Hank, and Dennis laid over a day at high camp, I strongly suspect that this was socially precipitated rather than an indication of excessive physical weakness or illness. Clark's party, even when accompanied by the poorly acclimated John Russell, maintained a strong pace while hiking toward the summit. There seems to be a general consensus that the second summit party left high camp with sleeping bags and other extra gear at about 3:00 PM on July 17. At 4:40 PM, Jerry radioed Eielson from above Denali Pass. If they had begun this climb at 3:00 PM, then they would have reached the pass within an hour and a half. By comparison the July 15 party took only an hour; however, the MCA party on July 29 took two full hours for the same hike. It appears that Clark's group made it to the ridge behind Archdeacon's Tower by about 9:30 PM, even though they were hiking in a whiteout and experiencing considerable route-finding difficulties. A time of 5 hours from Denali Pass to Archdeacon's Tower is a healthy pace on a clear day. From the known facts and their radio communications, there is no significant evidence that any members of Clark's summit group were either ill or abnormally weakened by altitude.

CRITICISM: Poor radio communications contributed to the disaster.

EVALUATION: From an armchair point of view it seems that good radio communications would have been of critical importance to Clark's party during the storm siege. Perhaps someone would have been able to advise them on what to do or how to get down or maybe pinpoint an air-drop of essential supplies. Considered in the light of logic, these possibilities lose a great deal of glamour. Huddled in the snow high on the mountain, it is extremely unlikely that anyone to whom Jerry could talk over the radio could give him a better assessment of where he was and how to get down than he could himself. Jerry had a compass and a copy of Washburn's topographical map, the most accurate instruments which would be available to anyone below. It is also improbable that the Park Service would have rendered advice; there were no McKinley veterans on the **park** staff and, after all, Jerry was the most knowledgeable of the condition of his men and their circumstances. In what way would radio communications have aided the rescue? Had the storm been of short duration, radio contact would have been beneficial in the air-dropping of food and fuel, replacements for lost or wet gear, and directing low camp climbers to their aid. As it was, however, radio contact would have only informed the world of their peril: by the time that the winds calmed enough for a plane to fly near the mountain, the struggles to survive were likely ended. At the time, I thought that a high overflight would have had a chance of observing the upper group; yet attempting an air-drop through the high winds and blowing snow from an extremely high altitude would likely have been futile. Radio contact may have been of some help in alerting the low camp sooner of the situation which could have inspired us to try to return to high camp earlier. This action may have saved two lives at 17,900 feet, although it's unlikely that anything could have been done for Clark's party. Outside radio contact may, however, have inspired the upper party with hope, bracing them up to better help themselves. In final analysis it is significant to note that in 1967, although we were required to carry radios, radios were not a general requirement for parties climbing McKinley.[5] Also

---

5. All expeditions climbing Mount McKinley in subsequent years were required to carry a two-way radio (regulation rescinded in November 1980).

most groups who took radios communicated with Fairbanks or some other outside station, and some did not bother to establish a reliable schedule. (We were perhaps the first group to talk directly to the park rangers.) Thus, it was not unusual for climbers high on McKinley not to have radio communications.

CRITICISM: Some people speculated that Clark's group had actually planned to camp on the summit in an effort to gain publicity. A few even suggested that the entire tragedy was a calculated risk to assure news media coverage.

EVALUATION: Three of the five climbers in Clark's party had written me previous to the trip specifically stating that they were neither interested in publicity nor camping on the summit; in fact, they were very much opposed to both. One thing should be remembered with clarity. During pre-trip planning, only Steve and I thought seriously of camping on the summit, and I, alone, considered publicity as a feasible means to help finance the expedition. Although publicity and summit camping were ultimately not objectives of the expedition, they did, because of the misunderstanding with Bradford Washburn, succeed in creating a great deal of suspicion—so much so that it would appear that such activities associated with a climb of Mount McKinley are abnormal. In reality, this does not seem to be the case. Previous to 1967, at least two other expeditions found significance in camping on the summit of Mount McKinley,[6] and there may have been others in the

6. The Meiji University Alaska Expedition of 1960 and the Mountaineering Club of Alaska McKinley-Hunter Traverse of 1963 both planned to and did establish camps on the summit of Mount McKinley. Three climbers in the Winter Expedition (1967) had also considered bivouacking on the summit.

years since 1967 (there have been several times as many ascents during the years since 1967 as in all of the preceding years).

I think that mountaineering should be a free expression of aspirations unencumbered by the chains of societal expectations. If a man finds significance in signaling a friend across the depths of space between the summits of a great mountain or in unrolling his sleeping bag on the doorstep of heaven, can there be any argument? Can one in honesty and truth declare inconsequential and trivial that which is of personal significance to another? Is there, in reality, an absolute scale? If so, then it must be in casting judgment to the tide of humanity. I doubt that the mountaineering fraternity is willing to submit to such arbitration. In the arena of public scrutiny, a mountaineer has difficulty justifying his simplest venture. He stumbles and stammers when fielding the inevitable question and thinks himself smug if he disarms his inquisitor with an original or unexpected reply. Under such universal analysis, the entire mountaineering quest loses a great deal of significance and practicality. Mountaineers are certainly viewed as being more akin to daredevil skydivers and motorcyclists than uninhibited artists, and indubitably more like lemmings running to the sea than magnanimous men lifted by exalted purpose.

While most Mount McKinley climbing trips proceed unnoticed by the public, scattered publicity is not entirely uncommon. Besides Washburn's publicized ascents of the peak, several other groups have received public notice in various forms: magazine articles, newspaper reports, features, pictorials, and television documentaries. The type of money-raising publicity which I envisioned for the expedition was a television documentary. (A pictorial feature in a newspaper would not have raised money but it was thought that it might have secured the loan of radio transceivers.) It is interesting to note that in 1974 a television documentary was filmed of a Muldrow climb and aired over a Seattle station. It became part of an adventure series, "Exploration Northwest".[7] I enjoyed viewing the program as well as other less rigorous trips such as backpacking treks into the northwoods and was not in the least offended that they were not the accounts of extraordinarily fantastic ventures. Judging from the success of the program (it was repeated), apparently many other people are content to be entertained by the activities of "ordinary" adventurers.

More important, however, than the philosophical questions of the publicity myth surrounding our 1967 expedition was its functional ramifications. There is evidence that some persons directly involved with the rescue efforts had adverse attitudes toward the expedition as a result of exaggerated and distorted gossip. Whether or not the skeptical attitudes of rescue personnel affected or delayed their responsiveness and conscientiousness, and/or whether this had any effect on the final outcome of the disaster, is a matter which is difficult to determine. Suffice it to say that, whether they choose to or not, people in immensely respected positions of public trust have tremendous influence. They should be cognizant of the fact that their involvement in folly can explode beyond reason, creating many far reaching prejudices which can conceivably endanger the lives of climbers in legitimate and desperate need of assistance.[8]

---

7. "Exploration Northwest," Channel 4 TV, Seattle, Washington.

8. Bradford Washburn's misjudgment of our 1967 expedition was, I feel, an isolated error and should not discredit the immense contributions which he has made in the exploration of Mount McKinley. Over the years no person has provided more valuable information to McKinley mountaineers than Bradford Washburn.

CRITICISM: One Mount Everest veteran indicated: "Leaving a
                  man in high camp alone is unforgivable."

EVALUATION: As leader of the expedition, I was philosophically
                  opposed to leaving a lone man in camp,
                  particularly if he was ill. In practice, however,
                  functional practicability seemed a more important
                  factor. On July 7, I agreed to leave Jerry Lewis
                  alone at Camp IV rather than weaken our pack
                  team strength by leaving another man with him.
                  At high camp on July 17, Clark's party was
                  faced with a more significant situation. To leave a
                  man with Steve Taylor at high camp would
                  virtually forfeit that man's chances of reaching the
                  summit: a goal for which each person had invested
                  a great deal of time, money, and energy; a goal for
                  which each man had already endured a great deal
                  of danger and adversity; a goal which, at the time,
                  seemed only a gentle stroll away. The mild danger
                  of leaving a lone man in camp for a few hours was
                  greatly overshadowed. Steve likely realized the
                  imposition and probably insisted that he be left
                  alone. It, apparently, is not uncommon for a weak
                  man to be left alone at high camp on Mount
                  McKinley expeditions as it occurred on at least
                  two other occasions during 1967.[9]

CRITICISM: Clark's party did not take enough equipment or
                  food on their summit climb.

EVALUATION: This criticism only makes sense in retrospect.
                  Actually Clark's party was much better equipped
                  than most summit groups. In addition to warm
                  clothing and parkas, full water bottles and extra
                  food which most groups take, Clark's group also

9. When the Western States Expedition climbed to the summit on
July 27, they left Ivan Kletka alone at their 17,200 foot high camp, and
Vin Hoeman's Humanitarian Climb left Ed Boulton alone at their 18,200
foot high camp during an August 27 summit climb.

had sleeping bags, a snow shovel, a snow saw, a radio, and probably a stove. By comparison our July 15 summit party took no sleeping bags, snow shovels or stoves, which seems to be the normal pattern for summit groups both before and after 1967. I, however, would go much better prepared were I to make the same climb in the future. Personal experience is a very effective teacher.

CRITICISM: The men caught in the storm did not know how to dig in to save themselves.

EVALUATION: Lack of knowledgeable use of mountaineering techniques has, on some occasions, precipitated mountaineering tragedies. Men have died because they did not know how to effect something as simple as prussiking. However, on this expedition every member of Clark's party had first-hand experience in the construction and use of snow caves, and Dennis Luchterhand had refreshed his knowledge earlier in the expedition with an elaborate structure at 12,100 feet. Steve Taylor and John Russell likely did not dig in at 17,900 feet because the high camp shovel was with Clark's group.[10]

CRITICISM: Snow caves should have been used instead of tents at 15,000 feet and 17,900 feet.

EVALUATION: The pre-expedition M-23 reads in part: "In exposed campsites we will construct alternate shelters, such as snow caves or block huts." This regulation was meant to apply to the camp on Karstens Ridge and camps on the Harper. A snow cave was constructed on Karstens Ridge, but none at 15,000 feet, although a comparable amount of

10. Two snow shovels were taken to high camp on July 14; however, the Colorado snow shovel may have been carried back to Camp VI on July 17.

energy was expended in building elaborate latrines. No snow cave was constructed at 17,900 feet. Why were snow caves not constructed at locations specified by the expedition regulations? At 15,000 feet it was probably the good weather, and the fact that we felt that one could be constructed easily if needed. The ease of digging in the snow may also have been a factor at 17,900 feet; however, at this altitude lassitude likely played a significant part. At low elevations there is excess energy to expend in folly; while under the mental and physical drain of extreme altitude, only essential tasks are considered, and some of these may unreasonably be rationalized into postponement. The advantages of a snow cave are several. First of all, it is *in* the mountain rather than *on* the mountain; it is out of the wind that can destroy a tent. It is also quiet, lacking the incessant flapping of a tent. At very low temperatures a snow cave can even be warmer than a tent. Even with their many advantages over tents, snow caves do not offer a panacea. In shallow snow or deep powder it may be difficult to effect a reliable structure. A heavy snowfall can deposit several feet of snow over the cave, a suffocating threat if the cave is unattended. A high wind on the other hand can remove several feet of snow and weaken the roof of a snow cave in deep powder, with possibly tragic results to its occupants. (A snow block hut would not be as susceptible to these hazards. However, suitable snow for a block hut is not always easy to find.) Also snow caves cannot be folded up and transported. A new one must be dug at each campsite and likely on the return trip as well. Unattended caves rapidly fill with drifted snow. Occasionally, snow caves can be reoccupied. However, on our descent, I found no evidence of our latrines at 15,000 feet or of Dennis' giant snow cave at 12,100 feet.

Snow caves at the Harper camps could have made a great difference in the chances of the two climbers at 17,900 feet. Besides giving the occupants of the high camp a better chance of self-preservation, a well-rested low camp would have been better disposed to return to the high camp. It is doubtful, however, that anything more could have been done for Clark's party.

A fair question is whether or not most expeditions build snow caves on the Harper. I do not have access to the logs of all Muldrow expeditions, but those I do have indicate that many and probably most expeditions do not dig snow caves, but rely on tents as we did. This seems to be true not only for McKinley, but also for other mountains of higher elevation. With my present knowledge and experience, I would not again venture high on McKinley or advise others to do so without extensive snow shelters—for I know that no tent can endure Denali's most extreme winds. It is also significant that such shelters must be constructed in fair weather, before they are desperately needed. In the height of the storm at 15,000 feet, it was impossible to even stand up, let alone effect any digging action. This futility would have been magnified higher on the peak.

CRITICISM: If John Russell did hike down to the high camp alone, then this was a very foolish action.

EVALUATION: Hiking alone on a glaciated mountian is seriously dangerous; however, at the time, two things apparently appeared more important. First of all, it would have been impossible to persuade John not to descend once he had determined to do so and to send someone down with him would have forfeited that man's summit chances. Secondly, the route to high camp was then well wanded and no significant crevasses had been encountered. As improper as it may appear, hiking alone or unroped near the top of McKinley is not entirely unheard of. In 1970, Naomi Uemura made a solo ascent of the mountain and the log of the 1963 McKinley-Hunter Traverse led by Vin Hoeman reads in part: ". . .Tom heads off for the south summit unroped with the HMC[11] party in late morning. . ." The 1967 Winter McKinley Expedition lost an unroped climber in a crevasse, yet later in the climb Art Davidson climbed to Denali Pass and above unroped.

CRITICISM: An experienced Himalayan mountaineer suggested that Clark's group was not aware of the immense danger of bivouacking en route to the summit, an action that weakens men beyond their comprehension. There was already a breakdown in their reasoning processes which failed to warn the men that they were making a fatal decision.

EVALUATION: There is little doubt that an open bivouac on a high mountain is a grave proposition. When such bivouacs occur accidentally, the results are almost certain frostbite, often with subsequent loss of toes or even death. To choose willingly such an outing seems a little beyond the rationale of mentally competent men. Only one thing could have persuaded Jerry Clark to engage in such an action, if he considered the endeavor camping. The group had a shovel for digging snow caves, each man likely had his sleeping bag, and they probably had a stove and extra food. Such a situation is certainly more descriptive of a camp than an open bivouac. The highest bivouac in mountaineering history occurred on Mount Everest on the night of May 22-23, 1963 (another high Mount Everest bivouac occurred in October, 1979). Four men (two who had climbed the South Col route to the summit, and two who had climbed the West Ridge

---

11. Harvard Mountaineering Club.

and traversed the peak) were caught by darkness and forced to bivouac at an elevation of more than 28,000 feet. The men, who earlier in the day knew the probability of a forced bivouac yet continued climbing toward the summit, knew the danger which they were inviting. As stated in the official account of the ascent: "In a whole year's cycle of Everest nights there are no more than a handful in which unsheltered men at 28,000 feet could conceivably live to see the morning."[12] They did survive with two of them losing their toes. During the summer of 1969 I chanced to have a lengthy conversation with one of these four men, Willie Unsoeld, a West Ridge climber who had lost his toes in the ordeal. I was astounded and even shocked when during the course of the discussion Willie indicated that he and his West Ridge companion, Tom Hornbein, felt that they could have still made the summit, even had they been forced to bivouac during the *ascent*. At least, they were committed to try. "We figured that we could just barely make it," Willie replied to my amazed response.[13]

What is it that drives a man to accept such extreme risks? On Everest it is probably the fact that a chance at the top of the world is a once-in-a-lifetime proposition, a coveted mountaineering goal worthy of pushing to the physical stops and beyond. On McKinley the summit drive would appear less; for surely if the goal were missed, the mountaineer could return another year for another try. Yet, as I review the men in Jerry Clark's summit party, I find that few if any had aspirations for future expeditions. To them, Mount McKinley was a once-in-a-lifetime chance. This *was* their Mount Everest. To try to justify a

12. *Americans On Everest*, page 273.
13. Willie Unsoeld was killed in an avalanche on Mount Rainier, March 4, 1979.

bivouac from a practical point of view would make no more sense than trying to justify mountaineering itself. It needs no explanation or apology.

CRITICISM: Weather reports were not available to the expedition.

EVALUATION: This is certainly a valid criticism. Despite Jerry Clark's pre-expedition efforts, we were unable to secure regular and reliable weather information. Forecasts, when we got them, were for Anchorage and hardly pertinent to the upper slopes of Mount McKinley. Weather at various elevations can be strikingly different as many Northwest climbers can verify. On a number of occasions I have begun climbing Mount Rainier in a wet drizzle, only to be greeted by calm sunshine before reaching high camp, with the storm completely below me. On other occasions I have battled dense clouds with windy horizontal sleet high on the mountain only to discover upon my descent that I had been hiking in a lenticular cloud cap, while the rest of the countryside had been basking in calm sunshine. There are two things of paramount importance in a weather forecast designed for mountaineers. First, the predicted winds aloft can advise a climber of whether or not an immobilizing ground blizzard is likely. High velocity winds will also dangerously accentuate the wind chill factor. Secondly, the existence, temperature, and elevation of moisture-laden air masses is of extreme importance. This information tells the climber the probability of expecting heavy snowfall which can cover trails, caches, collapse tents, and reduce visibility—and the possibility of whiteouts which can make route-finding impossible. When a relatively warm, moisture-laden air mass flows over the cool snow surface of a mountain, precipitation or a whiteout is inevitable, like the condensation of moisture on the side of a summer glass of lemonade. The lifting and consequent cooling of moist air as it passes over a mountain range also often causes precipitation.

Clearly, the weather information needed by the mountaineer is normally not available through radio and television reports. Information distributed by the Federal Aviation Administration, U.S. Air Force, and National Weather Service is more useful, yet even this information is not compiled for the mountaineer. Its primary responsibility is directed toward aviation and marine travel.[14] It is a good rule to always expect bad weather whenever a storm system approaches. Even if it seems relegated to lower elevations, high winds are likely above. The more subtle weather conditions are harder to predict. The uniqueness of the mountaineer is that he is sometimes at the birthplace of weather. While he trips lightly along listening to a Weather Service report of clear skies aloft, a thin whiteout may spontaneously generate along the snow surface at his feet and engulf him in a dense fog. Or a frigid gale may suddenly descend from a sunny sky and whip up a treacherous ground blizzard, while sea-level citizens are swimming and golfing or perhaps expressing disappointment that there is insufficient wind for kite flying. Although intense, adverse weather generated by the mountain itself is usually of short duration and no grave threat to the prepared climber. There is a danger, however, that such weather may conceal the approach of major storm systems of considerable length. When climbing a particular mountain, the mountaineer should always study the area weather patterns and solicit additional information from those who have ventured there before. In addition,

---

14. Correspondence with the National Weather Service in Alaska has revealed considerable improvement in mountaineering weather forecasts in recent years, and has raised interest in additional improvements.

he must be cognizant of possible abnormal weather conditions; for it is the exception which catches people unprepared—and it is the exception which kills. [15]

CRITICISM: Some people have contended that the circumstances of the two bodies below Archdeacon's Tower indicated that the upper group had been overcome with panic, that they separated and blindly stumbled down the slope casting aside their ice axes, ropes, and packs—each man left to get back to the high camp as best he could on his own. Had Clark's party dug in well, then they would have walked off the mountain when the storm passed.

EVALUATION: Such an assessment displays a great deal of ignorance of the men involved. Nor do I believe that these critics realistically appreciate the implications of the severe storm. If I were asked for advice on the best action to take when caught in a high altitude windstorm, I would say, "dig in and wait." If I had been asked before the 1967 McKinley expedition, I would have replied the same. I am certain that every member of Clark's party was of the same opinion. I cannot imagine them considering any course of action other than digging in. Why then, were bodies found in positions that would suggest that the climbers were trying to make a run for high camp? Several things could have forced the upper group to leave their snow caves and try to descend. In their circumstances great physical exertion would have been expected. Such exertion at high altitudes can

---

15. The summit whiteout of July 17 was somewhat atypical. When the warm air of day meets cold snow, a whiteout is common, although it characteristically dissipates when the air cools at night. The whiteout behavior of July 17 indicates the appearance of a new air mass with considerably more moisture, as verified by the National Weather Service.

cause pulmonary edema which often requires an immediate drop in elevation to prevent death. A more probable explanation is that they tried to get down to high camp during the brief July 20 "calm." By then they would have been out of food and water and desperate to get down. (Had I been with Clark's party, I certainly would have taken advantage of the brief clear weather.) Caught in the open by sudden and extreme winds, the group was either unable to dig in or suffered extensive frostbite in doing so. Trying to function in 150-200 mile per hour winds at 19,000 feet completely escapes my imagination. During the height of the storm I'm not sure that I could have constructed a snow cave at 15,000 feet, 4,000 feet lower on the peak. If Clark's party was caught in the open, it would have been miraculous if they could have managed any kind of shelter or have even stayed on the mountain. After such a pounding, it would have just been a matter of time before the weakened climbers acquiesced to the elements. Actually considering the magnitude of the July 1967 windstorm, most criticisms of Clark's party lose a great deal of validity and appear rather petty. Certainly no one is qualified to judge the actions of the lost climbers, since no living person has ever endured such an ordeal. The conditions faced by Clark's party were certainly adequate to panic all but the calmest and most disciplined men, men who were aware of the ingredients of survival. I firmly believe that the lost party struggled against the storm as a group, at least until such time as death seemed assured. Then their actions could make little difference. Dying quietly in a snow cave or dropping in stride while floundering down a steep slope, both promised the same ultimate end. In comfort and security one may write of how to face death nobly, yet in reality no one knows how he will react when the time arrives. When it comes to dying, we are all amateurs.

CRITICISM: The rescue of the upper party was not initiated immediately and vigorously.

EVALUATION: The bivouac and subsequent summit climb of Clark's party had me in alternate states of apprehension and confusion on July 18 and 19. By the evening of July 19 a clear danger was evident, and I initiated rescue activities. By noon of July 20 I had requested air support for the upper camp; an action which in and of itself constituted a rescue situation according to Park Service policy. Then and for many days to follow, agencies and officials termed the situation an emergency rather than a rescue. Throughout the entire organization and execution of rescue procedures, two truths emerged. First, aside from Wayne Merry's strong commitment to a full effort, rescue organizations seemed to be dragging their feet. (My point of view may have been somewhat distorted by the fact that when a need is great, it never seems like enough is being done.) I became very irritated that certain definite rescue requests which I made, such as a high altitude overflight, were seemingly ignored by the powers that be, even after I had called an all-out rescue. I certainly do not feel that any public official has the moral right not to comply with the request of an expedition leader who, of course, is in a much better position to ascertain the condition and needs of his group. Several things may have retarded the bureaucratic efforts. Communications were a major problem throughout the rescue operations with marginal contacts with the MCA, intermittent radio communications within McKinley **Park**, and disrupted telephone service to Anchorage. Often critical information had to be relayed by people with little or no understanding of the desperateness of the situation, and even some of those shouldering the responsibility for decision making lacked adequate mountain rescue experience. It sometimes required a couple of days for information originating at one source to reach all of the rescue agencies involved, and much longer for collaboration of ideas and efforts. Individually, people were genuinely concerned; functionally, they were highly victimized by the bureaucracy. Another possible controlling factor was the fear of public backlash, such as resulted from calling an all-out rescue for the three Winter Expedition climbers a few months earlier. Some people apparently thought that the rescue had been called prematurely. Reportedly, the climbers for whom the rescue was called, were not initially certain that they wanted to board a rescue helicopter, although they were hiking down the mountain with severely frostbitten toes. These facts together with the publicity myth surrounding our expedition were more than enough to make officials highly skeptical of calling a premature rescue. However, even without these considerations, a bureaucracy continuously exposed to public scrutiny cannot be expected to act with decisiveness and conviction. Mountaineers should be aware that outside help takes time, more time than most high altitude emergencies can endure. In such a situation an expedition should realize that it is the best and perhaps the only immediate source of rescue action for any of its members who may be in peril.

The second truth which seems undeniable is that regardless of the official agency responsiveness, it is doubtful that anything could have been done to aid the upper party; for, contrary to my assessment and hopes at the time, the wind was so severe high on the peak that even in clear weather a high altitude observation flight probably could not have seen through the ground blizzard. Had massive rescue operations been initiated as early as July 20, it is unlikely that experienced and acclimated personnel could have been assembled and transported to the upper slopes of the peak before the death drama was completed— probably no sooner than the MCA's ascent. Only a clear calm day allowing an air-drop could have saved Clark's party, and, of course, had they had a clear calm day the besieged party most likely could have rescued themselves without an air-drop. The lesson seems to reiterate itself: whenever a part of an expedition is suspected to be lost from camp at high elevations, there is not enough time to solicit outside help. Lives hang in the balance of hours and minutes, waiting several days or a week for help is certain to be fatal. An expedition must itself make every desperate effort at search and rescue which it can and without delay.

A common question after the expedition was whether or not I, as leader, had made any decisions or had observed any events that could have foretold the tragedy, decisions that I would make differently if permitted to turn back the clock. I have had many occasions to ponder this question over the years. There are some things which I feel should have been done differently, yet I do not see them as in any way precipitating the tragedy. The expedition seems to have been quite normal in most respects. The disaster hinges on a single day: had the expedition schedule been advanced one day, the second summit attempt would have occurred before the storm. There are a hundred ways we could have gained or lost a day: the rest day at 15,000 feet, a storm day on Karstens Ridge, and another at Camp II, the extra day which we took at Wonder Lake, the breakdown of the Green Bomb, the extra day we spent in Puyallup, ad infinitum. We could not have foreseen the flow of fate which aligned our expedition with disaster.

I have adjusted to eternity's choice of history; yet, there is still one nagging doubt which remains in the back of my mind. Could we in the lower party have rendered more aid to the upper group? Although it is only an academic question now, it does have futuristic implications. Despite the massive objective evidence supporting the immensity of the storm and fully aware that friendship can cloud logic, I still firmly believe that we might have been able to climb to the high camp on the evening of July 19 when I first suggested it to the other climbers at 15,000 feet. My inability to convince the others of the desperate need for such a trip and letting abrasive personalities control the situation was poor leadership. During an emergency it is the leader's responsibility to inspire courage in the faint-hearted. I should have exhausted all avenues of reasoning and diplomacy and if that failed then I should have made the hike alone. Had we climbed to high camp on that evening, we probably could have saved the two men there. Even having passed up this opportunity, we might have been able to climb back to the high camp after regrouping on July 23, although we probably would have been delayed a few days by the continuance of the storm high on the mountain.

Perhaps these seem like bold statements, considering the condition of Jerry Lewis, my hampered hands, the hectic descent and swim of the McKinley River, and the necessity of airlifting the remainder of the low party. Several things need to be clarified.

First of all, the exhaustive descent was unnecessary in terms of the lower party. Jerry Lewis was the only man in need of immediate evacuation. There are many places on the Muldrow where a helicopter could have landed and picked up Lewis. For that matter, eventually a helicopter could have landed in the vicinity of the 15,000 foot camp. This occurred in 1974 to evacuate an ill climber. The rest of the low party could have taken a leisurely and well-rested descent, spending several days at Camp III, and a week or so at McGonagall Pass if need be. My initial and primary concern for a rapid descent was the high party. If I got out quickly, I could dry my gear and be airlifted back to the rescue group, or accompany an overflight of the mountain, or at least spur the rescue operations. In my anxiety I hiked beyond my safe endurance level, and when confronted with the unexpected flooding rivers, found myself foolishly and almost fatally overextended.

My hands were not frostbitten and complete recovery would likely have occurred even if I had stayed at high elevations.

On July 23 I feel that Anshel and one other strong climber could have successfully assisted Lewis down Karstens Ridge. This would have freed two climbers to return to the high camp. A climb back to high camp, however, could not have been made without sacrifices, for we were somewhat fatigued and storm weary. The cost most likely would have been some frostbite, but we *were* capable of getting there and back if only "just barely." It was my feeling then and now that we were morally committed to the upper party and that we were obliged to make the return climb. As Lute Jerstad, a conquerer of Mount Everest, wrote: "One must have regard for his fellow man, be willing to submerge his desires to the need of the moment. If that need is the risking of his neck in order to save another man, I will be sure that my fellow climber is willing to undertake that task, and that he is capable of performing it."

To my knowledge I have not been criticized for not attempting to return alone to the high camp, yet such a trek was feasible. In 1972 Michiko Sekita was left at 12,500 feet on the mountain due to a severe cold and fever while three members of the party climbed to the summit. When they failed to return, Michiko, although weakened, was able to carry out a solo search of the upper part of the mountain as high as 19,500 feet. Admittedly in the storm I would have faced more desperate yet compelling odds, with questionable chances of survival.

It has been said by some that the 15,000 foot party made a gallant effort to aid the upper group, that we were nearing our physical and emotional limits, and had done all that could reasonably be expected; logic justified our descent. The sober reality, however, is that we were not in a "reasonable" situation. Fate had come to claim the lives of our companions. Extraordinary needs require extraordinary efforts. For rescue is pushing beyond limits; rescue is rising above circumstances that have overcome others; rescue is the conversion of anxiety into action; to go in darkness and storm where one would not choose to go in calm sunlight; to answer the desperate call of another, perhaps a stranger or even a foolhardy person, not out of friendship or commitment to a group, but motivated by an empathetic commitment to humanity—because you would want that person to do the same for you should your roles be reversed.

To say that the lower party would have been too exhausted to render aid had they returned to the high camp is to plead ignorance of the rescue phenomenon. For, more than wind and cold, it is the loss of hope that destroys the will to live. This has been proven time and again not only on mountains, but in prisoner-of-war camps and lifeboats at sea. The interjection of an outside contact: a person, an air-drop, or just a radio broadcast at a moment when all seems lost can cause a resurgence of hope, defying logic. To know that others are concerned, hoping, and praying, improves beyond measure a group's chances of rescuing themselves. It brings out the finer metal of consciousness that can send a timid mother into a burning building or spur a frantic father to a four-minute mile.

It is conceivable that some of the strong climbers in Clark's party could have survived if they had abandoned the weaker members, and certainly Steve and John passed up excellent opportunities to descend from the high camp. In dire circumstances, where rendering aid to others requires the sacrifice of safety, perhaps toes, fingers, feet, hands, or even life itself, no man can morally expect another to respond heroically. The decision to forsake personal welfare must come from within, exposing supreme character. Man cannot bring back a life once it is gone, but occasionally he has an opportunity to prolong the life of another. It is when a man's compassion is so exalted in love that he most clearly exhibits his kinship to God.

APPENDIX

Memorandum

While *WHITE WINDS* responds to the most common misconceptions concerning the expedition, it is not the intention of this writing to refute lengthy compositions of error. For those who may have an intricate interest in such matters I have prepared a separate dissertation available through the publisher entitled: *A Reader's Guide to the Hall of the Mountain King.*

Wind Chill Chart

The body loses heat in several ways: evaporation of perspiration; convection cooling; and through the lungs during breathing. The "coldness" that a person experiences is a function of his clothing, health, and metabolism and is directly related to the rate at which his body is losing heat. In cool and cold weather most body heat is dissipated through the convection cooling of exposed body surfaces. This cooling is greatly accentuated by the presence of wind. Through research, scientists have devised charts which correlate a given temperature and wind velocity with a lower equivalent "calm" temperature which would have a similar effect on exposed flesh. This "wind chill" is more pronounced for low temperatures. The following chart to $-45°F$ and 45 miles per hour is from the National Climatic Center. Partial extention of the chart to $-60°F$ was obtained from *Elements of Meteorology* (Miller and Thompson) and partial extension of the chart to 50 miles per hour was obtained from the National Oceanic and Atmospheric Administration.

Few wind chill charts include wind velocities in excess of 40-50 miles per hour. This is because extreme winds are seldom encountered and because the rate of wind chill effect moderates significantly after about 40 miles per hour. A speculation of the most severe actual conditions faced by Jerry Clark's summit party would be $-15°F$ with 200 mile per hour winds. An extrapolated wind chill equivalent temperature would probably be lower than $-100°F$.

TEMPERATURE (°F)

WIND VELOCITY (MPH)	45	40	35	30	25	20	15	10	5	0	-5	-10	-15	-20	-25	-30	-35	-40	-45	-50	-55	-60
4	45	40	35	30	25	20	15	10	5	0	-5	-10	-15	-20	-25	-30	-35	-40	-45	-50	-55	-60
5	43	37	32	27	22	16	11	6	0	-5	-10	-15	-21	-26	-31	-36	-42	-47	-52	-57	*	-68
10	34	28	22	16	10	3	-3	-9	-15	-22	-27	-34	-40	-46	-52	-58	-64	-71	-77	-83	*	-95
15	29	23	16	9	2	-5	-11	-18	-25	-31	-38	-45	-51	-58	-65	-72	-78	-85	-92	-99	*	-112
20	26	19	12	4	-3	-10	-17	-24	-31	-39	-46	-53	-60	-67	-74	-81	-88	-95	-103	-110	*	-124
25	23	16	8	1	-7	-15	-22	-29	-36	-44	-51	-59	-66	-74	-81	-88	-96	-103	-110	-118	*	-133
30	21	13	6	-2	-10	-18	-25	-33	-41	-49	-56	-64	-71	-79	-86	-93	-101	-109	-116	-125	*	-140
35	20	12	4	-4	-12	-20	-27	-35	-43	-52	-58	-67	-74	-82	-89	-97	-105	-113	-120	-129	*	-145
40	19	11	3	-5	-13	-21	-29	-37	-45	-53	-60	-69	-76	-84	-92	-100	-107	-115	-123	-132	*	-148
45	18	10	2	-6	-14	-22	-30	-38	-46	-54	-62	-70	-78	-85	-93	-102	-109	-117	-125	*	*	*
50	*	*	0	-7	-17	-24	-31	-38	-47	-56	-63	-70	-79	-88	-96	-103	-110	-120	-128	*	*	*

WIND CHILL EQUIVALENT TEMPERATURE

*Data not available from investigated references.

McKinley Fatalities

(From the files of Mount McKinley National Park)

Year	Month	Name(s)
1932	May	Allen Carpé Theodore Koven
1954	May	Elton Thayer
1967	January	Jacques Batkin
1967	July	Jerry Clark Hank Janes Dennis Luchterhand Mark McLaughlin John Russell Steve Taylor Walt Taylor
1969	June	Gary Cole
1970	April	John Luz Jerrold Smith
1971	June	Robert Bullard
1971	August	Eugene Jaidinger
1972	June	Mitsuko Toyema Sachiko Watanabe Nobue Yajima
1974	May	Yoshikaza Okada
1974	June	Tamo Hatakenaka
1976	July	Edward Guleke
1976	July	Joseph Ebner Richard Rose
1976	July	Gunther Schmidt
1979	May	Sang-Don Ko Ii-Kyo Lee

Route	Elevation	Cause
Muldrow	10,000 feet	fall (crevasse)
Muldrow	12,700 feet	fall (Karstens Ridge)
West Buttress	8,000 feet	fall (crevasse)
Muldrow	17,000 - 19,000 feet	windstorm (Class 6)
West Buttress	17,200 feet	pulmonary edema
South Face	13,500 feet	fall
Muldrow	9,300 feet	fall (crevasse)
West Buttress	17,200 feet	pulmonary edema
West Rib	19,000 feet	fall
Cassin Ridge	12,200 feet	fall
West Buttress	12,500 feet	cerebral edema
West Buttress	14,200 feet	pulmonary edema
Pioneer Ridge	18,000 feet	fall
West Buttress	17,200 feet	fall
West Rib	18,000 feet	fall

McKinley Fatalities continued

Year	Month	Name(s)
1980	May	Gerold Herrmann
1980	May	Manfred Loibl Margret Huschke
1980	June	Jiri Novotny
1980	July	Dave Carroll Allen Chase George Manson Sean Lewis

Route	Elevation	Cause
West Buttress	17,500 feet	fall
West Buttress	19,300 feet	exposure
Muldrow	16,100 feet	* illness
Cassin Ridge	* * 10,000 feet?	* * avalanche?

*   Autopsy unavailable at publication date.
* *   Expedition of four climbers vanished (no trace found at publication date).

Mount McKinley
White Winds Index[1]

High winds striking the upper reaches of Mount McKinley are usually immensely increased by the orographic disruptions of the mountain massif: lenticular airfoiling, funneling, and turbulence. Although the mountain undoubtedly responds somewhat differently to various wind directions and velocities, in a very general sense, the following index suggests a method of converting "predicted" 500 millibar (18,000 foot or 5,500 meter) winds to "expected" maximum gusts for the summit region. General winds can be expected to be near the lower range of the index while winds on highly exposed ridges and at Denali Pass (especially if the wind direction is directly into the pass) can be expected to be near the maximum of the index. It should be understood that, while reasonably accurate, wind forecasts can sometimes be in error. Climbers should also be aware that lengthy, life threatening windstorms occasionally and sometimes unpredictably blast the upper slopes of Mount McKinley. All summit parties would be well advised to travel with adequate emergency equipment and provisions.

---

1. The *White Winds Index* is intended for the summit region of Mount McKinley, but can probably be adapted somewhat for other elevations and other mountains. Localized influences can be expected to become increasingly dominant as elevation decreases from the summit.

WIND FORECAST (18,000 FEET)			WHITE WINDS INDEX (EXPECTED WINDS)			
Knots[2]	Miles Per Hour	Meters Per Second	Knots	Miles Per Hour	Meters Per Second	Wind Alert
33	38	17	50-65	58-75	26-34	Yellow
40	46	21	60-80	69-92	31-41	Yellow
45	52	23	70-90	81-104	36-46	Yellow
50	58	26	75-100	86-115	38-51	Yellow
55	63	28	85-110	98-127	44-57	Yellow
60	69	31	90-120	104-138	46-62	Red
65	75	34	100-130	115-150	51-67	Red
70	81	36	105-140	121-161	54-72	Red
75	86	38	115-150	132-173	59-77	Red
80	92	41	120-160	138-184	62-82	Red
85	98	44	130-170	150-196	67-88	Red
90	104	46	135-180	155-207	69-93	Red

YELLOW ALERT: Extreme Caution—danger of even well-placed wands being blown away; danger of immobilizing ground blizzard (even in otherwise clear weather); danger of forced bivouac for summit parties; danger of high camp tent failures; precautionary snow shelters recommended; summit climbing *not* recommended.

RED ALERT: Critical—immobilization of climbers virtually certain; danger of climbers in highly exposed areas being blown from the mountain.

PURPLE ALERT: Significant Windstorm Expected—Wind Alert (Yellow or Red) predicted for four or more consecutive days; life-threatening danger to summit climbers who are caught and trapped.

---

2. Winds aloft forecasts are normally given in knots. One nautical mile (about 6,076 feet) is the surface distance of one minute of arc of a great circle of the earth.

Mount McKinley Expeditions can obtain 500 millibar (18,000 foot) wind forecasts by arranging to have information relayed through their outside radio base or by establishing a telephone patch through their radio base directly to a National Weather Service station:

Anchorage (907) 271-5105
Fairbanks (907) 456-7596
McGrath (907) 524-3177
(All stations provide 24-hour personal contact forecasts.)

The McGrath winds aloft forecast is limited to that locale; however, if the winds are westerly, the forecast can be very indicative of conditions on McKinley. McGrath winds aloft forecasts are also available through the National Weather Service Forecast Offices at Anchorage and Fairbanks. Another often used source of winds aloft data is Elmendorf Air Force Base, Anchorage (907) 752-4903. At the present time the National Weather Service Forecast Office in Fairbanks seems the most enthusiastic about providing mountaineering weather forecasts.

An expedition can request that the Weather Service notify their radio base whenever the 18,000 foot wind forecast is 33 knots or higher, although the most crucial monitoring should occur in preparation for the final summit assault. Common outside radio bases are Radio Anchorage and Radio Fairbanks. Both are out of line-of-sight for parts of most climbing routes, however, reflection of radio signals usually permits some communication.

Climbers contacting a Forecast Office should state their location and elevation on the mountain and describe the weather which they have experienced during the past few hours. Forecasters can then provide a precise description of the 18,000 foot wind pattern and give an expected trend in weather conditions (getting better, worse, or no change) for the next couple of days. The National Weather Service uses the *White Winds Index* and windstorm study to assist them in predicting possible significant windstorms.[3] It should be understood, however, that the final responsibility for interpreting and utilizing all weather forecast information lies with the expedition on the mountain.

---

3. Mount McKinley National Park is also investigating possible uses of the weather study.

Notes

Picture Credits
In the confusion following the expedition many of the pictures (slides) of the trip were mixed up. Although in some cases it is possible to determine the photographer by a process of elimination or by knowing the composition of a given rope team, there are still a few pictures with uncertain photographers. Credit is given whenever the photographer of an individual picture is known or suspected. The absence of a credit indicates that the photographer is not known. It is believed that all members of the expedition except Jerry Lewis, John Russell, and Steve Taylor contributed pictures for this publication.

All pictures of climbers in the Tribute were taken by Anshel Schiff. Wayne Merry provided the photograph of Mount McKinley with a double lenticular cloud cap. The cover picture of the author was taken by Jon R. McIntyre and the back endflap picture was taken by Anshel Schiff. The front cover photo was taken on Karstens Ridge by Jerry Clark. A few of the photographs were damaged and have been retouched.

Elevations and Distances
Most elevations specified in *WHITE WINDS* are approximations determined by referring to contour maps and are indicated to the nearest 100 feet. (A 16,000 foot altimeter was transported as far

as Camp V, but was seldom used.) Elevations reported with more accuracy are points specifically noted on the topographic contour maps. Distances reported are believed to be accurate to within ½ mile on the tundra, and ¼ mile on the mountain above McGonagall Pass. There are a few guesses to the nearest 1/8 mile.

Miscellaneous

References for the mountain proper were taken from Bradford Washburn's Reconnaissance Topographic Map. For the surrounding area, United States Geological Survey maps were examined. In his illustration of Mount McKinley, Gus Swanberg used some artistic license (in particular, foreshortening of the foreground) in order to depict the entire route of the expedition.

Wind velocity reports by people *on* the mountain, while believed to be reasonably correct, are human approximations. A small wind gage was taken which could have measured the lighter winds; however, it was apparently never used.

Spelling, punctuation and arithmetic errors in quoted documents have been corrected unless thought to be intentional.

Acknowledgements

Any undertaking as immense as this book eventually became draws so much upon the resources of vast numbers of people and documents, that it is doubtful that any comprehensive list can be compiled that will not inadvertently omit a notable contribution. It is with a deep sense of indebtedness to those listed and a sincere apology to anyone who may have been overlooked that I make this effort.

First and foremost are the expedition members—most of whom provided documentation through correspondence, expedition radio communications, and pictures—and all of whom provided the adventure and drama of this story. The expedition members were: Jerry Clark, Hank Janes, Jerry Lewis, Dennis Luchterhand, Mark McLaughlin, John Russell, Anshel Schiff, Paul Schlichter, Howard Snyder, Steve Taylor, Walt Taylor, and Joe Wilcox. I am especially indebted to Anshel Schiff who has examined and commented on the manuscript and fully supports its accuracy. I would also like to express my gratitude to the families of the climbers who died on this expedition. Although they were unaware of my writing, my concern that they know as completely as possible the circumstances of the tragedy has been a major motivation for this documentation.

Additional persons and organizations directly involved with the expedition were: The Mountaineering Club of Alaska Expedition

496

(Bill Babcock, Jeff Babcock, Chet Hackney, John Ireton, and Gale Nienhueser), Mount McKinley National Park, The Alaska Rescue Group, Talkeetna Air Service (Don Sheldon), United States Air Force, Alaska Aeronautical, Rescue Coordination Center (Major Stevens), Alaska Helicopters Inc. (Pat Gray), The South Face Expedition, The Western States Expedition, and the Humanitarian Climb (Ed Boulton, Chuck Crenchaw, Ray Genet, Grace Hoeman, Vin Hoeman, and Dick Springgate). A special thanks must be extended to the Mount McKinley National Park rangers —Wayne Merry and Dick Shields at Wonder Lake, Gordon Haber and George Perkins at Eielson Visitor Center. The *Rescue Log* kept by Wayne and the *Radio Log* and radio tapes kept by Gordy and George were invaluable in documenting the tragedy. A special thanks must also be extended to Marion Millett and Cheryl (Wilcox) Tripp for their great assistance to the expedition.

Other people providing assistance before, and/or during, and/or after the expedition and/or documents were: Father Abele, Hap Allen, Kenneth Bateman, Norm Benton, Bruce Bleckert, Cricket Bourasssa, Malcolm Bourne, George F. Budd, Steven W. Buskirk, Richard R. Carr, Sid Childers, Dwight Cotton, Ann Crosby, Art Davidson, John E. Duggan, Boyd Everett, Benjamin J. Ferris, William O. Field, Duane Fuerstenau, Paul Gerhard, Robert A. Gerhard, Roy Gibson, George A. Hall, Leo Hannan, Gary Hansen, Arthur J. Hayes, Ray E. Heller, Morley and Sheila Horder, Jesse T. Hull, George Jacobson, Lute Jerstad, Darrell Johansen, Takeichi Katano, Ken Kessler, Wolfgang Klemperer, Daniel R. Kuehn, Marjorie Maagoe, Berle Mercer, Manard Miller, Tom Patrick, Alvin H. Proctor, Al Randall Jr., Al Randall Sr., C.A. Robertson, George Robinson, Joseph Rychetnk, Lee Ryker, Peggy Sandberg, Elwill M. Shanahan, William Smart, Kent Smith, Paul Sondrup, Elvis J. Stahr, Willie Unsoeld, Bob Wandesforde, Charles Warner, Bradford Washburn, Dave Wilson, Ginny Wood, Steve Wunsch, and M. Zalewski.

Other groups, institutions, organizations, and suppliers providing assistance and/or documents and/or items were: Alaska Mountain Expeditions, Alp Sport, Alpine Hut, American Geographical Society, *Anchorage Times*, Auburn High School, Brigham Young University, Carlson-Hatton & Hay Inc., Communications Equipment and Service Co., Copy Mart, Custom Photo Service, Donner Mountain Corporation, Eastman Kodak Company, Eugene

Canvas Products, Exim International Ltd., Gerry Mountain Sports, Green River Community College, Hales', Heath Company, Holubar, Institute of Arctic Biology, Jet Color Lab, J & J Office Supplies, Kansas State College of Pittsburg, Kelty Pack Inc., Kansas State University, Lafayette Co., Lund's Garden Corner, National Weather Service Forecast Office—Seattle, Neodesha High School, Northwest Copy Company, Northwest Weather Service, Pacific Color Inc., Perma-Pak, Photo & Sound Company, Print 'N Pak, Recreational Equipment Inc., Robi's Camera, Richcolor, Sportman Products Inc., State of Kansas Executive Department, Steel Sales, *Summit,* Swarthmore Denali Trip—1966, Tacoma Community College, Tacoma Public Library, Tacoma Reprographics, *Time,* Trailwise, Typographic Service Inc., United States Department of Commerce—National Climatic Center, University of Alaska, University of Kansas, University Sports, University of Washington, and Washington Photo.

The major manuscript typist was Carol (Thompson) Menka. Other typists were: Priscilla Davis, Holly Waters, and Helen Wilcox. All typists, Don Bender, Roy Campbell, Christy Duvauchelle, Jodi Eshom, Jini Kemp, Kathy Riley, and Sarah Weems were involved in proofreading the manuscript.

Gus Swanberg's illustration of Mount McKinley is excellent. For tireless weeks Gus diligently labored to artistically synthesize numerous photographs, maps, and my insistence on maintaining the accuracy of recollected detail. The resulting rendering is sure to receive significant recognition beyond its inclusion in this publication. Other artists contributing the best of their skills in the preparation of the manuscript were Lowell Egman and Bruce Walters. The cover was designed by the author.

A special thanks is extended to meteorological consultant, Robert M. Kinzebach for his professional review of the weather research. The weather study was also reviewed by the National Weather Service at Anchorage, Fairbanks (Ted Fathauer and Richard Hoopes), and McGrath; and the National Oceanic and Atmospheric Administration (Dick Davis, William McMurray and Daniel B. Mitchell).

Geologist Gerald Miller also offered professional advice.

The following people have provided encouragement and/or have influenced my life apart from the writing of this book: Jake

Amershek, John Barainca, Diana Beall (sister), Greg and Linda Brown, Peggy Burns (sister), Kenneth and June Carey, Paul Cox, Dave and Sue Cross, Bill and Kathy Daily, Kevin and Mary Alice Daley, Dick and Ann Davis, George Dixon, Darrow and Terry Dolan, Ken Ford, Don German, Don Hasting, Fred Johnson, Gus and Gloria Kehr, Bruce Knudson, Polly Mebus, Sandy Murphy, Sally (Gordon) Nielson, Steve Peterson, Loren Stienhower, Kim Turley, Dorothy Vaughn, Ted Wight, Harold and Dorothy Wilcox (parents), Sandy Wilcox, and Roger Wynne.

Daughters, Amanda Jo and Sarah Kasandria sometimes assisted in sorting manuscript copies.

A kind thanks to those who endured the writing with me. The completion of *WHITE WINDS* required the channeling of vast quantities of time and energy. The understanding and support of those around me was greatly appreciated.

Memoriam

Valiant men challenged and failed, gambled and lost. If their passing has a singular significance, it is to sustain the awesome reality of the experiences which they sought. They dared to demand naked honesty in their living at the colossal cost of tempting its last culminating mystery and were prepared to accept their engulfment into the universe as life's natural fulfillment.

WHITE WINDS is not my story. I am only the instrument of its telling. It is the story of seven whose words have been silenced, seven who cannot speak for themselves. But for fate and the unreasoned grace of God, I would lie in a frozen tomb while another told my story.

As a living memorial to my lost friends, I have directed that one-half of my royalties beyond expenses be relegated to the White Winds Outdoor Academy. I feel that this medium will serve to introduce many people to the uncomparable depth of soul offered by outdoor adventure: the principles by which seven men lived—and for which they died.